Veritas Press

PHONICS MUSEUM

MARLIN & LAURIE DETWEILER
DIANE COLEMAN
NED BUSTARD
EMILY FISCHER
ERIC VANDERHOOF

Third Edition

Veritas Press

Lancaster, Pennsylvania

www.VeritasPress.com
(800) 922-5082

ISBN-10: 1-932168-61-3
ISBN-13: 978-1-932168-61-7

Printed in the United States of America.

PHONICS
MUSEUM

Dear Friends,

We are very excited to be a part of your efforts to teach your students to read. Learning to read is a great thrill for young people. And what greater joy than to know that your children can read God's Word themselves. Upon completion of this program your child should be able to read the Scriptures. A portion of a canticle from an 1855 book based on an ancient verse expresses this well:

Christ His Cross shall be my speed!
Teach me, dear Mamma, to read
That I may in Scripture see
What His love hath done for me.
. . . Teach me letters—A B C.

After reviewing various phonics curricula, and after years of experience working with many of them and then doing extensive research of historical standards and methods, we became convinced that children would be much better off if the content they were reading had some meat to it. Consequently, we set out to create a program that had Biblical and historical content and also made use of the soundest phonetic principles and methods.

Teaching children to read is not a complex or complicated process. We know that alphabet tablets date back to the time of ancient Egypt and were baked tiles that had been scratched or etched. Looking back to the founding of Plymouth Colony, we see that children were taught to read from a hornbook. The hornbook was an alphabet board which was covered in front with a thin sheet of horn to prevent it from being soiled. The horn, harvested from cattle, was heated to make it malleable and then pressed until thin and translucent. Hornbooks were used because actual books were so precious children were not permitted to use them.

We want students to love reading by *quickly* learning to read early in the program. That is why the first book they read has so few consonants and only one vowel. We have found that this quick success helps them to love reading and effectively captures their interest in books. We have seen incredible results with this program. Not only do students read their first book in a matter of a few weeks, but the complexity builds to where they can actually read most anything by the end of the program.

As we surveyed the market we found that most phonetics readers were Dick and Jane*ish*—offering no real story. We thought this an unfortunate waste and sought to create readers (which we call *primers*) that had connections to meaningful events and stories. Some of these stories may not be familiar to you. In every case there is an explanation on the back cover to familiarize you with the event or topic of the primer. **You should read the back cover before the student reads the book.**

The difficulty of some words in the primers is intentional. You will be teaching phonetic word attack. Students will benefit from sounding out some unfamiliar words for which they do not know the meaning. Another great side-benefit is that they will develop their vocabulary by learning the meaning of these "new" words. There is great historic precedent for this approach from several hundred years ago, when many children learned to read with only the Bible. **After the first reading you should review the vocabulary words listed in the Teacher's Manual for that lesson and teach the meanings of the words to the students. Vocabulary cards for the most useful of these words are provided in Appendix 15.** Note that the meanings given for these words and phrases are *only* in the context of the story. The definitions are for comprehension of the story and are not all the definitions a word might have.

Have the students read each primer more than once. Don't expect immediate fluency. And realize that there are some books that are bigger jumps in difficulty from the prior book than others.

Teaching reading should be fun and interesting—captivating the students' interest and love, hopefully for life. We have provided you with the tools to do this. The music is a supplement to help your children learn the rules. Memorization is most easily done with music. The various styles of music should not be ignored, as they provide an ancillary learning opportunity. The games are also intended to draw the student in to learn what he must to be a great reader. This Teacher's Manual provides you with a multitude of teaching ideas. Please do not rely solely on the student worksheets—much of the teaching is found in the Manual. The flashcards, like the music, will teach letters and sounds and will also introduce the student to outstanding works of art. Finally, the museum itself is intended to put the entire program into a category of something that a student will seek out in his free time, as well as when he is "schooling."

Consult the Overview that follows the Table of Contents for more specific guidance for using the Phonics Museum.

Marlin Detweiler
Laurie Detweiler

TABLE OF CONTENTS

Phonics Museum Overview

This brief overview is intended to provide you with a quick orientation to this thorough program.

1. Using the enclosed packing list, identify everything to acquaint yourself with the name and description of each item.

2. Open the teacher's manual (start with Kindergarten, if you have both) and familiarize yourself with it. Pay particular attention to the page that explains the icons (this page appears after the Table of Contents) as the icons will be used extensively throughout the manual.

3. Open the student workbook (again, Kindergarten if you have both). The lesson numbers in the teacher's manual will correspond to the student workbook worksheet numbers. For example, Lesson 54 in the teacher's manual corresponds to worksheets 54A, 54B, and 54C.

4. Vocabulary cards and definitions for many of the words used in each primer are found in Appendix 15 in the back of the Teacher's Manual. These cards should be photocopied (or hand-copied by the student, if possible) to be reviewed occasionally for comprehension and for phonetic word attack. Remember that some of these are intentionally difficult words and are there for the purpose of promoting decoding skills pronunciation. It is important for the student to build confidence in pronouncing unfamiliar words. After making the cards you may want to go over the unfamiliar words, allowing the student to sound out each word and explaining the meaning as found on the back of the cards.

5. Set up the pop-up museum by folding at the creases and gathering the inward folds together in the center. Use paper clips to fasten these "inside corners" together. When properly assembled, the museum will have four "rooms" and, when viewed from above, will look like four spokes of a wheel. The museum is intended for the children to play in a museum just like they would play with a doll house. The paper dolls are intended for this activity. Encourage them to hang up the fine art cards as they study each of their letters. For example when studying the letter P, they might hang up the pig card. Sticky tack works well for attaching the cards. Note the game board portion. Refer to the packing list, if

necessary to determine which side is the game board. When you are ready to play a game, remove the paper clips and flatten the museum on a table with the game board up.

6. Make the museum bag. Take the iron-on sheet and iron this onto an old pillow case or even a fabric bag. Heat your iron to medium heat, lay the transfer squarely on the surface of the bag with the rough side down and iron over the sheet. The heat will cause the transfer to stick to the bag. This will be used as your student makes his own museum, hunting for objects that begin with the sound of the letter he is studying. If you are using this in a classroom, you will find a sheet in **Appendix 2** that explains the activity to parents. You will want to provide them each a copy.

7. Become familiar with each of the games. Look in the appendix of the teacher's manual for explanations.

8. **Appendixes 9** and **11** are pages for handwriting practice. Unlike in the Kindergarten manual, the First Grade manual has two pages because the students will be transitioning from the wider to the narrower lines this year.

9. Find the letter formation strips in **Appendix 10** of either teacher's manual. Write the student's full name on it, so he can see how to form his name correctly. You may want to laminate this and tape it to his desk or have it available where he can see it.

10. Punch out the puzzle boards. We have found that a plastic box with different compartments is a good way to organize these. Place a different letter in each one. For Kindergarten if you write the uppercase letter in permanent marker on the bottom of each slot it allows the child to play an upper and lowercase matching game.

You are now ready to begin with the first lesson! We have tried to answer the most frequently asked questions, but please feel free to call us if you have others. May your new adventure be a blessing to you and your students.

ICON LEGEND

Whether it is the Alphabet Quest or one of the primers, this icon will alert you to the fact that it is time to read a book.

Singing is an important element in learning with this reading program. You will be alerted that it is time for a song with this icon.

This icon indicates when it is time to remind the students of concepts like paper position when writing.

Fine art flashcards are pivotal in the Phonics Museum. The flashcard icon will show you when it is time to incorporate these cards in the teaching process.

Fun and insightful instructions for better teaching are indicated by this "bright idea" icon.

This icon tells you that it is time to hang a painting in the museum and allow the students time to collect items to make their own museum. The paintings to hang are the 2.25" square cards with the fine art reproductions printed on them. These cards should be hung with sticky tac.

The fine art coloring pages found in the back of the student workbooks are able to be used at any time but this icon shows where the coloring activity fits best in the overall program.

This icon shows the teacher where tests can be introduced to help evaluate the student's progress.

The puzzle piece icon refers to the letter puzzles. These puzzle pieces are used to teach the concepts of how different sounds link together to create words.

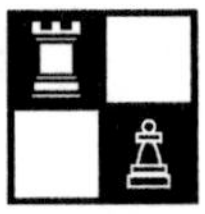

All work and no play makes learning dull. There are many games to play in the Phonics Museum and this icon reminds you to play games on a regular basis, though the games can be used at any time.

Get out your scissors and glue! This icon means that it is time for an art activity. Read through the directions before class.

In the first grade, sign language is used at several points along the way and this icon alerts you to that use.

The key icon indicates a rule that needs to be put to memory hat will help in "unlocking" reading for the students.

This phonics program can be taught with or without the use of breves and macrons. This icon indicates when breves and macrons are to be used.

PHONICS MUSEUM

LESSON 1
INTRODUCTION AND REVIEW

ACTIVITY 1: INTRODUCTION

Discuss with the children the various ways we use our language every day: listening, talking, singing, writing, and READING! Remind them that the most important thing we can do with our language is glorify God—by listening to and reading His Word, talking, singing, and writing about Him to and with others.

Many people in the past were unable to read God's Word for themselves. Today, we are all able to learn how to read and this is a wonderful blessing and privilege.

Draw their attention to the flashcards around the room. Ask if anyone remembers why the pictures are important (they are there to remind them of the sounds made by the letters). Praise correct responses.

Tell them you will start the year by reading the book *The Alphabet Quest*. Read the story aloud. This will either act as a review from last year or be a new introduction to the idea of a museum for studying phonics.

Ask if anyone remembers the song which was used last year to teach the letter names. Play the Alphabet Song, inviting children to sing along. After playing the Alphabet Song, ask if anyone remembers the song which was used to teach the letter sounds. Play the The Museum Song, inviting children to sing along.

Tell the new students in your class that they are not required to sing at this time. Assure them that they will catch on very quickly and can sing along as soon as they feel confident. You may need to reassure them frequently in the first few weeks about many components of the program with which they are unfamiliar.

ACTIVITY 2: WRITING REVIEW

Tell the children that reading and writing go together, so often they will be writing the letters and words which they are reading. Remind them at this time about the "FOUR P's" of writing: Pencil grip, Paper position, Posture, and Pressure. Discuss and demonstrate each in turn, having the children model your example. Tell them you will be watching these things carefully as they do their work.

THE FOUR P'S

First, teach the children that there are four things they must remember when they are writing. These are called the "FOUR P's." They are: Pencil grip, Paper position, Posture, and Pressure.

Pencil grip should be demonstrated at this time. It is a three-point grip, with the pencil resting on the third finger, the thumb and index fingers grasping the pencil on either side just above the "paint line." Fingers should not be on the bare wood—this is too close to the point for good control, nor should fingers be too far up the shaft of the pencil, for the same reason. Their hands should rest comfortably on the desk with the pencil at an approximate 45 degree angle from the plane of the desk (not straight up).

Children should be instructed to use good posture. The free hand should be used to hold the paper in position. Remember that children's fine motor skills all develop at different times. Initially this may be a difficult task, but success can be gained with practice. Some children tend to press very hard when writing, which makes erasure more difficult and messy. Help children to have a firm, but not tense, grip on their pencils and gentle pressure. If they are writing correctly, their hands won't get tired so easily!

Be patient and encourage them to do their best. If you find they are having difficulty, consider using a washable marker as they flow over the page easier.

Draw their attention to the letter formation strips on their desks. The letter formation strip can be found in **Appendix 10**. Instructions for forming each letter appear in Appendix 12.

Worksheet 1A
Name
Hearing
Writing
REVIEW
INSTRUCTIONS
After reading *The Alphabet Quest*, write the beginning letter for each museum picture below.

Write the following upper case letters on the board:

D, G, T, R, U, H, F, I, Q, B, X, J.

To the right of each letter, draw guide lines and perimeter lines. Demonstrate how each letter is made, numbering and describing your strokes as you form each letter. Invite students to come to the board and make the letters on their own. Monitor stroke direction and order carefully, especially with new students.

Worksheet 1B
Name
Hearing
Writing
REVIEW
INSTRUCTIONS
After reading *The Alphabet Quest*, write the beginning letter for each museum picture below.

Worksheet 1A and 1B: Read the instructions aloud. Allow students to check the stimulus pictures on display and copy the letters as necessary. This is a good way to monitor printed-to-written carryover. Also, please remind students that the picture for X uses it as an ending sound, not a beginning sound.

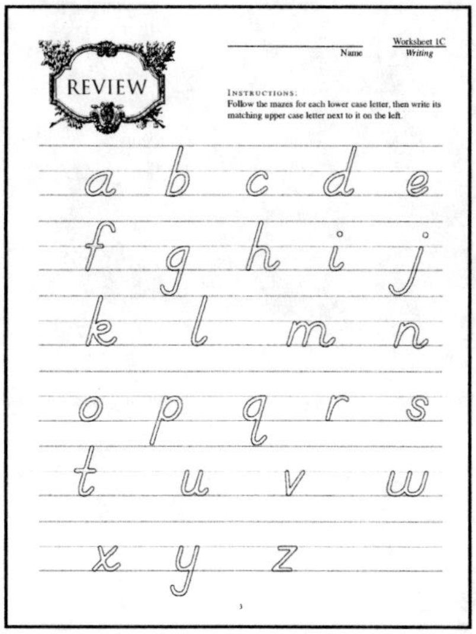

Demonstrate the formation of the letters as above and invite children to come up by threes or fours and practice writing upper case letters, especially those who have not been in this program previously. Repeat this with the lower case letters.

Worksheet 1C: Read the instructions aloud and monitor carefully as they work independently.

Lesson 2
Review

ACTIVITY 1: HEARING AND WRITING

Write the following letters in lower case on the board (number and describe your strokes as you do so):

D, J, A, K, U, E, N, V, H, C, B, T, G, S, Q, W.

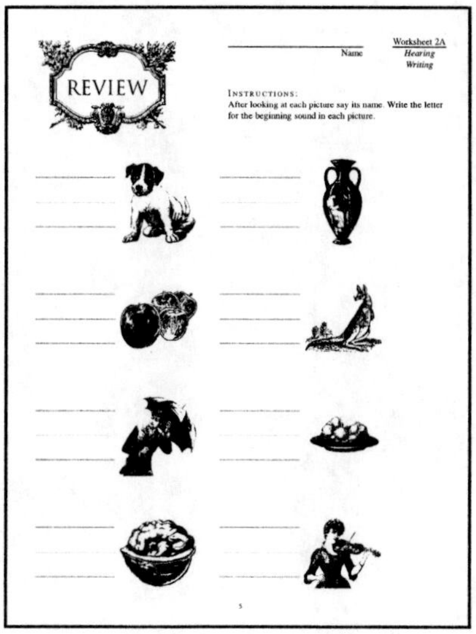

Review the letter names and the sounds with the children, calling special attention to the vowel sounds and the two sounds of A (short as in "cat" and "ah" as in "watch").

Use the flashcards to review the stimulus words and their initial sounds (such as A is for apple, B is for bull). Ask the children for examples of words which begin with each of the letters. Write these words (two or three for each) under the corresponding letter on the board. Have children come up and circle the initial letter in each word.

Invite children to come up to the board and make the lower case letters. Number and describe their strokes as they do so.

Worksheets 2A/2B: Read the instructions aloud. Call on students to label the pictures. Remind them to work from left to right across the page, rather than in up/down columns. Monitor their letter formation carefully, especially with new students.

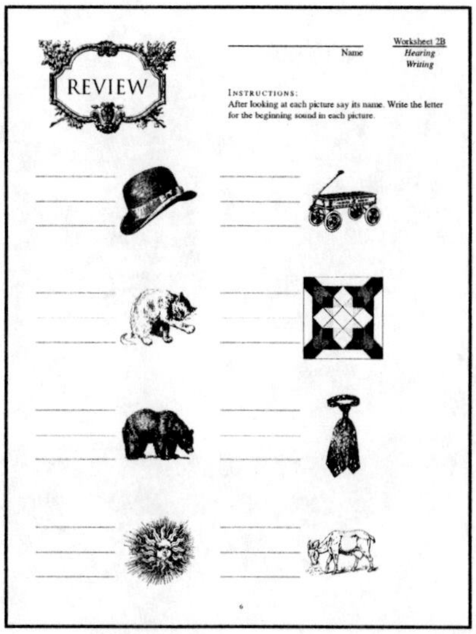

Row 1 (2A): dog, jar
Row 2: apples, kangaroo
Row 3: umbrella, eggs
Row 4: nut, violin

Row 1 (2B): hat, wagon
Row 2: cat, quilt
Row 3: bear, tie
Row 4: sun, goat

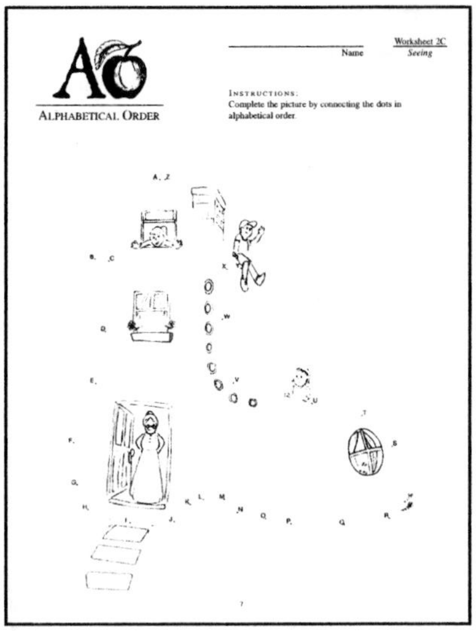

ACTIVITY 2: ALPHABETICAL ORDER

Sing the Alphabet Song a second time today with great ENTHUSIASM! Have students point to the letters as they are singing (this will be quick!)

Write all the students' names on the board. Have each student come up and circle the initial letter in his name. Guide the class through the task of alphabetizing all the names, calling the students to the perimeter of the room to form a line in alphabetical order. Place a check mark beside each name as it is used and the student is called into the line.

When all the students are assembled, they may go back to their desks one at a time, saying the initial letter of their names as they do so. You should point to the stimulus picture on the flashcard for that letter also, reinforcing the concept.

Worksheet 2C: Read the instructions aloud. Monitor the students' progress as they work independently.

LESSON 3
REVIEW

ACTIVITY 1: MIDDLE SHORT VOWELS

Ask if anyone can tell you what the five vowels are by their letter names. (A,E,I,O,U) Affirm correct answers. Write these in lower case on the board.

Now ask if anyone can tell the class what "short" sound is made by each of the letters. The sounds given should be as follows: A as in "apples," E as in "elephant," I as in Indian, O as in "ox," and U as in "umbrella." Ask for examples of these sounds at the beginning of words and write several of these on the board, highlighting the initial letter in each one.

Erase the board and ask students if they remember that these sounds don't always like to be the "leader" in words—often they would rather be in the middle! Read the following list:

sat bag ram bad map

Ask which of the short vowels they heard in each of the words. Repeat if necessary. Praise correct responses and have the students echo the list. Write them on the board, circling or highlighting the medial vowel "a."

Continue in the same manner with the following lists for each vowel:

ten	leg	wed	met	den
fig	him	sin	tip	lid
hot	mop	rob	dot	pop
gum	hug	rut	fun	bus

Leave the display on the board as you present the worksheet.

Worksheet 3A: Read the instructions aloud. Assist with labeling as necessary, but do not give any further letter or sound clues. Monitor their work, especially letter stroke formation.

ACTIVITY 2: READING SENTENCES AND COMPREHENSION

Write the sentences from Worksheet 3B on the board. Call on different children to read them out loud. Then allow the students to proceed to Worksheet 3B.

Worksheet 3B: Read the instructions aloud. Assist the children to read the sentences and guide them in their selection of the corresponding pictures.

LESSON 4 REVIEW

ACTIVITY 1: HEARING AND SEEING

Play the Museum Song for the children encouraging them to sing along while pointing to the corresponding letters on the flashcards.

Write the following on the board: SH, CH, WH, TH. Ask the children what they see which is the same in each of the letter pairs. (H)

Give them each a piece of paper. Demonstrate for them how to fold it into four quarters. Open it up and flatten on the desk. On each quarter, have the children write one of the four digraphs above. Give each student a cup of 20 Cheerios. Tell them you will be reading a list of words and they are to place a Cheerio in the square on the paper with the letter pair which makes the beginning sound for each word. Tell them to listen carefully—some of them may be tricky!

chase	share	whip	chain	thumb
shower	when	choice	what	Thursday
thing	shield	child	those	shadow
shed	thank	whisk	chew	whopper

The children should have five Cheerios in each quarter section of the paper. Tell them to eat the Cheerios!

Worksheet 4A: Read the instructions aloud. Assist to label the pictures as needed, but give no other letter or sound clues.

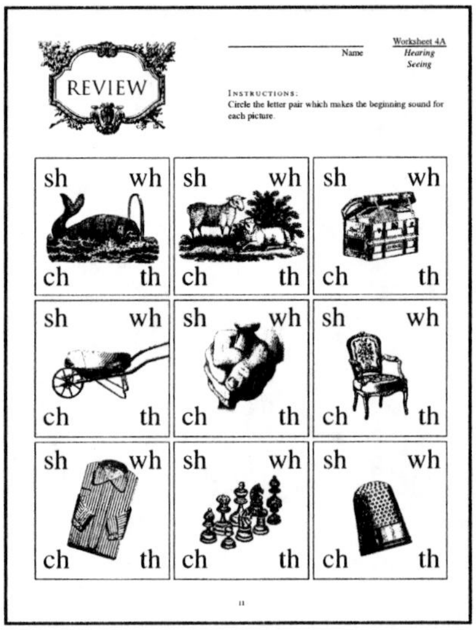

ACTIVITY 2

Place lines and perimeter lines for enough letters to accommodate the longest first or last name in your class on the board. Invite students to the board to write their first and last names. Make sure they use upper case for the first letters of each. Remind them about stroke direction and order according to the letter formation directions.

Worksheet 4B: Read the instructions aloud and Monitor the students' progress as they work independently.

You may want to discuss the picture at the bottom of this page with the children. Books on doing Cat's Cradle are available if you'd like to teach this as a leisure activity at another time.

Lesson 5
Review

Play the Alphabet Song for the children encouraging them to sing along while pointing to the corresponding letters on the flashcards.

ACTIVITY 1: ART ACTIVITY: HEARING AND SEEING

Show the students a completed Museum Alphabet Book. Go through it page by page, naming the pictures, beginning letters, and sounds. Show the children how it was assembled.

Display the Worksheets 5A–5H. Tell them they will begin to look for pictures in magazines which start with each of the letter sounds and glue them on the proper column on the worksheets. AFTER all the pictures are glued, the book will be cut out and assembled.

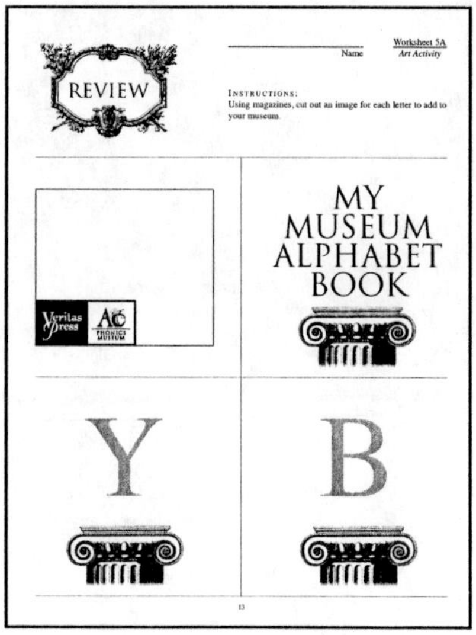

It would probably be a good idea to staple packets together for each child which include all the Museum Book Worksheets. That way each student's work will stay together, and he may glue pictures as he finds them.

Worksheets 5A–5H: Distribute the packets to the children. Allow 45–60 minutes for them to locate, cut out, and glue appropriate pictures. If doing this in a classroom setting, send the project home for the students to complete.

Lesson 6
Target Sound: NG

ACTIVITY 1: HEARING AND SEEING

Tell the children you will be playing the riddle game today in order to help them discover today's new sound. Read the following and write the children's correct answers on the board in a column with the letters lined up beneath one another:

I am the top man in the land. I am married to the queen. I wear a crown and carry a scepter. Who am I? (king)

I am the part of a bird which allows it to fly. I am covered with feathers. There are two of me on every bird. What am I? (wing)

I am a piece of jewelry which goes on your finger. I sometimes have a precious gem, sometimes a beautiful design. Men and women often give one of me to each other when they marry. What am I? (ring)

Draw the children's attention to the words on the board and say them again, having the children echo after you. Ask if anyone can tell you the sound which all of the words have in common. (ng)

Do not focus on the vowel I right now.
Draw attention only to the NG.

Have a student come to the board and circle all the NG letter pairs.

Describe that although N and G are used to write this sound, it really isn't an N or a G sound. Tell them the NG sound is different from either N or G alone or even when the two sounds are together. Make the N and G sounds distinctly, but close together. Then make the NG for comparison.

Have them make NG several more times, using the short vowel I before it, to reinforce this.

Now ask them what else is the same in each of the words. (short I). Draw attention to the fact that the three words are said to "rhyme" because all their ending sounds are alike. Read the following to further demonstrate this concept:

We went to the king
with a peacock wing
and a diamond ring.

You may want to do a side lesson for enrichment using some rhyming poetry this week.

Erase "king" and "wing." Erase the I from the word "ring" and replace it with A. Assist the children to decode the new word formed: rang. Call on a student to use this word in an original sentence.

Erase the R and replace it with S. Assist the children to decode the new word formed: sang. Call on a student to use it in an original sentence.

Erase the A and replace it with O. Assist the children to decode the new word formed: song. Call on a student to use it in an original sentence.

Write all the above words in a column on the board, one under the other: ring, rang, sang, song. Discuss the fact that only one letter and sound changed in each word, but they all mean different things.

Have a child come to the board and underline the NG at the end of each word. Have another child come up and circle the entire "vowel + NG" letter group in each word.

ing/ang
/ong

Name

Worksheet 6A
Seeing

Instructions:
Circle the "ing," "ang," or "ong" in the following words.

king	rang	song
ring	sang	gong
sing	bang	dong
wing	hang	pong
ding	gang	long

21

Worksheet 6A: Read the instructions aloud and monitor their work.

Talk to them about the story *The Alphabet Quest* and give them their museum bag. Allow them time to go through the house and collect items that have the NG sound to make their own museum. If you are teaching in a school setting, instruct the children to take the bag home and bring in objects the following day.

ACTIVITY 2: READING

Present the puzzle pieces for S and R, and ING, ANG, and ONG. Link them together to form the words on Worksheet 6B, guiding children in decoding. Use the words in original sentences.

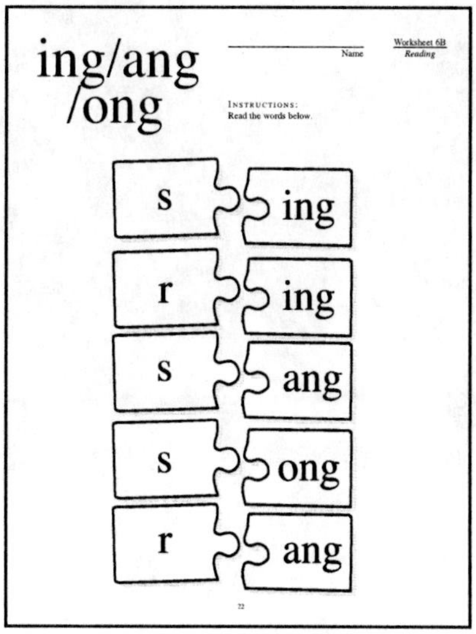

ing/ang /ong

Name

Worksheet 6B
Reading

INSTRUCTIONS:
Read the words below.

s ing

r ing

s ang

s ong

r ang

72

Two of the word pairs here (ring/rang, sing/sang) differ in meaning because of tense. You may want to call this to their attention by asking such questions as "Which one of these would we use if we performed a song yesterday?" (sang) "What would describe the sound of a bell if we heard it right now?" (ring)

Worksheet 6B: Read the instructions aloud. Assist the children to read the words top to bottom, then bottom to top.

Variations for prompting the reading of words on this sheet include: numbering the words and calling on students to read them by the designated number, verbal "fill-in-the-blanks" (This morning I heard a _______ on the radio.), pointing to the written letter on the board and having students point to the corresponding printed letter on the sheet, riddle clues, categorizing on the basis of beginning sound or ending letter group.

You may want to give the students the coloring page along with the flashcard. Read the information about the artist to your students before they color the picture.

LESSON 7
TARGET SOUND NG

ACTIVITY 1: SEEING

Start the lesson by singing a simple song aloud to the children. After you are done ask "What am I doing?" (singing) Write the word "sing" on the board.

Start singing again. Ask again "What am I doing right now?" (singing) Repeat the word "singing." Clap out the two syllables of the word. Point to the word "sing" on the board. Say it and clap the single syllable. Ask the children if the word on the board is "singing." (NO)

Play the Ing Ang Ong Song for the children encouraging them to sing along while pointing to the corresponding letters on the flashcards.

In a different color, write the additional ING on the end of the word "sing" to form "singing." Remark that this word needs TWO ING's on it! Underline "sing" and read it. Then run the pointer under the entire word "singing" and read it.

Again, it is necessary to explain the concept of tense here. Affirm that the ING is added to the word when the action is going on RIGHT NOW!

Write the word "ring" on the board and have a student read it aloud. If you have a bell, ring it for the students. If not, ask what you would have to add to this word if a bell was making that sound right now. (ING) Add the second ING to the word, forming "ringing"

Continue in the same manner with the words "bang," "hang," and "wing" (this one may need some explanation, it is another term for flying).

Now tell the children that you are going to play "charades." Call on students to come to the front of the room. You will whisper to them what they should demonstrate and the rest of the class will guess what they are doing. Use the following charade actions: hum, hop, rub, tap, sit.

Each time a correct answer is offered, write the base word on the board. Ask the performing child to continue the activity and ask "What is she doing right now?" and "What must I add to this word to make it say that?" Add the ING to each of the words in this manner, using a different color to highlight it.

You will need to double the final letter in each base word before adding the ING. Observant children will notice this and probably ask about it. Although this spelling rule is not being addressed in this lesson, you should acknowledge the correctness of their observation and affirm that this is a rule, which they will learn more thoroughly later on. Tell them it does not change the way the word is spoken or read. For now, they need only focus on the addition of ING. Have students come to the board and circle the final ING in each of the words.

Write the following on the board: begging, dipping, hugging, puffing, rocking. Assist the children to decode and invite students to come to the board and circle the final ING in each word. Discuss meanings and use in original sentences.

ing/ang /ong

Name

Worksheet 7A
Seeing

INSTRUCTIONS:
Circle the "ing" in the following words

hopping	humming
huffing	winning
singing	begging
budding	

23

Worksheet 7A: Read the instructions aloud. Monitor the students' progress as they work independently. Watch the word "singing"—they should only circle the last ING letter group.

ACTIVITY 2: READING

Prepare a finished example of Worksheet 7B. Present this to the children, demonstrating how the words are formed when the strip is drawn through the slits. Assist the children to decode the words.

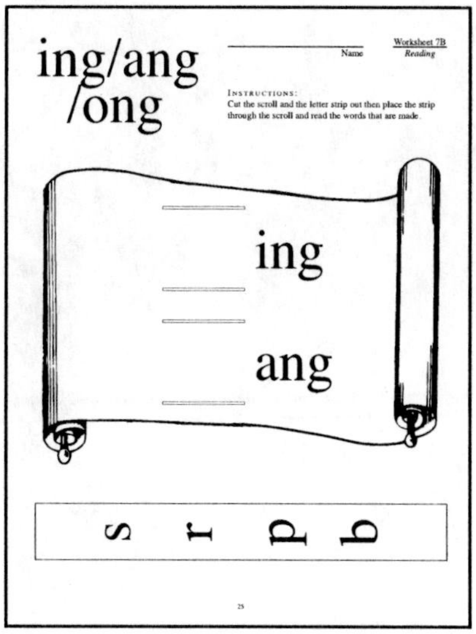

ing/ang
/ong
Name
Worksheet 7B
Reading
Instructions:
Cut the scroll and the letter strip out then place the strip through the scroll and read the words that are made.
ing
ang
s r p b

Worksheet 7B: Read the instructions aloud. The children may need assistance to cut the slits in the scroll—show them how to do this by folding the paper lengthwise where the lines are located and cutting through from the folded edge. Assist them as needed to insert the strip properly.

Tell them to take the page home to their parents to read tonight!

Bingo: Initial Sounds

Lesson 8
Target Sound NG, Special Exhibits and Review

Play the Ing Ang Ong Song for the children encouraging them to sing along while pointing to the corresponding letters on the flashcards.

In the Special Exhibit wing of the *Phonics Museum* you will find odd and unique words. We call them "Special Exhibits" because we recognize that we cannot identify them by their letter sound like Percival did in the museum. These words can not be explained or sounded out. They must be memorized. Appendix 5 lists the Special Exhibit words used for each primer. In Appendix 1, you will find empty frames to be copied and filled in with the Special Exhibit words you are studying at that time and colored by the students. These can be pasted in a Special Exhibit book, stapled to a bulletin board or made into magnets and placed on the refrigerator (self adhesive magnet tape can be found in a local craft store).

Activity 1: Reading

Write the following word on the board: sing. Decode with the children. Ask what you would say if someone did this yesterday. (sang) Call on a student to tell you what must change in the word "sing" to form the word "sang." Invite a child to the board to make the change.

Ask what you would say if someone was doing this right now. (singing) Call on a student to tell you what must be added to the word "sing" to form "singing." Invite a child to the board to make the change. Monitor letter stroke direction and order each time.

Follow the same procedure for the word "ring."

Write the word "hop" on the board. Ask what you would have to add if someone was doing this right now. Add the extra "p" to the word before inviting a child to come up and add the "ing." When alert children ask about the addition of the extra "p," affirm that this is a spelling rule and that they will see words like this often in their reading.

Write the word "love" on the board. Remind them that this was a Special Exhibit for last year and have the children echo it several times. Tell the children that God is loving His people all the time. Show them that when we add ING to this word, we must take off the E first. Tell them this is another spelling rule which they do not need to remember yet, but that they will see this word in their reading. Help them to decode the word "loving."

You can "force" the decoding of "loving" based on the use of short O, although the sound is formed as short U in spontaneous speech. By using short O, however, students will be able to come to the correct pronunciation and meaning.

Worksheet 8A: Read the instructions aloud. Guide the children through reading the words by various forms of prompting as previously described. Discuss the meanings of any words which may be unfamiliar.

ing/ang/ong

Name

Worksheet 8A
Reading

INSTRUCTIONS:
Read up and down the word columns. After this you will be able to read *Ella Sings Jazz*.

sing	pong	napping
king	lungs	getting
swing	sung	buzzing
bing	singing	begging
ping	hopping	itching
sang	huffing	budding
gang	puffing	humming
bang	dipping	zinging
songs	rocking	like
long	swinging	loving

When students come to the word "lungs," guide them to use the short U as they have been taught, along with the NG sound and the final S (which will be voiced like Z). This will be a good indication to you of how well they are applying the decoding skills from last year. You may want to ask why the S is added (pluralization) and briefly affirm the fact that we have two lungs!

Variations for prompting the reading of words on this sheet include: numbering the words and calling on students to read them by the designated number, verbal "fill-in-the-blanks" (This morning I heard a ________ on the radio.), pointing to the written word on the board and having students point to the corresponding printed word on the sheet, riddle clues, categorizing on the basis of beginning sound or ending letter group, etc.

ACTIVITY 2: REVIEW

Give each child four index cards. Write SH on the board and have the children write this letter pair on one card. Continue with CH, WH, and TH. Ask if anyone can tell you what is the same about each of these letter pairs. (h) Point out the differences in each one. Draw attention to the stimulus pictures on the flashcards for each of these sounds. Have the children echo them several times. Remind the children that these letter pairs make sounds which are different from either letter sound alone.

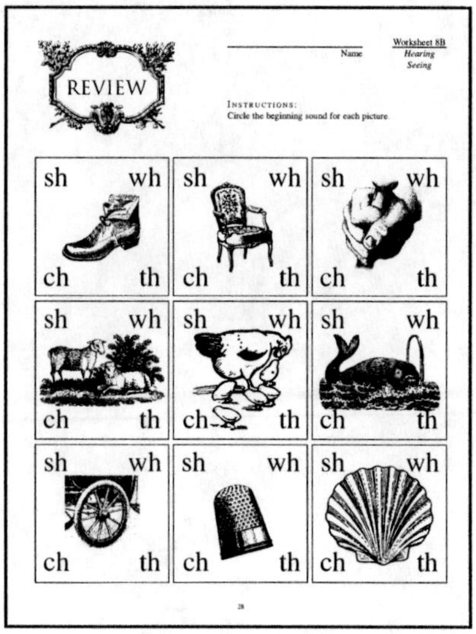

Do not worry about the differentiation of voiced and unvoiced TH. Either will do for demonstration purposes. Be careful with WH however. Make sure your examples begin with the letter pair WH and not W alone.

Give examples of words which start with each one and write them on the board. Solicit suggestions from students to add to the display words. Invite children to come up and circle the letter pair at the beginning of each word.

Worksheet 8B: Read the instructions aloud. Assist with labeling the pictures as needed, but give no further letter or sound clues.

Row 1: shoe, chair, thumb
Row 2: sheep, chicken, whale
Row 3: wheel, thimble, shell

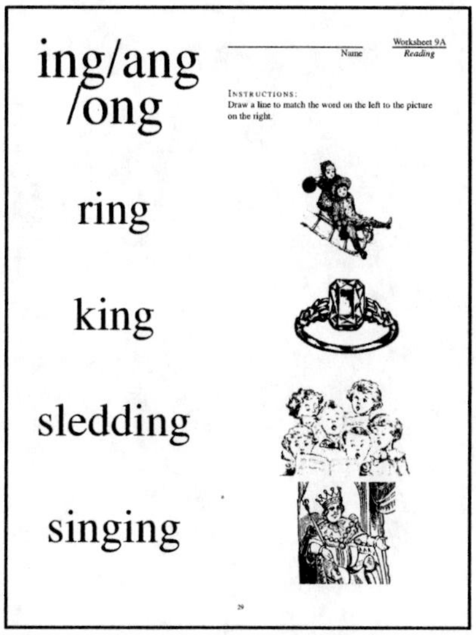

Lesson 9
Target Sound NG
and Reading ELLA SINGS JAZZ

ACTIVITY 1: READING AND WRITING

Ask who remembers the sound for the week: ng. Write the letter pair on the board.

Write I to the left of the letter pair NG. Ask the children to decode the letter group formed: ING. Continue in the same manner with ANG and ONG.

Brainstorm with the children to come up with words which end with each of the letter groups. Write these words under the appropriate letter group. Invite students to come up and circle the entire three-letter group in each word.

Use the words in original sentences. Have students add additional ING to appropriate words to show ongoing action. Invite them to circle the additional ING also.

Worksheet 9A: Read the instructions aloud. Monitor the students' progress as they work independently.

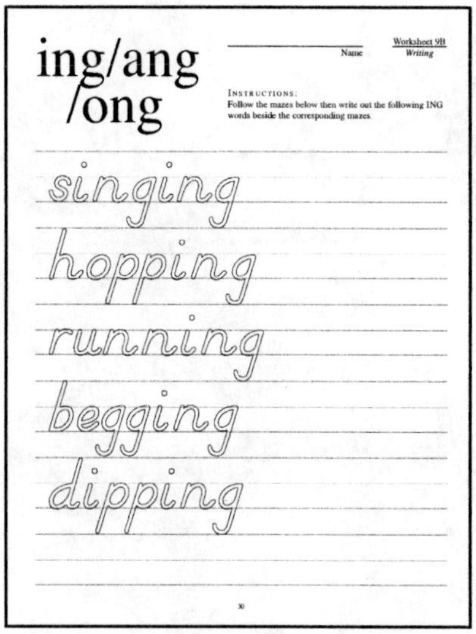

ACTIVITY 2: WRITING

Write on the board the word "rocking," along with guide lines. Demonstrate the writing of each letter, calling attention to stroke direction and order. Invite children to the board to write the word.

Worksheet 9B: Read the instructions aloud and monitor their work.

ACTIVITY 3: READING ELLA SINGS JAZZ

Throughout this program's primers, you may find unusual words and phrases. This is due to the sequence of when sounds and concepts are introduced. For example, one primer read in Kindergarten was entitled *Pepin the Not-Big*. Because the students had not yet learned the SH sound, we rendered "short" as "not-big."

Before you read this story, you may want to briefly review the Master Special Exhibit page in Appendix 5.

This story is about Ella Fitzgerald, the jazz singer. It contains strings of nonsense syllables—skat singing—lifted from actual songs sung by Ella Fitzgerald. You may pronounce these in any way you want, just keep them "jazzy." (Maybe you'll want to listen to Ella's music first to get an idea of what this is like!) In addition, the following words are used which will require your assistance during the children's reading:

Chick Webb—jazz band director
gang—those who are dancing
huffing and puffing, dipping and rocking—dancing
bebop—musical form used in jazz
swing—type of instrumental jazz music
king of swing—the top man in jazz music
got the hall hopping—caused people to dance to the music
hall—large auditorium
pop—short for "popular," another musical form
itching—wanting, anxious
budding—beginning, just starting
zinging—peppy, full of energy
top lungs—a great voice
tip top—best

Please note that exclamation points are used in this story. For this reason, a quick review of end marks may be in order.

Direct the children through the reading of the story in "round robin" style. Encourage fluency and expression in their reading. Discuss as necessary.

Some questions for comprehension may include: Did the fans like it when Chick and Ella performed together? Where did they perform? Did the fans like "bebop" singing right away? Did that discourage her?

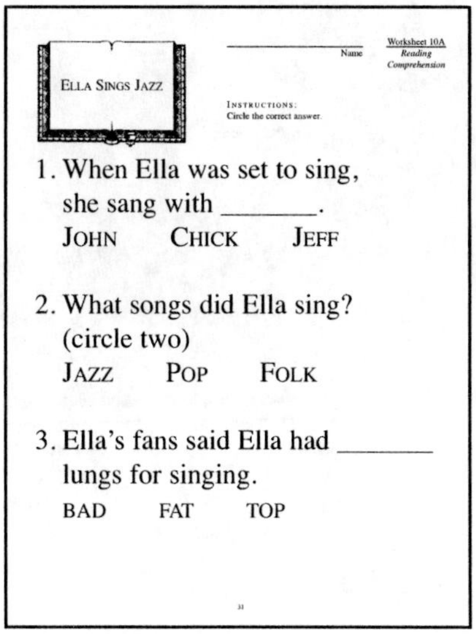
Ella Sings Jazz

Name

Worksheet 10A
Reading Comprehension

INSTRUCTIONS:
Circle the correct answer.

1. When Ella was set to sing, she sang with _______.
   JOHN CHICK JEFF
2. What songs did Ella sing? (circle two)
   JAZZ POP FOLK
3. Ella's fans said Ella had _______ lungs for singing.
   BAD FAT TOP

LESSON 10
READING COMPREHENSION

Play the Ing Ang Ong Song for the children encouraging them to sing along while pointing to the corresponding letters on the flashcards.

ACTIVITY 1: REVIEW

Lead the children in a brief review of yesterday's story. Draw attention to the characters, main ideas, and order of events.

Worksheet 10A: Read the instructions aloud. Assist children to read the questions to themselves and answer as directed. Monitor their work.

ACTIVITY 2: ART ACTIVITY

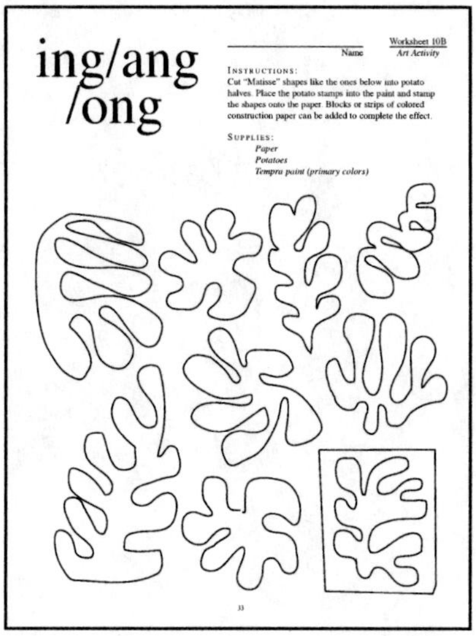
ing/ang /ong

Name

Worksheet 10B
Art Activity

INSTRUCTIONS:
Cut "Matisse" shapes like the ones below into potato halves. Place the potato stamps into the paint and stamp the shapes onto the paper. Blocks or strips of colored construction paper can be added to complete the effect.

SUPPLIES:
Paper
Potatoes
Tempra paint (primary colors)

Prepare an example of a finished print as described on Worksheet 10B and shown in the book *Ella Sings Jazz*. Set up a table with the necessary art supplies and monitor carefully. The teacher should pre-cut the designs into the potatoes.

Worksheet 10B: Read the instructions aloud. Call attention to the display model you have prepared. Assist children to complete the project as described.

LESSON 11
TARGET: R BLENDS

Play the Alphabet Chase Song for the children encouraging them to sing along while pointing to the corresponding letters on the flashcards.

ACTIVITY 1: HEARING AND SEEING

Ask the children if they have ever heard a rabbit "roar." You may get lots of interesting answers to this! Affirm that rabbits do not roar, but that "rabbit" and "roar" both start with the same sound—the R sound.
Sustain the R sound deep in your throat like a growl. Invite the children to "growl" with you. Tell them that when we pretend to growl, we often use two sounds: GR. Growl several times with less emphasis on the R and more on the G. Modify this into a genuine GR blend, eliminating the sustained R. Have the children echo the GR blend in the same manner.

You may still have children in your class who are unable to accurately produce the R sound since it can be late to develop. Encourage any effort toward approximation of the sound, remind them that the lips are not rounded like a W. Pairing G with R can sometimes stimulate more accurate production, due to the fact that both sounds utilize the back of the tongue.

Tell them to wiggle their good listening rabbit ears when they hear the GR blend at the beginning of any of the following words:

lace	grace	Granny	rain	gain	grain
grow	found	ground	win	grin	goose
rooster	grass	was	rose	go	grows

Give the students their museum bag. Allow them time to go through the house and collect items that have the R blend sound to make their own museum. If you are teaching in a school setting, instruct the children to take the bag home and bring in objects the following day.

Tell them that the letter R likes to follow after other "leader" letters in other words also. Wrap your arms around you as if you are cold and shivering. Say "brrrrr" several times. Ask if they hear the R sound. Challenge them to tell you what sound is before the R when you say BR. (b) Have them pretend to be cold also and echo "brrr" several times. Tell them this will be the indication gesture for BR when they hear it at the beginning of any of the following words:

brown	bone	rope	rake	break
bake	bread	red	brother	mother

Write the letter pairs GR and BR on the board. Ask what is the same in each one. (r) Tell them that these types of letter pairs are called "blends."

Tell them that these letter pairs are easier than the ones they have had before because each of the letters makes its own sound. The sounds "blend" together, like the harmony of a song. Have the children echo and then say the blends independently as you point to them.

Instruct them that R will come after several other sounds which they already know and form other blends. Challenge them to decode the following: cr, fr, pr. Affirm that the two letters make their own sounds and they are spoken smoothly together when in a blend.

Give examples of simple words which begin with the blends CR, FR, and PR. Solicit examples from the children. Write them on the board and circle the R blend in each one.

The following two blends are tricky. TR is often distorted into a CH sound and DR is distorted into a J in spontaneous speech. Try to avoid these distortions and produce them clearly and distinctly when you model them. Encourage the children to do the same. These are also more difficult for the child who is unable to produce R due to the change in tongue position required.

Write TR and DR on the board. Say each one very clearly, making sure the initial sounds are distinct. Have the children echo each several times.

Give examples of simple words which begin with each blend. Invite the children to think of words also. Write them on the board and circle the DR or TR in each one.

Write WR on the board. Tell the children that this is the easiest of all, because W hardly makes a sound. They may round their lips just a little bit when they say WR but R does all the talking in this letter pair!

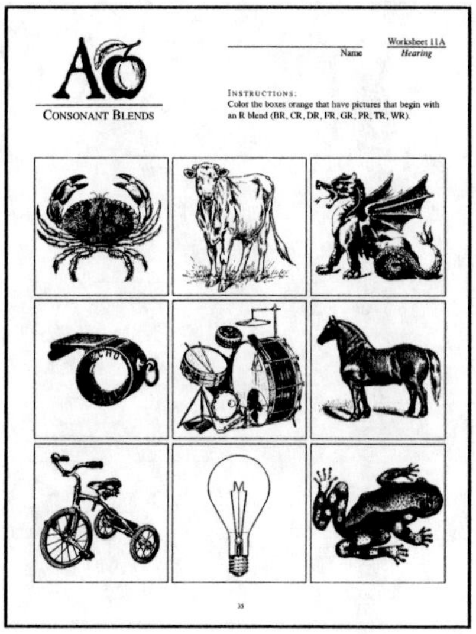

Give examples of words which begin with WR: write, wrestle, wrong. Write them on the board and circle the WR in each one. Tell them that when they see WR together, they will hear and readR. The W is silent.

These are the most difficult types of words for children with R difficulty. Most will completely eliminate the R sound and substitute "w." Remind them that R is the "talker" in this blend, but expect this pattern to persist until they mature in their production of R.

Worksheet 11A: Read the instructions aloud. Tell the children they will be working on this sheet together. Label the pictures for them and tell them to put a small dot of orange in the corner of the ones which start with an R blend. They may then go back and color in the picture when all the pictures have been labeled.

Row 1: crab, cow, dragon
Row 2: whistle, drums, horse
Row 3: tricycle, lightbulb, frog

Consonant Blends

Name

Worksheet 11B
Seeing

In some words, the letter R comes after another letter, like in *frog*. To say these words you blend the sound of the first letter with the sound of R.

Instructions:
Circle the blend at the beginning of each word

frog	crop	drum
brag	crush	grab
bred	drab	grin
brig	dress	grub
crib	drip	trot

Worksheet 11B: Read the instructions aloud. Monitor the students' progress as they work independently. Draw attention to the examples on the board as necessary.

Variations for prompting the reading of words on this sheet include: numbering the words and calling on students to read them by the designated number, verbal "fill-in-the-blanks" (This morning I heard a ________ on the radio.), pointing to the written word on the board and having students point to the corresponding printed word on the sheet, riddle clues, categorizing on the basis of beginning sound or ending letter group, etc.

Lesson 12
Target: R blends

Play Crash! Swing! Squash! for the children encouraging them to sing along.

ACTIVITY 1: SEEING AND READING

Write the following across the top of the board: GR, CR, BR, PR, TR, DR, FR, WR. Tell the children to listen carefully while you read a list of words. You will call on someone to come to the board and point to the blend which begins each word. You will then write the word in the correct section of the board under its beginning blend letter pair.

friend	crown	brain	trees	drop	prize
grin	proud	frame	wrote	crazy	wrist
drizzle	broken	cream	prince	growl	wren

Invite children to come to the board and circle the beginning letter pair blend in each word.

It is not important that students cannot decode most of the above words. You want them to be focused on the two initial letters only.

You may want to "accidentally" put one or two of these in the wrong section under the wrong letter pair. Encourage children to alert you when these "mistakes" are made to reinforce their editing skills.

On index cards, write the following words: dug, sing, ram. Show them one at a time and ask if they should be written on any of the lists on the board. (NO) Ask why not and affirm that they do not start with an R blend.

On index cards, write the following: shin, chop, this, what. Show them one at a time and ask if they should be written on any of the board lists. (NO) Ask why not—after all, they all begin with a letter pair! Affirm to the children that these letter pairs are not R blends, that they make new and different sounds and are not blends of the letters in them. Have students read each word and reinforce that these are not blends.

Leave the board display for reference while they do the next worksheet.

Worksheet 12A: Read the instructions aloud and Monitor the students' progress as they work independently.

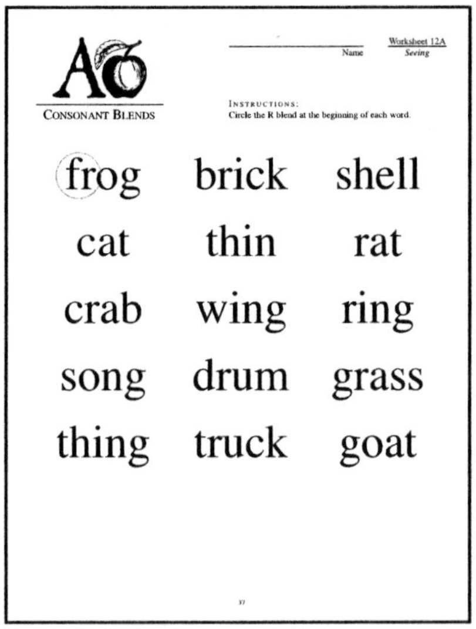
Worksheet 12A
Seeing
Name
Consonant Blends
Instructions:
Circle the R blend at the beginning of each word.

frog	brick	shell
cat	thin	rat
crab	wing	ring
song	drum	grass
thing	truck	goat

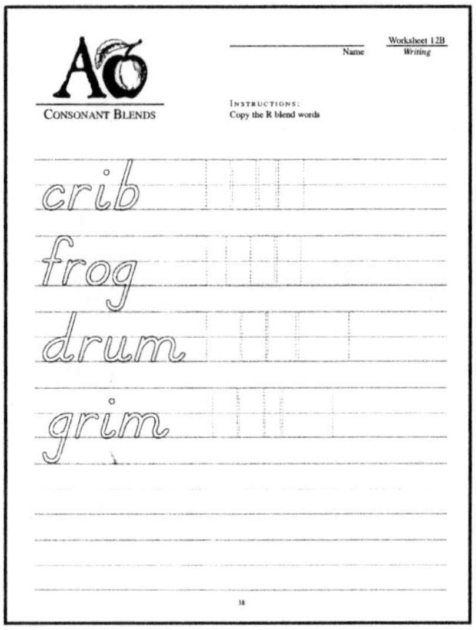
Worksheet 12B
Writing
Name
Consonant Blends
Instructions:
Copy the R blend words

crib
frog
drum
grim

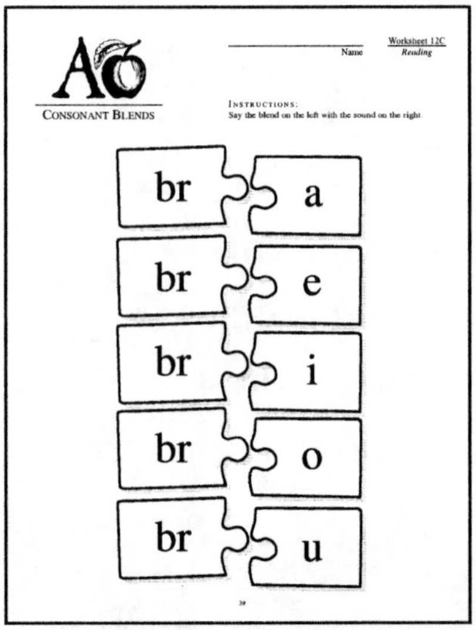
Worksheet 12C
Reading
Name
Consonant Blends
Instructions:
Say the blend on the left with the sound on the right

br	a
br	e
br	i
br	o
br	u

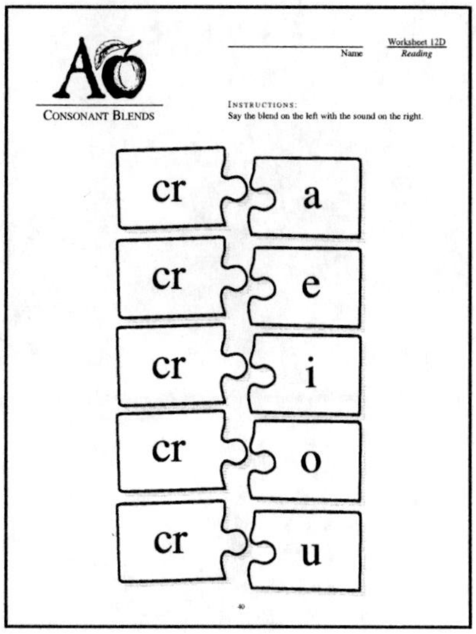
Worksheet 12D
Reading
Name
CONSONANT BLENDS
INSTRUCTIONS:
Say the blend on the left with the sound on the right.

cr	a
cr	e
cr	i
cr	o
cr	u

40

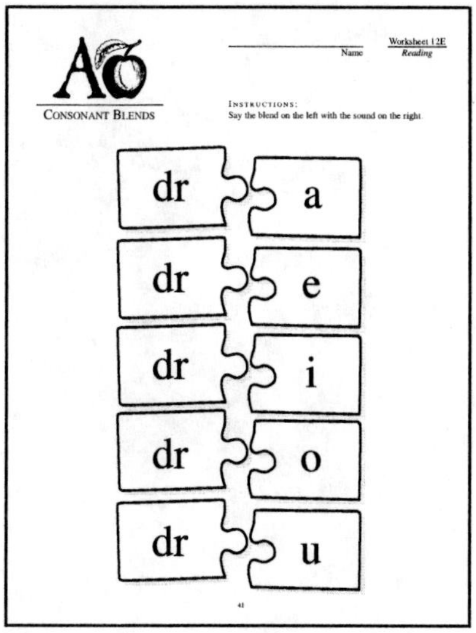
Worksheet 12E
Reading
Name
CONSONANT BLENDS
INSTRUCTIONS:
Say the blend on the left with the sound on the right.

dr	a
dr	e
dr	i
dr	o
dr	u

41

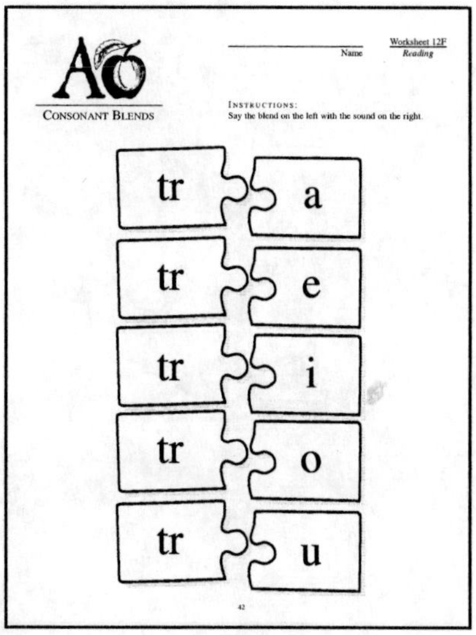
Worksheet 12F
Reading
Name
CONSONANT BLENDS
INSTRUCTIONS:
Say the blend on the left with the sound on the right.

tr	a
tr	e
tr	i
tr	o
tr	u

42

ACTIVITY 2: WRITING

Write on the board the following words: crib, frog, drum, grim. Draw guidelines and perimeter lines to the right of each one. Invite children to the board to write the words. Describe and number their strokes as they form each letter.

Worksheet 12B: Read the instructions aloud. Monitor the students' progress as they work independently.

Remind your students about the "FOUR P's" of writing if you have not done so recently.

ACTIVITY 3: READING

Display the BR puzzle piece. Have the children echo it several times. Present the puzzle pieces for each of the short vowel sounds in this order: A, E, I, O, U. Have the children echo them for you, then say them independently as you display or point to them randomly.

Place the U to the right of the BR and assist the children to sound out the syllable which is formed. Continue in the same way with the rest of the vowels, linking them to the beginning BR sound.

Present the CR, DR, and TR pieces and repeat the above exercise.

Worksheets 12C–12F: Read the instructions aloud. Have the students number the syllables in order from top to bottom on each sheet. Call on students to read the syllable you specify by number. Do this for each page one at a time.

You may also ask if they can come up with words which begin with any of the syllables. (Some will be easier to do this with than others.) Affirm correct answers. Monitor their proper use of short vowels in each instance.

Lesson 13
Target: R blends

Play Crash! Swing! Squash! for the children encouraging them to sing along.

ACTIVITY 1: HEARING AND WRITING

Give each child a sheet of paper. Have them fold it into quarters, then open it flat on the desk.

Draw a square divided into four quarters on the board. On each quarter, write one of the following: DR, TR, FR, TR. Instruct the children to label their papers in the same manner.

Give each child a cup with 12 Cheerios. Tell them you will be reading a list of words and that they are to place a Cheerio in the proper section of the paper for the beginning letter pair blend for each word. They may eat the Cheerios when the activity is completed.

Read the following aloud, allowing time for response:

crib	dragon	frost	trip	trust
drill	crumb	from	crayon	drain
freeze	trail			

Write the words in the squares on the board after each child has responded to each one. Monitor that the Cheerios are properly placed. At the end of the game, they should have three Cheerios in each square.

Worksheet 13A: Read the instructions aloud. Tell them that there will be more than one picture in each row which begins with the blend on the left. Assist with labeling as necessary. Monitor their work.

Row 1: cat, apples, crab, crown
Row 2: drum, horse, duck, dress
Row 3: fish, frame, frog, sun
Row 4: train, top, trophy, tricycle

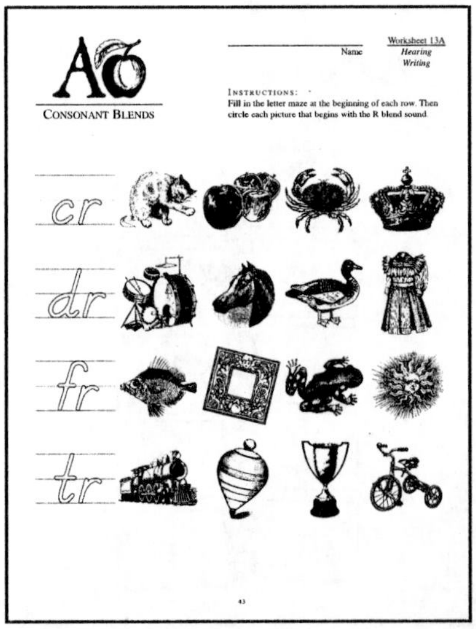

ACTIVITY 2: READING WORDS

Present the puzzle pieces for each of the R blends and the puzzle pieces for each of the short vowels. Have available the puzzle pieces for G, M, B, P and two S's.

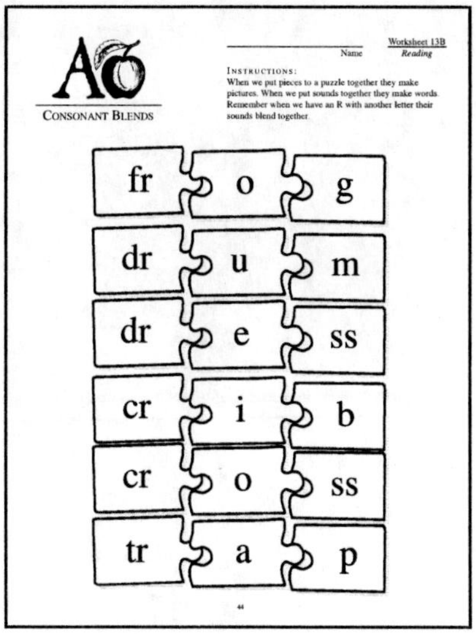

Demonstrate for the children how you would assemble the pieces to form the word "frog." Sound it out as you go, selecting the pieces you need based on the sounds. Link them together and read the word fluently.

Invite students to use the same method to form the words found on Worksheet 13B. Encourage distinct pronunciation of each R blend, especially in the case of TR and DR.

Write the words on the board as they are formed. Leave this on display.

Worksheet 13B: Read the instructions aloud. Have students read the list using any of the previously suggested variations.

Variations for prompting the reading of words on this sheet include: numbering the words and calling on students to read them by the designated number, verbal "fill-in-the-blanks" (This morning I heard a ________ on the radio.), pointing to the written word on the board and having students point to the corresponding printed word on the sheet, riddle clues, categorizing on the basis of beginning sound, middle vowel, or ending letter group, etc.

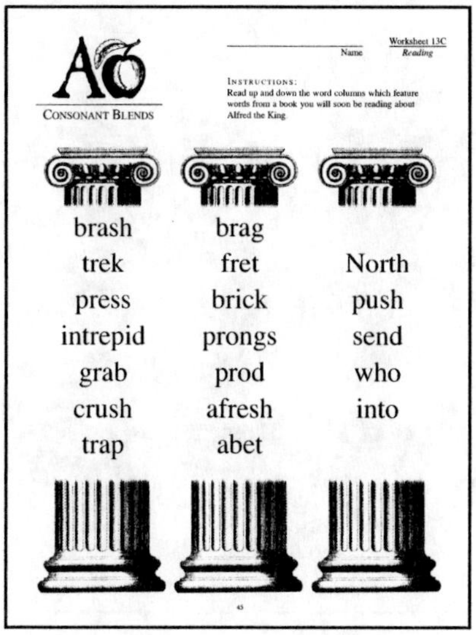

ACTIVITY 3: SPECIAL EXHIBITS AND VOCABULARY

Write the words on Worksheet 13C on the board in columns just as they are presented on the worksheet.

You will need to remind the students about the two sounds of A which were taught at the end of kindergarten: short A as in "cat" and "ah" as in "watch." They can decode "afresh" and "abet" on this list using the "ah" sound. (Although it is a schwa in spontaneous speech, decoding it with "ah" will suffice.)

Worksheet 13C: Read the instructions aloud. Assist the children to decode the words from top to bottom of each column, following along on the worksheet as you point to the corresponding written word on the board. Repeat the activity going from bottom to top of each column. Finally, point randomly to the words on the columns and call on students to read them.

Have students point to the word on their sheets which matches the word you point to on the board, without hearing it read.

Erase the words from the board and then have students point to or circle the correct word as you randomly say them. You may want to do this on an individual or small group basis to more carefully monitor their responses.

Discuss the meanings of the more uncommon words. Use the words in sentences.

Lesson 14
Target: R blends

Play Crash! Swing! Squash! for the children encouraging them to sing.

ACTIVITY 1: HEARING

Tell the children to put on their "rabbit ears" again and listen for any R blends at the beginning of the following words:

trouble	box	drink	crest	long
brass	fudge	green	prank	friend

Praise their GR and listening!

Worksheet 14A: Read the instructions aloud. Permit the children to select any color they wish. Assist them in labeling the pictures and responding as directed.

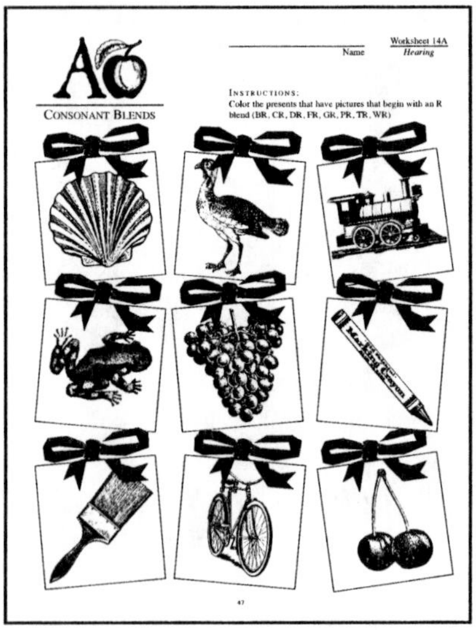

Row 1: shell, bird, train
Row 2: frog, grapes, crayon
Row 3: brush, bicycle, cherries

ACTIVITY 2: READING

Write the following words on the board: crack, Fran, drops, brass. Call on students to decode and use in original sentences.

Call attention to the upper case F in the word "Fran." Ask why you must use upper case at the beginning of this word. (It is a proper name.) Review the use of final CK, SS, and pluralization as necessary.

Worksheet 14B: Read the instructions aloud. Monitor the students' progress as they work independently.

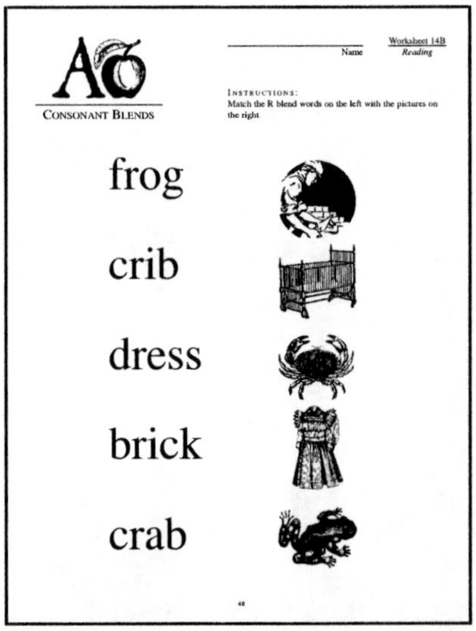

Archives: Beginning Blends Edition (use only those cards with R blends).

Lesson 15
Target: L blends

Play Crash! Swing! Squash! for the children encouraging them to sing.

ACTIVITY 1: HEARING AND SEEING

Write the following letter pairs on the board: BR, CR, GR, FR, PR. Review the sound made by each blend.

Write the following words under the corresponding letter pair: bred, crock, grass, frog, prod. Assist the children to decode and read each one. Discuss meanings and use in original sentences.

Write lower case L on an index card. Ask the children what sound is made by this letter. Now tell them to watch carefully as you cover the R in the word "bred" with the L card, forming the word "bled."

Tell the children that we blend the two sounds B and L in the same way we did with B and R. Read the word "bled" for the children and have them echo it.

Affirm that the letter pair at the beginning forms the blend BL. Call their attention to the fact that the meaning of the word changes with this letter change. Discuss the meaning of "bled" and use it in an original sentence. Write the word "bled" under the word "bred," highlighting the BL by writing in another color.

Follow the same pattern with the other words, forming "clock," "glass," "flog," and "plod." Lead the children to decode and read these words. Discuss their meanings and use them in original sentences.

Tell them that one other letter likes to "team up" with L to form a blend at the beginning of words. That is the letter S. Write a big S on the board and ask the children what sound is made by this letter. Add an L beside it and challenge them to blend the two sounds to make SL.

Write the word "sled" under the SL and assist the children to decode and read it. Ask the children if they can think of any other words which may begin with the SL blend. Write a few of them on the board also, highlighting the SL in another color.

Erase the board. Write the words found on Worksheet 15A on the board for display while you do the worksheet.

Worksheet 15A: Read the instructions aloud. Monitor as they circle the blends in each word. Call on students to read the words according to any of the variations below.

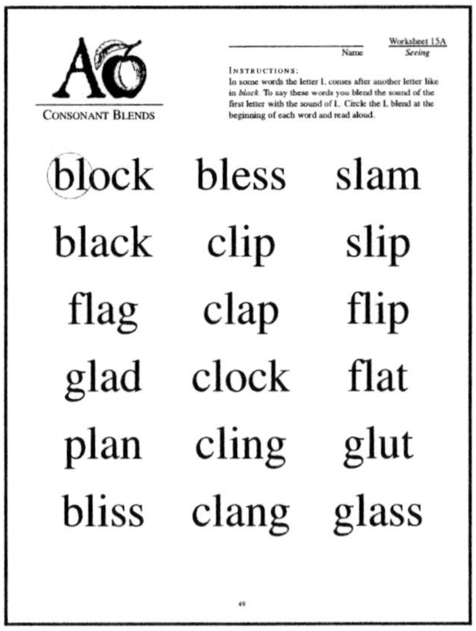
Consonant Blends

Name

Worksheet 15A
Seeing

Instructions:
In some words the letter L comes after another letter like in *black*. To say these words you blend the sound of the first letter with the sound of L. Circle the L blend at the beginning of each word and read aloud.

block	bless	slam
black	clip	slip
flag	clap	flip
glad	clock	flat
plan	cling	glut
bliss	clang	glass

Variations for prompting the reading of words on this sheet include: numbering the words and calling on students to read them by the designated number, verbal "fill-in-the-blanks," pointing to the written word on the board and having students point to the corresponding printed word on the sheet, riddle clues, categorizing on the basis of beginning sound, middle vowel, or ending letter group, etc.

ACTIVITY 2: WRITING

Write the beginning blends CL and BL on the board with guidelines. Call on students to come to the board and write the letter pairs. Remind them about stroke direction and order as necessary.

Worksheet 15B: Read the instructions aloud and monitor their work.

Consonant Blends

Name

Worksheet 15B
Writing

Instructions:
Follow the mazes for the L blends, then make them on your own.

bl

bl

clang

clock

black

Archives: Beginning Blends Edition (use only those cards with R and L blends).

Lesson 16
Target: L blends

Play Crash! Swing! Squash! for the children encouraging them to sing.

ACTIVITY 1: HEARING

Tell the children that they must be good listeners again today. You are going to read a list of words. Some of them will begin with one of the L blends we have been studying. When they hear a word with an L blend at the beginning, they should "flag it down" by pretending to wave a flag in the air.

Write the six L blend letter pairs on the board (GL, PL, BL, CL, SL, FL) Review the sound of each blend with the children and have them echo them. Read the following list of words:

plum	pocket	feed	flea	said	sled
climb	come	back	black	lack	glad
game	flame	slow	blow	clamp	please

Praise their careful listening!

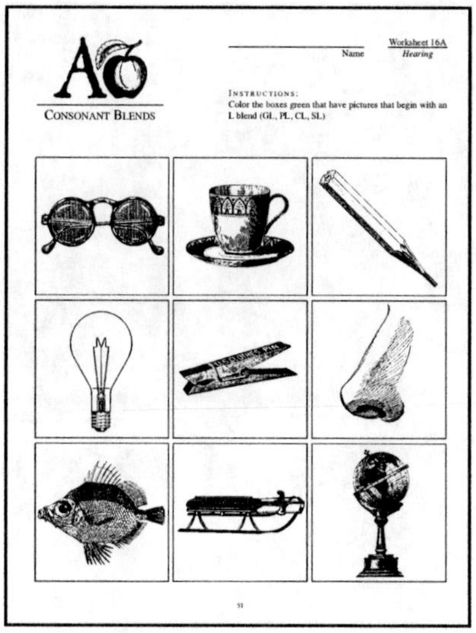

Worksheet 16A: Read the instructions aloud. Assist them to label the pictures and monitor as they respond as indicated.

Row 1: glasses, cup, pencil
Row 2: lightbulb, clothespin, nose
Row 3: fish, sled, globe

ACTIVITY 2: READING SYLLABLES

Display the BL puzzle piece. Have the children echo it several times. Present the puzzle pieces for each of the short vowel sounds in this order: A, E, I, O, U. Have the children echo them for you, then say them independently as you display or point to them randomly.

Place the U to the right of the BL and assist the children to sound out the syllable which is formed. Continue in the same way with the rest of the vowels, linking them to the beginning BL blend.

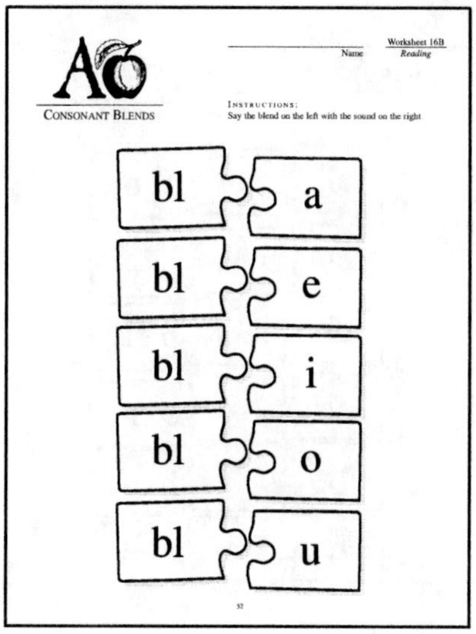

Continue in the same way with the blends CL, FL, and SL.

Worksheets 16B–16E: Read the instructions aloud and elicit student response.

Lesson 17
Target: L blends

Play Crash! Swing! Squash! for the children encouraging them to sing.

ACTIVITY 1: HEARING AND WRITING

Write the following across the top of the board: CL, GL, SL, PL. Review the sound made by each of these blends.

Read the following word list. After each word, invite a child to come to the board, point to the blend which is heard at the beginning of that word, then copy the letter pair which makes this blend.

class	glass	plot	slot	slam	clam
plan	sled	club	glad	pluck	Glen

Discuss the replacement of the lower case G with upper case "G" for the proper name "Glen."

Worksheet 17A: Read the instructions aloud. Assist the children to label the pictures as necessary. Remind them that there will be more than one picture to circle in each row. Monitor their work.

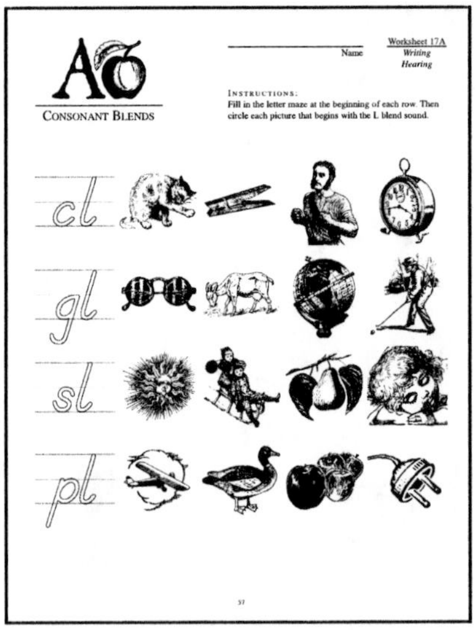
Worksheet 17A
Name
Writing
Hearing
CONSONANT BLENDS
INSTRUCTIONS:
Fill in the letter maze at the beginning of each row. Then circle each picture that begins with the L blend sound.
cl
gl
sl
pl

Row 1: cat, clothespin, man, clock
Row 2: glasses, goat, globe, golf
Row 3: sun, sled, pear, sleep
Row 4: plane, duck, apples, plug

ACTIVITY 2: READING

On the board, write the words from the above word list (which you used in the last teaching activity, not the worksheet words). Assist the children to decode and read aloud. Discuss meanings as necessary and solicit original sentences for each word. You may need to remind them about the decoding of final CK.

As a brief review of pluralization, add S to any appropriate word on this list and discuss how the meaning is changed.

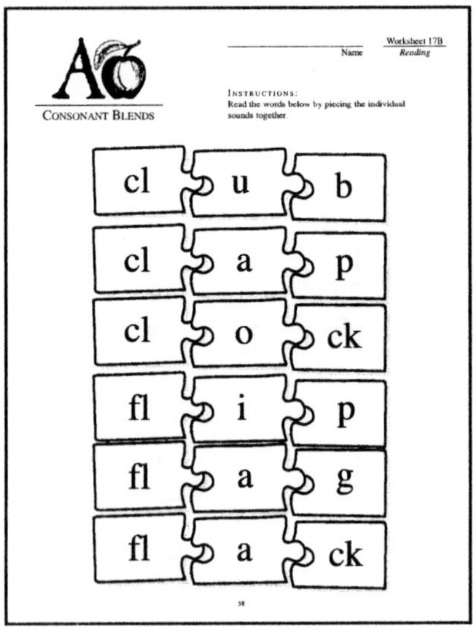
Worksheet 17B
Name
Reading
CONSONANT BLENDS
INSTRUCTIONS:
Read the words below by piecing the individual sounds together

cl	u	b
cl	a	p
cl	o	ck
fl	i	p
fl	a	g
fl	a	ck

Present the puzzle pieces needed to form the words on Worksheet 17B. Before passing out the worksheet, read each of the words on the worksheet and challenge the students to find and link the sounds which are necessary to form each word.

This is the first time students will be actually forming entire words with the puzzle pieces from dictation. Give them plenty of assistance with this.

Worksheet 17B: Read the instructions aloud. Elicit student response using any of the previous techniques.

Variations for prompting the reading of words on this sheet include: numbering the words and calling on students to read them by the designated number, verbal "fill-in-the-blanks," pointing to the written word on the board and having students point to the corresponding printed word on the sheet, riddle clues, categorizing on the basis of beginning sound, middle vowel, or ending letter group, etc.

ACTIVITY 3: READING VOCABULARY WORDS

Write the words on Worksheet 17C on the board in columns just as they are presented on the worksheet.

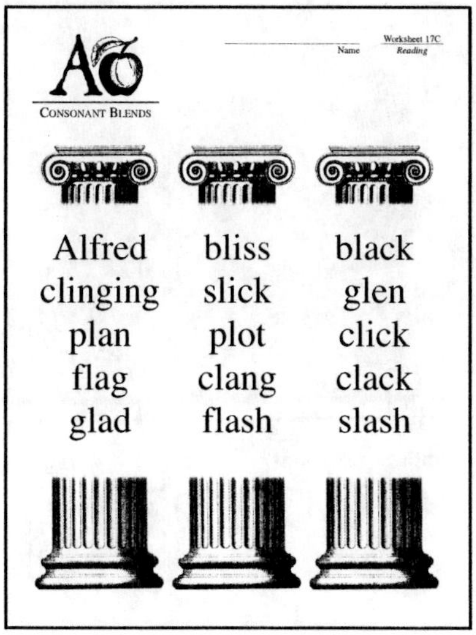

Worksheet 17C
Name
Reading
CONSONANT BLENDS

Alfred	bliss	black
clinging	slick	glen
plan	plot	click
flag	clang	clack
glad	flash	slash

Worksheet 17C: Read the instructions aloud. Assist the children to read the words from top to bottom of each column, following along on the worksheet as you point to the corresponding written word on the board. Repeat the activity going from bottom to top of each column. Finally, point randomly to the words on the columns and call on students to read them.

Pay particular attention to the words "Alfred" and "clinging." These will probably require additional assistance to decode. You may want to divide these into syllables and decode each syllable separately, then recombine to form the larger word.

Have students point to the word on their sheets which matches the word you point to on the board, without hearing it read.

Erase the words from the board and then have students point to or circle the correct word as you randomly say them. You may want to do this on an individual or small group basis to more carefully monitor their responses.

Discuss the meanings of the more uncommon words. Use the words in sentences.

You may have children come to the board and copy the shorter words as additional reinforcement.

Archives: Beginning Blends Edition (use only those cards with R and L blends).

LESSON 18
TARGET: L BLENDS

ACTIVITY 1: HEARING, SEEING AND WRITING

Give each child four index cards. Write the following on the board: PL, GL, CL, SL. Instruct the children to write one letter pair on each card.

Tell them you will be reading a list of words, and they are to hold up the card with the letter pair which makes the blend they hear at the beginning of each word. Read the following words, one at a time, allowing time for student response:

slow	plan	clap	glow	please	slim
clip	glue	sleet	plant	glove	close

Worksheet 18A: Read the instructions aloud. Assist the children to label the pictures, but give no other letter or sound clues. Monitor their work.

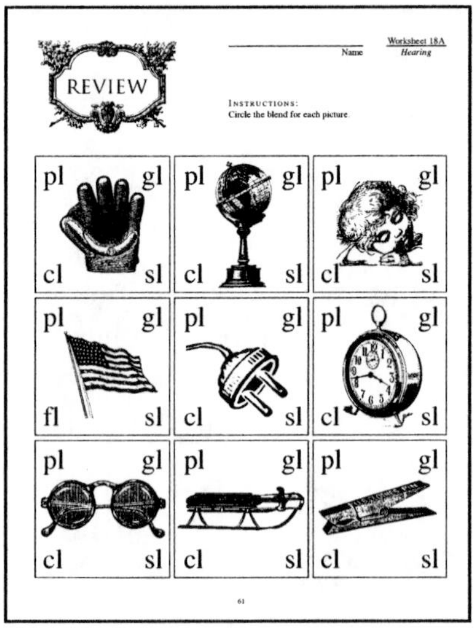

Row 1: glove, globe, sleep
Row 2: flag, plug, clock
Row 3: glasses, sled, clothespin

ACTIVITY 2: WRITING AND READING

Write the words from Worksheet 18B, on the board along with guide lines. Invite students to the board to write the words. Remind them about stroke order and direction.

Worksheet 18B: Read the instructions aloud. Monitor the students' progress as they work independently.

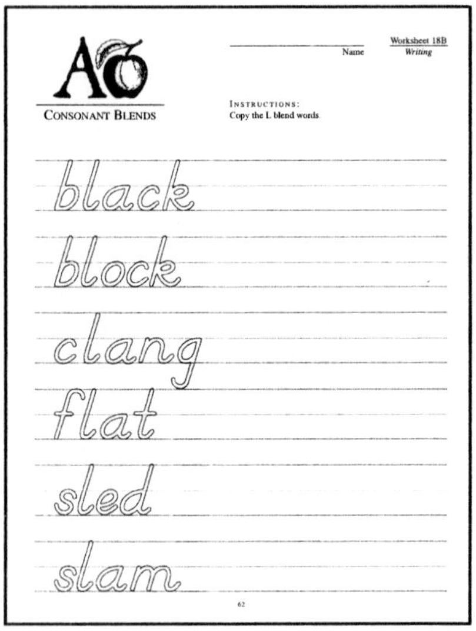

Remind about the "FOUR P's" if you haven't done so in a while!

ACTIVITY 3: ART ACTIVITY

Prepare a completed sound wheel as indicated on Worksheets 15C and D. Show the children how it works and prompt them to read the syllables formed.

Worksheets 18C and D: Read the instructions aloud and assist children as necessary to make their own wheels.

Bingo: Use R and L blends. The Bingo cards (found in the Appendix) should be filled by the students with the following blends: BR, CR, DR, FR, GR, PR, TR, WR, BL, CL, FL, GL, PL, and SL. The teacher will then call out words containing any of the above blends.

LESSON 19
TARGET: L AND R BLENDS, READING ALFRED THE KING

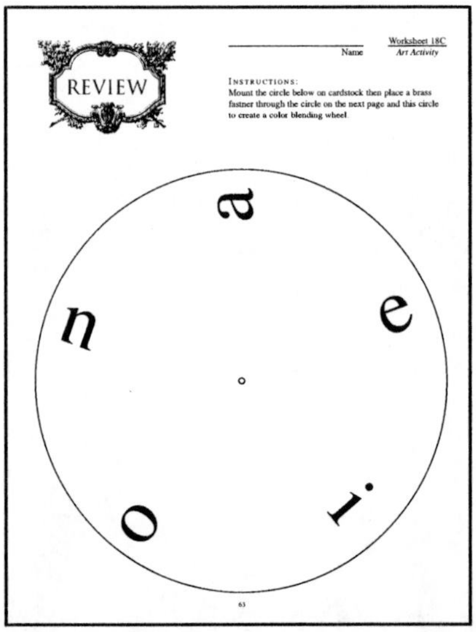

ACTIVITY 1: READING WORDS

Use the riddle game to prompt answers which require the use of the words on Worksheet 19A. For instance, tell the children "I am thinking of something which we use to tell time. Sometimes it has an alarm or bell in it to wake us up. What is it?" (clock)

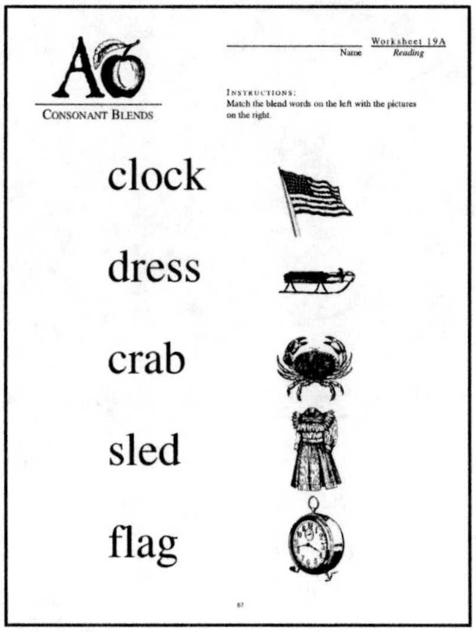
Worksheet 19A

Name Reading

CONSONANT BLENDS

INSTRUCTIONS:
Match the blend words on the left with the pictures on the right.

clock

dress

crab

sled

flag

When the correct answer is offered, call on that student to come to the board and write the letter pair blend which begins that word. Invite another child to write the letter for the vowel sound which is heard in the middle. Invite a third child to finish the word with the final letter or letters.

They will need help with final CK and SS. Guide them through the process of determining the sounds used (K and S), then give assistance in deciding how it is spelled. Once again, this is essentially spelling from dictation and is a very new skill for them.

Worksheet 19A: Read the instructions aloud and Monitor the students' progress as they work independently.

ACTIVITY 2: READING ALFRED THE KING

This story chronicles the battle between the Saxons and the Vikings during Alfred's reign in England (Wessex) in the late 800's. The following vocabulary and expressions are used, which may require clarification to students as they read:

Saxons—the people who lived in Britain at this time
bliss—happiness, joy
brash—aggressive
North Men—Vikings
trash—destroy
trek—trip, long journey
clash—fight
quell—stop
fifth son—usually an older sibling takes the throne
grab and crush—fight in combat
gruff—angry, harsh
fret—worry
brag of their sin—glorify their evil deeds
dull god—powerless non-deity
glen—clearing in the forest
glum—sad
click and clack—the sound of axes in battle
sun slips by—it is getting dark
gravel—dirt
slick with red—covered with blood
bless—praise
clinging to the flag—believing in the flag
match—beat
rush—charge
prep—to get ready

Special Names:
- Egburt
- Athelwulf
- Guthram

Special Places:
- Wessex
- Sussex
- Essex

Guide the children through the "round robin" reading of this story. Encourage fluency and expression. Call attention to end marks and proper voice inflection for questions and exclamations.

Discuss pictures, characters, main ideas and events as you go along.

Lesson 20
Reading Comprehension and Review

ACTIVITY 1: ART ACTIVITY

Prepare a finished crown as directed on Worksheet 20A and show the children how it was made.

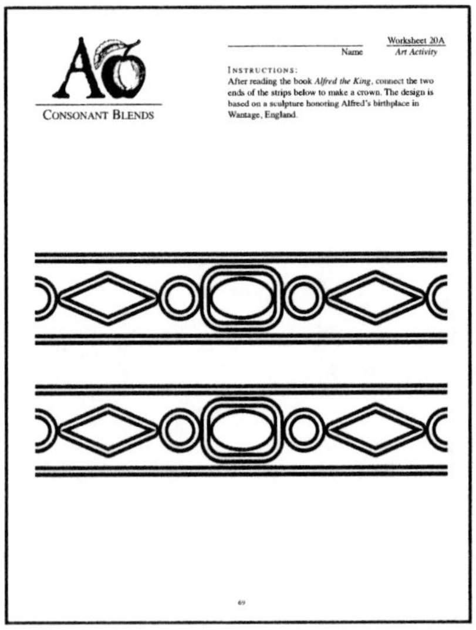

Worksheet 20A: Read the instructions aloud. Have the children color the strips before cutting them out. Assist as needed to adjust the crown strips to fit the children's heads.

ACTIVITY 2: READING COMPREHENSION

Review and discuss yesterday's story. Go over the characters and main events in order. Write the special names of people and places on the board for reference.

Worksheet 20B: Read the instructions aloud. Monitor as they read the sentences to themselves and respond as indicated.

ACTIVITY 3: REVIEW

Tell the children that they will each have a chance to be the "teacher" today! You will give them each a word written on an index card to read to the class. They will call on someone to tell the beginning sound and letter for that word. The "teacher" will then use the pointer to point to the stimulus picture on the flashcard for that letter/sound and write the letter in lower case on the board.

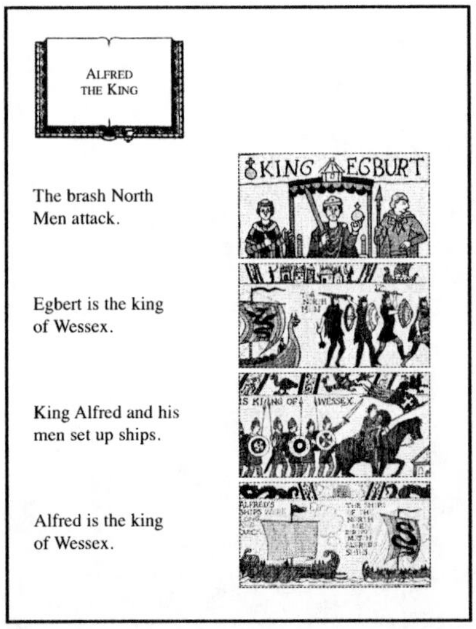

Alfred the King
King Egburt
The brash North Men attack.
Egbert is the king of Wessex.
King Alfred and his men set up ships.
Alfred is the king of Wessex.

The child they have called on will then become the "teacher."

Monitor to make sure every child has an opportunity to be the "teacher" and every child has had a chance to respond.

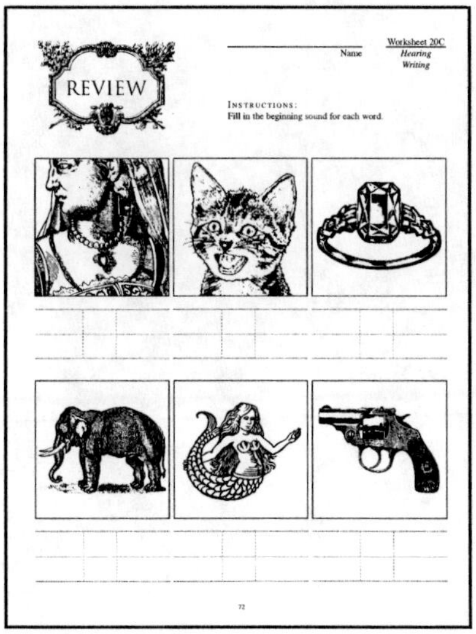

Write the following words on index cards:

gum	neck	cap	rang	exit	mat
hop	pass	big	gong	sell	are
what	shop	chin	nap	fun	tack
lips	ham	cash	Jim	zip	you
ill	up	on	quit	thin	this

fox *(remind them this is for the final X sound)*

Worksheet 20C: Read the instructions aloud. Monitor the students' progress as they work independently.

Worksheet 20D: Test. This test is optional and is added to evaluate your students if you feel it is necessary at this time. The answers are worth 10 points each.

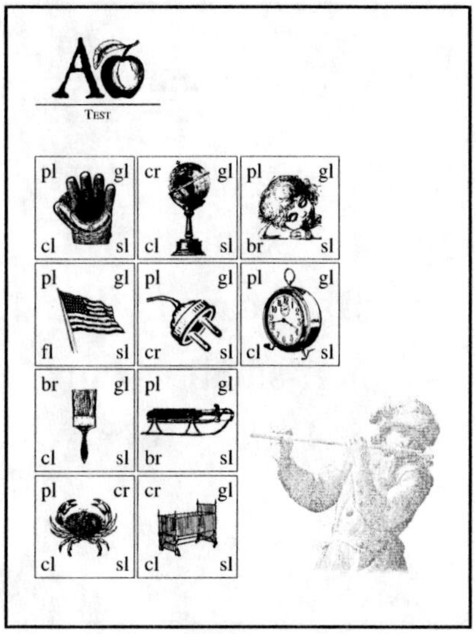

LESSON 21
TARGET: S BLENDS

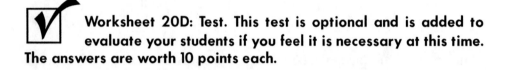

Play Crash! Swing! Squash! for the children encouraging them to sing.

ACTIVITY 1: HEARING AND SEEING TWO-LETTER S BLENDS

Write a BIG upper case S on the board. Brainstorm with the children to come up with a dozen or so words which begin with S. Write these on the board around the letter. If students offer words with S blends at the beginning, this is fine. In fact it will contribute to the lesson.

Look carefully at the list. If there are no words starting with the blends ST, SC, SK, SM, SN, SP, or SW, add the following to the list: stem, smack, scab, skill, snap, switch, spot. Underline the beginning S in each word.

Now challenge the children. Tell them that in some of these words, S has taken along another consonant to help as the leader. Remind them that a consonant is any letter which is not A, E, I, O, U. Call on students to come to the board and point to the words with S + consonant at the beginning. Circle the two-letter blend, say it aloud and have the children echo it after you.

Tell them that these letter pairs are like the L blends and the R blends: the two sounds run together and work as a "team."

Erase the board. Across the top of the board, write each of the two letter S blends. Invite students to say the blends as you point to them randomly.

Tell them that two of these letter pair blends are "sound twins"—they do not look alike, but they sound alike. Challenge them to find the "twins" by reading the blends again. The "twins" are SC and SK. Praise correct answers and point out that they will see both spellings used in their reading, but the blended sound will be the same.

Have the children move their finger through the air in a squiggle like a snake when they hear the sound of S. Tell them to use this gesture to indicate to you when they hear one of the S BLENDS at the beginning of any of the following words:

soap	small	stone	tape	skip	snail
soon	swap	scoot	sick	spit	stick
smoke	sail	sneak	scout	sell	swell

Write the words found at the beginning of this lesson under the appropriate letter pair headings on the board. Call on students to come to the board and circle the letter pair in each word and decode it. Discuss meanings as necessary and use in original sentence.

Worksheet 21A
Seeing
Name
CONSONANT BLENDS
INSTRUCTIONS:
In some words the S comes before another letter like in the word *stop*. To say these words you blend the sound of S with the sound of the letter that comes after it. Circle the blend at the beginning of each word.

stop skip spin
stuff scat swim
stick scan swam
skin smell swing
snug

Worksheet 21A: Read the instructions aloud. Monitor the students' progress as they work independently.

ACTIVITY 2: HEARING AND SEEING THREE-LETTER S BLENDS

Erase the SM, SN, SK and SW from the board, along with their stimulus words. Erase the stimulus words under the ST, SC, and SP.

Tell them you are now going to show them something they have never done before. In a different color, write R after each of the two-letter blends on the board.

Ask the children: "NOW, how do you think we are going to say these three letter blends? Let's try it and see what we get." Read each of the blends and have the children echo after you.

Now write the following under the appropriate letter triplet: strong, scrap, spring. Call on students to come to the board and circle the three-letter blend at the beginning. Assist the students to decode the words. Discuss meanings and use in original sentences.

Tell them there are two more blends they will learn today. One starts with S and the other starts with SH. Write each of these on the board.

Ask them to listen carefully to this word: squirt. Challenge them to think of the letter which makes the KW sound in this word. Agree that it sounds like it could be just K, but call their attention to the W which can be heard after the K sound. Ask them what letter they have studied makes the KW sound. (Q) Praise correct answers and write the Q after the S.

Now, challenge them to think of the letter which Q ALWAYS takes with it when it gets in the letter line which makes up a word. (U) Praise correct responses and write the U after the Q. Tell them these are the letters they will see in their reading when the SKW sound is used.

Point to the SH. Ask someone to tell the class what sound is made when S and H stand together. Praise correct responses and affirm that this is not a blend of S and H, but is an entirely new sound.

Write R after the SH on the board. Ask them: "Based on what we did with the three-letter blends STR and SPR, what do you thing this will sound like?" Assist the children to decode SHR. Give the following words as examples of this sound at the beginning: shred, shrink, shrimp.

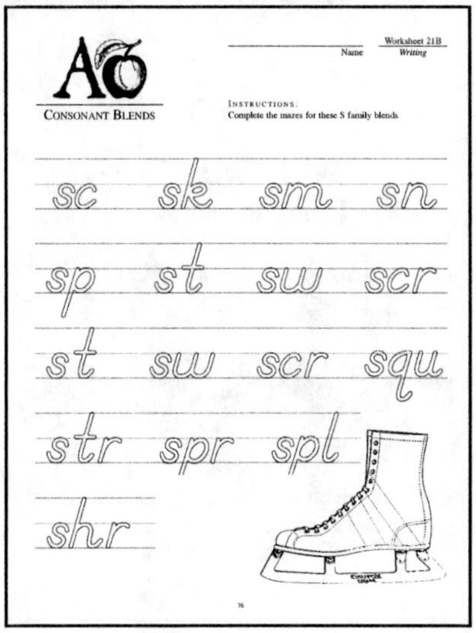

Now tell them there is only one more S blend to be studied today. Erase the R from the blend SPR and replace it with L. Challenge them to blend the three sounds to make SPL. Give the following words as examples of this sound at the beginning: splash, split, splendid.

ACTIVITY 3: WRITING S AND SH BLENDS

Write the blends listed on Worksheet 21B on the board. Invite students to come to the board and write the letters. Remind them about stroke direction and order as needed. Have them say the blend as it is completed.

Worksheet 21B: Read the instructions aloud and monitor their work.

Archives: Beginning Blends Edition (use only those cards with R, L, and S blends covered to this point).

Lesson 22
Target: S Blends

Play Crash! Swing! Squash! for the children encouraging them to sing.

ACTIVITY 1: HEARING AND WRITING

Write the following four S blends across the top of the board: SK, SM, SN, SW. Tell the children that you will be reading a list of words which will begin with one of these S blends.

Read the following list. After each word, call on students to repeat the blend at the beginning of it and come to the board to write the word under the correct letter pair (with your assistance with spelling as necessary).

skip	smell	snap	swatch	skit
smog	snip	swell	smack	swim

Remind about stroke direction and order as needed.

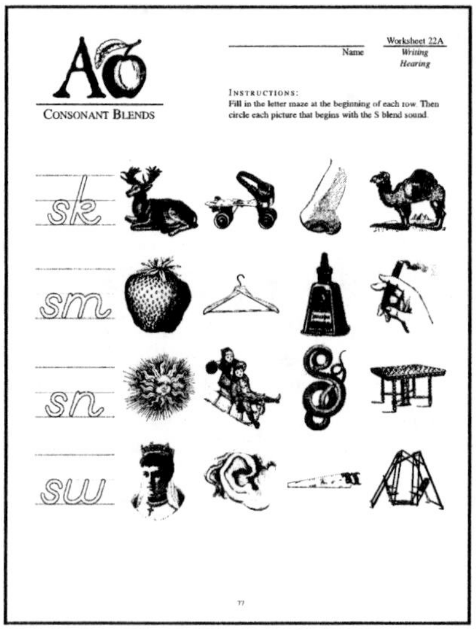

Worksheet 22A: Read the instructions aloud. Assist the children to label the pictures, but give no other letter or sound clues. Tell them to be careful; some of the labels are S blend words, but not the blend written at the beginning of the row! Monitor their work.

Row 1: deer, skate, nose, camel
Row 2: strawberry, hanger, ink, smoke
Row 3: sun, sled, snake, table
Row 4: queen, ear, saw, swing

ACTIVITY 2: READING SYLLABLES

Display the SM puzzle piece. Have the children echo it several times. Present the puzzle pieces for each of the short vowel sounds in this order: A, E, I, O, U. Have the children echo them for you, then say them independently as you display or point to them randomly.

Place the U to the right of the SM and assist the children to sound out the syllable which is formed. Continue in the same way with the rest of the vowels, linking them to the beginning SM sound.

Follow the same pattern for presenting SN, SC/SK, SP, ST, and SW.

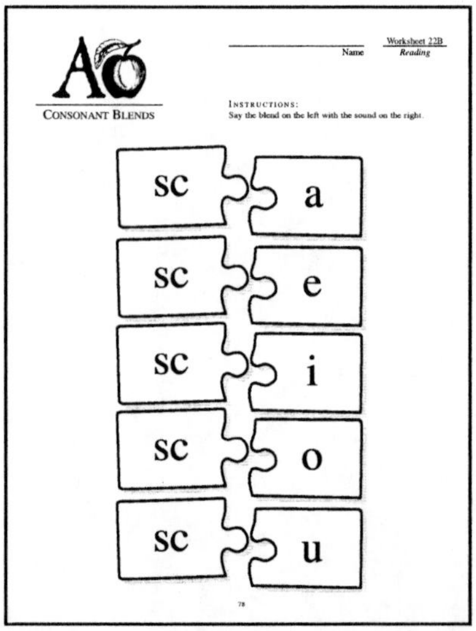

Worksheet 22B–H: Read the directions aloud. Direct the children to read the syllables in various ways: in order, randomly, pointing to them as you say them randomly, etc.

LESSON 23
TARGET: S BLENDS

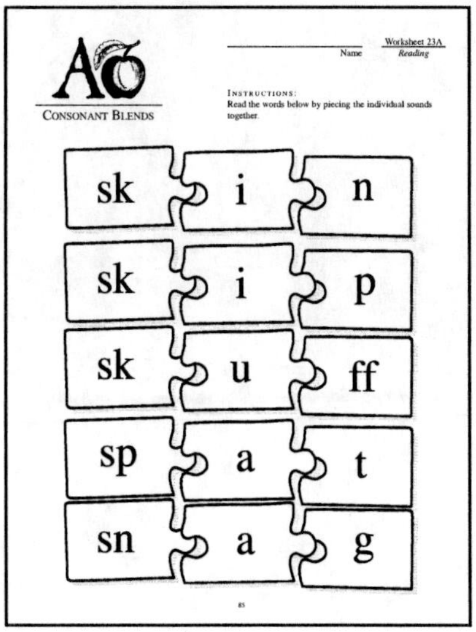

ACTIVITY 1: READING WORDS

Tell the children they will be using the puzzle pieces today to form words using the S blends. Write the following across the top of the board: sk, sp, sn. Review the sounds made by each blend.

Present the puzzle piece for SK, A, I, U. Ask which vowel piece you will need to form the syllable "ski." Praise correct responses and invite a student to link the I piece with the SK piece.

Present the puzzle pieces for N, M, P, and LL. Ask which one of these will need to be added to the SKI syllable to form the word "skin." Praise correct responses and invite someone to link the N piece with the SKI syllable. Call on students to read the word and use it in an original sentence.

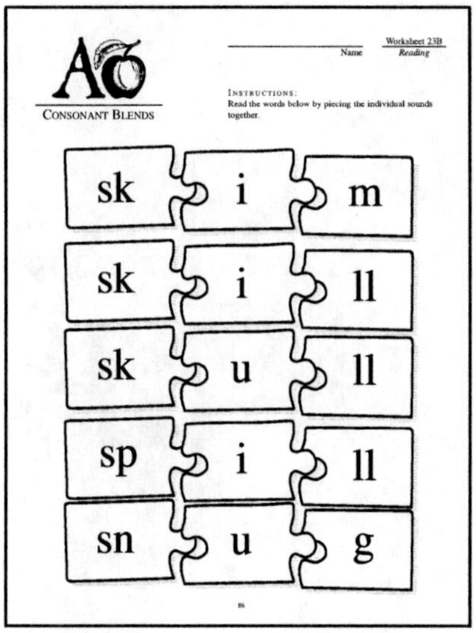

Continue in the same way to form the words "skim," "skip," and "skill." Discuss the meanings of these words and use in sentences.

Present the puzzle piece for SP, I, LL and N. Form the words "spill" and "spin" in the same way as above.

Finally, present the puzzle piece for SN, A, U, G and P. Assist the children to form the words "snap," "snag," and "snug." Discuss meanings and use in sentences.

Worksheet 23A/B: Read the instructions aloud and elicit student response in any of the previous ways. You may want to write the words on the board to further reinforce printed-to-written matching.

ACTIVITY 2: WRITING

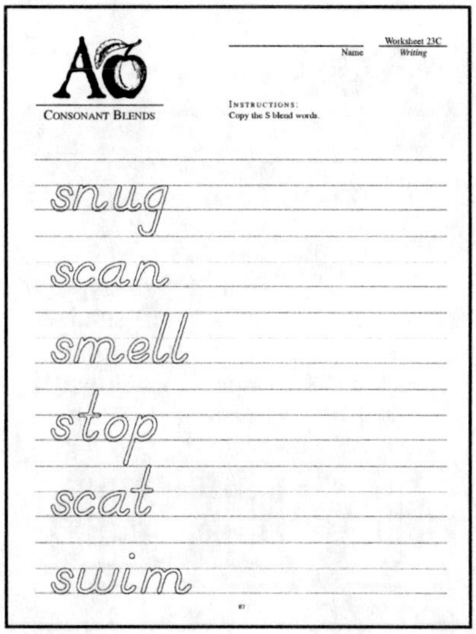

Write the words found on Worksheet 23C, along with guidelines on the board. Invite children to the board to write the words. Remind as necessary about stroke direction and order.

If you are noticing some students persisting in incorrect letter formation, additional monitored practice may be necessary. Stroke direction and order are important for future transition to cursive.

Worksheet 23C: Read the instructions aloud and Monitor the students' progress as they work independently.

Lesson 24
Target: S blends

ACTIVITY 1: HEARING

Write the following across the top of the board: SL, SC/SK, SM, ST, SN, SW. Review the sounds made by each blend. Remind them that SC and SK make the same sound and are used in words according to spelling rules.

Tell them you will be reading a list of words and you will call on students to tell you what letter pair makes the beginning sound of each word. They will then come to the board and copy the letter pair under the example. Reassure them that you will tell them whether to write SC or SK when the SK sound is heard.

scale	smoke	sled	swing	stamp
skunk	skate	snake	stove	sweet
small	stone	scat	slip	slow

Praise their careful listening!

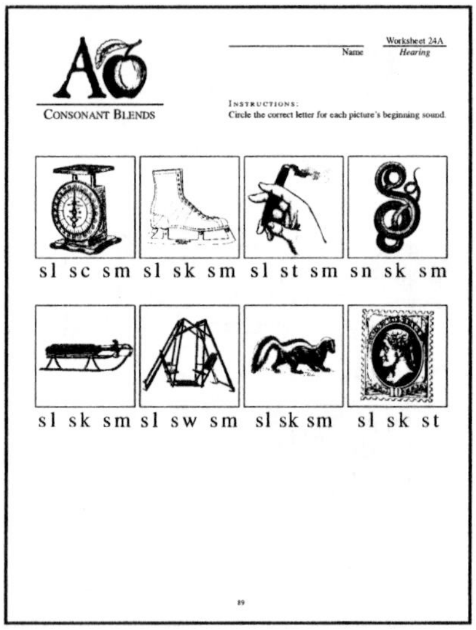
Worksheet 24A
Name
Hearing
Consonant Blends
Instructions:
Circle the correct letter for each picture's beginning sound.

sl sc sm | sl sk sm | sl st sm | sn sk sm

sl sk sm | sl sw sm | sl sk sm | sl sk st

Worksheet 24A: Read the instructions aloud. Assist them to label as necessary. Reassure them that when the SK sound is heard, the choices will not include both SC and SK, but only the one which is used to spell that word. Monitor their work.

Row 1: scale, skate, smoke, snake
Row 3: sled, swing, skunk, stamp

ACTIVITY 2: READING WORDS

Across the top of the board write the following: SCR, SPR, STR. Review with the children the sound made by each of these three-letter blends. Give examples of words which use each one: scrub, sprout, strap, etc.

Write the words on Worksheet 24B on the board in columns just as they are presented on the worksheet. Have students come to the board and underline all the two-letter blends and circle all the three-letter blends. They may want to do this on the worksheet as well just to highlight these letter combinations.

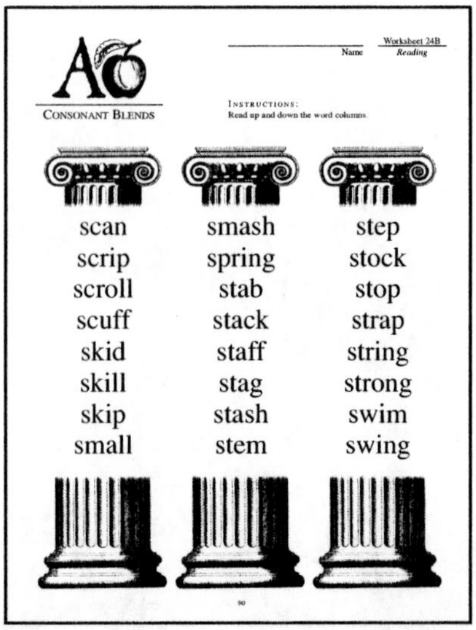
Worksheet 24B
Name
Reading
Consonant Blends
Instructions:
Read up and down the word columns.

scan	smash	step
scrip	spring	stock
scroll	stab	stop
scuff	stack	strap
skid	staff	string
skill	stag	strong
skip	stash	swim
small	stem	swing

Worksheet 24B: Read the instructions aloud. Assist the children to read the words from top to bottom of each column, following along on the worksheet as you point to the corresponding written word on the board. Repeat the activity going from bottom to top of each column. Finally, point randomly to the words on the columns and call on students to read them.

Have students point to the word on their sheets which matches the word you point to on the board, without hearing it read.
Erase the words from the board and then have students point to or circle the correct word as you randomly say them. You may want to do this on an individual or small group basis to more carefully monitor their responses.

Discuss the meanings of any of the more uncommon words. Use the words in sentences. You may have children come to the board and copy entire words from their sheets for further reinforcement.

Lesson 25
Target: Three-letter S blends and THR

ACTIVITY 1: HEARING AND SEEING

Across the top of the board write the following: SCR, SPR, STR. Review the sounds made by each blend. Give examples of words which start with each one: scribble, sprain, strike, etc.

Remind them that in each case, all three letter sounds are heard and they all work together in a team to form the blended sound.

Now write the following on the board: SH, TH. Ask if they remember what sounds these letter pairs make. Praise correct responses.

Add an R after each of these letter pairs, forming SHR and THR. Underline the SH and TH. Guide the children through the decoding of these blends, using the proper sound for the initial letter pair and blending with the R. Give examples of words which use these blends: shrink, shrimp, throw, thrush. Define the words as needed and use in original sentences.

Give the students two index cards and ask them to write SHR on one and THR on the other. Tell them you will be reading a list of words and they are to hold up the card with the letter group on it which makes the beginning sound. If neither sound is heard, they should not hold up either card. This is tricky so they must listen carefully!

ship	shrunk	thin	threw	shrub
thank	throw	shape	throb	shred

Present the puzzle pieces for SCR, SPR, SHR, THR, and all the vowels. Call on students to form various syllables by linking the correct pieces according to the syllable you say. Use random syllables, varying blend and vowel used.

Present the puzzle pieces for B, P, D, and G. Call on students to link them to the proper blend+vowel syllable to form the words on Worksheet 25A. Write the words formed on the board.

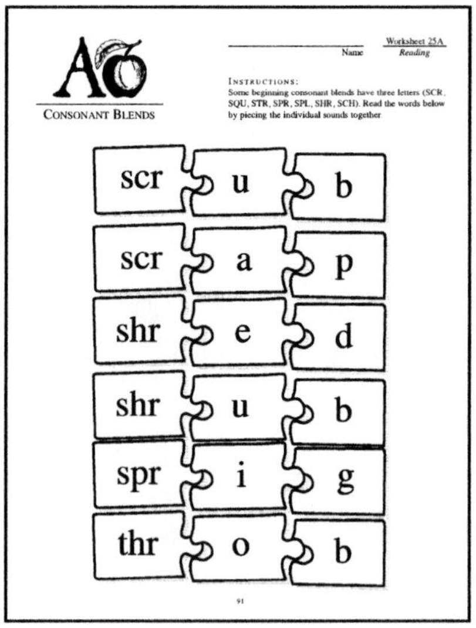
Worksheet 25A
Name Reading
CONSONANT BLENDS
INSTRUCTIONS:
Some beginning consonant blends have three letters (SCR, SQU, STR, SPR, SPL, SHR, SCH). Read the words below by piecing the individual sounds together.
scr u b
scr a p
shr e d
shr u b
spr i g
thr o b
91

Worksheet 25A: Read the instructions aloud. Assist the children to read the words using any of the variations previously suggested. Discuss meanings and use the words in original sentences.

Variations for prompting the reading of words on this sheet include: numbering the words and calling on students to read them by the designated number, verbal "fill-in-the-blanks," pointing to the written word on the board and having students point to the corresponding printed word on the sheet, riddle clues, categorizing on the basis of beginning blend, middle vowel, or ending letter, etc.

ACTIVITY 2: WRITING

Tell the children there is one S blend that has not been talked about for a while. Read the following words and challenge them to try to figure out what this blend might be: squish, squid, squall, squawk.

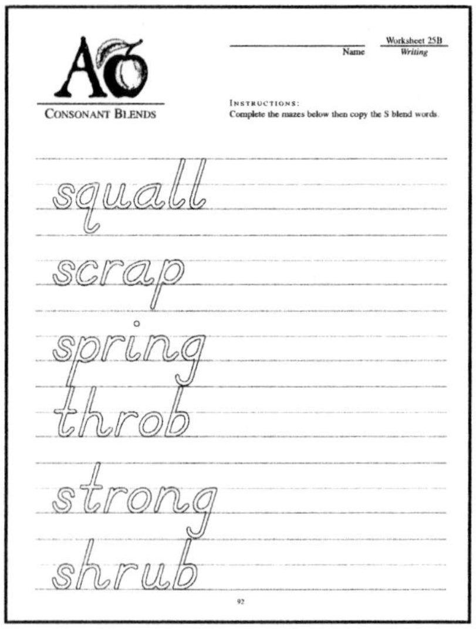
Worksheet 25B
Name Writing
CONSONANT BLENDS
INSTRUCTIONS:
Complete the mazes below then copy the S blend words.
squall
scrap
spring
throb
strong
shrub
92

The children might think it is SKW, but guide them to realize that QU is needed to make the KW sound. Write SQU on the board and have them echo it several times.

Write the three-letter blends found on Worksheet 25B on the board. Call students to the board to write them. Reinforce the sounds made by each.

Worksheet 25B: Read the instructions aloud. Monitor the students' progress as they work independently. Call on students to read the words formed, define as necessary and use in original sentences.

LESSON 26
REVIEW

Play Crash! Swing! Squash! for the children encouraging them to sing.

ACTIVITY 1: HEARING AND WRITING

Write the following across the top of the board: BL, GL, CR, DR. Call on students to read the blends and give you an example of a word which starts with each.

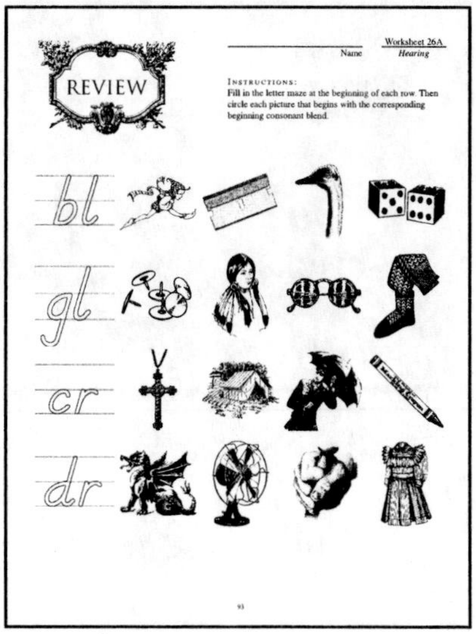

Make sure DR is pronounced clearly (not as J).

Tell them it is listening time again. You will read some words and call on students to come to the board and copy the letter pair which makes the beginning blend of each word, under the example on the board.

glasses	blade	crab	cross	drum	black
drug	dragon	crayon	blow	glossy	glad

Worksheet 26A: Read the instructions aloud. Assist the children to label the pictures, but give no other sound or letter clues. Monitor their work.

Row 1: elf, blade, ostrich, dice
Row 2: tacks, Indian, glasses, socks
Row 3: cross, tent, umbrella, crayon
Row 4: dragon, fan, thumb, dress

ACTIVITY 2: HEARING AND WRITING

Erase the board. Write the following across the top: FR, TR, SC, SK. Review the sounds made by each and invite them to give you examples of FR and TR words. Ask which two make the same blended sound (SC and SK). Move the SC and SK together to show their sound similarity. You should offer examples of SC and SK based on proper spelling.

Make sure TR is pronounced clearly (not as CH).

Tell them you will be reading words which will start with one of these blends. They must come to the board when called upon and write the letter pair which makes the blend heard at the beginning of each word. Assure them you will help when it comes to SC or SK, but they must know that it is one or the other!

frame	train	scale	skunk	frog
trip	scout	skirt	frost	trick

Worksheet 26B: Read the instructions aloud. Assist the children to label as necessary. Monitor their work.

Row 1: elephant, tiger, frame, dog
Row 2: shoe, train, jacks, ring
Row 3: sun, scale, unicorn, walrus
Row 4: rabbit, faucet, skunk, quilt

ACTIVITY 3: READING

Little or no instruction should be needed for most students to complete the next worksheet. Those who may need additional assistance can be taken aside into a small group. For those students you could write the worksheet words on the board and guide them through the decoding before presenting the worksheet for independent reading.

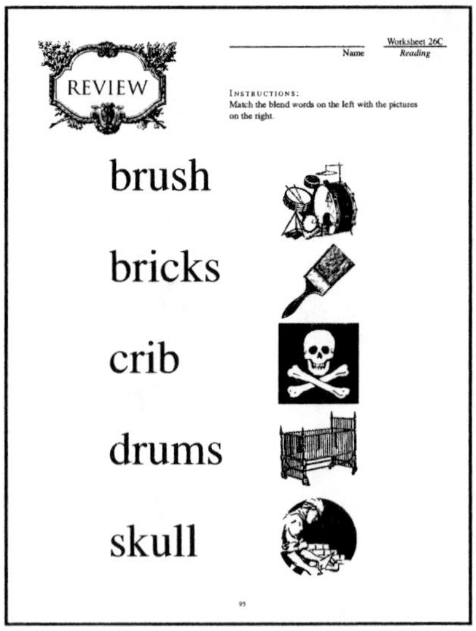
Worksheet 26C
Name Reading
REVIEW
INSTRUCTIONS: Match the blend words on the left with the pictures on the right.

brush
bricks
crib
drums
skull

Worksheet 26C: Read the instructions aloud. Monitor the students' progress as they work independently.

Percival's Pairs: Using ING, ANG, ONG, and R, L, S blends.

LESSON 27
TARGET: TW/DW BLENDS, REVIEW, AND SPECIAL EXHIBITS

ACTIVITY 1: HEARING AND SEEING

Write the blend SW on the board. Ask someone to tell you what sound is made by this letter pair. Write the following two word examples on the board under the letter pair: swig, swell. Discuss the meanings of these two words and use in original sentences.

Tell the children that there are two more blends which they must recognize in order to read some of the words in their next book.

Erase the S in "swig" and replace it with a T. Remind the children that the sounds of the letters in a blend run together and act as a "team." Assist the children to decode the word "twig" using the TW blend. Discuss the meaning of this word and use it in a sentence.

Now erase the S in "swell" and replace it with a D. Assist the children to decode "dwell" using the DW blend. Discuss the meaning and use it in a sentence.

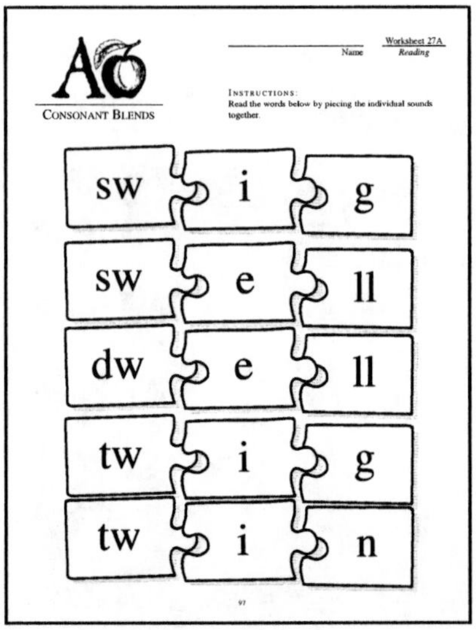
Worksheet 27A
Name Reading
CONSONANT BLENDS
INSTRUCTIONS: Read the words below by piecing the individual sounds together.

sw	i	g
sw	e	ll
dw	e	ll
tw	i	g
tw	i	n

Again, in spontaneous speech, these two blends often are somewhat slurred into CH and J sounds followed by W. Try to produce the blends as clearly as possible for teaching purposes, even though the distortions are commonplace and understandable in standard spoken English.

Worksheets 27A: Read the instructions aloud and elicit student response.

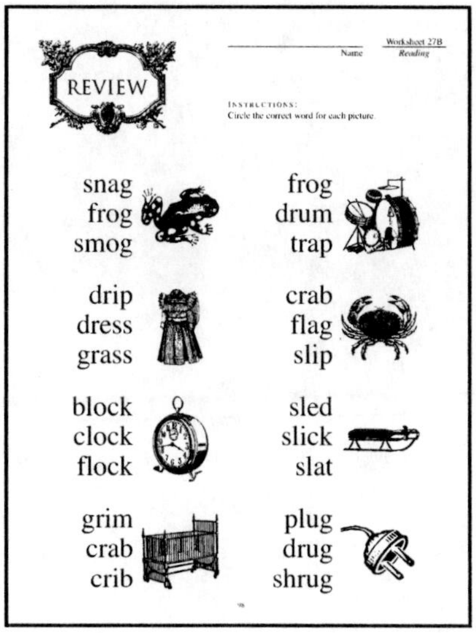

ACTIVITY 2: REVIEW

Write the words found in the first group on Worksheet 27B on the board in a vertical column. Tell the children that they must be careful listeners and readers today. You will be reading one of the words on the board and they must choose which word is the one you have read. Read the word "smog." Call on a student to come to the board and circle the correct word. After the correct response is completed, have students read the other words also to reinforce reading skills.

Using the words as they are presented on Worksheet 27B, continue this activity. Do NOT read the words which are used as stimulus pictures on this worksheet, but choose one of the other two in each example.

Worksheet 27B: Read the instructions aloud. If students have trouble determining the label for any picture, encourage them to decode and read the word choices first and pick the one which best fits. Do not label the pictures for them.

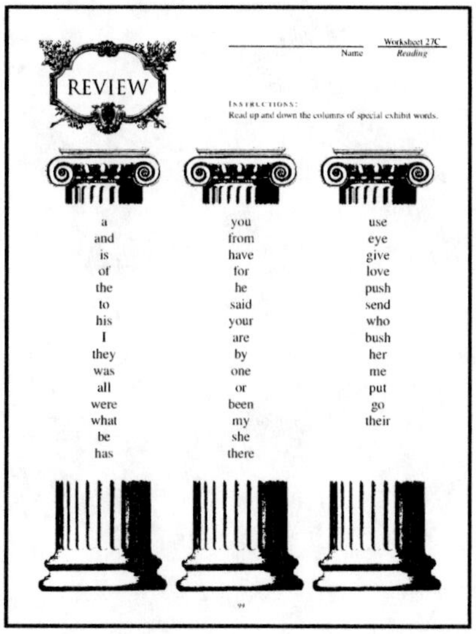

ACTIVITY 3: SPECIAL EXHIBIT REVIEW

Write the words on Worksheet 27C on the board in columns just as they are presented on the worksheet. You may want to do this in sections, there are a lot of words on this page!

Pay special attention to the words "she" and "bush." These are new to the children. Help them to decode "she" based on the previous word "me," and "bush" based on the previous word "push."

Worksheet 27C: Read the instructions aloud. Assist the children to read the words from top to bottom of each column, following along on the worksheet as you point to the corresponding written word on the board. Repeat the activity going from bottom to top of each column. Finally, point randomly to the words on the columns and call on students to read them.

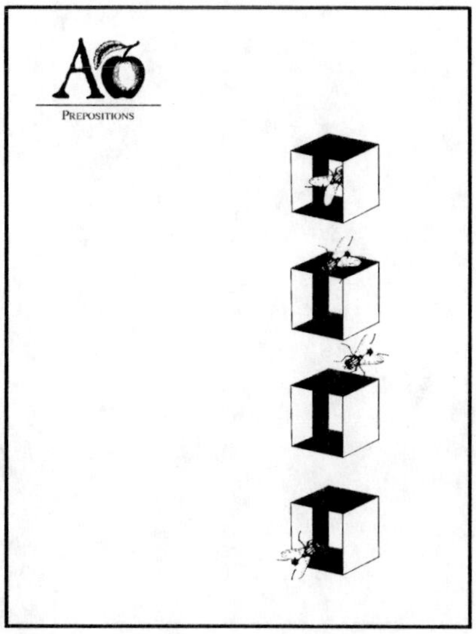

Have students point to the word on their sheets which matches the word you point to on the board, without hearing it read.

Erase the words from the board and then have students point to or circle the correct word as you randomly say them. You may want to do this on an individual or small group basis to more carefully monitor their responses.

Discuss the meanings of any of the more uncommon words. Use the words in sentences. You may have children come to the board and copy entire words from their sheets for further reinforcement.

Worksheet 27D: Read the instructions aloud. Monitor the students' progress as they work independently.

Lesson 28
Reading MY CLARA

ACTIVITY 1: READING

This story is an example of fantasy. It features a magical bird (thrush) which is an enchanted nix (water sprite in Germanic folklore). You may want to discuss briefly with the children that such tales are only make-believe. Reassure them that magical stories are entertaining, but that only our God has true power and total control over all of life!

The children will encounter the possessive ITS in this story. Observant children may notice that it does not have an apostrophe, like the other possessive forms they have studied. Affirm their observation and tell them this is an exception to the apostrophe + S rule. They will understand why in future lessons (when they get to contractions).

There are also two end marks used together at one point in this story: "What!?" When you get to this, tell them that both are used to emphasize that the question is asked in a surprised manner. Demonstrate using proper inflection. Also, the superlative form "biggest" is used. Children will be able to decode it, but you may want to discuss how the EST is added to mean "the most."

The following vocabulary and phrases are used:

bit hot—a little warm
snapdragon—a kind of flower
spit spot—without a trace of dirt
linens—sheets, bedclothes
drill—practice
splendid—wonderful
thrush—small bird
long spell—long time
shrub—low growing bush
shrill—high pitched sound
twitch—quick, startled movement
strip—take off
status—state of being
snag—catch
flash—sudden burst of bright light
flit—short flight
smock—loose fitting dress
thicket—dense growth of bushes and woods
trod—walked along
moss—a small, leafy-stemmed plant that grows on moist ground
thrust—to throw off with force
black walnut—a type of tree with walnuts for fruit

swish—the sound a bird makes with its wings (an onomatopoeia)
squish—to squeeze
attic—top part
splash—the sun's rays shine
swell—great
spin—turn around
switch—turn into
lass—girl
nix—sprite; fairy-like fantasy creature
gloss—shiny surface
spring-fed—watered by a spring
skillfull—able to do something well

Assist the children in their reading "round robin" style. Encourage fluency and expression. Discuss characters, main ideas and events as you proceed through the book.

Some discussion questions may include: Why was the thrush silent at the beginning of the story? Why did Clara follow the thrush? Would YOU have done the same thing—why or why not? Do you think Clara will return to the walnut tree? Would YOU?

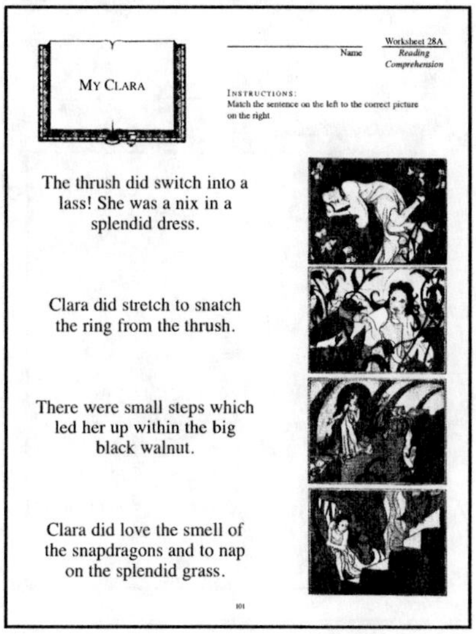
MY CLARA

Name

Worksheet 28A
Reading Comprehension

INSTRUCTIONS:
Match the sentence on the left to the correct picture on the right

The thrush did switch into a lass! She was a nix in a splendid dress.

Clara did stretch to snatch the ring from the thrush.

There were small steps which led her up within the big black walnut.

Clara did love the smell of the snapdragons and to nap on the splendid grass.

101

ACTIVITY 2: READING COMPREHENSION

Recap the events of the story in order, discuss the characters and main ideas.

Worksheets 28A: Read the instructions aloud. Monitor the students' progress as they work independently.

ACTIVITY 3: ART ACTIVITY

Worksheets 28B: Color the trunk of the tree and the bird. Then paste torn green tissue paper on the page to form the leaves of the tree.

Percival's Pairs: Using ING, ANG, ONG, and R, L, S blends.

MY CLARA

Name

Worksheet 28B
Art Activity

INSTRUCTIONS:
Color the trunk of the tree and the bird. Then paste torn green tissue paper on the page to form the leaves of the tree.

103

Lesson 29
Reading Comprehension: MY CLARA

Play Crash! Swing! Squash! for the children encouraging them to sing.

ACTIVITY 1: READING COMPREHENSION

Worksheet 29A: Read the instructions aloud. Assist the children in reading the questions.

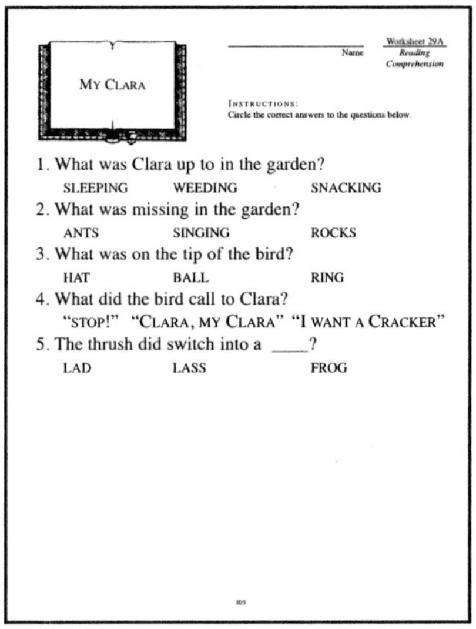
MY CLARA

Name

Worksheet 29A
Reading Comprehension

INSTRUCTIONS:
Circle the correct answers to the questions below.

1. What was Clara up to in the garden?
   SLEEPING WEEDING SNACKING
2. What was missing in the garden?
   ANTS SINGING ROCKS
3. What was on the tip of the bird?
   HAT BALL RING
4. What did the bird call to Clara?
   "STOP!" "CLARA, MY CLARA" "I WANT A CRACKER"
5. The thrush did switch into a ____?
   LAD LASS FROG

105

ACTIVITY 2: ART ACTIVITY

Remind the students what a fairy tale is and give them some examples of other classic fairy storylines to fuel their imagination in creating the illustration of a 'prequel' to the story *My Clara*.

Worksheets 29B: Read the instructions then let the children work independently.

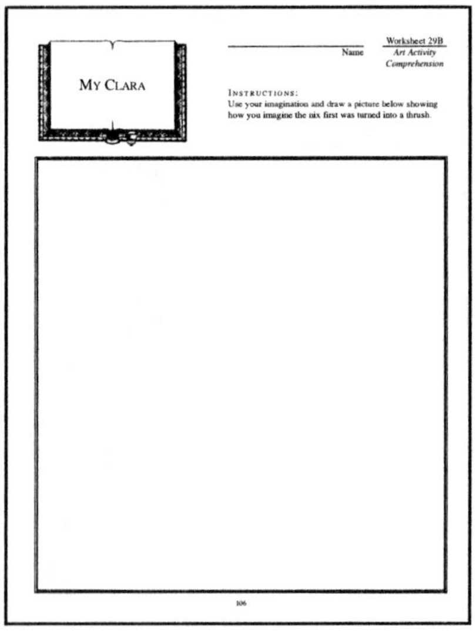
MY CLARA

Name

Worksheet 29B
Art Activity Comprehension

INSTRUCTIONS:
Use your imagination and draw a picture below showing how you imagine the nix first was turned into a thrush.

106

Archives: Special Exhibit Edition

Lesson 30
Reading Comprehension: MY CLARA and Review

ACTIVITY 1: DRAMA

Read alternate pages from the story *My Clara* and have the students act out what was read to them then allow them to act out what happens next, alternating between reading a page then acting out a page. If you are teaching in a school setting, have the children read round robin, with two students acting out the parts who are next to the reader. As the reader changes then so do the actors.

ACTIVITY 2: REVIEW

Worksheets 30A: Read the instructions then let the children work independently.

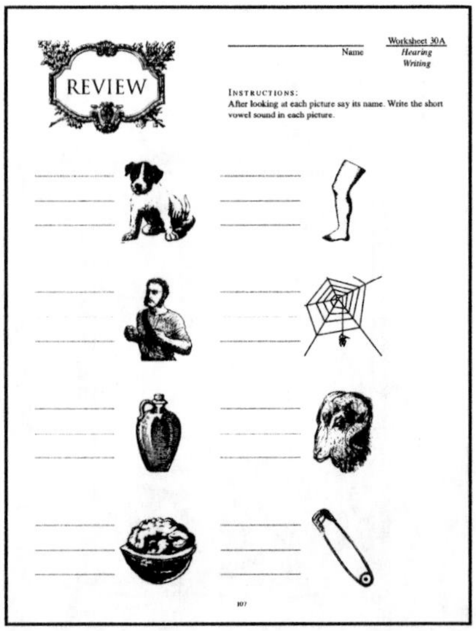
REVIEW

Name

Worksheet 30A
Hearing Writing

INSTRUCTIONS:
After looking at each picture say its name. Write the short vowel sound in each picture.

107

Percival's Pairs: Using ING, ANG, ONG, and R, L, S blends.

Lesson 31
Target: Ending Blends

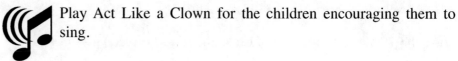

Play Act Like a Clown for the children encouraging them to sing.

ACTIVITY 1: HEARING AND SEEING

Write the letter pair ST at the top of the board, once on the right side and once on the left side. Review the sound made by this blend.

Brainstorm with the children to come up with words which start with ST. Write the words on the board, under the ST on the left side. When there are eight or ten, invite children to the board to circle the ST letter pair at the beginning of each word.

Affirm that in all of these words, the ST letters work as a team to start the word. Even the word "STart" has the ST blend!
However, tell them that this letter pair also likes to come at the end of words. Write the following on the board under the ST on the right side: dust, fist, nest, past, lost. Read the words and have the children echo them. Ask if they can hear the ST at the very end of each word.

Call on students to come to the board and circle the final ST in each of these words.

Give each student an index card and have them write ST on it. Tell them they will have to be very good listeners today. You are going to read a list of words. All of the words will have the ST blend in them, but sometimes it will be at the beginning and sometimes it will be at the end. If they hear it at the beginning, they are to hold up the ST card with their left hand, just like the board display. If they hear it at the end, they are to hold up the card in their right hand. Demonstrate this for them, standing with your back to them for proper orientation.

star	mist	stove	stem	fast	list
steam	post	still	must	cast	stick
stew	west	pest	starve	stiff	mast

Praise their careful listening!

Erase the words from the board. Tell them that two more S blends like to do the same thing. Erase the T in each blend and replace it with K. Call on a student to tell you what blend is formed by SK.

Challenge them to tell you if the following words have SK at the beginning or end, and on which side of the board they should be written:

desk	skate	skunk	risk	mask	skull
skin	ask	skim	task	brisk	tusk

Erase the words from the board. Erase the K and replace it with P.

Challenge them to tell you if these words have SP at the beginning or end, and on which side of the board they should be written:

spell	gasp	lisp	spin	spot	grasp

Now tell them that there are other letter pairs which blend together at the end of words which never like to be the leader in words! They will only see these at the very end.

Write these words on the board: hand, pant, damp, silk, soft, belt, next, exact. Underline the letter pair blends at the end of each word. Read the words, emphasizing the blending of the two final sounds. Have the children echo them after you.

Remind them that blending these letter sounds is very simple. They just must say each one and allow them to run together. Since they know the individual sounds of each of the letters, it is easy to sound out the blends they make when they are paired up!

Prevent students from making this harder than it is! Guide them carefully to see the sounds as a team, each doing its part, but working together. The two letter sounds together are no more difficult than any other sound combinations which they use all the time in their reading.

They will encounter other final blend letter pairs in their reading that are not introduced here. If they are reminded to simply blend the two sounds, they should do fine without any further formal instruction.

Erase the board and write the following: NG. Remind them that this is another letter pair which doesn't ever begin words, but is only found at the end. Write the following: ring, sang, long. Call on students to read these words and come to the board and circle the final NG.

Now tell them there is one more like this. Erase the words and the G after the N. Replace the G with K. Write the following: bank, link, sunk. Have the children echo the words after you, emphasizing the NK. Affirm that this blend sounds slightly different from a true N + K, just like NG sounds a little different. When they are blending the sounds and decoding the words, their tongues will know what to do!

Consonant Blends

Name — Worksheet 31A *Seeing*

Instructions:
At the end of some words two letters appear together. To say these words, sound the sounds together. Circle the blend at the end of each word (ST, SK, ND, NK, NT, MP).

dust	mask	pump
desk	nest	crank
risk	hand	plant
fist	bank	skunk
task	band	sink

109

The N sound used in the blends NG and NK is produced with the back of the tongue and is not truly N. Students may try to decode these using the tip of the tongue for N, but will intuitively change this tongue placement when they realize what the word is and say it as they have heard it spoken. It will not be necessary to belabor the sound difference.

Worksheet 31A: Read the instructions aloud. Monitor the students' progress as they work independently. Call on students to read the words aloud. Define as necessary and use in original sentences.

ACTIVITY 2: WRITING

Write the words found on Worksheet 31B on the board. Invite students to come to the board and write the words. Monitor stroke direction and order. Read the words and use in original sentences.

Worksheet 31B: Read the instructions aloud and Monitor the students' progress as they work independently.

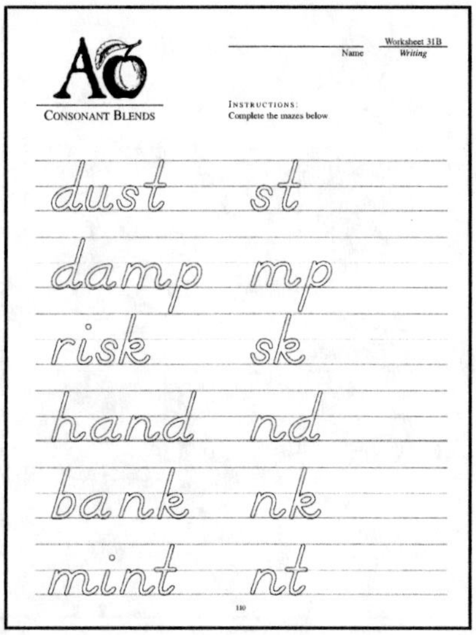
Consonant Blends

Name — Worksheet 31B *Writing*

Instructions:
Complete the mazes below

dust st
damp mp
risk sk
hand nd
bank nk
mint nt

110

Lesson 32
Target: Final Blends

Play Act Like a Clown for the children encouraging them to sing.

ACTIVITY 1: HEARING, SEEING, AND WRITING

Write these final blend letter pairs on the board: ST, SK. Under each, write a decodable example of each word. (Do not use words found on Worksheet 32A.) Highlight or underline the final blend in each word.

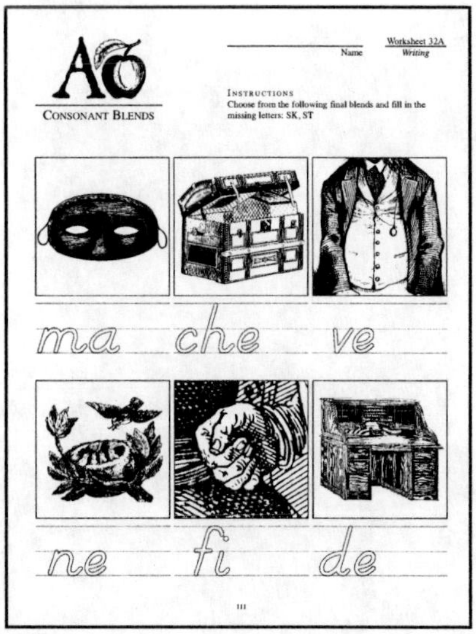
Consonant Blends

Name — Worksheet 32A *Writing*

Instructions
Choose from the following final blends and fill in the missing letters: SK, ST

ma che ve
ne fi de

111

Worksheet 32A: Read the instructions aloud. Tell the children you will be labeling the pictures for them and they must decide which letter pair makes the blend at the end. After they have filled in all the blends, they may go back and follow the letter mazes to complete the words.

Row 1: mask, chest, vest
Row 2: nest, fist, desk

ACTIVITY 2: READING WORDS

Present the puzzle pieces for the ST and SK blends. Present the pieces for the short vowels and review the sounds made by each. Connect each of the vowels in turn to the final blends, sounding out the syllables as you do so.

Now present the pieces for L, T, R and M. Present the syllable IST with the linked pieces. Challenge the children to find the beginning sound which will be needed to form the word "list." Praise correct responses. Continue in the same manner for the word "mist."

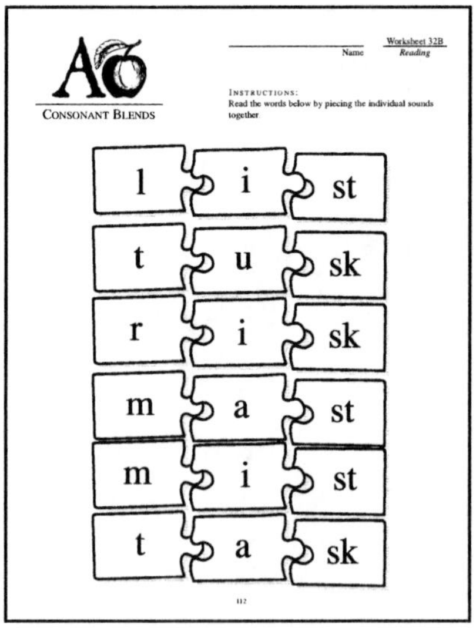

Follow the same procedure to form the words found on Worksheet 32B. Write the words on the board as they are formed.

Worksheet 32B: Read the instructions aloud. Call on students to read the words. Use any of the previous variations for eliciting student response. Make sure students understand the meanings of the words and can use them appropriately in sentences.

Lesson 33
Target: Final Blends

Play Act Like a Clown for the children encouraging them to sing.

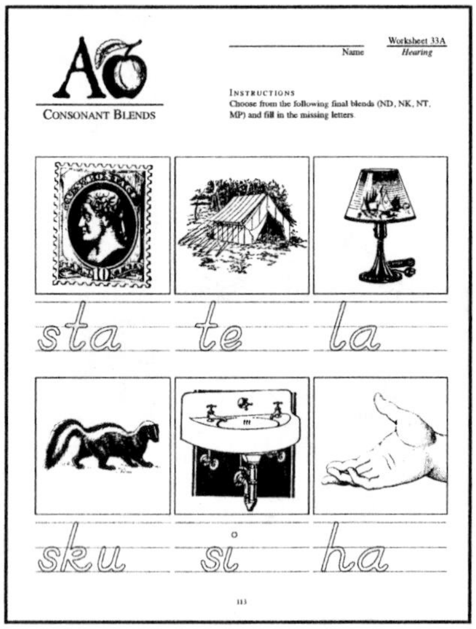

ACTIVITY 1: HEARING, SEEING, AND WRITING

Write these final blend letter pairs on the board: ND, NT, MP, NK. Under each, write a decodable example of each word. (Do not use words found on Worksheet 33A.) Highlight or underline the final blend in each word.

Worksheet 33A: Read the instructions aloud. Tell the children you will be labeling the pictures for them and they must decide which letter pair makes the blend at the end. After they have filled in all the blends, they may go back and follow the letter mazes to complete the words.

Row 1: stamp, tent, lamp
Row 3: skunk, sink, hand

ACTIVITY 2: READING WORDS

Present the puzzle pieces for the NT, ND, MP, and NK blends. Present the pieces for the short vowels A and U and review the sounds made by each. Connect each of the vowels in turn to the final blends, sounding out the syllables as you do so.

Now present the pieces for B, D, L and the blends PL and SL. Briefly review the blends.

Present the syllable AND with the linked pieces. Challenge the children to find the beginning sound which will be needed to form the word "band." Praise correct responses. Continue in the same manner for the word "land."

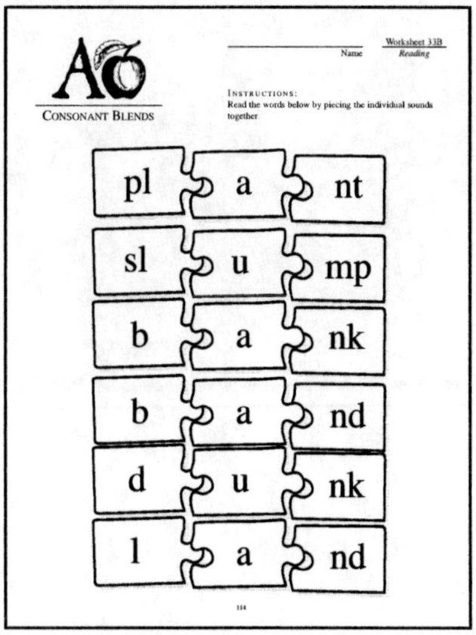

Worksheet 33B
Reading

CONSONANT BLENDS

Name

INSTRUCTIONS:
Read the words below by piecing the individual sounds together.

pl	a	nt
sl	u	mp
b	a	nk
b	a	nd
d	u	nk
l	a	nd

114

Follow the same procedure to form the words found on Worksheet 33B. Save the words with blends at the beginning until last.

Write the words on the board as they are formed.

Worksheet 33B: Read the instructions aloud. Call on students to read the words. Use any of the previous variations for eliciting student response. Make sure students understand the meanings of the words and can use them appropriately in sentences.

Lesson 34
Review, Special Exhibits, and Reading A Grand Cat

Activity 1: Hearing and Seeing Review of Ending Blends

Write the following words on the board: gasp, last, ask, send, sent, jump, milk, theft, felt, next, expect, swept, help, self, ink.

Have students come to the board and underline the ending letter pairs which make the final blends in each word. Assist the children to decode the words and use them in original sentences.

Although they have not encountered all of these letter pairs in the last lessons, the concept of blending the two final sounds, whatever they may be, should be encouraged at this point in the curriculum. Exceptions to this will be addressed later.

Worksheet 34A: Read the instructions aloud. Assist the children in reading through the list, defining vocabulary as necessary and using the words in original sentences. All of these words are decodable and have a variety of final ending blends.

REVIEW

Name

Worksheet 34A
Reading

INSTRUCTIONS:
Read up and down the columns of words found in the next book you will read.

Holland	shelf	theft
kept	black	rend
Atlantic	felt	slink
land	last	next
along	stilt	assist
windmill	distant	diligent
pump	swift	spunk
dampness	hand	grasp
blond	crumb	luck
glint	gust	pluck
blink	sent	swept
bunk	whisk	glint
blink	swept	jump
slept	twist	gasp
prompt	plunging	bolt
stand	second	pelt
climb	crest	wilt
except	kept	limp
plant	instant	wimp
bulb	halt	grand
milk	grump	

115

Sometimes the verbs on this list will appear in the story with ING added. If you like, you may write some of these on the board, adding the ING for additional review and practice.

Activity 2: Special Exhibits, Special Vocabulary, and Compound Words

Write the following on the board: she, he, me. Ask if anyone remembers how these Special Exhibits are pronounced. Affirm correct answers. Now write the word "we." Challenge them to tell you how this word would be read. Praise correct responses and use the word in a complete sentence.

Write the following on the board: to. Ask someone to read this Special Exhibit aloud. Now write the word "do." Challenge them to say this word to rhyme with "to." Ask "DO you know how to DO this?" They should catch on right away!

Write the following on the board: watch. Ask if anyone remembers what sound the letter A makes in this word. (ah) Affirm correct answers. Tell the children that the letter A often makes the "ah" sound when it is the leader in the word.

Write the following on the board: along, aloft, assist, across, alas. Assist the children to decode each one. Define them and/or use in original sentences. Make sure they hear that the two A's in "alas" make different sounds!

While the A in these words is often a schwa in conversational speech, "ah" is sufficient for decoding purposes and students will comprehend the appropriate word.

Finally, write the following on the board: Holland, Atlantic. Assist the children to decode these words (they can do it!) Use a map to point out the geographical location of the Atlantic Ocean and the Netherlands and briefly describe how the Dutch must pump the water from their land in order to farm it.

ACTIVITY 3: READING A GRAND CAT

A review of vocabulary has been done in the preceding activity. In addition, the following expressions have been used in this story and may need additional explanation:

Atlantic—ocean between North America and Europe
Holland—a country in Europe, also called The Netherlands
windmill—a machine that grinds or pumps using the wind for power
pumping the dampness—excess water
dwelling—home, place to "dwell"
Dutch—from Holland
Da—nickname for father or Dad
slack—lazy
glint—sparkle or flash of light
blink—to open and close the eyes quickly
bunk—bed
spring—jump
loft—an upper room under a sloping roof
habit—common way
but for the tick-tock of the clock—it was quiet except for the sound of the clock
munch—a bite to eat
stilts—two poles with foot supports for walking above the ground

swift—speedy, quick
flicking—pushing aside quickly
scraps—bits of food; crumbs
sudden—quick, unexpected
aloft—into the air
whisk—the sound his hat made as it flew off his head (an onomatopoeia)
alas—a word used to express sorrow, grief or concern
for a second—for a short time
dipping and falling—the hat was falling and rising on the blade of the windmill
swept—passed over
instant—short time
halt—stop moving
lit—fell upon, saw
lifting and sinking—going up and coming down
spun—went around and around
toss—throw
gusting—sudden strong blasting of wind
grump—depressed or grumbling way
get by with theft—get away with stealing
rend—tear away
grasp—tight hold
slinking—walking slowly in a crouch
expect—to plan on; anticipate
lap—to lick up
fend for—take care of
spunk—spirit, mettle
snatch—to seize suddenly
tact—being careful of somone else's feelings
nicks and dents—the windmill hit the stilt and damaged it
shred—destroy
hissing—making a wound like the letter "s" (an onomatopoeia)
gasping—taking sudden, short breaths
astonishment—amazement
clutching—seizing, grabbing
black as ink—dark and cloudy
pelt—hit with fierce blows
big wet drops—raindrops
wilt—lose its shape and droop
dampness—rain
limp—without stiffness or firmness
grip—hold
plunk—the sound of the hat hitting the ground (an onomatopoeia)
brisk—quick
gallant—brave, high-spirited
grand—magnificent, splendid

Guide the children through the "round robin" reading of the story. Encourage fluency and expression. Discuss the people and events as they occur in the story.

Some questions for discussion might be: Why and how does Frans' opinion of Wim change from the beginning of the story to the end? Have you ever changed your opinion about something or someone after you learn more about it (or him)? (Don't get into details about personalities here—keep the discussion upbeat! You could direct this toward things like going to camp, eating a certain kind of food, etc.)

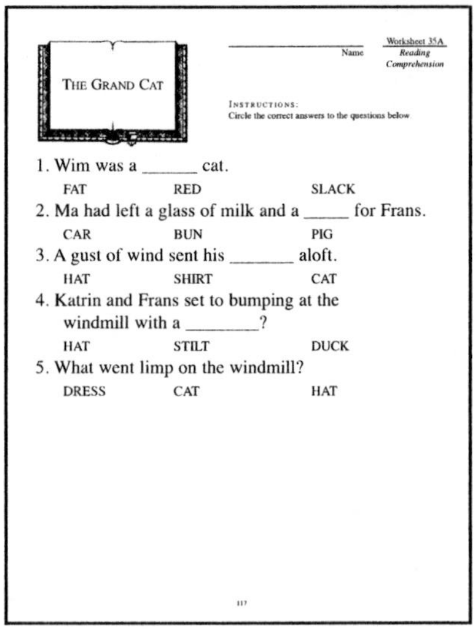

Lesson 35
Reading Comprehension

ACTIVITY 1: ORDER OF EVENTS

Lead a discussion on the main ideas, characters, and order of events in the story A GRAND CAT.

Worksheet 35A/B: Read the instructions aloud and Monitor the students' progress as they work independently.

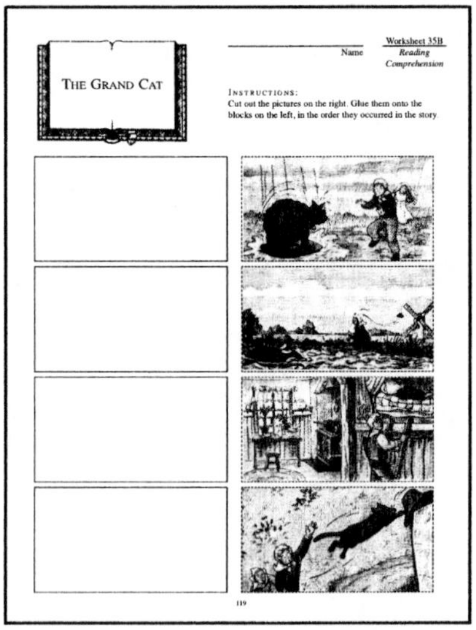

ACTIVITY 3: ART ACTIVITY

Display a finished windmill. Prepare a table with the necessary art supplies.

Worksheet 35C: Cut the square paper from the corners as shown by the dotted lines on Worksheet 34B. Fold the top right corner towards the center then repeat with with the next three corners. Run a fastner through the center of the pinwheel and then aagin into the milk carton, bending back the fastners inside the carton to keep the pinwheel attached. Paint or use markers to decorate the exterior of the carton like the windmill in the story.

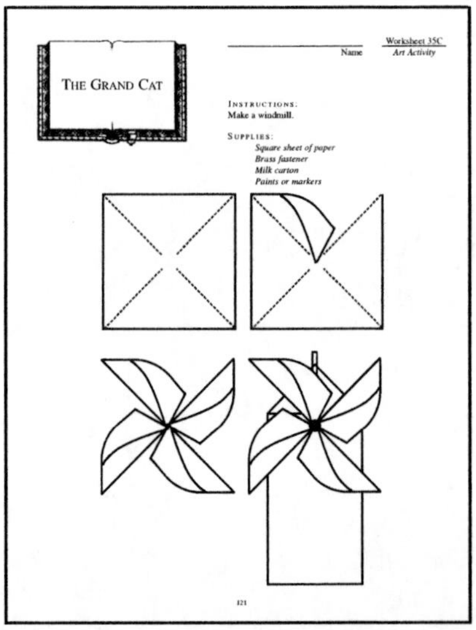

Lesson 36
Target: Vowels + R

Write a large R on the board. Ask the students what sound is made by this letter.

Write the word "her" on the board. Up to this point, this has been a Special Exhibit. Call on a student to read it aloud. Underline the ER.

Call to their attention that when they say "her," they use H and R together. The vowel E isn't even heard!

Now tell them "Guess what? If we put any of these vowels in front of R, we still will hear only R!" Write the following: ir, ur. Tell them that all of these letter pairs make the same sound and it is simply R!

Write the following words on the board: fir, fur. Read them and have the children echo them. Ask if they hear any difference in how the words sound. (NO) Point out to them that these words, however, mean different things just because they are spelled differently. Define each and use them in the following sentences: I have a fir tree in my back yard. She has a fur coat.

Now show them how silly these sentences would be if you used the wrong spelling. Say "I have a fur tree in my back yard." while you point to "fur." Ask them if this would make sense if you used that spelling. Enjoy the absurdity of this with the children. Now say "She has a fir coat." and point to "fir." Ask if this one makes any more sense. Affirm that the spelling of these words is important to its meaning.

Write the letter A on the board. Ask if anyone remembers the two sounds made by A. (short A and "ah") Write A in front of the R. Tell them that when A comes before R, it will use the "ah" sound. In fact, the syllable AR just says the name of the letter R!

Now write the word "or" on the board. Up to this point this has been a Special Exhibit. Tell the children that this letter pair likes to come in the middle and end of words also. Write the word "for." This has been a Special Exhibit also. Affirm that the OR sounds the same in this word.

Write the following on the board: horn, corn, born. Use a different color to write the OR in each one to highlight it. Ask students what the ending sound is in each of these words. (N) Have them echo the ORN syllable.

Have them echo the word "horn." Using that as a pattern, have them decode "corn" and "born." Praise their fine reading!

Tell them that for now when they see AR it will sound like the letter name, when they see OR it will sound like OR and anytime they see ER, IR, UR, it will just say R!

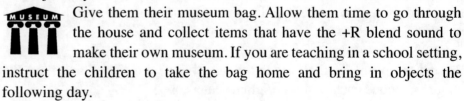

MUSEUM Give them their museum bag. Allow them time to go through the house and collect items that have the +R blend sound to make their own museum. If you are teaching in a school setting, instruct the children to take the bag home and bring in objects the following day.

Erase the board and write the words found on Worksheet 36A. Invite students to come to the board and circle the vowel + R pairs they see in each word. Read each word and have them echo them. Use the words in original sentences.

Worksheet 36A: Read the instructions aloud and monitor the students' progress as they work independently.

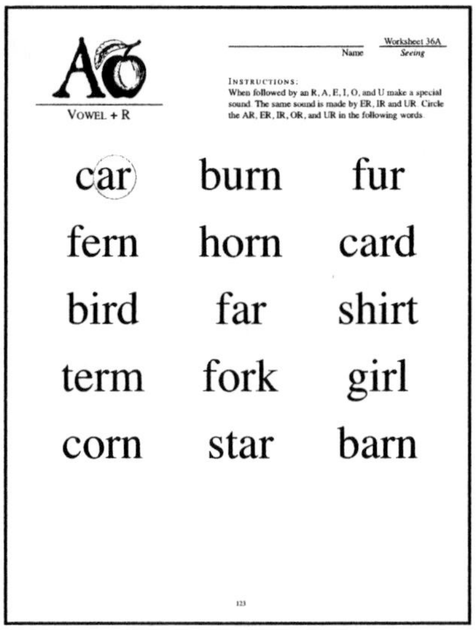
Name
Worksheet 36A
Seeing
Vowel + R
Instructions:
When followed by an R, A, E, I, O, and U make a special sound. The same sound is made by ER, IR and UR. Circle the AR, ER, IR, OR, and UR in the following words.
car burn fur
fern horn card
bird far shirt
term fork girl
corn star barn

ACTIVITY 2: WRITING

Write the words shown on Worksheet 36B. Call students to the board to write the words, using a different color for the vowel + R to highlight it.

Remind about stroke directions and order as needed.

Assist the children to decode the words. Define as necessary and use in original sentences.

Worksheet 36B: Read the instructions aloud. Monitor their work.

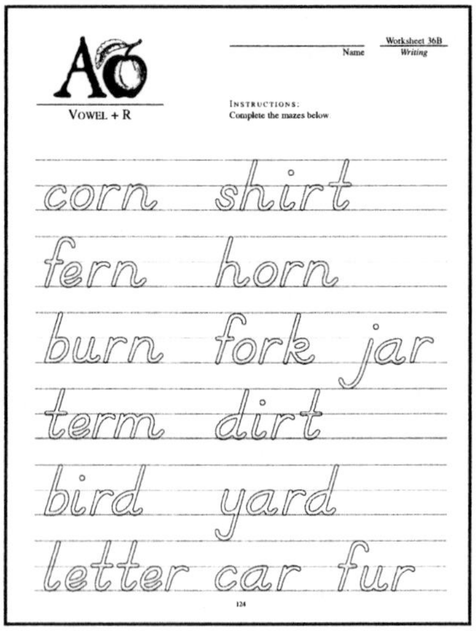
Name
Worksheet 36B
Writing
Vowel + R
Instructions:
Complete the mazes below
corn shirt
fern horn
burn fork jar
term dirt
bird yard
letter car fur

You may want to give the students the coloring page along with the flashcard. Read the information about the artist to your students before they color the picture.

Percival's Pairs: Using ING, ANG, ONG, blends and +R.

Lesson 37
Target: Vowel + R

ACTIVITY 1: READING

Present the puzzle pieces for the AR, ER, UR letter pairs. Review the sounds made by each. Now present the pieces for C, F and H.

Invite children to select the proper pieces to form the words "car," "her," "fur." Remind them that "her" has been a Special Exhibit and to try to remember how it is spelled. Tell them the "fur" to spell is the kind on an animal!

Present the piece for D. Form the words "herd" and "card" and have the children decode each. Use in original sentences.

Again, you want to make sure they understand the meaning of this spelling of "herd." Tell them that the word meaning "to hear" (past tense) is spelled differently and they will learn that later.

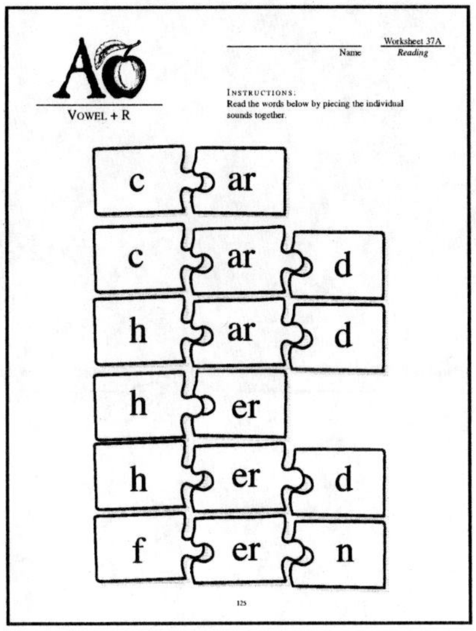
Worksheet 37A
Reading
Name
VOWEL + R
INSTRUCTIONS:
Read the words below by piecing the individual sounds together.

c	ar	
c	ar	d
h	ar	d
h	er	
h	er	d
f	er	n

Move the H from the word "herd" and use it to replace the C in "card, forming the word "hard." Call on a student to decode the new word.

Continue in the same manner to form the words found on Worksheets 37A/B. Write the words on the board as they are formed.

Worksheet 37A/B: Read the instructions aloud. Call on students to read the words. Use any of the previous variations for eliciting student response. Make sure students understand the meanings of the words and can use them appropriately in sentences.

ACTIVITY 2: HEARING AND READING MORE WORDS

Write the following words on the board in a vertical column: card, star, car. Tell the children that they must be careful listeners and readers today. You will be reading one of the words on the board and they must choose which word is the one you have read. Read the word "card." Call on a student to come to the board and circle the correct word. After the correct response is completed, have students read the other words also to reinforce reading skills.

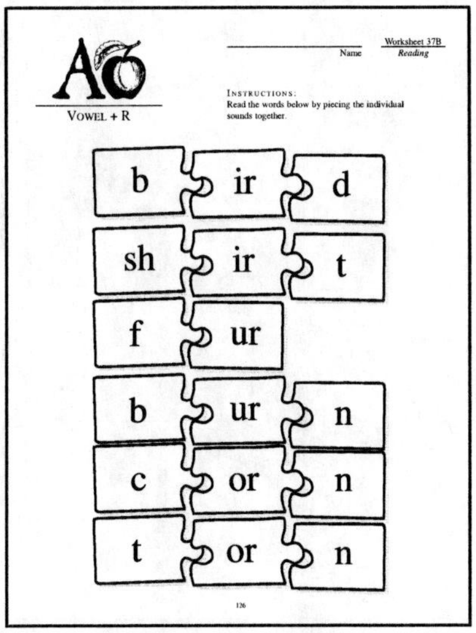
Worksheet 37B
Reading
Name
VOWEL + R
INSTRUCTIONS:
Read the words below by piecing the individual sounds together.

b	ir	d
sh	ir	t
f	ur	
b	ur	n
c	or	n
t	or	n

You may want to point out the small differences in the words, reminding them of past lessons when they learned that just one letter can change the entire meaning of a word.

Using the words as they are presented on Worksheet 37C, continue this activity. Do NOT read the words which are used as stimulus pictures on this worksheet, but choose one of the other two in each example.

Worksheet 37C: Read the instructions aloud. Monitor the students' progress as they work independently. Do not label the pictures for the students. Encourage them to read the words first and choose the word which best labels the picture they see.

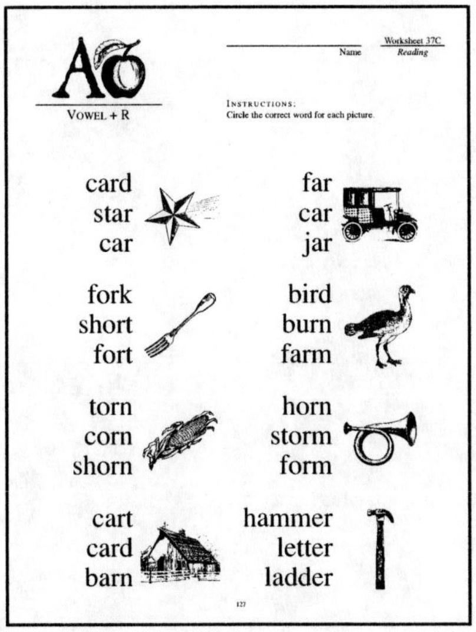

LESSON 38
TARGET: VOWEL + R

ACTIVITY 1: READING AND WRITING

Write the following words on the board: girl, farm, corn, shark, skirt, zipper, star, fork. Have students come to the board and underline the vowel + R in each word.

Challenge them to be detectives. Three of these things can be found in the classroom. (girl, skirt, zipper) Call on students to come to the board, point to and read the word, then show the example.

You may have examples of more of these words in your classroom or home. Feel free to incorporate them into the lesson as possible!

Assist the children to decode the rest of the words. Discuss their meanings and use in original sentences.

Draw guidelines next to each word and invite students to come to the board and copy them.

Remind them about letter sizing and spacing.

Worksheet 38A: Read the instructions aloud. Hint to them that there are two words shown in the instructions which will not be used in the pictures. Tell them to be good detectives again to find the right words for the pictures and leave out the two which are not labels!

ACTIVITY 2: USE OF FINAL ER TO FORM NOUNS

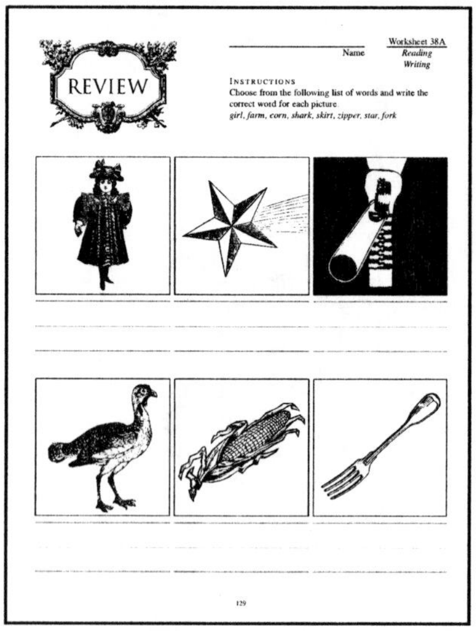

Write the following on the board: walk, ring, plant. Assist the children to decode the words and discuss their meanings as ACTION words!

It is very important that they be presented as verbs. The children may also give their meanings as nouns. Affirm that many words can be either, and today you will be using them as words that tell what someone DOES. Also, the above words were chosen because they do not require doubling the letter right away.

In a different color, add ER to the end of each word. Read the words formed and have the children echo them.

Explain that when we add ER to an action word, it now means "one who does" what the original word describes. So, a "walker" is "one who walks," a "ringer" is "one who rings (a bell)." Ask them to tell you what a "planter" would be.

Now write the following on the board: dig, trap, swim. Call on students to decode and read the words. Discuss meanings and use in original sentences. Ask the children what you will need to add to each word to mean "one who" does the thing described. Write an ER slightly to the right of each of the words.

Now remind them of the lesson when you added ING to words. Ask if anyone remembers what you had to do to the last letter in some words when you added ING (double it). Affirm correct answers, or remind them of this if no one remembers.

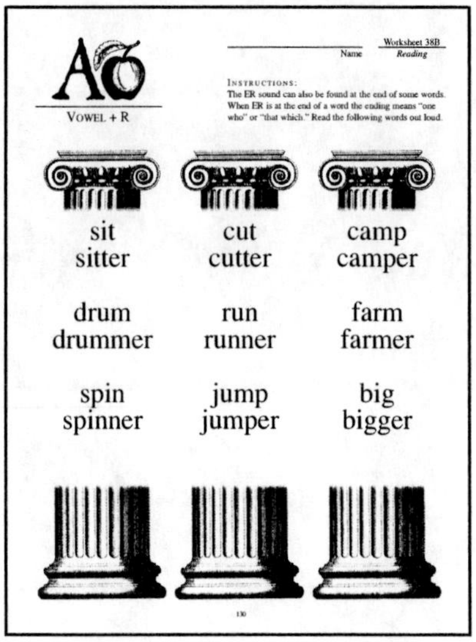
Worksheet 38B
Name Reading

A
VOWEL + R

INSTRUCTIONS:
The ER sound can also be found at the end of some words. When ER is at the end of a word the ending means "one who" or "that which." Read the following words out loud.

sit sitter	cut cutter	camp camper
drum drummer	run runner	farm farmer
spin spinner	jump jumper	big bigger

130

Double the last letter in each of the above words in the open space between the root and the "er."

Assure them that they will not have to remember this spelling rule right now, but they will see the words this way in their reading.

Worksheet 38B: Read the instructions aloud. Have the children underline the final ER where it occurs. Assist them to read the words aloud, using in original sentences. Draw attention to the difference between the word which means ACTION, and the word which means a PERSON or THING.

Sometimes OR is used in this same way. Examples include words like "sailor," "visitor," "pastor," "actor." In spontaneous speech, this use of "or " is pronounced "er." Children can decode such words using OR, but should be prompted after decoding to pronounce the words in the more commonly heard way. They will encounter several instances of this in the vocabulary of the next story.

Lesson 39
Target: Vowel + R
Vocabulary and Review

ACTIVITY 1: REVIEW

Write four or five of the upper case letters on the board, along with guide lines to the right. Invite children to come and write the letters, describing and numbering their strokes as they do so. Then ask them to independently write the corresponding lower case letter to the right of each upper case letter. Continue in this way with all of the 26 alphabet letters.

Worksheet 39A: Read the instructions aloud and monitor their work.

ACTIVITY 2: VOWEL + R VOCABULARY

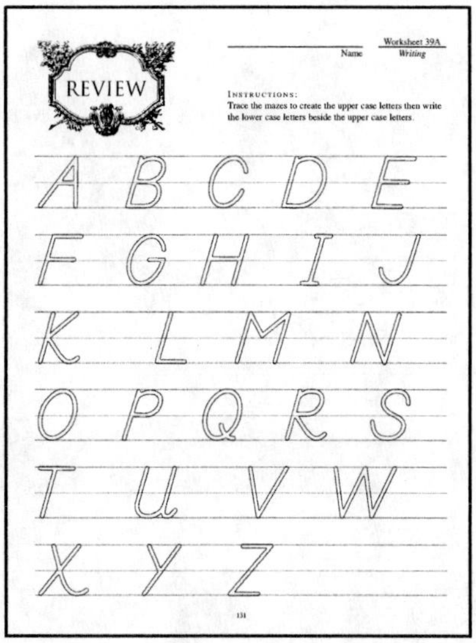
Worksheet 39A
Name Writing

REVIEW

INSTRUCTIONS:
Trace the mazes to create the upper case letters then write the lower case letters beside the upper case letters.

A B C D E
F G H I J
K L M N
O P Q R S
T U V W
X Y Z

131

Write the following on the board: rob, win, sin. Call on students to read the words aloud.

Ask if anyone remembers what we will add to "rob" to make a new word which will mean "one who robs." (ER) Affirm the correct answer. Write this slightly to the right of the end of the word "rob."

Tell the children that you must also double the B in this word to follow a spelling rule. Add the second B in the open space. Invite a child to read the word aloud.

Continue in the same way with the other two words. Now tell the children that we can use final ER in another way. Write the following on the board: big, fast, rich. Call on students to read each of these words.

Explain that these words DESCRIBE something or someone. Use the following sentence as an example: Yesterday he ate a big sandwich for lunch. What was "big"? (the sandwich)

Now tell them that if we want to say that something is MORE "big" than something else, we can add ER to the end. Double the G and add ER to the end of "big." Call on a student to read the word formed. Use it in the following sentence: Today he ate a bigger sandwich for lunch. Ask the children how today's sandwich was different from yesterday's.

Explain that by adding ER to many words like this, we can use them to compare one thing with another. Solicit sentences from the children using the words "fast" and "rich." Modify the sentences to use the comparative form of each with the ER. Add the ER to these words as you use them.

Worksheet 39B: Read the instructions aloud. Elicit student response in any of the ways previously described. Define words as necessary and use in complete sentences.

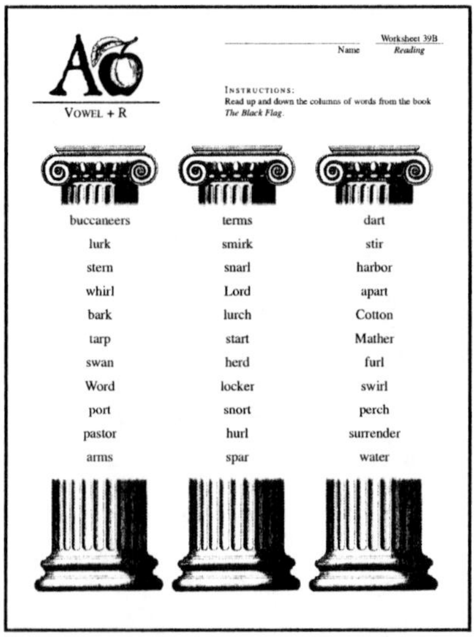

Worksheet 39B
Reading

Name

Vowel + R

Instructions:
Read up and down the columns of words from the book *The Black Flag*.

buccaneers	terms	dart
lurk	smirk	stir
stern	snarl	harbor
whirl	Lord	apart
bark	lurch	Cotton
tarp	start	Mather
swan	herd	furl
Word	locker	swirl
port	snort	perch
pastor	hurl	surrender
arms	spar	water

As previously mentioned, this list includes several words in which OR is pronounced as ER. Correct student pronunciation as needed. The most unusual instance of this is in the word "Word!" Do call attention to the use of the upper case—it is the very Word of God and is a very proper name! (The word "Lord" should be presented likewise.) You may also want to call their attention to the pronunciation of AR in "dollars" as ER. The word "stern" has two meanings in the next story: as the back of the ship, and as firm or harsh. The word "port" has two meanings also: as the left side of a ship, and as a harbor. Three words use A as "ah": apart, water, swan. You can compare "apart" with other beginning "ah" words which they had in the last story and "watch" with Special Exhibits "was" and "what." Some words are used as verbs in the story which may be more familiar to the children as nouns. Examples include: dart, start, storm, bark. Check the teacher background information in the next lesson for additional examples of words which may be used in unfamiliar ways. Finally, the word "buccaneers" is central to the story, although it uses the long E sound spelled "ee." The children should be able to decode all of it except for this last syllable. Present this as a Special Exhibit to the children, pointing out the pronunciation of the last syllable.

Percival's Pairs: Using ING, ANG, ONG, blends and +R.

Lesson 40
Reading THE BLACK FLAG

ACTIVITY 1: READING AND COMPREHENSION

This story describes an act of piracy in the early days of the American colonies and the efforts of Cotton Mather, the preacher and evangelist, to bring the offer of salvation to the captured buccaneers. The story is fictional, but the evangelistic efforts among the pirates by Rev. Mather are not. Mather would preach in the convicted pirate's hearing every day, pray daily with them and see that they were catechized. The following special words and expressions are used:

Places and People:

Boston

Cotton Mather, pastor of Boston's Old Church

Vocabulary and expressions:

cutter—swift single-masted sailing vessel
hurling—the cutter was moving quickly through the water
turning curls—making waves
lurking—hiding
brig—a two-masted, square-rigged sailing ship
set with a black flag—a black flag was flying from the ship's mast
buccaneers—pirates
swinging guns and sharp swords—making threatening gestures with their weapons
port—the left side of the ship
whirling—hitting with great force
rigging—sails, ropes, etc.
lurching—abruptly swaying
gun blasts—cannon balls hitting the brig
in short order—quickly
mast—the tall pole on a ship to which the sails are attached
furl—roll up
winners—the victors in the battle against the other ship
spars—poles that support sails and rigging
larder—pantry, where food is stored
sorting—arranging according to kind
deck—the upper level floor of the ship
carting—carrying
charts—maps
tarps—protective canvas covers
richer—the pirates rob the cutter to get wealthier
locker—storage chest
silver dollars—coins made of silver
top man—the look-out up on the mast
smirk—insincere smile
stern—1) back of the ship; 2) firm, grim
darting—moving suddenly

swirling—twisting
mist—fog
arms—guns, cannons, ammunition
fort—a place strengthened with defensive armor and military men
start or stir—move
perch—high sitting place
barking—commanding loudly and sharply
terms of surrender—requirements for giving up
herding—forcing them to walk in a group
harbor—a place of calm water where ships may anchor or tie up to a dock
Port of Boston—a harbor in Massachusetts
Boston's top men—the ones in authority in that city
stern punishment—severe penalty for a crime
order—command
hang—to suspend by the neck until dead
pastor—a teaching elder in the church
Word of God—the Bible
mark the words—listen carefully
hard sinners—wicked men who are set in their ways
stand apart—are separated from
turn your black flags into the color of swans—the Lord can wash away their sins and make them white as snow (a metaphor)
spat—past tense of "spit"
snort—an angry laugh
with the Lord ever after—go to heaven

New Compound Word:
flagship of the King—leading ship in the King's navy

Assist the children to read the story "round robin" style. Discuss vocabulary, characters, events, main ideas as you proceed through the book.

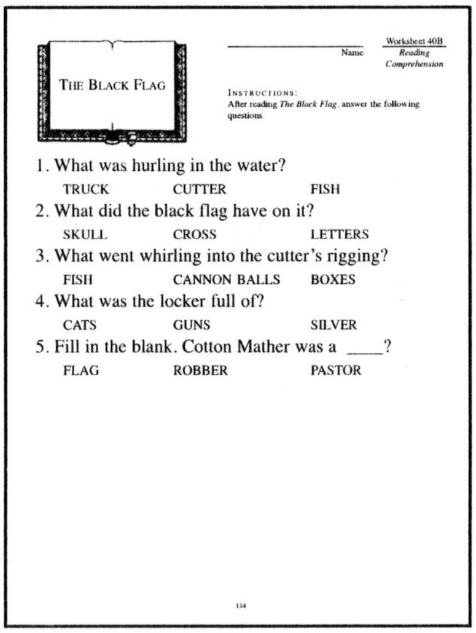

Some questions for discussion might be: The flagship which caught the buccaneers belonged to a king; what country ruled the American colonies during its early years? (England) What is it called when the Lord calls someone to be sorry for his sins and turn to him? (repentance) (Westminster Shorter Catechism Question 87: "What is repentance unto life? Repentance unto life is a saving grace, whereby a sinner, out of a true sense of his sin, and apprehension of the mercy of God in Christ, doth, with grief and hatred of his sin, turn from it unto God...")

Worksheet 40A/B: Read the instructions aloud. Monitor the students' progress as they work independently.

Worksheet 40C: Test. This test is optional and is added to evaluate your students if you feel it is necessary at this time. The answers are worth 5 points each.

Lesson 41
Target: Final Silent E

Show the children the flashcard with the long vowel on it. Have them hear the sound of long I as in "pipe."

ACTIVITY 1: HEARING AND SEEING/THE E TRAIN

Lead the children in a recitation of the short vowel sounds: A, E, I, O, U. Ask what other sound is made by the letter A. (ah)

Give the children index cards and assign different children to write the following letters on their cards: H, A, T, K, I, N, O, R, D, B, M, U, E. Have two children write P on their cards.

The child with E on his card will have a lot to do during this demonstration. With that in mind, assign this letter to a child who is reliable at following directions and able to stay on task.

Say the word "tap." Ask the children if they have a letter which makes a sound in this word. The three children with the letters T, A and P should come to the front of the class. Help them to line up and put their cards together in the proper order to make the word when viewed by the class. Instruct the children to repeat the word over and over as they walk around the room linked like a train.

Now call up the child who has the card with E on it. Have this child link on the right (end) of the line of children forming "tap." Have him place his E card next at the end of the word. Explain that adding another car to the train slows it down and changes the sound it makes as it goes down the tracks.

Tell them that this new car on the train is absolutely quiet (make sure he is!). He likes to join the line of letters in a word, but he doesn't make a sound. However, when he joins the word, he makes the other vowel (in this case, A) say its name!

Now, ask the children in the line to say the sounds of their letters in order, reminding the A child that now he has to say his letter's NAME, not the short sound, or the "ah" sound.

When you come to the "silent E" child, have him cover his mouth with his hand. He doesn't say a sound!

Echo the sounds again, blending them into the word "tape." Have the children echo this after you.

Have the E child move away from the others. Ask the children what the word is now. (TAP) Have the E child come back and join the train. Ask what the word is now. (TAPE)

If you are doing this at home introduce this lesson when there are other family members around who can assist. If this is not possible, you can make a train out of empty oatmeal containers, using sticky-tac to attach the letter cards to the train.

Continue in the same manner with the formation of the words: kit/kite, not/note, rid/ride, tub/tube, dim/dime, bad/bade, ton/tone, pip/pipe. Discuss the meanings of any of these words as necessary and use in original sentences to further define.

Impress upon them that every time the final E shows up as the second vowel in these words, the first vowel in the word has to say its name. When it does this it is called a "long" vowel sound.

Another way to introduce this concept is to cut a 1" x 11" strip of black board to be used as a macron. Introduce the black paper macron to the children. Tell them that this is the sign for a vowel to say its name. Give the "silent E" child the black paper macron and permit him to reach across and place it over the head of the A child. Ask the A child to name his letter. He will use the long A sound to do so. Inform the children that they will not see a macron in their reading, but that often it is in the dictionary to tell them how to pronounce words. It may be a good idea to show the children a few dictionary entries which use the macron. Tell them that every time they see this, it means that vowel says its name.

BULLETIN BOARD IDEA: Make a bulletin board with trains on it. One train would have the word "tub" on it and one train would have the word "tube" on it. Then place curvy train tracks linking those trains to pictures of the objects the words represent on the far end of the bulletin board.

Worksheet 41A: Read the instructions aloud. Tell the children they are only to circle the words with the E at the end. Have them read the words as you point to them on your copy, or as you write them on the board. Call their attention to and read aloud the rule at the bottom of the page.

LONG VOWELS

Name — Worksheet 41A *Seeing*

INSTRUCTIONS:
Circle the words that have two vowels, with the second one being an E.

hat	ride	bad
hate	rid	bade
kite	tub	ton
kit	tube	tone
not	dime	pipe
note	dim	pip

The letters a, e, i, o, and u are called vowels. We have learned the sounds of these letters but sometimes they may sound different. There is a rule that will help know when to make the different sound: *A, E, I, O and U usually keep their names, when a silent final E is near—as in cute and bike and game.*

137

A, E, I, O and U usually keep their names, when a silent final E is near—as in cute and bike and game.

Give them their museum bag. Allow them time to go through the house and collect items that have long vowels to make their own museum. If you are teaching in a school setting, instruct the children to take the bag home and bring in objects the following day.

ACTIVITY 2: HEARING LONG A

Tell them they will be listening for only the long A sound today. You will read a list of words and they will indicate when they hear it by putting the tips of their index fingers together at an angle like the top of the upper case letter A. Read the following words aloud:

scale	back	bake	scat	skate	map
ape	vase	bat	fan	cake	Kate
take	tack	tame	tam	pan	pane

Praise their careful listening!

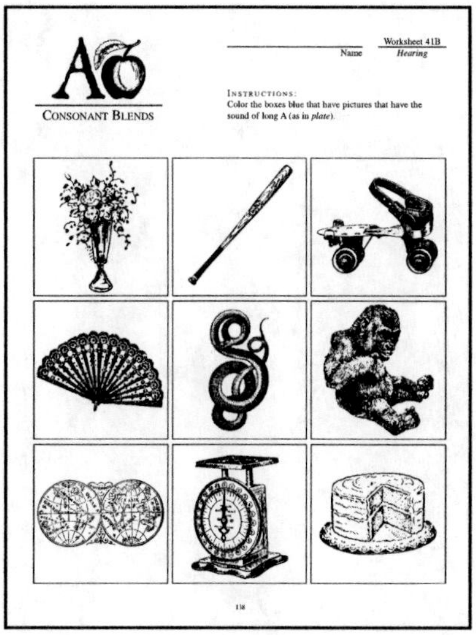
Worksheet 41B
Hearing
Name
CONSONANT BLENDS
INSTRUCTIONS:
Color the boxes blue that have pictures that have the sound of long A (as in *plate*).

Worksheet 41B: Read the instructions aloud. Tell them you will label the pictures for them while they place a dot of blue in the corner of the ones with the long A sound. They may then go back and color in the marked boxes.

Row 1: vase, bat, skate
Row 2: fan, snake, ape
Row 3: map, scale, cake

ACTIVITY 3: WRITING

Write the words found on Worksheet 41C on the board, along with lines. Invite children to come to the board and copy the words. Have them read the words aloud after writing them. Define as necessary and use in original sentences.

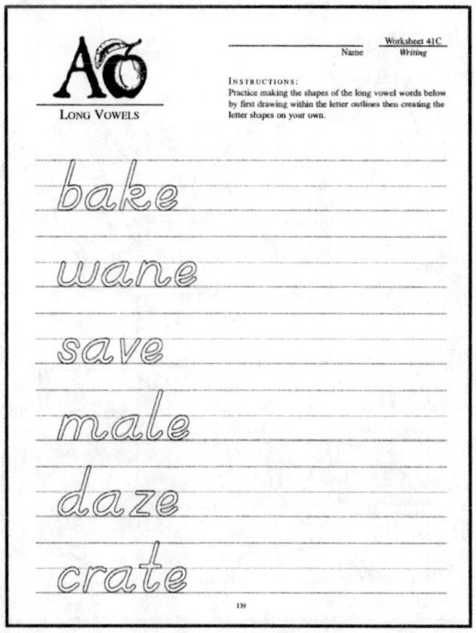
Worksheet 41C
Writing
Name
LONG VOWELS
INSTRUCTIONS:
Practice making the shapes of the long vowel words below by first drawing within the letter outlines then creating the letter shapes on your own.

bake
wane
save
male
daze
crate

Worksheet 41C: Read the instructions aloud and Monitor the students' progress as they work independently.

Monitor stroke direction and order, letter and word spacing, and the "FOUR P's!"

You may want to give the students the coloring page along with the flashcard. Read the information about the artist to your students before they color the picture.

Lesson 42
Target: Final Silent E

ACTIVITY : HEARING

Write the following on the board: rip, ripe. Ask someone to read the first word aloud. Now ask if anyone remembers how the second word will sound, with the E at the end. Praise and affirm correct responses. Call on a student to tell the class how he decoded the second word. Rephrase the rule if necessary. Remind them about the line of children making words yesterday and the child who played "silent E." He always made the other vowel say its name!

Tell them that today they will be listening only for the long I sound in words. When they hear it, have them make the finger spelling gesture for I: little finger raised, all other fingers folded down. Remind them they are listening for I to say its name in these words:

lip	kit	kite	bike	pipe	dim
dime	win	wine	fine	fin	pin
pine	bide	bid	bit	bite	vine

Praise their great listening!

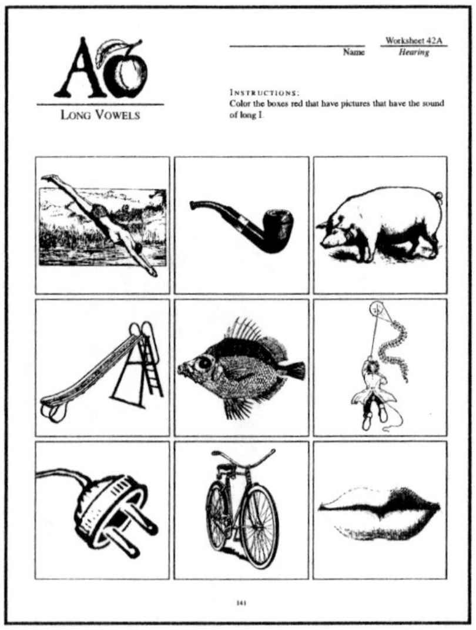

Worksheet 42A: Read the instructions aloud. Tell them you will label the pictures and they should put a dot of red in the corner of those pictures with the long I sound. They can then go back and color them in.

Row 1: dive, pipe, pig
Row 2: slide, fish, kite
Row 3: plug, bike, lips

ACTIVITY 2: READING

Present the puzzle pieces for M, A, and N. Have a child read the word "man."

Now ask what you must do if you wanted to form the word "mane" (like the mane of a lion). First ask what sound is made by the letter A in this new word (long A). Now ask what you will need at the end of the word to make the letter A say its name like this (final silent E). Add the E piece. Have the students link and unlink the E, pronouncing the word properly depending upon its presence or absence.

Continue in the same way to form the other words found on Worksheet 42B.

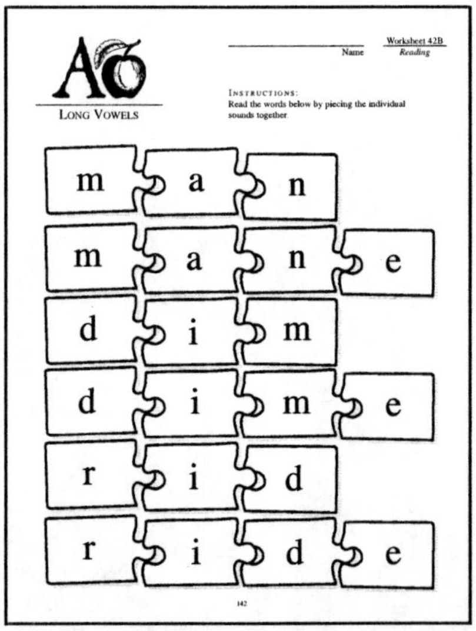

Worksheet 42B: Read the instructions aloud. Have the children read the words using any of the previous variations for eliciting student response.

Variations for prompting the reading of words on this sheet include: numbering the words and calling on students to read them by the designated number, verbal "fill-in-the-blanks," pointing to the written word on the board and having students point to the corresponding printed word on the sheet, riddle clues, categorizing on the basis of beginning sound, middle vowel, or ending letter group, etc.

Archives: Long E Edition

Lesson 43
Target: Final Silent E

Play the How Many Sounds? song for the children encouraging them to sing along.

ACTIVITY 1: HEARING

Write the following on the board: hop, hope. Ask someone to read the first word aloud. Now ask if anyone remembers how the second word will sound, with the E at the end. Praise and affirm correct responses. Call on a student to tell the class how he decoded the second word.

Rephrase the rule if necessary. Remind them about the train of children making words and the child who played the silent E caboose. He always made the other vowel say its name!

Tell them that today they will be listening only for the long O sound in words. When they hear it they will form a big O with their two hands, fingertips together. Remind them they are listening for O to say its name in these words:

top	tone	code	cod	mop	mope
dote	dot	pop	pope	robe	rob
slop	slope	tot	tote	rod	rode

Write some of the long O words above, along with lines. Invite children to the board to write the words.

Worksheet 43A: Read the instructions aloud. Label the pictures for the children and monitor as they respond independently. Watch their letter spacing at the bottom.

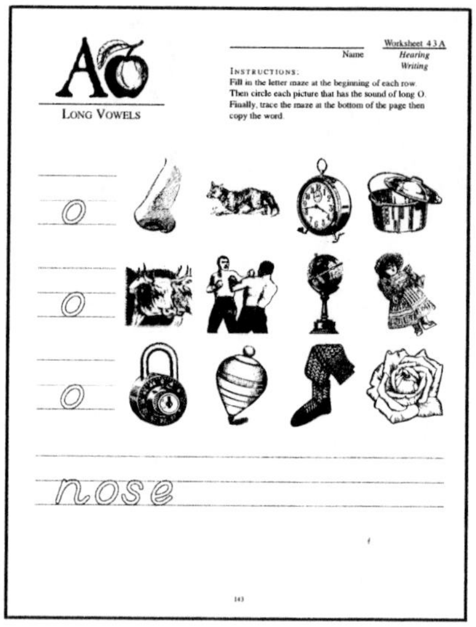

Row 1: nose, fox, clock, pot
Row 2: ox, box, globe, doll
Row 3: lock, top, socks, rose

ACTIVITY 2: READING

Present Worksheet 43B. Tell the children you will be working on this together today.

Worksheet 43B: Read the instructions aloud. Call on students to read each word pair. Guide them to determine which word labels the picture and circle it as directed. Discuss the meaning of any words which are unfamiliar.

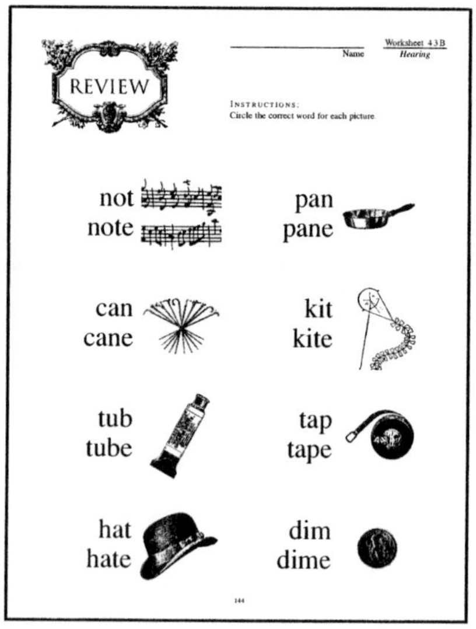

ACTIVITY 3: WRITING

Some words with long U are pronounced using the true letter name (as if a Y precedes the U, as in the words "cute," "use," "fume," etc.) and some are pronounced as if the long U was simply OO (like "moo," in words like "tune," "June," "rude,") Children may decode either way, but help them to pronounce the word properly after they have worked through it phonetically. Most children will correct their pronunciation spontaneously once they realize what the word is.

On the board write the following: mule, wore, yoke. Challenge the children to read the words as you point to them randomly. Remind them about the sound made by OR if necessary. Tell them that silent E doesn't have to make O say its name in this word—it already does! Define the word "yoke" for the children.

Review a little grammar here! Discuss briefly that words have different jobs in sentences. Ask the children if they can find the word on the board which tells what someone does (wore). Ask which words name things. (mule, yoke).

Add the words "the" and A to the words on display. Challenge the children to rearrange the words to form a sentence which will make sense. Remind them about using upper case for the first word and a period at the end!

Worksheet 43C: Read the instructions aloud. Carefully monitor letter and word spacing as they copy the entire sentence on their papers. Encourage them to be neat and take their time!

LESSON 44
TARGET: FINAL SILENT E

ACTIVITY 1: HEARING

Write the following on the board: tub, tube. Ask someone to read the first word aloud. Now ask if anyone remembers how the second word will sound, with the E at the end. Praise and affirm correct responses. Call on a student to tell the class how he decoded the second word.

Tell them that today they will be listening only for the long U sound in words.

You may want to explain that sometimes it will sound like long U (OO) and sometimes it will sound like "yu" (you), but don't make it complicated. Reassure them that either way, it is the long U and the letter is "saying its name."

Write the Special Exhibit "YOU" on the board and tell the children that they may indicate when they hear long U by pointing at "YOU" (on the board!) Read the following aloud:

cut	cute	flute	rude	cube	cub
duke	duck	fuzz	fuse	mute	mutt
run	rune	prune	dune	use	tune

Worksheet 44A: Read the instructions aloud. Assist the children to label the pictures and respond as indicated. Allow them to go on to the writing at the bottom independently.

Row 1: tube, duck, cup
Row 3: mules, nut, flute

ACTIVITY 2: READING

Write the following on the board: can, hid, tot, cub. Have students read each word. Define as necessary and use in original sentences.

Invite children to the board to add E to the end of each word and place a macron over the first vowel. Call on students to read the new words formed, using the proper long vowel sounds. Define the new words as needed and use in original sentences.

Worksheet 44B: Read the instructions aloud. Elicit student reading responses using any of the previous variations. Discuss the meanings of any unfamiliar words.

An additional activity with this sheet would be to have students go through and place macrons over all the vowels which will have the long sounds.

Archives: Long E Edition

Lesson 45
Target: The Vowel Sounds of Y and Syllabication

Play the Funny Butterfly song for the children encouraging them to sing along.

ACTIVITY 1: HEARING AND SEEING

If there are any children in your class with names ending in Y, add them to the list of names used in this lesson!

Challenge the children to be great "sound detectives" again today and tell you what sound is the same in all of the following:

Andy Billy Sammy Jenny Wendy

Praise the response that the ending sound is the same and it sounds like long E.

Now draw their attention to the board as you write each of the names in a vertical column, lining up all the final Y's, reading them aloud as they are written. Ask a student to come to the board and circle the letter which is the same in all of the names. (Y)

Have the children echo the names again. Now ask them: "What letter in each of these names is making the long E sound?" (Y) Praise correct responses.

Affirm that sometimes Y likes to pretend to be long E. Write the following on the board: bunny, puppy, candy. Assist the children to decode the words and use in original sentences.
Erase the board. Now write the following previously taught Special Exhibits: my, by. Ask the children what sound they hear at the end of each of these words. (long I) Affirm the correct answer and explain that Y sometimes likes to pretend to be long I also!

Write the following on the board: why, cry, fly. Call on children to decode each one, following the pattern for "my" and "by." Have them use these words in original sentences.

Show the students how to make an E in sign language. Tell them this is the sign we will use when we hear Y making the sound of long E. Then show the students how to make an I in sign language. Tell them this is the sign we will use when we hear Y making the sound of long I.

Give each child two index cards. Have them write E with a macron over it on one card and I with a macron on the other.

Tell them that you will be reading a list of words. They will hold up their hand forming an E or an I to indicate which sound they hear at the end of each of the following words:

lady	pony	funny	shy	family
baby	dry	sky	tiny	silly

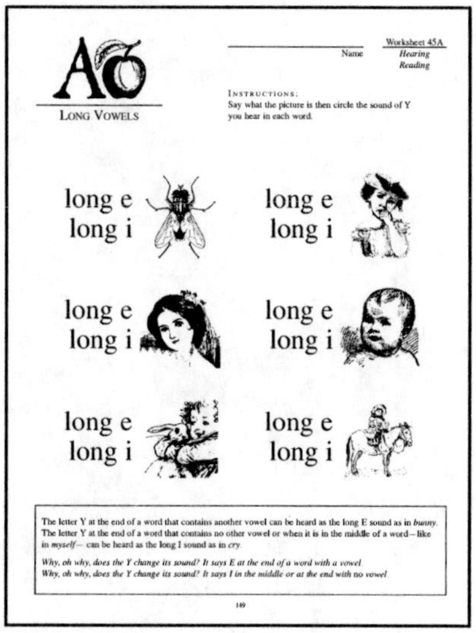
Worksheet 45A
Hearing
Reading

LONG VOWELS

Name

INSTRUCTIONS:
Say what the picture is then circle the sound of Y you hear in each word.

long e
long i

long e
long i

long e
long i

long e
long i

long e
long i

long e
long i

The letter Y at the end of a word that contains another vowel can be heard as the long E sound as in *bunny*. The letter Y at the end of a word that contains no other vowel or when it is in the middle of a word—like in *myself*— can be heard as the long I sound as in *cry*.

Why, oh why, does the Y change its sound? It says E at the end of a word with a vowel.
Why, oh why, does the Y change its sound? It says I in the middle or at the end with no vowel.

149

Worksheet 45A: Read the instructions aloud. Call on students to label the pictures, assisting as needed. Monitor as they respond as indicated.

Read the following rule to the children.

Why, oh why, does the Y change its sound?
It says E at the end of a word with a vowel.
Why, oh why, does the Y change its sound?
It says I in the middle or at the end with no vowel.

Write the following on the board as examples of the first part of the rule: silly, funny. Have students come up and underline the first vowel in each of these words. Tell them because this word has another vowel which comes before the Y, the Y makes the long E sound.

Write the following on the board as examples of the second part of the rule: sky, dry, shy. Ask them if they see any other vowels in these words. In cases like this, the Y makes the long I sound.

ACTIVITY 2: SYLLABICATION AND READING

Do a brief review of pluralization of nouns as an introduction to syllabication. Write the following on the board: mat, dish. Have a student read these words. Ask the students how you would say each word if there were more than one mat. (mats).

Add the S to the end of "mat." Have the students say the word. Ask how many beats they hear when this word is spoken. (one) Have them clap as they say the word both in the singular form and the plural form. Affirm that adding the S to this word does not change the number of beats in this word.

Now ask them how you would say "dish" if there were more than one of them. (dishes) Have them clap out the beats in both words, contrasting the single beat for the singular form with the two beats needed for the plural form. Ask if anyone remembers what must go with the S at the end of this word to form the word "dishes." (E + S) Praise correct responses.

Review that the two beats in the word are called "syllables." Syllables are just groups of letters which blend together. Words can be made up of two, three, four, or more syllables! Each syllable makes a beat and has at least one vowel in it.

Words can be broken into syllables to make them easier to read. Write the word "puppy" on the board. Lead the children in clapping it out. Affirm that it has two beats. Ask a child to come to the board and underline the first vowel in this word.

Tell them that because Y sounds like long E, it acts just like a vowel in this word. Have a student come up and underline the Y also. Compare the two clapping beats with the two vowels.

Ask the children to look carefully at the word and tell you what comes between the two vowels. (PP) Tell them that all the letters which are not vowels are called consonants. Tell them "Here's the rule for a word like this:"

When two consonants come between two vowels, the first one goes with the first syllable and the second one goes with the second syllable.

Draw a slash between the two P's. Draw their attention to the fact that each syllable on either side of the slash has a vowel. Say the word slowly, breaking it into the two syllables as shown. Have the children echo this after you. Do it again, clapping the beats.

Write the word "bunny" on the board. Ask how many syllables it has and clap them out. Invite a child to come to the board and underline the vowels U and Y. Challenge them to tell you where the slash should go to separate the two syllables. (between the N's) Invite a child to come to the board and put the slash in the correct location. Say the word slowly, breaking it into the syllables shown, clapping the beats, and having the children echo.

Now explain that some words are a little different. Write the following on the board: lady. Ask how many beats they hear in this word. (2) Then ask how many syllables it has. (2) Lead them to the conclusion that since it has and underline the two vowels. (A and Y) Ask them why Y is a vowel. (because it makes the long E sound)

Have them look carefully at the word. What do they see between the A and the Y? (D) Ask if this is a consonant or a vowel. (consonant)

Explain that now we have a word with only one consonant between the vowels. Where is it going to go?

Tell them you are going to experiment a little bit. Cover the Y with your hand. Ask them how they would read the syllable they see. (lad) Tell them this cannot be right because the word "lady" doesn't use the short A like in "lad." (She's not a "laddy!") So the D will not go with the first syllable. Instead it will go with the second syllable and pair up with the Y. Place a slash between the A and the D.

Tell the children that when this happens, the vowel at the end of the first syllable usually says its name, just like when silent E is around!

Say the word "lady," clapping out the syllables and having the children echo it several times. Emphasize the long A in the first syllable.

Now challenge the children to do this again with a new word. Write "pony" on the board. Ask the following: How many vowels does this word have? Underline them. How many syllables does it have? Where do we divide the syllables? Does the O make a short vowel sound or does it say its name? Why?

Praise their wonderful attentiveness!

Worksheet 45B: Read the instructions aloud. Assist the children to read the words and respond as indicated. Tell them to watch out—one of the words does not have a picture to match!

Worksheet 45B
Name
Reading
LONG VOWELS
INSTRUCTIONS:
Match the words on the left with the pictures on the right.

fly

lady

puppy

cry

bunny

pony

LESSON 46
TARGET: FINAL SILENT E AND ALPHABETICAL ORDER

ACTIVITY 1: ALPHABETICAL ORDER

Sing the Alphabet Song with enthusiasm today, especially if you haven't sung it in a while!

Write the following words on index cards: bun, fun, sun. Give these to three students.

Tell each student to read the words on his card aloud. Each must name the beginning letter and the sound made by that letter in his word. Place the flashcards on a desk in a pile and have each of the students find the flashcard that represents his letter.

Call attention to the order of the children in the room. Ask who is first, next, last. Have the children hold up their words and ask "In alphabetical order, which of these words will come first? (next? last?)

Have the children give you their cards as they return to their seats. Affix them to the board. Ask the children again which one was first and write a "1" beside the word "bun." Continue with "2" for "fun," and "3" for "sun."

Continue in the same manner with the following groups of words: cap, mask, zoo; fox, egg, dime. The last one will be tricky—they will be side by side!

Remind the children that knowing the order of the alphabet will be a great help to them later on when they begin to look things up in dictionaries.

Worksheet 46A: Read the instructions aloud. It may be helpful to allow the children to write the numbers "1," "2," "3" above or below the three words in each group, then copy onto the appropriate lines. Monitor their work and assist as necessary.

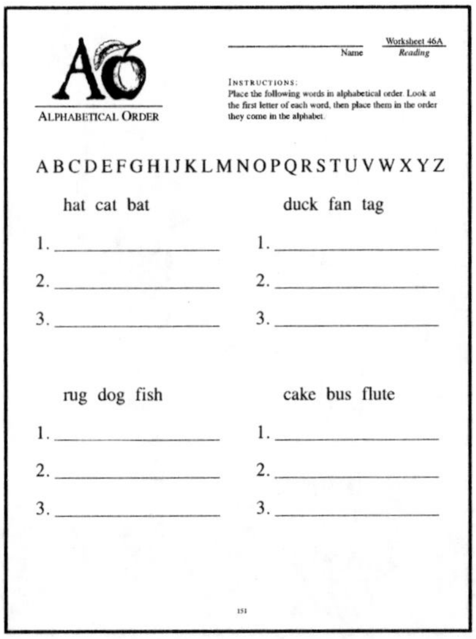
Alphabetical Order

Name ______ Worksheet 46A Reading

Instructions: Place the following words in alphabetical order. Look at the first letter of each word, then place them in the order they come in the alphabet.

A B C D E F G H I J K L M N O P Q R S T U V W X Y Z

hat cat bat
1. ______
2. ______
3. ______

duck fan tag
1. ______
2. ______
3. ______

rug dog fish
1. ______
2. ______
3. ______

cake bus flute
1. ______
2. ______
3. ______

ACTIVITY 2: SPELLING LIST 1

Write the following in a vertical column on the board: make, ride, note, cube. Draw guidelines to the right of each word. Invite students to the board to copy the words. Monitor their stroke direction and order and letter spacing.

Remind them about the final silent E rule. Call on students to read the words aloud. Define them as necessary and use in original sentences.

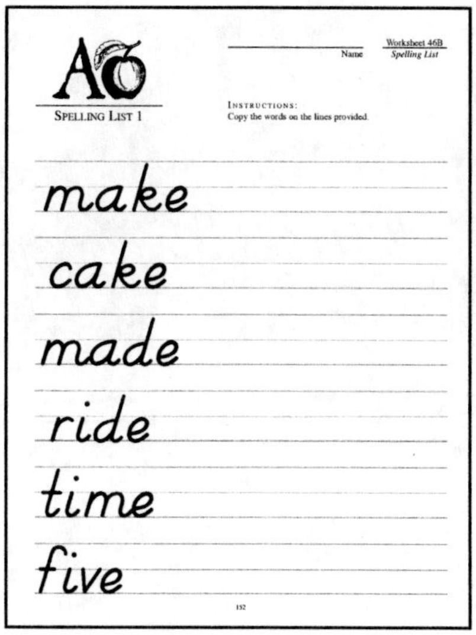

AO

SPELLING LIST 1

Name

Worksheet 46B
Spelling List

INSTRUCTIONS:
Copy the words on the lines provided.

make
cake
made
ride
time
five

152

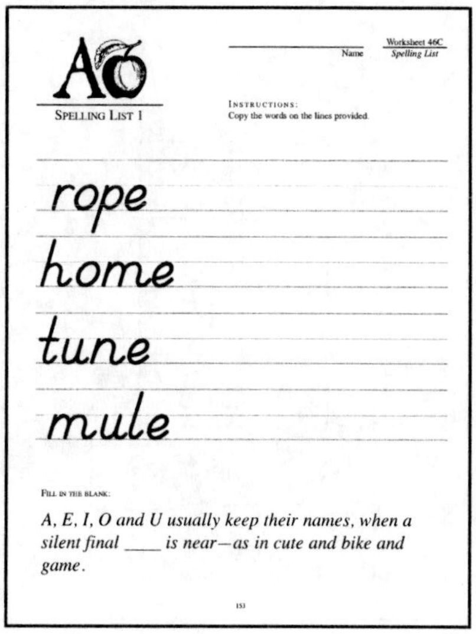

AO

SPELLING LIST 1

Name

Worksheet 46C
Spelling List

INSTRUCTIONS:
Copy the words on the lines provided.

rope
home
tune
mule

FILL IN THE BLANK:

A, E, I, O and U usually keep their names, when a silent final ____ is near—as in cute and bike and game.

153

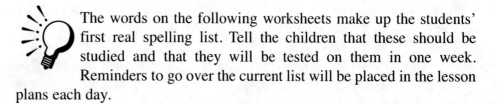

The words on the following worksheets make up the students' first real spelling list. Tell the children that these should be studied and that they will be tested on them in one week. Reminders to go over the current list will be placed in the lesson plans each day.

Worksheet 46B/C: Read the instructions aloud. Monitor their work carefully.

Remind about the "FOUR P's." Encourage neatness and accuracy. Excessively sloppy or malformed letters should be erased and redone.

LESSON 47
TARGET: FINAL Y, SYLLABICATION, AND LONG VOWELS IN OPEN SYLLABLES

ACTIVITY 1: READING

Write the following previously taught Special Exhibits on the board: my, by. Ask the children to read them aloud. Ask them what sound is made by the ending Y in each word. (long I).

Play the riddle game. Tell them you are thinking of a word which tells what a baby does when it is hungry or needs some attention. Affirm the correct answer ("cry") and challenge the children to determine what letters will be needed to spell this word. It will have the same pattern as the words on the board.

Do the same thing to stimulate the words "fry," "dry," "sky."

Write the following on the board: duty, glory, tiny. Do NOT read or say the words yet! Ask the children how many vowels they see in these words. Remind them to include the Y! Review the sound made by Y at the end of words which contain other vowels. (long E).

Call on a student to tell you how many syllables are in each of these words. Do NOT say them; base this answer ONLY on the number of vowels present.

Review the syllabication rule for words which contain one consonant between two vowels.

When two consonants come between two vowels, the first one goes with the first syllable and the second one goes with the second syllable.

Invite a student to come to the board and put the syllable slash between the first vowel and the following consonant in each word.

Now, ask if anyone remembers what happens to the sound of the first vowel when it comes at the end of the first syllable. (It says its name and becomes a "long" sound.) Affirm correct answers.

Ask what sign we can use over the first vowel to show that it now says its name. (a macron)

Worksheet 47A: Read the instructions aloud. Use any of the previous variations for eliciting student response.

ACTIVITY 2: MORE SYLLABICATION (LONG VOWELS IN OPEN SYLLABLES)

Tell the children that there are many words which will follow this pattern:

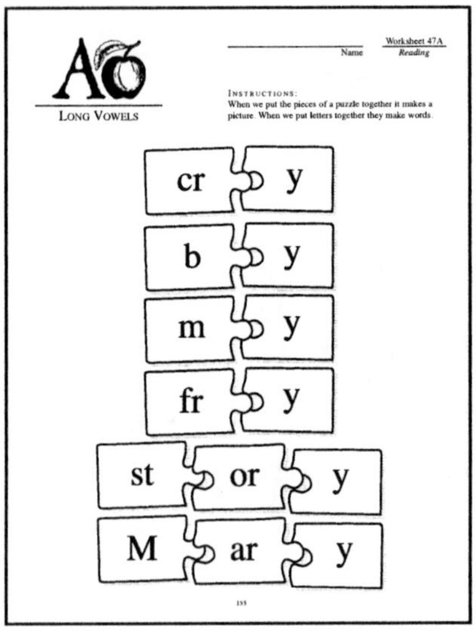

When a consonant falls between two vowels, sometimes it goes with the second syllable and the first vowel will be 'long.'

The words don't have to end in Y to do this.

Write the following on the board: favor, paper, clover. Do NOT say them. Invite students to come to the board and underline the two vowels in each word.

Ask how many syllables will be in each word. Tell them that the consonant in between the vowels will go with the second syllable. Invite students to come up and put the syllable slash between the first vowel and the following consonant in each word.

Now, ask if the first vowel will make the short sound, or if it will say its name and be "long." Affirm that the sound will be the long sound. Invite students to come to the board and write macrons over the first vowel in each word.

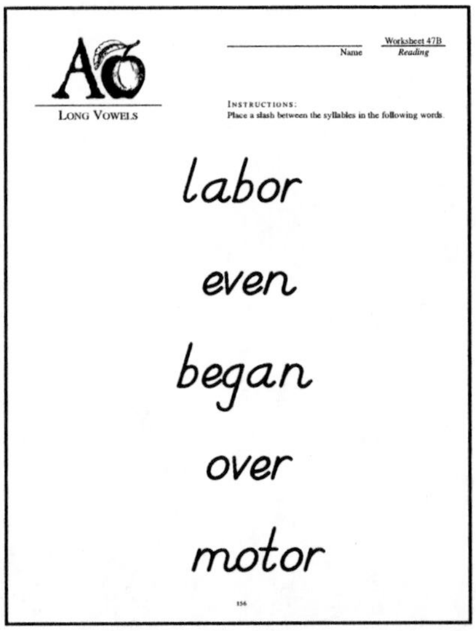

Challenge them to decode and read the words aloud. Praise their fine reading!

Worksheet 47B: Read the instructions aloud. Monitor the students' progress as they work independently.

Remind the children to study the spelling words introduced in Lesson 46. Keep the list posted in the room and do a short spelling bee daily to assist them in their learning.

LESSON 48
DECODING VCV (VOWEL-CONSONANT-VOWEL) WORDS, SIGHT AND SPECIAL WORDS

ACTIVITY 1: DECODING VCV WORDS

Distribute puzzle pieces : L, B, R, V, N, B, G, M, T, A, E, O. Instruct the students to assemble the letters: B, E, G, A, N in that order.

Ask the students how many vowels are in this word. (2) Therefore, how many syllables does it have?

Tell them to separate the puzzle pieces between the G and A. Have the class decode the two syllables using all short vowels, then blending the syllables to form a word. Is the word formed one that they know and understand? (NO)

Some children may say "yes," thinking that it is the word "beggin'" (begging). Write "begging" on the board for comparison in this case and show that it is the action word "beg" plus the ING ending. The word being formed by the children is different.

Ask if you are in the right place. (NO) Remind them of the pattern they learned yesterday:

When a consonant falls between two vowels, sometimes it goes with the second syllable and the first vowel will be 'long.'

Ask them where the break should be in this word. (between the E and the G). Each student should reassemble the puzzle pieces then break the word between the E and the G.

When distributing the puzzle pieces, give each child a paper clip to act as the macron. Ask the children where it needs to go. (over the E) Place it over the head of the E puzzle piece. Ask what sound the E will make now. (long E).

Now ask the class to decode and read the word formed. Define it and use in an original sentence. Follow the same procedure with the words "labor," "even," "over," and "motor."

It is very important that the children attempt to decode the word using short vowel sounds first. They will encounter words in their reading which follow the VCV pattern, which utilizes short vowels in the first syllable. Since their decoding up to this point has been focused on using short vowels, it doesn't need to be specially taught. The VCV decoding pattern is new and requires the long vowels, which is what is being emphasized in these lessons.

Now write the following on the board: river, model. Tell the children to decode these using short vowels. Do they make words which they understand? (YES) Affirm that these are words which do NOT follow the pattern. Yet they can be easily read by using the short vowel sounds which they know so well!

ACTIVITY 2: SPECIAL EXHIBITS

Write the following previously taught Special Exhibits on the board: love, have, give, one, were, there, where. Call on students to read each one.

Tell the children that these are "buccaneer" words—named after the pirates in THE BLACK FLAG. They do not obey the rules or follow the law.

Ask the question: What rule do they break? Do not answer this right now. Instead ask them to read the words aloud again. Do they hear the final E in each word? (NO)

Remind them about the activity when the E caboose came at the end of the word train. He placed his hand over his mouth and didn't make a sound. When he did this what sound did the first vowel make? (long)

Does the first vowel make the long sound in these words? (NO) That's the rule they break and that is why they are BUCCANEERS! Tell them that there is a band of "buccaneers" in our language and their "pictures" hang in the Special Exhibit gallery so we will recognize them. They don't all break the same rule, but none of them follow any set pattern. They will see some more in the next story.

Write the following on the board: some, Orville, many, also. Read them aloud and have the children echo them after you. Define them and use in complete sentences.

ACTIVITY 3: READING UP IN THE SKY

This story chronicles the experimentation of the Wright Brothers and the first sustained flight of an aircraft in 1903. The following vocabulary and expressions are used:

larks, storks and robins—kinds of birds
hike—travel on foot

glide—fly smoothly and without effort
whirl—turn, spin
labor—work
copper—a reddish-brown metal
a bang and a clang—the sounds of hitting metal with a hammer (an onomatopoeia)
rubber—an elastic substance
bumper—a horizontal metal guard that protects the front or the back of a car
shed—an out-building
lumber—planks of wood
tire—become weary or weak
model—smaller version, toy
lurch—a sudden swaying to one side or the other
jerk—a quick, sharp pull
flying crafts—airplanes
suffer harm—become damaged
motor—an engine that would propel the plane
gas—fuel
propellers—turning panels, like a windmill
shore—beach
thumping and humming—the sounds of th motor (an onomatopoeia)

Assist the children in their round robin reading. Discuss characters, main ideas, and events as they occur.

Some questions for discussion include: What kinds of skills did Wilbur and Orville practice in order to be able to build an airplane? Why did they make a model first? Why was a motor important? What made the beach a good place for launching a plane? Have you ever flown? What was it like?

Remind the children to go over Spelling List 1. Assign pairs of students to quiz one another for review.

Lesson 49
Reading Comprehension and Review

ACTIVITY 1: READING WORDS REVIEW

Praise the children today for all the fine reading they have been doing. Remind them that as they learn more and more patterns for decoding and reading, they will be able to read more and more wonderful things, including and especially, the Bible. This is the ultimate goal!

Review with them all the special patterns they have learned so far: consonant blending, vowel + R, ING, ANG, ONG, adding ING and ER to action words, adding ER to description words (adjectives) to form comparatives, final Y as long I and long E, final silent E and the use of the long sound (with a macron) for the first vowel. Write examples of each on the board and call on students to read them aloud.

Feel free to refer back to previous worksheets to find clear examples of each of these patterns. You may also solicit examples from the class, but screen them carefully to make sure they are fully decodable by the students and use the patterns correctly!

They have mastered quite a few "Special Exhibit" words which are "buccaneers" in our language! Write a few of these and try to determine what "law" they are breaking (if it is one they know) or how they are pronounced differently. Tell them they will use these skills over and over again as they continue to read.

Worksheet 49A : Read the instructions aloud. Remind the children to look for the patterns and apply them to read the words on the page. Monitor the students' progress as they work independently.

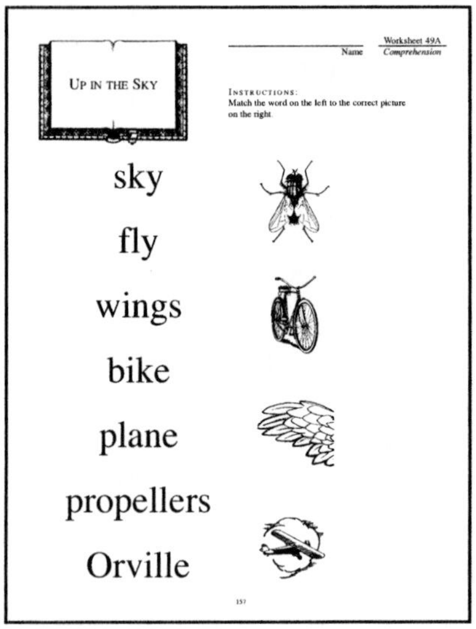
Up in the Sky

Name

Worksheet 49A
Comprehension

Instructions:
Match the word on the left to the correct picture on the right.

sky
fly
wings
bike
plane
propellers
Orville

157

This is a good time to watch carefully to see if all the paradigms are being applied and experimented with appropriately. Students who are showing difficulty with any of these concepts at this point should be given further practice and support before moving any further in the curriculum.

ACTIVITY 2: READING COMPREHENSION

Review the characters, events, and main ideas of the story UP IN THE SKY. Discuss further any of the questions from the last lesson as needed.

Worksheet 49B: Read the instructions aloud. Monitor the students' progress as they work independently. Affirm that they are to write an entire word on the last lines to answer Question 4. You may need to guide them to the correct answer for this. (The answer is GOD!)

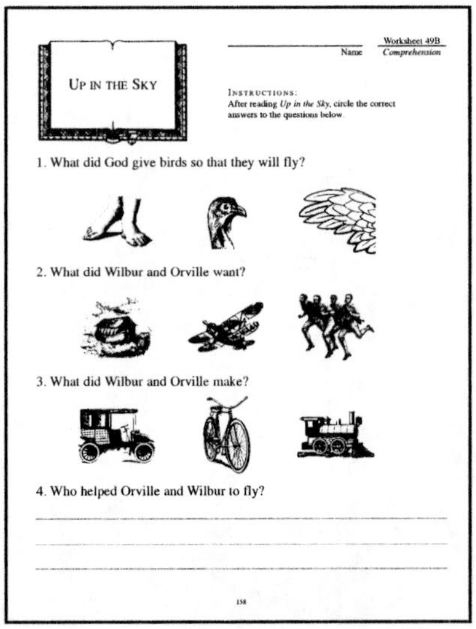
Up in the Sky

Name

Worksheet 49B
Comprehension

Instructions:
After reading *Up in the Sky*, circle the correct answers to the questions below.

1. What did God give birds so that they will fly?
2. What did Wilbur and Orville want?
3. What did Wilbur and Orville make?
4. Who helped Orville and Wilbur to fly?

158

Lesson 50
Targets: ARE Words, Final BLE Words, S as Z

ACTIVITY 1: ARE WORDS

Write the following on the board: car, far, mar, star, scar, spar. Call on students to read the words, using the AR sound as they have been taught. Discuss the meanings of the words and use them in original sentences.

Ask the children what will happen to the sound of A (pronounced as "ah" in these words) when final silent E is added. (the sound will become "long")

Add final E to the word "car." Guide the children to decode the new word "care," using long A. (It will almost sound like it has two syllables.)

Tell the children that in words like this, the A is really not pronounced as long A, but is turned into short A instead. So the word "car," which uses A as "ah," becomes "care" with the A pronounced as short A.

Practice this by adding E to the end of the rest of the AR words, pronouncing them clearly and having the children echo them after you.

ACTIVITY 2: FINAL BLE WORDS

Write the blend BL on the board. Ask the children to give you several words which begin with this blend.

Now tell the children that BL can be at the end of words also, but when it is, final silent E always goes along. Write an E after the BL blend on the board. Affirm that the sound is still BL and that the E doesn't make any sound at all.

Now write the following on the board: able, table, fable, cable.

Ask the children how many vowels are seen in these words. (2) Invite a student to come to the board and underline the two vowels.

Ask the children how many syllables will be heard in each of these words and why. (2—because there are two vowels)

Tell the children that because the BL is a blend and the two sounds work together as a team, they will not be broken apart by the syllable slash. Place the syllable slash between the first vowel and the "b" in each of the words.

Ask what often happens to the first vowel when it is at the end of the first syllable. (it says its name) Assist the children to apply this rule to the words on the board and decode them. Define as necessary and use in original sentences.

Inform the children that many L blends behave this way at the end of words. Write the following on the board: circle, rattle, tickle, drizzle, steeple, ladle, ruffle. Invite children to the board to underline the consonant + LE at the end of each word. Assist the children to decode and read the words. Define as necessary and use in original sentences.

ACTIVITY 3: TARGET: S PRONOUNCED AS Z

Write the following previously taught Special Exhibits on the board: is, was, as.

Ask the children what letter they see at the end of each word. (S) Tell the children to be fantastic listening detectives today.

Read the words aloud, emphasizing the S as Z at the end of each word. Ask the children if they hear S or Z at the end of these words. (Z) Praise their great listening!

Affirm that in these words S makes the Z sound. Remind them that this same thing happens in some plural words. Write the following on the board as examples: ribs, lands, pins. Read each one and emphasize the Z sound at the end of each.

When pluralization was taught at the end of the kindergarten year, the pronunciation of the final S as Z was not discussed in order to avoid confusion. Decoding more advanced words, however, will sometimes require it. Therefore, it is introduced at this time.

Challenge the children to tell you what the difference is between the S sound and the Z sound. (Z is voiced and S is not) Have them place their hands on their throats to confirm the use of the voice with Z. Explain that because they are so alike, S will sometimes use the Z sound and they will often say it that way without even realizing it!

Write the following previously taught Special Exhibit on the board: use. Ask a child to read it aloud. Affirm that the S in this word makes the Z sound also.

Ask them if the final E makes any sound. (NO) Because of that, the word only has one syllable, even though they see two vowels. Final silent E is never spoken, so it never makes a syllable. Remind them that all of the final silent E words they have studied are like this.

However, it does make the first vowel say its name. Say the word "use" again and emphasize the long U at the beginning.

Ask the children what symbol can be placed over the U to show it is long. (macron). Invite a child to the board to write the macron over the U.

Tell them that they will now learn two more words which follow this pattern. Write the following on the board: these, those, wise.

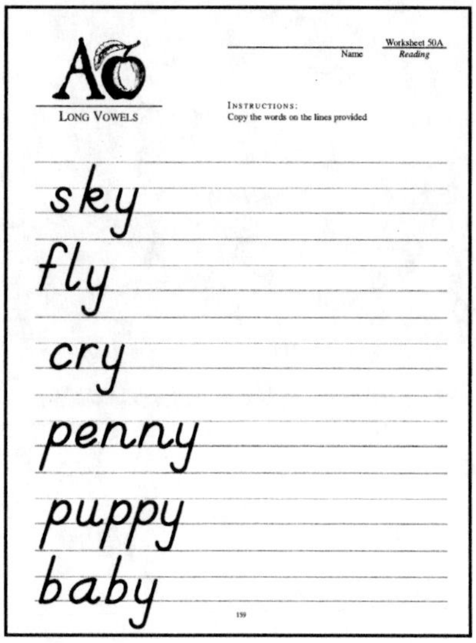
Worksheet 50A
Reading
Name

Long Vowels

Instructions:
Copy the words on the lines provided

sky
fly
cry
penny
puppy
baby

159

Affirm that the S will make the Z sound, and the final E is silent. Ask what sound will be made by the first vowel. (long) Have a child come to the board and write the macron over the first vowels in each word.

Assist the children to decode and read the words. Use them in original sentences to define them.

Worksheet 50A: Read the instructions aloud. Encourage them to be neat and take their time!

Continue to review Spelling List 1 in preparation for tomorrow's test!

Worksheet 50B: Read the instructions aloud. Use any of the previous variations for eliciting student response.

Worksheet 50B
Reading
Name

Long Vowels

Instructions:
Read up and down the word columns.

time	more	anger
alive	blame	angry
some	rage	debate
Bible	relate	silent
life	state	abide
dare	riding	Jesus
brave	revere	inquire
page	is	relate
share	was	here
pore	as	assembly
over	alone	close
bade	holy	never-ending

160

Percival's Pairs: Using ING, ANG, ONG, blends, long vowels and Y as I.

Lesson 51
Reading THE BRAVE MONK

ACTIVITY 1: READING ALOUD

This story chronicles the calling of Martin Luther to initiate the Reformation through the posting of 95 theses on the door of the chapel at Wittenburg Castle. The theses outlined the doctrinal errors of the Roman Catholic Church and put Luther in great danger. He was "kidnapped" by supporters and kept in seclusion in a hidden location for a period of time to protect him and allow him to continue his writing. His "protest" against Roman Catholicism led to the establishment of "Protestantism," although his true goal was to reform Catholicism. The Lutheran denomination derives its name from Martin Luther.

The following vocabulary and expressions are used in this story and may need further explanation to students:

monk—a person who leaves normal life and joins a religious group in an attempt to be more holy
get to the Bible—have the opportunity to read it themselves
men of the Church—leaders in the Roman Catholic Church
holy—without sin and acceptable to God
dare—have the necessary courage
brave—courageous
paper—Luther's 95 Theses

square—a public area in the center of town (the door of the castle church in Wittenburg)
trade wares—sell or buy in the market
pore over—read carefully, think about
bade—requested, asked
debate—argue politely
Churchmen—leaders in the Roman Catholic Church
fixing stares—staring, glaring
state—say, write
spare the public your mistakes—do not lead the people astray
take back—deny, be sorry for
submit—obey
abide—live
inquire—ask
hare—rabbit
snare—trap
implore—fervently request
relate—tell
blades—swords
spades—shovels
manner—way
fare—do
smite—hit, strike
assembly—group
shade—twilight
mare—female horse
man close to—friend of
fortress—strong building, castle
rare—not common, outstanding
never-ending—eternal
spend time with the Bible—have the opportunity to read and interpret the Bible
note—take notice of, pay attention to
revere—love and honor

Guide the children through the round robin reading of the story. Note main characters, events, and main ideas as you proceed through the book.

This would be a good time to discuss the Westminster Shorter Catechism Question 86: What is faith in Jesus Christ? Faith in Jesus Christ is a saving grace, whereby we receive and rest upon him alone for salvation as he is offered to us in the gospel.

Questions for discussion may include: What did the Roman Catholic Church teach that men must do to earn eternal life? What did God teach Martin Luther through the Scriptures? Do you think he was brave for taking a stand against the Church and why? How did he spend his time in his hiding place?

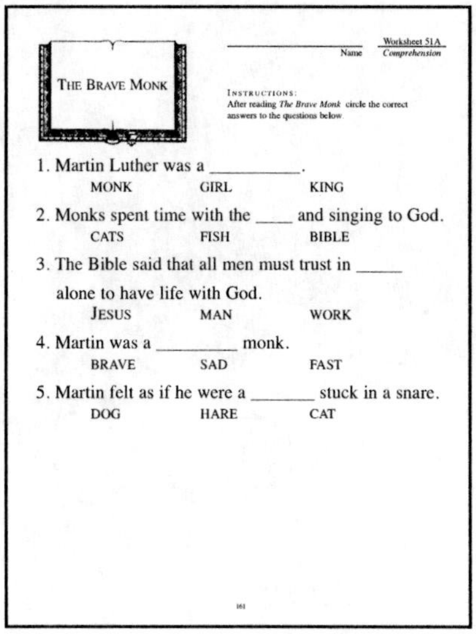

Name ____________ Worksheet 51A *Comprehension*

THE BRAVE MONK

INSTRUCTIONS:
After reading *The Brave Monk* circle the correct answers to the questions below

1. Martin Luther was a __________.
   MONK GIRL KING
2. Monks spent time with the ____ and singing to God.
   CATS FISH BIBLE
3. The Bible said that all men must trust in _____ alone to have life with God.
   JESUS MAN WORK
4. Martin was a ________ monk.
   BRAVE SAD FAST
5. Martin felt as if he were a _______ stuck in a snare.
   DOG HARE CAT

161

You may want to show the children some of the books and writings we have today which Martin Luther wrote during his lifetime.

Worksheet 51A: Read the instructions aloud. Assist as necessary and monitor their work.

ACTIVITY 2: SPELLING TEST 1

Name ____________ Worksheet 51B *Spelling Test*

SPELLING TEST 1

1. 7.
2. 8.
3. 9.
4. 10.
5.
6.

162

Worksheet 51B: Administer the test on Spelling List 1. Read each word once, use it in a sentence, then repeat it. Do not give any other sound or letter clues.

LESSON 52
TARGET: AI/AY

Listen to the song Play Everyday.

ACTIVITY 1: HEARING AND SEEING

Tell the children that today they will be learning a new letter pair. Write the following on the board: ma, pa, ha. Remind the children that each of these words uses the "ah" sound of A. Call on students to read them aloud.

Now ask if anyone remembers the other two sounds of letter A. (short and long A). Then add a Y to the end of each word. The Y is a silent buddy or partner, just like final silent E. It doesn't make any sound of its own in these words, but it makes the A before it long. Every time we see A and Y together, we know it is the long A sound.

If you have been using macrons, you should place one over each letter A.

Write the following on the board: SAY, TRAY, MAY, CLAY, HAY. Read them aloud and have the children echo them after you. Point to the words randomly and call on children to read them independently.

Now explain that the same thing happens in the middle of words. Write the following on the board: RAN, BRAN, MAN. Leave a small space between the A and the N. Call on students to read each word.

Now we are going to show how this A is long in the middle. In the middle of words, the letter I likes to be the silent partner for long A. Write an I to the right of each A in each word.

Tell the children that AY and AI both make the long A sound.

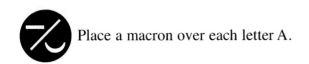

Place a macron over each letter A.

Invite students to come to the board and circle the letter pairs AI and AY in each of the words. Demonstrate how to draw a line through the silent I or Y in each letter pair. Tell them we do this to show that they are quiet in these words. Invite students to the board to draw lines through all the silent partners in all the words. Erase the board.

Worksheet 52A: Read the instructions aloud. Monitor the students' progress as they work independently. Lead the children through the reading of each word, first by echoing, then by independent decoding.

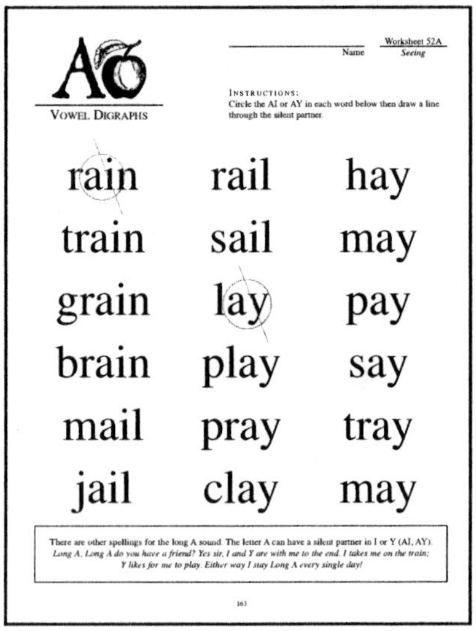

Worksheet 52A
Seeing

Name

VOWEL DIGRAPHS

INSTRUCTIONS:
Circle the AI or AY in each word below then draw a line through the silent partner.

rain	rail	hay
train	sail	may
grain	lay	pay
brain	play	say
mail	pray	tray
jail	clay	may

There are other spellings for the long A sound. The letter A can have a silent partner in I or Y (AI, AY). *Long A, Long A do you have a friend? Yes sir, I and Y are with me to the end. I takes me on the train; Y likes for me to play. Either way I stay Long A every single day!*

163

Long A, long A do you have a friend?
Yes sir, I and Y are with me to the end.
I takes me on the train;
Y likes for me to play.
Either way I stay Long A every single day!

ACTIVITY 2: FORMING AND READING AI/AY WORDS

Present the puzzle pieces needed for the formation of the words on Worksheet 52B. Remind the children that AY is used at the end of words and AI is used in the middle.

Say the word "train." Guide them through the selection of the proper puzzle pieces to form the word. Write the finished word on the board.

Invite students to form the rest of the words on Worksheet 52B.

You may want to add to this activity by forming additional words with the same pieces. Some possible combinations include: trail, pain, pail, main, rail, sail, saint, may, pay, tray. You may also want to bring students to the board to write the words for additional writing practice.

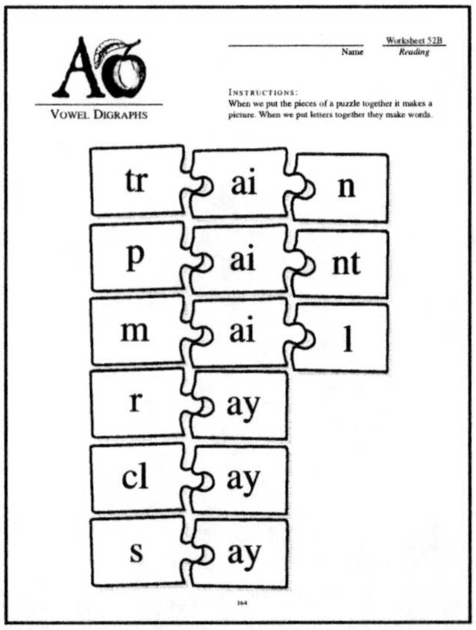

Worksheet 52B
Reading

Name

VOWEL DIGRAPHS

INSTRUCTIONS:
When we put the pieces of a puzzle together it makes a picture. When we put letters together they make words.

tr	ai	n
p	ai	nt
m	ai	l
r	ay	
cl	ay	
s	ay	

164

Worksheet 52B: Read the instructions aloud. Use any of the variations for eliciting student response. Use the words in original sentences.

Archives: Special Exhibit Edition. Use all the Special Exhibit words used to date.

LESSON 53
WRITING AI/AY AND REVIEW

Listen to the song Play Everyday.

ACTIVITY 1: WRITING AI/AY

Write the following on the board: gain, stay, pray, wait. Draw lines to the right of each word. Invite children to come to the board and copy the words.

Remind them about stroke direction and order as necessary.

Guide the children to decode and read the words formed, reminding them about the silent I or Y partners and the use of long A. Discuss meanings and use in original sentences.

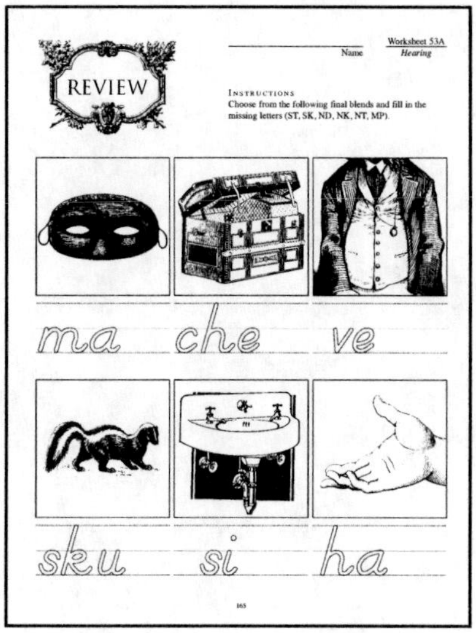

Worksheet 53A
Hearing
Name
REVIEW
INSTRUCTIONS
Choose from the following final blends and fill in the missing letters (ST, SK, ND, NK, NT, MP).
ma
che
ve
sku
si
ha

Worksheet 53A: Monitor as they copy the words independently. Call on students to decode and read them, solicit original sentences from the children.

ACTIVITY 2: REVIEW

Play a little rhyming game today. Say the following word: pink. Have the children come up with as many words as they can which rhyme with "pink." Write them on the board as they are offered. (Try to keep up!)

Make up a silly poem using some of the rhyming words like:

A pink sink
Full to the brink
Of a mink with a drink
Made me wink

A cover is in Appendix 3 that can be copied and folded around 8.5" x 11' sheets of paper. On these pieces of paper write the poems that the students come up with to make a NK poem collection.

Invite students to the board to underline the final letter pair NK in each word. Remind them that this is called a blend and that the two letters run together and act like a sound team.

Play the same game with the words "stamp," "pest," "band." Assist as necessary to come up with words which follow the correct final blend spelling patterns.

Write some of these words on the board without the final blend. Invite students to come up and write the appropriate letter pair to complete the words.

Worksheet 53B: Read the instructions aloud. Caution the children that not all of the letter pairs listed will be used in the words. Assist as necessary to label, but do not give any other letter or sound clues. Monitor their work.

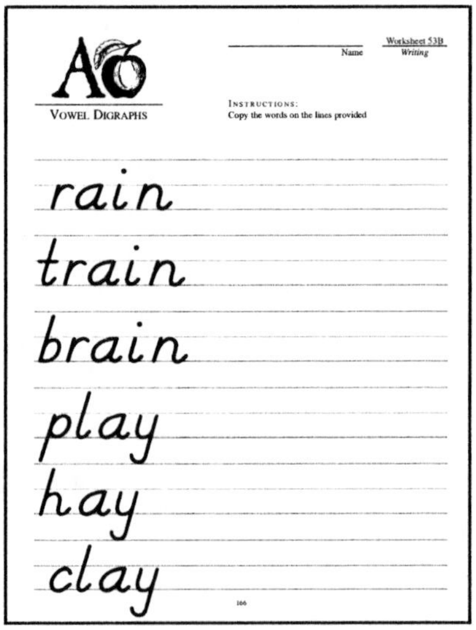

Worksheet 53B
Writing
Name
Vowel Digraphs
Instructions:
Copy the words on the lines provided

rain
train
brain
play
hay
clay

Archives: Combine the cards for the beginning blends, ending blends and long vowel editions.

Lesson 54
Target: EE/EA as Long E

Play The E Partnership song for the children encouraging them to sing along.

ACTIVITY 1: HEARING AND SEEING

Tell the children that today we will learn how to recognize another letter pair. Write the following on the board: met, step, pep. Leave a small space between the E and the final letter. Call on students to read each word. Use in original sentences.

Ask what sound of E is heard in each of those words. (short E) Ask if E has another sound. (long E) Affirm correct answers.

Tell them that we will put another letter after the E and this letter will make the first E say its name. This letter will not make a sound. What do we call letters like that? (silent partners or silent letters)

For these words, the silent partner for E is its twin—another E! Write in the second E in each word. It doesn't make a sound, but even if it did, they would say the same thing!

Read the words formed and have the children echo them. Use them in original sentences.

Write the following on the board: deep, beef, sheep. Call on students to decode and read each one.

Draw a macron over the E in each word. Ask what this symbol means. (that the E will be long, or say its name)

Challenge the children to pronounce each word using the long E sound. Do they hear words which make sense? (YES) Discuss the meanings of the new words they hear.

Now remind them that we do not use macrons in our writing or see them in our reading. So we have to have another way to show that the long E sound is used in these words.

Invite students to the board to circle the EE in each word.

Demonstrate how to draw a line through the silent partner and have students come to the board and do the same with each display word.

Now tell them that sometimes the E twin doesn't want to go along. Sometimes another letter follows E instead. It is still silent and still lets the first E say its name.

Write the following on the board: seat, beam, feast. What letter do they see now following the E? (A)

Draw one over each E.

Invite children to come to the board, circle the letter pair EA in each word, and draw a line through the A.

Challenge the children to read each of the words. Define as necessary and use in original sentences.

Now tell them that these letter pairs EE and EA can also be found at the end of words. Write the following on the board: tree, see, tea, pea. Invite students to circle the letter pairs in each word.

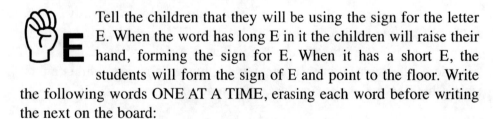

Tell the children that they will be using the sign for the letter E. When the word has long E in it the children will raise their hand, forming the sign for E. When it has a short E, the students will form the sign of E and point to the floor. Write the following words ONE AT A TIME, erasing each word before writing the next on the board:

deed	tree	met	leap	led	week
sheep	bet	bean	fed	sleep	red
bed	beef	feet	teach	Ned	least

Finally, ask the children if they remember the lesson when they studied UR and IR. Write these two letter pairs on the board. Remind them that they sounded the same, but made a difference sometimes in the meaning of words. Remind them about the words "fur" and "fir" and the silly sentences you made when you used the wrong spelling. (Lesson 36)

Tell them that EE and EA sometimes do the same thing. They sound the same, but can be used to change the meaning of words!

Write these word pairs on the board: see/sea, tea/tee, meet/meat. Read them aloud for the children. Do the words in each pair sound the same? (YES) Yet they do not mean the same thing! Define each word in each pair and use in original sentences to further clarify their meanings. Affirm that the spelling makes the difference in how each word is used. When we read these words like these, we will understand them only by the way they are spelled.

Assure them that they will not need to remember how to spell words like this right now, but that they will be practicing how to read and understand them.

Worksheet 54A: Read the instructions aloud. Monitor as they respond as indicated. Assist the children to read through the words listed. Define as necessary and use in original sentences.

Long E, long E do you have a friend?
Yes sir, E and A are with me to the end.
E keeps me on my feet;
A gives me a seat.
Either way I stay Long E, which really is a treat!

Worksheet 54A
Seeing
Name
VOWEL DIGRAPHS
INSTRUCTIONS:
Circle the EE or EA in each word below then draw a line through the silent partner.

tree	meet	each
deep	sheep	cream
free	green	beat
peep	bean	feast
beef	leaf	least
steep	seat	beast

Long e can also have silent partners. The first is another E as in feet. Or E can have A as a silent partner as in meat. *Long E, long E do you have a friend? Yes sir, E and A are with me to the end. E keeps me on my feet; A gives me a seat. Either way I stay Long E, which really is a treat!*

167

ACTIVITY 2: READING MORE WORDS

Present the puzzle pieces for the words shown on Worksheet 54B. Place the EE on display. Invite children to link the appropriate pieces together to form the EE words found on the worksheet. Do the same for the EA words.

Do not require that students choose between EE and EA in this exercise. That will require the independent application of spelling patterns based on meaning, which they have not acquired yet. Instead, you may want to reinforce the meaning/spelling connection by interchanging EE and EA in some of these words. For instance: "meet/meat," "feet/feat," and "peek/peak." This will provide further vocabulary and receptive language practice, while emphasizing that the two letter pairs make the same sound.

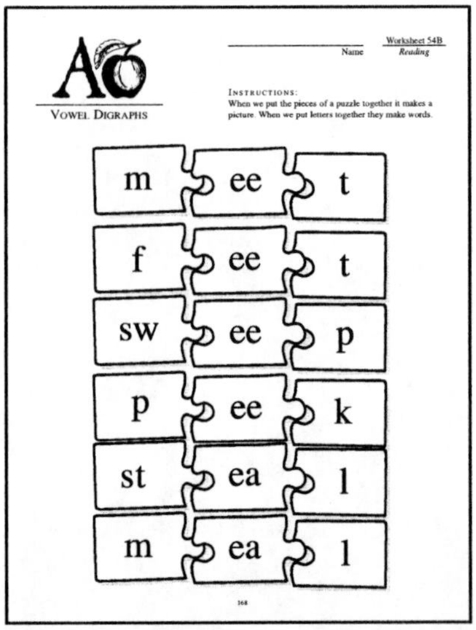
Worksheet 54B
Reading
Name
VOWEL DIGRAPHS
INSTRUCTIONS:
When we put the pieces of a puzzle together it makes a picture. When we put letters together they make words.

m	ee	t
f	ee	t
sw	ee	p
p	ee	k
st	ea	l
m	ea	l

168

Worksheet 54B: Read the instructions aloud. Elicit student response using any of the previous variations. Define and use in original sentences, paying particular attention to meanings based on spelling patterns.

LESSON 55
TARGET: EE/EA AND REVIEW

Play The E Partnership song for the children encouraging them to sing along.

ACTIVITY 1: READING

Write the words found on Worksheet 55A on the board.

Play the riddle game. Give the children clues to the meaning of one of the words on the board. Call on a child to come to the board, point to the word which they think answers the riddle, and read it aloud. Confirm the meaning by using it in an original sentence.

When all the words have been identified, invite students to the board to circle or underline each EE or EA letter pair in each word.

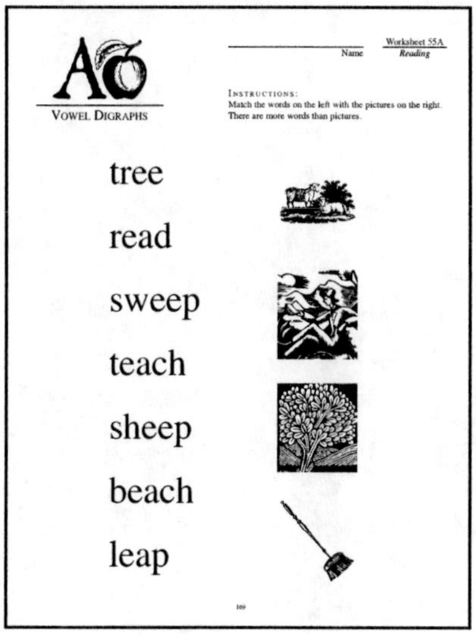

Worksheet 55A: Read the instructions aloud. Assist as necessary. Remind them that not all of the words have pictures which match!

ACTIVITY 2: REVIEW

Write the following on the board: SH, TH, WH, CH. Review the sounds made by each of these letter pairs. Confirm that the pairs SH, CH, and TH each make a new, unique sound, and that WH is just a "breathy W."

Invite children to give you examples of words which start with each of these sounds. (either voiced or unvoiced TH are fine) You may need to give examples since its use can be easily confused with W alone.

Now write the following on the board: "arp." Have someone sound it out. Challenge the children to put one the targeted sounds at the beginning of this letter group to form a word which means "pointed." (sharp)

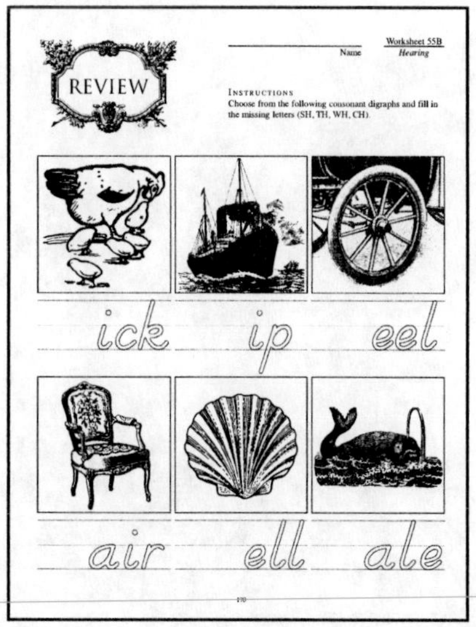

Continue in the same manner to form the words "chin," "shin," "thin," "why," "shy," etc.

Invite students to the board to copy these words. Remind them about stroke direction and order as necessary.

Worksheet 55B: Read the instructions aloud. Assist as necessary.

Percival's Pairs: Using ING, ANG, ONG, blends, long vowels and Y as I.

Lesson 56
Target EA as Short E and Long A

Play The E Partnership song for the children encouraging them to sing along.

ACTIVITY 1: HEARING AND SEEING EA AS SHORT E

Write the following on the board: deed, breed, sweet. Call on students to decode and read each one. Define and use in original sentences.
Ask what sound is made by the EE in each word. (long E) Does the second E make any sound in these words? (NO) Invite students to the board to circle the EE in each word and cross out the silent E partner.

Put a macron over the first E to designate the long sound of this vowel.

Now, remind the children that the letter E makes two main sounds. What is the other sound of the letter E? (short E)

Erase the macron over the E in "deed."

Ask the children to read this word using the short E sound. (It will sound like the word "dead.") Repeat this word and ask if it is meaningful. Use it in a sentence to reinforce its meaning.

Erase the second E and replace it with A. Circle the EA letter pair. Explain to the children that sometimes A will not make the E use the long sound. Sometimes it will make the E use its "short" sound. It will still be a silent partner, though. Draw a line through the A to show that it does not make a sound. This is the way we spell "dead."

Add the next step. When a letter makes the short sound, we have another symbol which we can use to show this. Although it will not be in their reading, it helps to know it when we look up a word which we are not sure how to pronounce. This symbol is a "breve." Write a "breve" over the E in "dead." Draw attention to the fact that it looks like a little "cup"—and the word "cup" uses a short sound (U) in the middle. On the other hand, the macron is a "line" and "line" uses a long sound. That may help them to remember which symbol denotes which kind of sound.

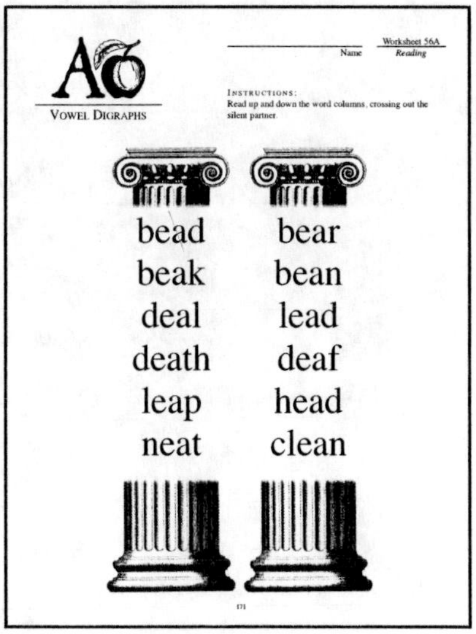

Follow the same procedure to decode the words "bread" from "breed, and "sweat" from "sweet." Use each of the words in sentences to reinforce meaning and part of speech.

Worksheet 56A: Read the instructions aloud. Monitor the students' progress as they work independently.

ACTIVITY 2: HEARING AND SEEING EA AS LONG A

Now tell the children that EA is a very tricky letter pair—it sometimes likes to play a "reverse" game. Sometimes the first E will be silent and make the A say its name!

Write the following on the board: STEAK, BREAK. Have students come to the board and circle the EA letter pair.

Now challenge the children to experiment a little.

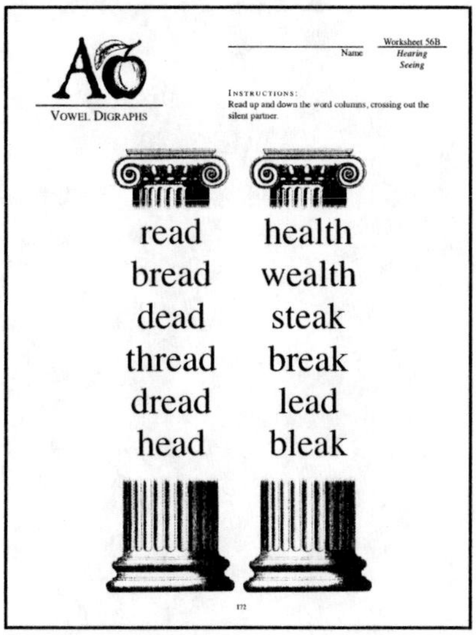

If using macrons, draw a macron over the E in each word.

Tell them to say the words with long E. Do they recognize either of these words as being meaningful? (NO) Affirm that the words pronounced this way are not real words. If using macrons, replace the macron with a breve.

Tell them to read the words using short E. Are they meaningful now? (NO) Explain that this means we must try another sound.

If using macrons, erase the breve and draw a slash through the E. Draw a macron over the A.

Guide the children to decode the words using long A. Now ask if they make sense. (YES) Affirm the meaning of each word and use in original sentences. Affirm to the children that EA as long A doesn't happen a lot and that most words with EA will be pronounced using long or short E.

Write the word "GREAT" on the board in upper case letters. Tell them that this is what kind of readers they are if they can decode it!

Worksheet 56B/C: Read the instructions aloud. Monitor the students' progress as they work independently.

ACTIVITY 3: WRITING

Draw lines on the board. Invite children to come to the board and write what you dictate to them.

Spell the following words aloud, letter by letter: beef, creek, feel, deal, bleak, leap, death, spread, heaven. Monitor as the children write the letters in order on the lines.

Call on and assist students to decode each word. Discuss meanings and use in original sentences.

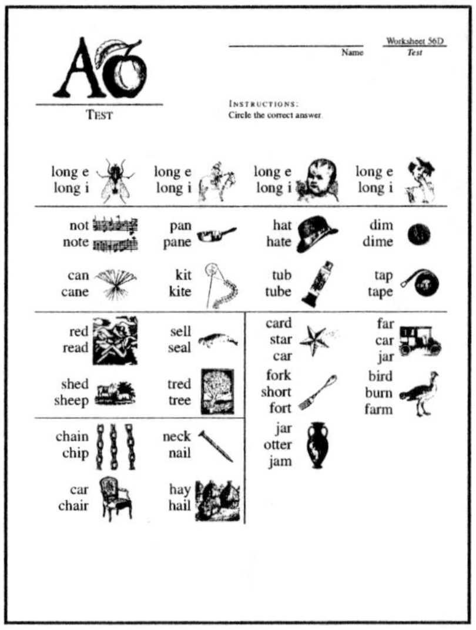

Worksheet 56D: Test. This test is optional and is added to evaluate your students if you feel it is necessary at this time. The answers are worth 5 points each.

LESSON 57
TARGET: OA/OW/OE AS LONG O

Play the South Sea song for the children encouraging them to sing.

Show the children the flashcard with the letters OA on it. Have them hear the sound of OA as in "boat."

ACTIVITY 1: HEARING AND SEEING

Do a quick review of the vowel digraphs (letter pairs) the children have studied so far. Write the following on the board: AI, AY, EE, and three sets of the pair EA. Ask the children what sound or sounds are made by each of the letter pairs. Each of the EA pairs should be designated as saying one of the three sounds made by this combination. (long E, short E, and long A)

Invite students to come to the board and circle the pairs, cross out the silent partner (depending on the sound made).

Draw a macron or breve over the vowel which is heard in each pair.

Write an example of each pair used in a word. Decode the words and use in original sentences.

Now tell the children that the letter O is another vowel which loves to have a silent buddy along.

Write the following on the board, leaving a small space between the O and the final letters: rod, got, blot. Call on students to read the words. What sound of O do they hear in the middle of each one? (short O)

Put a macron over each O. Now what sound will the O make? (long O) Call on students to pronounce the words using the long sound. Do the words make sense? (YES) Affirm their meanings.

Tell the children that in these words the letter A is the silent partner, just like in the EA letter pair. Write an A after the O in each word. Invite children to the board to circle the OA letter pair.

Draw attention to the macron over the O and then ask what you should do to the A to show that is does not make any sound. (draw a slash through it) Invite students to the board to do so.

Use the words in original sentences. Explain that this letter pair OA will only be found in the middle of words. The letter O likes to take other letters with it when it makes the long sound at the end of words.

Write the following on the board: doe, toe, hoe. Tell them that in these words the E is just like final silent E; it makes the first vowel say its name. Invite students to come to the board, circle the OA letter pair in each word.

Draw a backslash through the E, and put a macron over the O.

Call on students to decode and read the words. Use them in original sentences.

Now explain that there is one more letter which O likes to take along, especially at the end of words. Write the following on the board: glow, throw, window. Invite students to the board to mark the letter pair and O as above. Decode, read, and use the words in original sentences.

Long O, long O do you have a friend?
Yes sir, A, E, and W are with me to the end.
A looks like a toad;
E tickles my toe;
W helps to keeps us straight in a row!

Worksheet 57A: Read the instructions aloud. Monitor the students' progress as they work independently.

Give them their museum bag. Allow them time to go through the house and collect items that have the OA sound to make their own museum. If you are teaching in a school setting, instruct the children to take the bag home and bring in objects the following day.

Worksheet 57A
Seeing
Name

VOWEL DIGRAPHS

INSTRUCTIONS:
Circle the OA, OW, OE in each word below then draw a line through the silent partner.

load	soap	snow
loaf	goat	hoe
road	coat	toe
toad	tow	foe
bloat	slow	woe
oak	flow	

The letter O can have a silent partner, oa as in road, OE as in hoe or OW as in row.
Long O, long O do you have a friend? Yes sir, A, E, and W are with me to the end. A looks like a toad; E tickles my toe; W helps to keeps us straight in a row!

173

ACTIVITY 2: WRITING AND PLURAL OE WORDS

Write the following on the board: hoe, toe, foe. Call on students to read them aloud.

Ask what we would need to add to each of these words to mean more than one. (S) Invite students to come to the board and write S after each word.

Decode the plural words formed. Acknowledge that the S makes the Z sound in each of these words.

Now write "goes" on the board. Instruct the children to follow the pronunciation pattern of the other words shown to decode this word.

Have a student come to the board and circle the "oe" in "goes." Ask if they hear the E. (NO) Draw a backslash through the "e."

Do a mini-grammar lesson. Affirm that "goes" is an action word. Use "go" in a sentence, then use the word "goes" in a sentence, using proper subject/verb agreement. Remind the children how you added "es" to other action words which ended with SH or CH sounds when you wanted to describe what someone else was doing. Write two or three of these on the board as examples (rushes, patches) Use the singular (rush) and plural (rushes) forms in sentences to show the grammatical use differences.

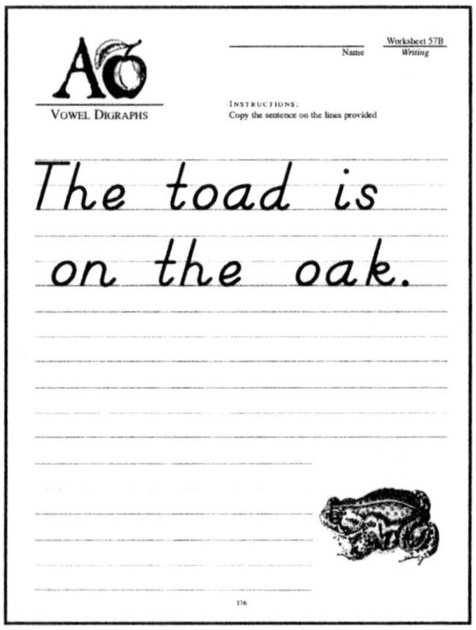

Call students to the board to write the display words independently on guidelines.

Worksheet 57B: Assist the children to read the sentence. Monitor as they copy the sentence on the lines provided. Carefully monitor letter formation, letter and word spacing.

You may want to give the students the coloring page along with the flashcard. Read the information about the artist to your students before they color the picture.

Percival's Pairs: Using ING, ANG, ONG, blends, long vowels Y as I, OA, OE and OW.

LESSON 58
TARGET: OA/OW/OE

Play the South Sea song for the children encouraging them to sing.

ACTIVITY 1: READING WORDS

Pass out the following puzzle pieces to each student: B, O, A, T, C, W, Y, two tiles of L, P, R, S, H, G, F, K, and J.

Using the words on Worksheet 58A (except "toast"), read each one aloud and then call out the letters needed to spell them. The children should assemble the puzzle pieces in the proper left-to-right order to form the word. Ask the children which is the silent letter in the word. Ask which vowel says its name. Have the students read the word and call on someone to give you an original sentence using that word.

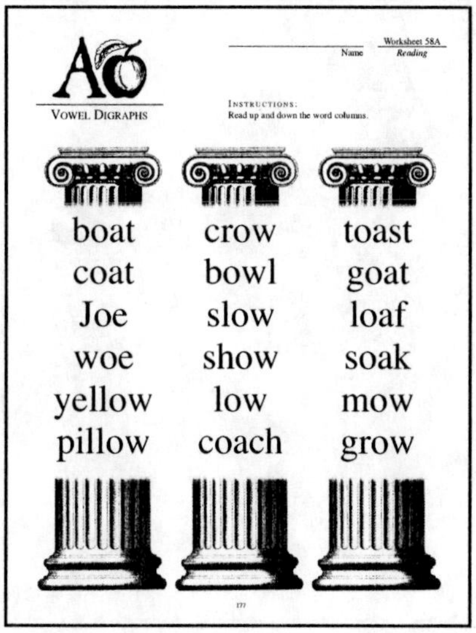
Worksheet 58A
Reading
Name
VOWEL DIGRAPHS
INSTRUCTIONS:
Read up and down the word columns.

boat	crow	toast
coat	bowl	goat
Joe	slow	loaf
woe	show	soak
yellow	low	mow
pillow	coach	grow

Continue with as many of the words on this list as you see fit, making sure to use at least two examples of each letter pair, the proper name "Joe," and also one of the words using the double L.

Remind them about the syllabication of the LL word and the use of the upper case "Joe."

Worksheet 58A: Read the instructions aloud. Use any of the previous variations for eliciting student response.

Variations for prompting the reading of words on this sheet include: numbering the words and calling on students to read them by the designated number, verbal "fill-in-the-blanks," pointing to the written word on the board and having students point to the corresponding printed word on the sheet, riddle clues, categorizing on the basis of beginning sound, middle vowel, or ending letter group, etc.

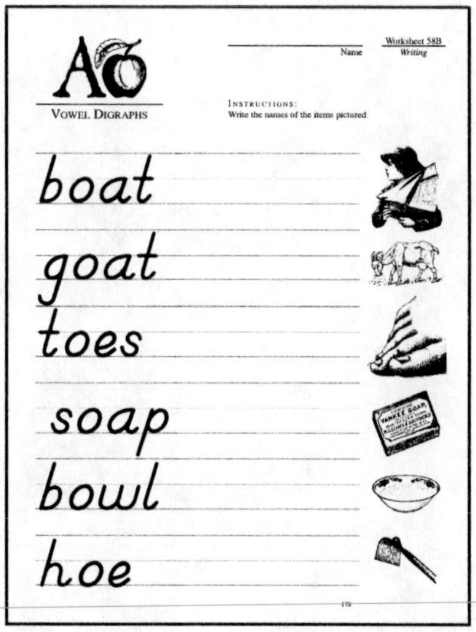
Worksheet 58B
Writing
Name
VOWEL DIGRAPHS
INSTRUCTIONS:
Write the names of the items pictured.

boat
goat
toes
soap
bowl
hoe

ACTIVITY 2: WRITING

Little or no instruction should be needed for this worksheet. You may wish to work with them more closely on an individual or small group basis.

Worksheet 58B: Read the instructions aloud and Monitor the students' progress as they work independently.

Lesson 59
Target: OA/OW/OE and Alphabetical Order

Play the South Sea song for the children encouraging them to sing.

ACTIVITY 1: READING OA/OW/OE WORDS

Tell the children you will be reading and writing some word pairs today and they must be careful lookers and listeners. Both of the words in each pair will have the long O sound. You will write both of them on the board, one on the left side and one on the right side. They will have to raise the hand which corresponds with the side of the board where they see the word you have read.

For example, write "toast" on the left side of the board and "toes" on the right side. Say the word "toast" several times. The children should raise their left hands to designate the word on the left as being the word you have spoken.

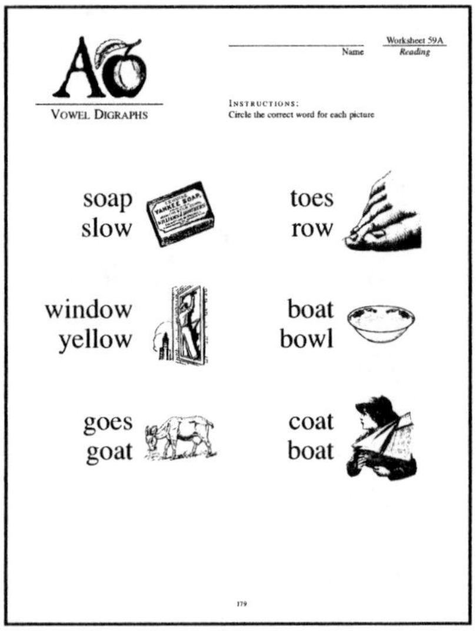

Proceed in this manner with the following word pairs:

yellow/hollow	elbow/oboe	own/groan
bowl/boast	toes/snows	oats/boats
throw/throat	doe/window	mow/hoe

Worksheet 59A: Read the instructions aloud. Monitor the students' progress as they work independently. Assist as necessary to label the pictures, but do not give the words as clues.

ACTIVITY 2: ALPHABETICAL ORDER

Sing the Alphabet Song today if you haven't done so in a while!

Pass out puzzle pieces required to form the following words: foam, low, toe (using the special OA and OW pieces). Have each student make the words on their desks, read it, and name its beginning letter. Ask "Which of these three words comes first in alphabetical order?" (foam) Which comes next? (low) Which comes last? (toe) Have the students move the words around on their desks to put the words in the correct order.

Repeat this procedure with these four words: goes, moan, oboe, shadow.

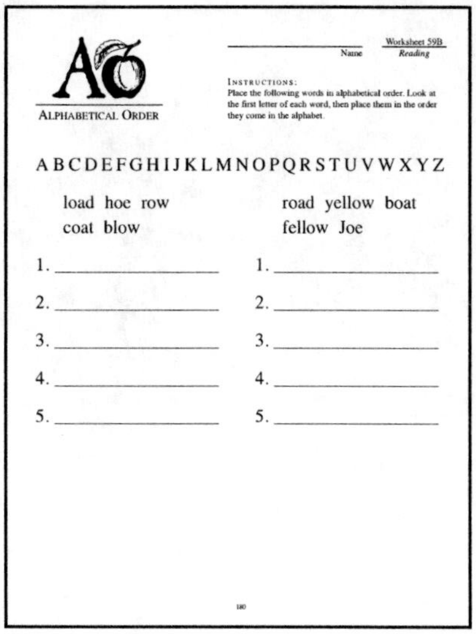

Worksheet 59B
Reading

Name ______

Alphabetical Order

Instructions:
Place the following words in alphabetical order. Look at the first letter of each word, then place them in the order they come in the alphabet.

A B C D E F G H I J K L M N O P Q R S T U V W X Y Z

load hoe row
coat blow

1. ______
2. ______
3. ______
4. ______
5. ______

road yellow boat
fellow Joe

1. ______
2. ______
3. ______
4. ______
5. ______

180

Worksheet 59B: Read the instructions aloud. Tell the children that they may place numbers over the words and then copy the words in the assigned order onto the lists. Have students read the words aloud after the worksheet is completed and use them in original sentences to reinforce meaning.

Lesson 60
Target: OA/OW/OE Words, Pluralization of Final Silent E Words, and Review

Play the South Sea song for the children encouraging them to sing.

ACTIVITY 1: READING AND WRITING

Draw guidelines on the board. Tell the children that you are going to play a fill-in-the-blank game today. Write the following sentence on the board, leaving the guidelines at the end of the sentence in the place of the final word:

My father works for the ______________.

Under the sentence, write the following words: oatmeal, meatloaf, railroad.

The words used in this activity require an application of many of the digraphs they have studied so far. Allow and encourage them to experiment as they decode the words, using the various sounds which they know can be made by the letter pairs they see. Monitor their ability to do this and praise them when they "hit" upon the correct pronunciation and determine the meaning of each word!

Assist the decoding of each of these words. Remind them as needed about the sounds made by the various letter pairs. Call attention to the fact that these are compound words—two short separate words which make up one long word. Each of the short words should be decoded separately and then verbally linked together.

When all of the words have been decoded, assist the children to determine which word should be written in the blank of the sentence. Invite a student to the board to write the word (railroad) on the guidelines.

Erase the sentence but leave the words on the board. Write the following sentence, leaving the blank at the end:

For breakfast in the morning, I like to eat ________________.

Discuss which word will best fit into the blank. (No, "meatloaf" is not a typical breakfast food!) Invite a student to come to the board and write the appropriate word (oatmeal) on the guidelines. Elicit original sentences from the children for the use of the word "meatloaf."

ACTIVITY 2: PLURALIZATION OF FINAL SILENT E WORDS

Write the following on the board: hop, tap. Call on students to read them aloud.

Read the following sentence: He hops around the block. Ask the children what they hear at the end of the word "hop." (S) Invite a student to come to the board to write the S at the end of the word "hop."

Read the following sentence: The bird taps on the window. Again, ask the children what is heard at the end of "tap" and invite a student to write the S at the end of this word.

Now, write the following on the board: hope, tape. Call on students to read them aloud. Remind about the final silent E patters if necessary.

Read the following sentence: He hopes to get a bike for his birthday. Ask what they hear at the end of the word "hope." (S) Invite a student to come to the board and write it in.

Read the following sentence: The teacher tapes the note to the board. Again, ask what is heard at the end of "tape" and invite a student to write the S at the end of this word.

Now, explain to the children that even though they see "es" at the end of these words, the E is still silent. Read them again aloud and clap out the single beat in each one. Affirm that each word only has one syllable. The E does not make any sound and does not make another beat.

Write the following on the board: rides, takes, stares. Read them aloud and have the children echo them after you. Ask how many beats are heard in each word.(L)

Explain that when they see words like this, the best thing to do is to ignore the S at first and just read the final silent E word. Then tack the S sound on at the end. Demonstrate this by covering the S in the above words. Have students decode the final silent E word, then reveal the S and have them repeat the word with the S (or Z) sound added to the end.

Write a few more examples on the board: rakes, saves, shares. Call on students to come to the board, cover the S, decode the final silent E word, then add the final S to pluralize the word.

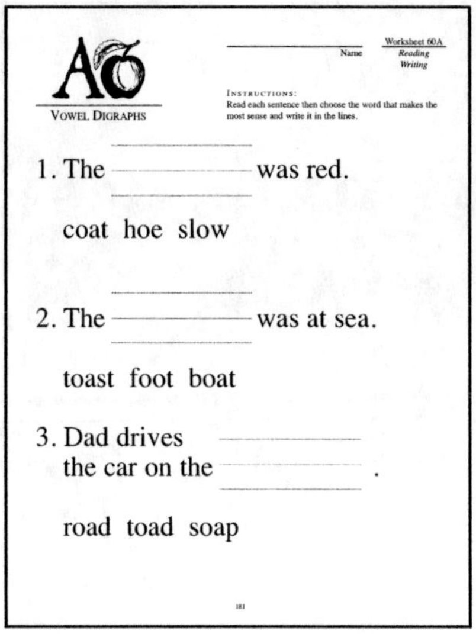
Worksheet 60A
Reading
Writing

Name

VOWEL DIGRAPHS

INSTRUCTIONS:
Read each sentence then choose the word that makes the most sense and write it in the lines.

1. The ____________ was red.

coat hoe slow

2. The ____________ was at sea.

toast foot boat

3. Dad drives ____________ the car on the ____________.

road toad soap

Worksheets 60A/B: Read the instructions aloud. You may elect to read the sentences aloud, leaving out the missing word, or call on students to do so. Do not read the words offered as choices. Monitor their selections and writing.

ACTIVITY 3: REVIEW OF BEGINNING SOUNDS

Worksheet 60C: Read the instructions aloud. Assist the children to label the pictures as necessary. Do not offer any other sound or letter clues. Alert children that there are two pairs of pictures in each box which start with the same sound! Reading left to right, labeled clockwise from upper left of each box.

Row 1 : zipper, baby, zebra, boat;
moon, bat, barrel, mermaid;
eggs, elf, hand, hat.

Row 2: ox, kangaroo, octopus, keys;
pig, penguin, watch, walrus;
fan, monkey, mittens, fox.

Row 3: apple, ax, duck, dog;
ram, ring, quilt, queen;
top, bird, tent, bell.

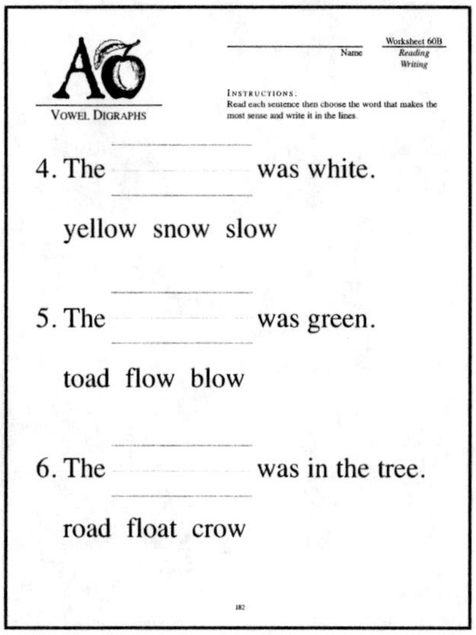
Worksheet 60B
Reading
Writing

Name

VOWEL DIGRAPHS

INSTRUCTIONS:
Read each sentence then choose the word that makes the most sense and write it in the lines.

4. The ____________ was white.

yellow snow slow

5. The ____________ was green.

toad flow blow

6. The ____________ was in the tree.

road float crow

LESSON 61
TARGET: OA/OW/OE WORDS AND REVIEW

Play the South Sea song for the children encouraging them to sing.

ACTIVITY 1: HEARING

Tell the children that it is time to be good listeners again today! You will be reading a list of words. When they hear the long O sound in any of the words, they should indicate by raising both hands over their heads and bringing their finger tips together, making a big "O" with their arms.

Read the following list:

boat	dish	snow	below	cat
show	sleep	foe	lady	grow
foam	silly	rabbit	load	doe

Worksheet 61A: Read the instructions aloud. Give clues to assist the children to label the pictures as necessary, but do not say the picture labels aloud. Monitor their work.

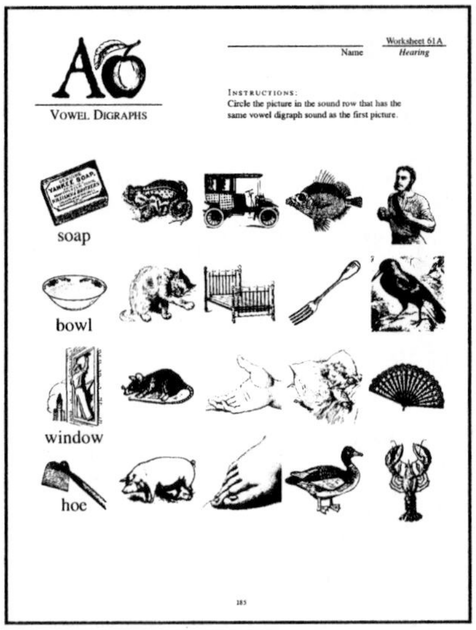
Vowel Digraphs

Name

Worksheet 61A
Hearing

Instructions:
Circle the picture in the sound row that has the same vowel digraph sound as the first picture.

soap

bowl

window

hoe

185

Row 1: toad, car, fish, man
Row 2: cat, bed, fork, crow
Row 3: rat, hand, pillow, fan
Row 4: pig, toes, duck, lobster

ACTIVITY 2: READING

Write the following on the board: roast, slow, doe, cream, see, health, steak, spray, pain.

Before they decode the words, review with them the sounds made by each of the letter pairs shown in the words, especially EA with its three sounds (long E, short E, and long A).

Assist the children to decode the words. Define as necessary and use in original sentences.

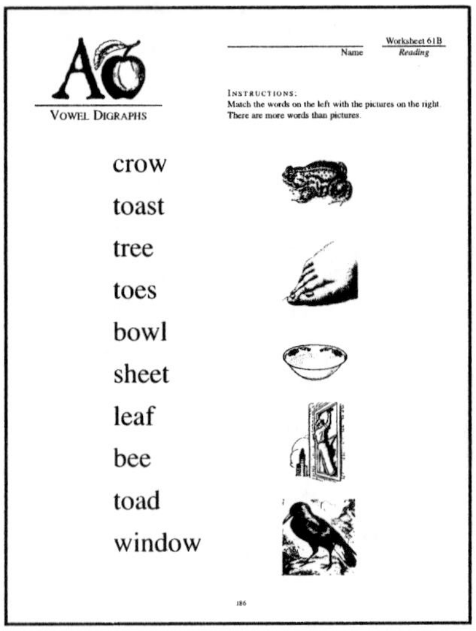
Vowel Digraphs

Name

Worksheet 61B
Reading

Instructions:
Match the words on the left with the pictures on the right. There are more words than pictures.

crow
toast
tree
toes
bowl
sheet
leaf
bee
toad
window

186

Worksheet 61B: Read the instructions aloud. Encourage the children to decode each word on the page to determine which one is the best label for each of the pictures shown. Monitor the students' progress as they work independently.

Percival's Pairs: Using ING, ANG, ONG, blends, long vowels Y as I, OA, OE and OW.

LESSON 62
REVIEW AND SPELLING LIST 2

Play The Alphabet Chase song for the children encouraging them to sing.

ACTIVITY 1: REVIEW

Review the sounds SH, WH, TH, and CH. Tell the children they must listen carefully again today. You will read a word aloud. Read the following words, one at a time, allowing time for students to respond with the beginning sound:

wheel	shovel	chain	thick
chop	them	what	shake
shell	chore	this	whistle

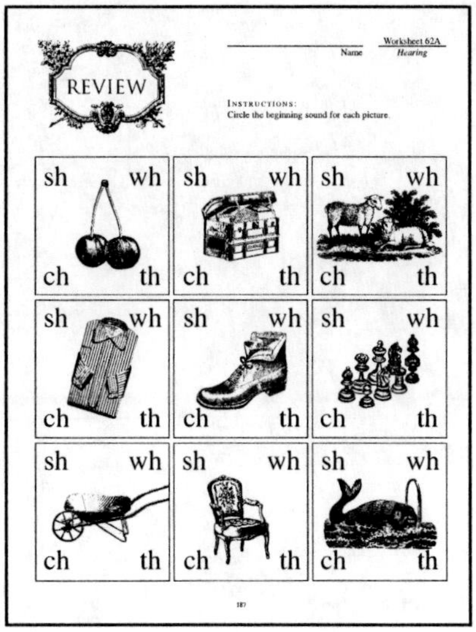

Worksheet 62A: Read the instructions aloud. Give clues for the labeling of the pictures, but do not say the picture labels aloud. Monitor the students' progress as they work independently.

ACTIVITY 2: SPELLING LIST 2

Write the spelling words found on Worksheets 62B and C on the board, with guidelines to the right of each word.

Call on students to read the words aloud and come to the board to copy them independently on the guidelines. Use each word in a complete sentence and solicit original sentences from the children.

Tell the children that this is their second spelling list. They must study them every day for the next week. They will have to know which letter pair to use in these words from now on.

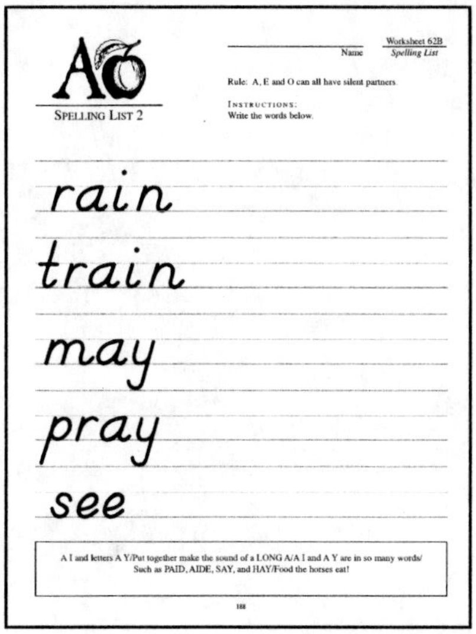

Worksheets 62B/C: Read the instructions and the rule at the bottom of Worksheet 62B. Monitor as they copy the words on the lines provided.

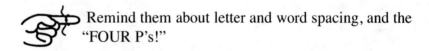

Remind them about letter and word spacing, and the "FOUR P's!"

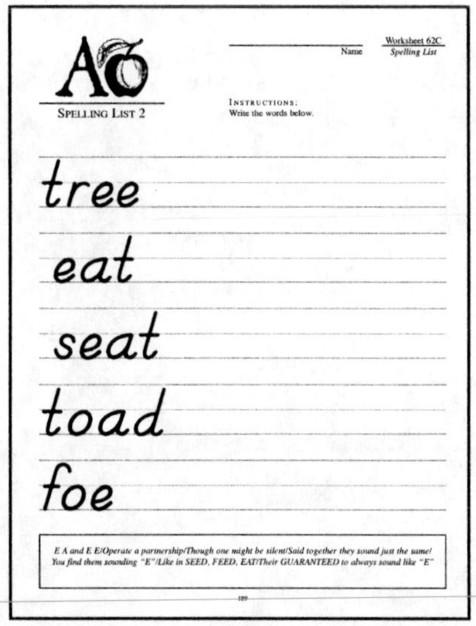

LESSON 63
TARGET: IE AS LONG I AND ALPHABETICAL ORDER

ACTIVITY 1: HEARING AND SEEING

Tell the children they will be learning a new letter pair today!

Write the following on the board: toe, doe. Ask the children what sound they hear in each of these words. (long O) Which letter is silent? (e) Affirm that the first vowel says its name in this letter pair.

Now, erase the O in each word and replace it with I. Tell them that the E is still silent and the first vowel will still say its name in these words.

Invite a student to come to the board, circle the IE in each word.

Draw a backslash through the E, and add a macron above the I.

Challenge the children to decode and read them, applying this information to these words. Affirm and praise correct decoding! Add these words to the list on the board: pie, lie. Call on children to circle the letter pair and backslash the E in each word. Use the words in original sentences.

Now, ask the children what you will have to add to each word to mean more than one of each of them. (S) Call on students to come to the board and add the S to each of the words.

Challenge the children to read the new words formed, using the final S (which will actually be the Z sound). Use the plural words in original sentences.

Now write the following on the board: sky. Remind the children about the two sounds of Y at the end of words. (long I or long E) Ask them which sound should be used in this word and why (long I, because there is no other vowel in the word) Call on students to read it aloud.

Tell them that "sky" is a thing. Ask how we would say it if we were talking about more than one of them. (skies) What letter would we need to add to the end of this word? (S) Write the S slightly to the right of the word "sky."

Explain to the children that in words like this which end in a Y which makes the long I sound, we take out the Y and replace it with the letter pair IE, which also makes the long I sound.

Erase the Y and replace it with IE. Do they see theIE letter pair here? Circle the IE and backslash the E. Read the word aloud.

Write the following on the board: cry, try, dry. Ask the children what kind of words these are: things or actions? (ACTIONS)

Ask the children "What if I wanted to say 'The baby cries'?" (Emphasize the Z sound at the end of the word "cries." What would I have to add to the word "cry?" (S) (If they say Z, ask what other letter makes the Z sound, especially at the end of words.)

Alert them that this word ends in a Y which sounds like long I. What else must they do to this word before adding S? (change the Y to IE)

Invite a student to come to the board, erase the Y, replace it with IE, and add the S. Read the word "cries" aloud and use it in another original sentence.

Follow the same procedure for "try" and "dry."

Tell them there is one more thing they must learn before they can do the worksheet.

Erase the S at the end of "tries," "dries," and "cries," and replace each one with D. Ask what sound is made by this letter.

Challenge the children to read the words now, with the D sound at the end.

Use these past tense words in original sentences. Explain to the children that when the D is placed at the end of some action words like these, it means that the action has already happened!

Remind them of the lesson when they added ING to action words to mean that the action was happening right now. Give the following examples: sitting, reading, watching. These are things they are doing right now.

In the same way, we add D to the end of some action words to show that the action happened in the past. When we do this to words which end in Y which sounds like long I, we use the IE letter pair to replace the Y and then we add D.

Assure them that they do not need to remember how to do this on their own yet, but they should be able to recognize how words like this look, are pronounced, and what they mean.

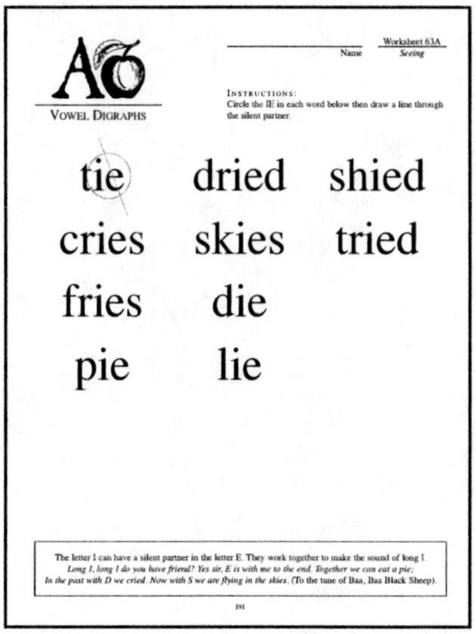
Worksheet 63A
Seeing
Name
VOWEL DIGRAPHS
INSTRUCTIONS:
Circle the IE in each word below then draw a line through the silent partner.

tie dried shied
cries skies tried
fries die
pie lie

The letter I can have a silent partner in the letter E. They work together to make the sound of long I. *Long I, long I do you have friend? Yes sir, E is with me to the end. Together we can eat a pie; In the past with D we cried. Now with S we are flying in the skies.* (To the tune of Baa, Baa Black Sheep).

191

Long I, long I do you have friend?
Yes sir, E is with me to the end.
Together we can eat a pie;
In the past with D we cried.
Now with S we are flying in the skies.

Worksheet 63A: Read the instructions aloud. Assist as necessary to complete the sheet as directed. Call on students to read the words aloud, using the sound pattern as marked. Define the words and use in original sentences.

ACTIVITY 2: ALPHABETICAL ORDER

Worksheet 63B: Read the instructions aloud. Monitor the students' progress as they work independently. Allow them to sing the Alphabet Song as they work.

Lesson 64
Target: CH as K, Long Vowels in "Wild Words," Writing and Reading

ACTIVITY 1: HEARING

Make the sound of CH several times for the children. Ask someone to come to the board and write the letter pair which makes this sound.

Remind the children that many of the letters can make more than one sound. Review with them the sounds of TH (voiced and unvoiced), S (voiced as Z and unvoiced as S), EA (long E, short E, and long A).

Explain that CH can make another sound also. Point to the flashcard of the K on the wall. Ask what sound is made by this letter. (K)

Tell them that this is another sound that CH sometimes likes to imitate. Write the following on the board: chorus, character, chord. Assist the children to decode each one, using the K sound for CH. Define these words and use them in original sentences.

Tell them that occasionally CH as K will be in other places in a word, or linked to S in a blend. Write the following on the board: ache, scheme, scholar. Assist the children to decode the words. Define and use in original sentences.

Alert students may notice that SCH is pronounced the same way as SK. Affirm that this is true, and that the use of SCH is a spelling pattern which they do not need to remember now, but should be able to recognize.

Assure them that CH doesn't say K very often, but when it does, the word will only make sense if it is pronounced that way.

ACTIVITY 2: MORE LONG VOWELS

Ask the children if they have ever watched a scientist do an experiment. Discuss with them the fact that scientists have to try many different things sometimes in order to get the result for which they are looking or to answer a question they have.

Tell them that reading is like that also. We must often try different sounds in order to find the ones which make certain words meaningful. Remind them how they have done this in past lessons with the different sounds of EA.

Write the following on the board: A, E, I, O, U. Review the main sounds of each of these vowels.

Remind them that they know that these vowels say their names and make their long sounds when some words are spelled a certain way, or when they are paired with other letters.

Write the following as examples: day, hear, pie, torn, flute, paper. Review the letter pairs and patterns which govern the pronunciation of each of these words (AY as long A; EA as long E; IE as long I; OR with long O; final silent E making the first vowel long; the first syllable ends with a vowel, making that vowel long). Tell them that there are, of course, many other examples which they have learned. Praise them for all the decoding skills they have acquired so far!
Now, explain that sometimes words will contain the long vowel sound even though they may not follow any of the patterns. It is only by experimenting with the sounds, noticing how they are used in sentences, and then seeing these words over and over that we learn how they are pronounced and what they are.

We will call these "WILD words" because the word "wild" is one of them! Write "wild" on the board. Affirm that we would probably first decode this word using short I. Say the word using short I. Ask if the word has any meaning pronounced like this. (NO) Direct the children to try using long I instead of short I. Now the word makes sense!

Very quick students may argue that the word "wild," pronounced with short I, is a word—the word "willed" (as in "God willed it to be so." Affirm that it does sound like that, but that the word "willed" is spelled differently (with the past tense ED on the end).

Tell the children that there are quite a few words like this in our language. Write the following on the board: kind, gold, pint, both, most. Instruct the students to be "word scientists" by experimenting with the different vowel sounds.

Read the words to them using the short vowel sounds. Affirm in each case that the words are not meaningful pronounced that way.

Now read the words using long vowel sounds. Affirm that the words are now recognizable. Define them and use in original sentences.

Ask the children if they notice anything about the vowels which are used in these words. (they are all I or O) Affirm that these are the two letters which they will see most often in words like this.

Ask if they notice anything else about the words. (they all have final consonant blends) Affirm that this is another clue that a word may be using the long vowel sound.

Worksheet 64A: Read the instructions aloud. Assist as necessary to complete the sheet as directed. Call on students to read the words aloud, using the sound pattern as marked. Define the words and use in original sentences.

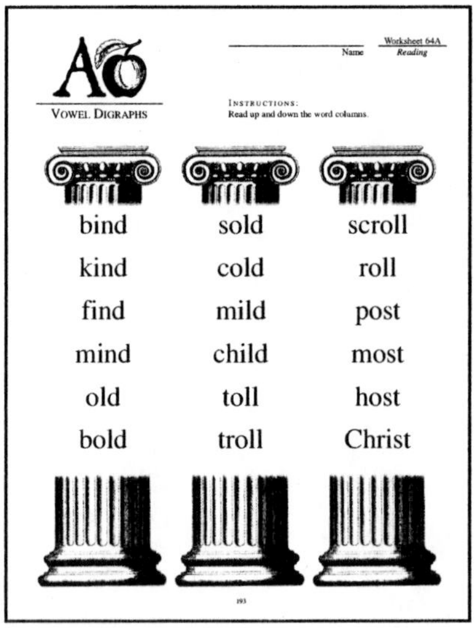

ACTIVITY 2: READING AND WRITING

Write the following sentence on the board, along with guidelines: *The old blind pony had many aches and pains.*

Assist the children to apply the decoding patterns they have learned, including the new ones, and read the sentence. Invite children to the board to copy the words of the sentence one-by-one onto the guidelines provided. Monitor letter formation and spacing carefully.

Worksheet 64B: Read the instructions aloud. Call on a student to decode and read the sentence. Monitor as they copy it onto the lines provided.

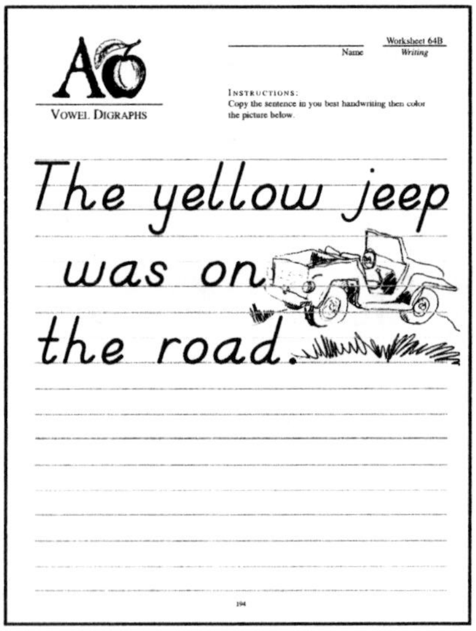

LESSON 65
READING THE SAILING SAINT

ACTIVITY 1: READING WORDS

Write the words found on Worksheet 65A on the board. Lead the children through the decoding and reading of the words. Discuss meanings and use in original sentences as needed.

Worksheet 65A: Read the instructions aloud. Use any of the previous techniques for eliciting student reading and response.

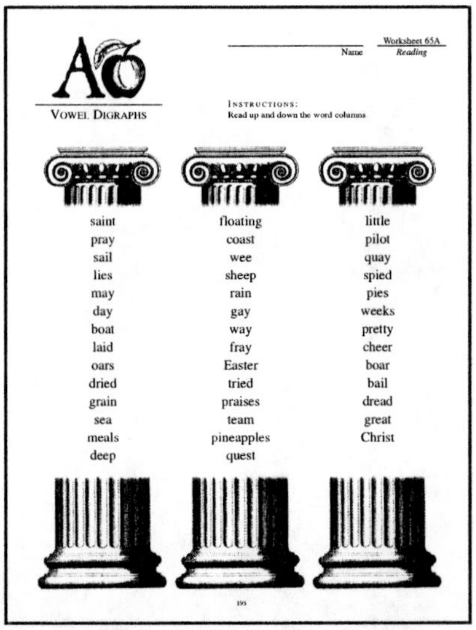

ACTIVITY 2: READING THE SAILING SAINT

This story recounts the voyages of Saint Brendan in the early 500's. He was born in County Kerry, Ireland, educated under monastic influences and became a priest. However, he had a great desire to travel which legend recounts in the popular ninth century medieval Latin text "The Voyage of Saint Brendan the Abbot." His journeys included exploration of the western and northern islands surrounding Great Britain, including the Hebrides, Shetland, and Faroe (Island of Sheep) Islands (where he established monasteries), passing by Iceland and Greenland, with a possible landing in Newfoundland and perhaps elsewhere in the New World. He also traveled to the continent of

Europe and to the Canary Islands. An island just south of the Antilles and west of the Cape Verde Islands was named St. Brendan's Island on 18th century maps and was presumed to have been his discovery.

There is much evidence in North and Central American Indian traditions of visitations from peoples of the northeastern Atlantic, including the report of an Irish-speaking tribe in Florida and the legend of Quetzalcoatl in Central America. This lends plausibility to the historic reality of St. Brendan's voyages.

Vocabulary and expressions used in this story include:

saint—one who is holy, set apart
(Biblically, all believers are properly called saints. It is also a title given by the Roman Catholic Church to individuals who are specially recognized for godliness.)
blest—shown favor
past the sunset—to the west
quest—journey in pursuit of a goal
tan skins—animal hides
oars—wooden poles with flat ends, used for rowing a boat through the water
sea moss—edible seaweed, kelp
God the One Person of the Three—Father, Son and Holy Spirit
pilot—guide, lead, direct (a Special Exhibit word)
coast—the shore, land next to the sea
wee land—island
dread—fright and sadness
spinning—turning quickly
cove—protected natural harbor
cheer—joy
Christ Mass—Lord's Supper celebrated on Christmas Day
boar—large wild pig
gay—happy
floating white hills—icebergs
quay—landing dock
frosty block—iceberg
had church—has a worship service
into the sunset—west
hills spat hot rocks—spewed lava (volcanoes)
fled the fray—ran away from the danger
Bread and Wine—elements of Communion
wake—waves
broke across the boat—waves swamped the boat
soaking—making wet
cloaks—clothes
bail—dump the water out of the boat by hand
pails—buckets
lush—filled with abundant vegetation

Hy Brasil—blessed land in Irish mythology
tribe—a community of people
tan lads and lasses—native peoples
green home—Ireland

Lead the children through the "round robin" reading of the story. Discuss pictures, main characters, events, and ideas as they occur.

Some possible questions for discussion include: What do you think was Brendan's main reason for going to other lands? What did he do first in every place they landed? Today, we have people who travel to other lands to share the Gospel—what do we call them?

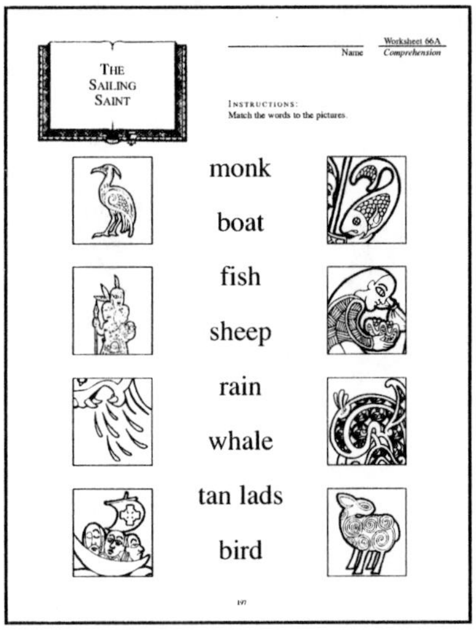

LESSON 66
READING COMPREHENSION

ACTIVITY 1: REVIEW OF STORY ELEMENTS

Briefly discuss yesterday's story. Lead the children in a retelling of the main events in order. Trace his voyage on a map and talk about the difficulties of such a long trip at sea in a small boat.

Worksheet 66A: Read the instructions aloud. Direct the children to read all the words first, then match words to pictures. Assist in labeling pictures as needed.

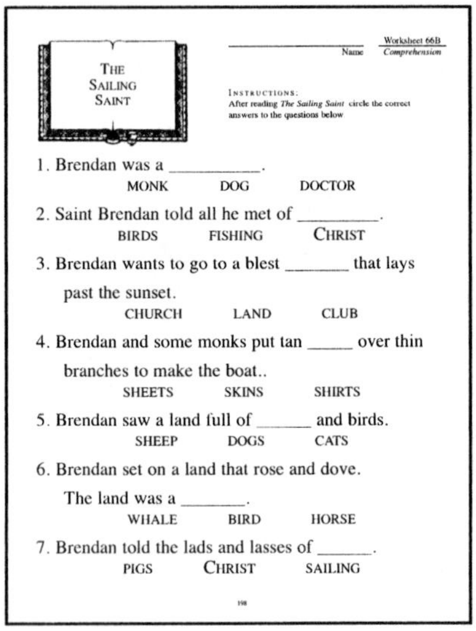

Worksheet 66B
Name
Comprehension

THE SAILING SAINT

INSTRUCTIONS:
After reading *The Sailing Saint* circle the correct answers to the questions below

1. Brendan was a ________.
MONK DOG DOCTOR
2. Saint Brendan told all he met of ________.
BIRDS FISHING CHRIST
3. Brendan wants to go to a blest ______ that lays past the sunset.
CHURCH LAND CLUB
4. Brendan and some monks put tan _____ over thin branches to make the boat..
SHEETS SKINS SHIRTS
5. Brendan saw a land full of ______ and birds.
SHEEP DOGS CATS
6. Brendan set on a land that rose and dove. The land was a _______.
WHALE BIRD HORSE
7. Brendan told the lads and lasses of ______.
PIGS CHRIST SAILING

198

Worksheet 66B: Read the instructions aloud. Monitor as the children read the sentences independently and choose the correct responses.

ACTIVITY 2: ART ACTIVITY

Draw an artist's palette on the board and color and label the paint "splotches" according to the key at the bottom of Worksheet 66C.

Worksheet 66C: Read the instructions aloud and call the students' attention to the palette on the board. Monitor as they work independently to color the picture according to the directions.

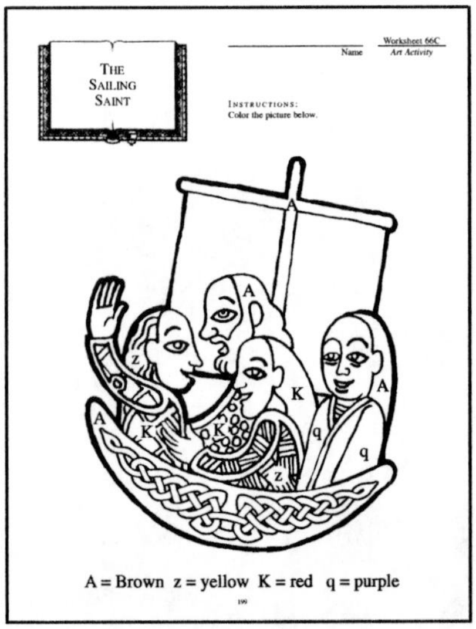

Make sure you review Spelling List 2 on Worksheets 62 B/C with the children in preparation for tomorrow's spelling test!

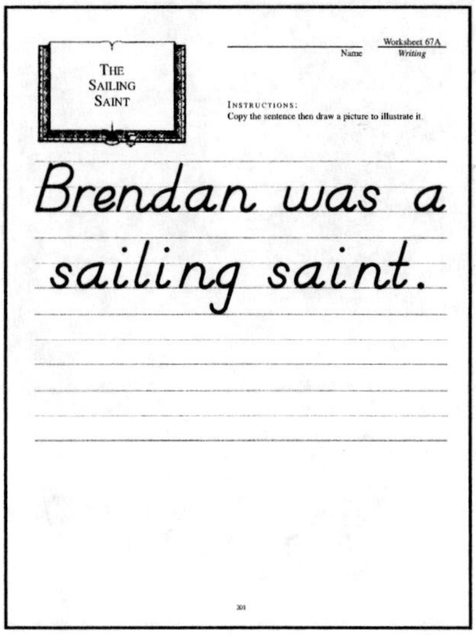

Lesson 67
Writing and Spelling Test

ACTIVITY 1: WRITING

Draw guidelines on the board. Place the letter for the word "Brendan" on the lines. Invite a student to come to the board and write the letters within the lines. Describe their stroke direction and order aloud as they write.

Continue in the same manner with the rest of the words in the sentence "Brendan was a sailing saint."

Call attention to the upper case letter in "Brendan" and the period at the end of the sentence.

Worksheet 67A: Read the instructions aloud. Monitor the students' progress as they work independently.

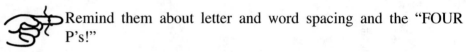

Remind them about letter and word spacing and the "FOUR P's!"

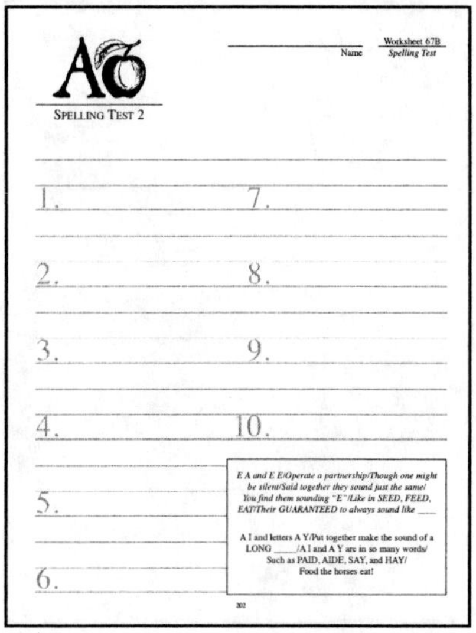

ACTIVITY 2: SPELLING TEST 2

Worksheet 67B: Administer the test on Spelling List 2. Read each word once, use it in a sentence, then repeat it. Do not give any other sound or letter clues.

Lesson 68
Review

Play the How Many Sounds? song for the children encouraging them to sing.

ACTIVITY 1: HEARING LONG VOWELS

If you have not taught macrons and breves, follow the directions below, allowing the students to raise their hand when they hear a long vowel sound rather than using the piece of yarn.

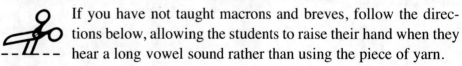

Give each student a piece of yarn or string approximately 3-4" long. Demonstrate and instruct them to hold the string at each end and pull taut horizontally to make a straight line. Tell them that this is a "macron" and will indicate a long vowel sound. Now allow the string to go slack, forming a shallow U shape. Tell them that this is a "breve" and will indicate a short vowel sound.

Tell them you will be reading some words aloud. They are to make either a macron or a breve with their strings, depending upon whether or not they hear a long or short vowel sound in each word.

lip	pile	sat	plate	boat	lot
pipe	cane	can	bee	bed	kit
kite	cake	not	nose	toes	toss
notes	hoe	hop	pin	hat	pain

Praise their careful listening!

Before presenting the worksheet, write the letter A with a macron over it in blue on the board, the letter O with a macron in red, and the letter I with a macron in yellow. This will serve as a visual key for coloring the pictures on the worksheet according to the directions.

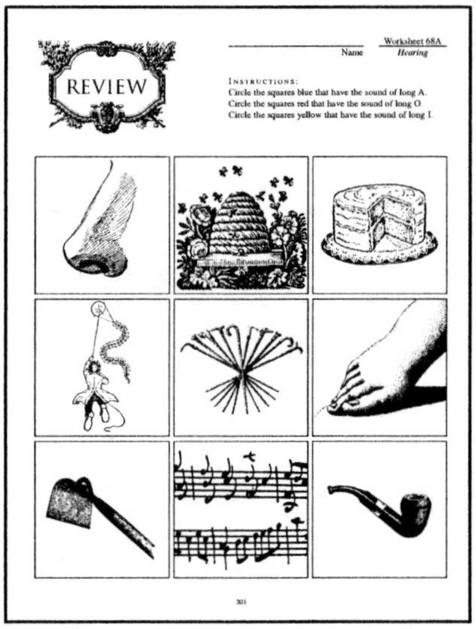

Worksheet 68A: Read the instructions aloud. Call attention to the letter/sound key on the board. Assist to label the pictures as necessary, but do not give any additional sound or letter clues. Monitor their work.

Row 1: nose, bees, cake
Row 2: kite, cane, toes
Row 3: hoe, notes, pipe

ACTIVITY 2: WRITING

Draw lines on the board. Tell the children that you will call them to the board to write one letter of their choice, either upper or lower case. They may then call on another student to come to the board and write that letter's match, in upper or lower case as necessary.

Monitor this activity to make sure all the letters are used and practiced and that all children have an opportunity to write on the board.

Worksheet 68B: Read the directions aloud. Monitor the students' progress as they work independently. Remind them that the upper case matches are to be written to the left of the lower case examples, and that the lower case matches are to be written to the right of the upper case examples.

Lesson 69
Review

ACTIVITY 1: HEARING R BLENDS

Write the following blends on the board: FR, BR, DR, TR. Review the sounds made by each blend and give examples of words which start with each one.

Tell the children that you will be reading a list of words and that they must decide which blend sound is heard at the beginning of each word. They will hold up their hand to answer which letter pair makes each blend sound.

frame	brown	drink	trip	brag
travel	dress	frown	breeze	drop
freckles	break	drizzle	treat	braces

Worksheet 69A: Read the instructions aloud. Assist to label as necessary, but do not give any other sound or letter clues. Monitor their work.

Row 1: broom, drums, trophy
Row 2: frame, bricks, frog
Row 3: train, dress, tricycle

ACTIVITY 2: REVIEW: READING WORDS

Write the following on the board: desk, pen, seat, board, paper, crayon, skirt, socks, hair, head. Do NOT read them aloud. Tell the children to read the word silently, then raise their hands if they can find that item in the room.

Call on students to point to the item written on the board as you point to it. They may then read the word aloud and use it in an original sentence.

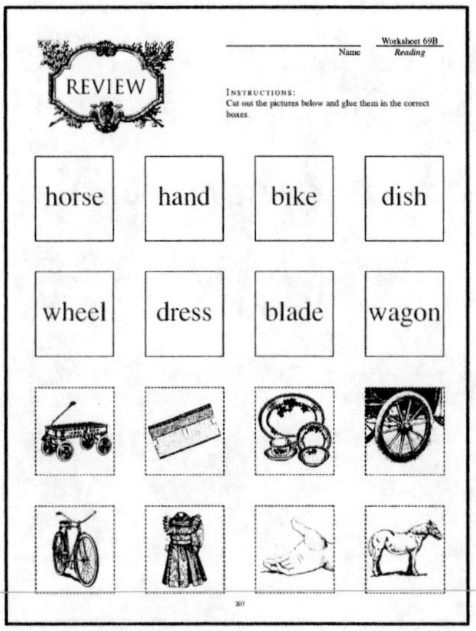

Worksheet 69B: Read the instructions aloud. Direct the children to cut across the page, separating the pictures from the rest of the paper. They may then cut out each individual picture and paste it in the proper box at the top half of the page.

Lesson 70
Review

ACTIVITY 1: READING WORDS

Select three or four of the less familiar words from Worksheets 70A/B to write on the board. Play the riddle game, giving clues for the meaning of each of the words in turn and calling on students to point to and read the words which answer the riddles. Allow students to use the words in original sentences.

Some students may be able to make up riddles of their own for some of the more familiar words on these lists. Permit them to do so and continue this activity as time allows.

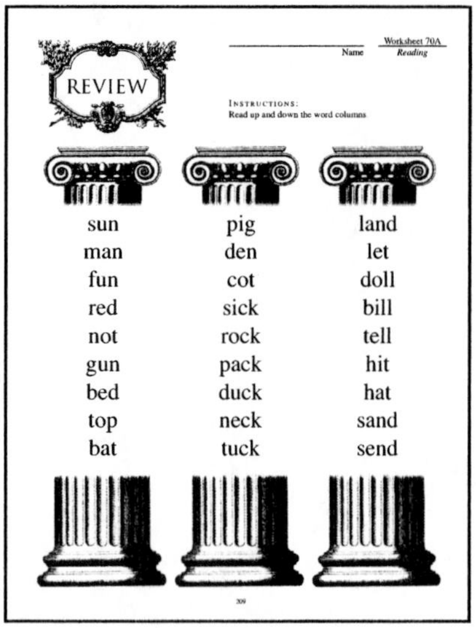
Worksheet 70A
Reading
Name
REVIEW
Instructions:
Read up and down the word columns

sun	pig	land
man	den	let
fun	cot	doll
red	sick	bill
not	rock	tell
gun	pack	hit
bed	duck	hat
top	neck	sand
bat	tuck	send

Worksheets 70A/B: Read the instructions aloud. Use any of the previous variations for eliciting student response.

The word "wind" on 70B can be read and understood when decoded with either short or long I. Discuss the change of meaning when the pronunciation is changed.

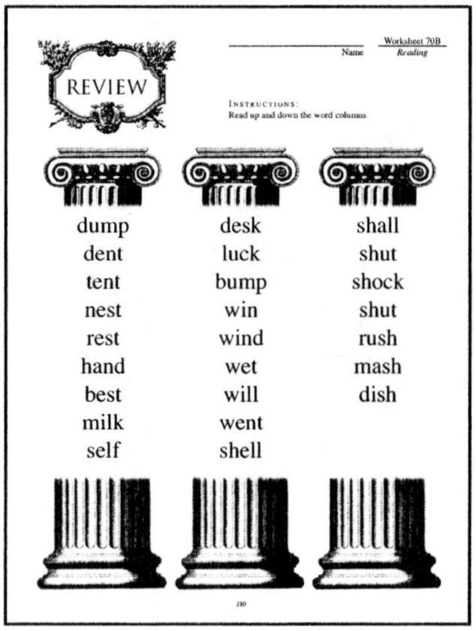
Worksheet 70B
Reading
Name
REVIEW
Instructions:
Read up and down the word columns

dump	desk	shall
dent	luck	shut
tent	bump	shock
nest	win	shut
rest	wind	rush
hand	wet	mash
best	will	dish
milk	went	
self	shell	

Variations for prompting the reading of words on these sheets include: numbering the words and calling on students to read them by the designated number, verbal "fill-in-the-blanks," pointing to the written word on the board and having students point to the corresponding printed word on the sheet, riddle clues, categorizing on the basis of beginning sound, middle vowel, or ending letter group, etc.

ACTIVITY 2: WRITING REVIEW

Invite children to the board as you think necessary to practice the writing of the words found in the sentence: The green tree sways in the breeze.

Worksheet 70C: Read the instructions aloud. Call on a student to read the sentence to the class. Monitor the students' progress as they work independently.

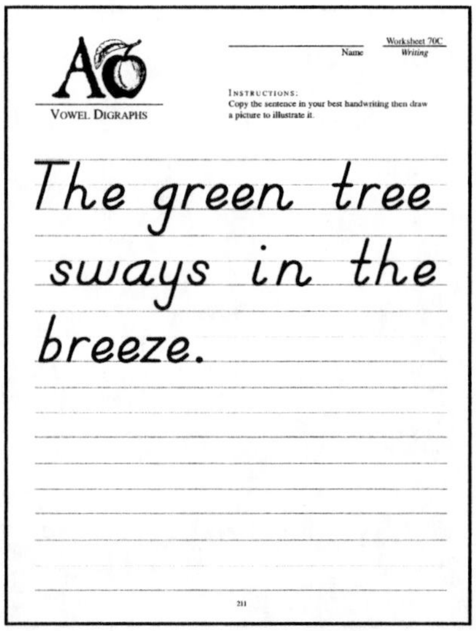
Worksheet 70C
Writing
Name
Vowel Digraphs
Instructions:
Copy the sentence in your best handwriting then draw a picture to illustrate it.

The green tree sways in the breeze.

Lesson 71
Alphabetical Order and Target: IE as Long E

Play the Alphabet Song for the children encouraging them to sing along.

ACTIVITY 1: ALPHABETIZING TO THE SECOND LETTER

Write the following on index cards, using blue for the beginning letter F, red for the middle vowels, and black for the ending consonants: fat, fed, fig.

Call students to the front of the room and give each of them one of the cards. Have them read the words aloud.

Ask the children what letter is at the beginning of each of these words. (F) Have all three students stand under the stimulus picture for F. Tell them that according to the first letter only, we can not put these words in any order since they all start with the same letter.

However, explain to them that we can order them according to the second letter. Call their attention to the letters in red, which are the second letters in each word.

Ask the children who are holding the cards to stand under the pictures which represent the red (or second) letters in the words they hold.

Tell the children that now the words are in alphabetical order based on the second letter of each word. When we must alphabetize words with the same first letter, we must look at the second letters to place them in the correct order.

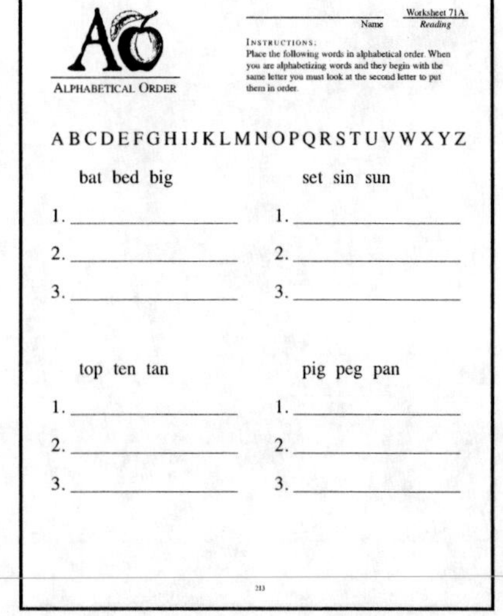
Name

Worksheet 71A
Reading

ALPHABETICAL ORDER

INSTRUCTIONS:
Place the following words in alphabetical order. When you are alphabetizing words and they begin with the same letter you must look at the second letter to put them in order.

A B C D E F G H I J K L M N O P Q R S T U V W X Y Z

bat bed big

1. ______
2. ______
3. ______

set sin sun

1. ______
2. ______
3. ______

top ten tan

1. ______
2. ______
3. ______

pig peg pan

1. ______
2. ______
3. ______

Repeat this activity with the words "map," "mix," "mop," using the same color coding of the letters to draw attention to the second letter in each word.

Worksheet 71A: Read the instructions aloud. Direct the children to place small numbers over the second letters in each word set according to their alphabetical order, then write them on the lines provided.

ACTIVITY 2: HEARING AND SEEING "IE" AS LONG E

Write the following on the board: steam, steak. Remind the children that in one of these words EA makes the long E sound and in the other it makes the long A sound. Challenge them to experiment like "word scientists" to determine the correct and meaningful pronunciation of each of the words. Praise correct responses. Use the words in original sentences.

Remind them that this is a letter pair which sometimes reverses itself and allows the second vowel to say its name instead of the first vowel. (Lesson 56)

Now tell them that the pair IE sometimes does the same thing. Sometimes the I will be long and say its name. However, with this letter pair, it is more likely that the E will do all the talking.

Write the following on the board: pie. In this word, IE will sound like long I.

Place a macron over the I and a backslash through the E.

Allow a child to read it aloud. Now add an R to the end of the word, forming "pier." Tell them that in this new word, E will say its name instead. Circle the IE.

Place a macron over the E and backslash through the I.

Read the word aloud and have the children echo it. Define and use in an original sentence.

Tell the children that there are quite a few words like this in our language. Write the following on the board: chief, field, grief, priest, shield, shriek, thief, yield. Invite children to the board to circle the IE pair.

Write a macron over the E and a backslash through the I in each word.

Challenge the children to read each word, pronouncing the IE as long E. Define the words and use them in original sentences.

Worksheet 71B: Read the instructions aloud. Call on students to read the first sentence aloud, leaving out the final word. Call on another student to read each of the word choices under the sentence. Ask them which word best fits the sentence. Monitor as they circle the correct selection. Continue in the same manner to complete the worksheet.

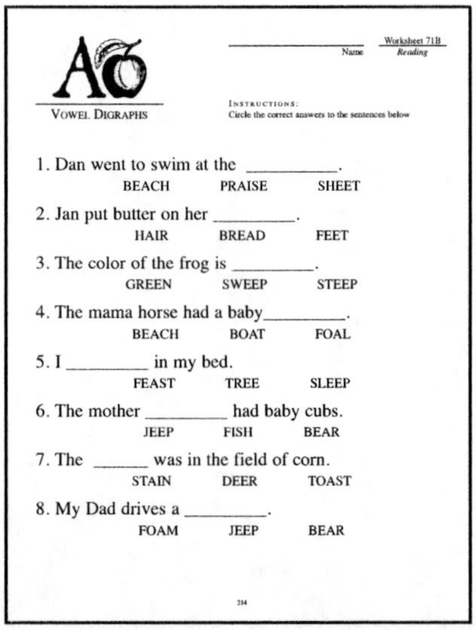

Vowel Digraphs

Name ______________ Worksheet 71B *Reading*

Instructions:
Circle the correct answers to the sentences below

1. Dan went to swim at the __________.
BEACH PRAISE SHEET
2. Jan put butter on her _________.
HAIR BREAD FEET
3. The color of the frog is _________.
GREEN SWEEP STEEP
4. The mama horse had a baby_________.
BEACH BOAT FOAL
5. I _________ in my bed.
FEAST TREE SLEEP
6. The mother _________ had baby cubs.
JEEP FISH BEAR
7. The ______ was in the field of corn.
STAIN DEER TOAST
8. My Dad drives a _________.
FOAM JEEP BEAR

214

Archives: Special Exhibit Edition. Use the list in Appendix 5 to select the Special Exhibit words that can be used to play the game at this point.

Lesson 72
Review

ACTIVITY 1: ART ACTIVITY

Write the following on the board:

bear = black
leaf and frog = green
trunk of tree = tan
horse and foal = gray
goat = white.

Call on students to read each of the word pairs. Explain what a “foal” is.

Tell them that this is their coloring key for the next worksheet.

Worksheet 72A
Name
Comprehension

COMPREHENSION

INSTRUCTIONS:
Color the bear black. Color the leaves on the tree green. Color the trunk of the tree tan. Color the frog green. Color the horse and the foal gray. Color the goat white.

Worksheet 72A: Read the instructions aloud. Monitor the students' progress as they work independently.

ACTIVITY 2: COMPOUND WORDS

Remind the children about some of the compound words they have been reading this year: within, into, upon, windmill, flagship. Draw a line between the two small words which make up each of these compound words. Remind them that compound words are just two smaller words linked together into one word.

Write the following on the board in a vertical column on the left side of the board: back, bath, bed, cup, pine, week. Call on children to read the words aloud.

Now write the following on the board in a vertical column on the right side of the board, with enough space between the columns to write the compound words which will be formed: end, cake, robe, pack, room, cone. Call on children to read these words aloud.

Challenge the children to match a word on the left with a word on the right to make a compound word which makes sense! This activity could get a little silly, but that's okay! When real words are formed, write them in the space between the two columns.

Define the words as necessary and use them in original sentences. Erase the two columns of words on either side of the board. Invite students to come to the board and copy the compound words on display.

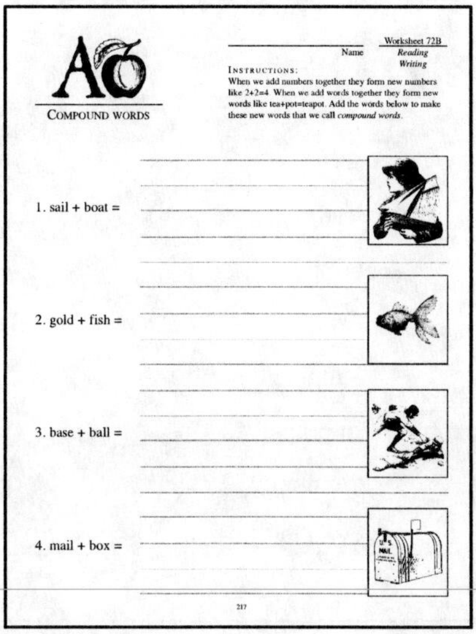

Worksheet 72B
Name
Reading
Writing

COMPOUND WORDS

INSTRUCTIONS:
When we add numbers together they form new numbers like 2+2=4. When we add words together they form new words like tea+pot=teapot. Add the words below to make these new words that we call *compound words*.

1. sail + boat =

2. gold + fish =

3. base + ball =

4. mail + box =

Worksheet 72B: Read the instructions aloud. Call on students to read the compound words as shown. Monitor as they copy them on the lines provided. Remind them that there should not be a space between the two small words when they write them as a compound word.

Lesson 73
Dropping Final Silent E to Add ING and Spelling List 3

ACTIVITY 1: DROPPING FINAL SILENT E TO ADD ING

Briefly play the "charades" game today. Write the following on the board: smile. Invite a child to the front of the room and ask him to demonstrate this for the class. Ask "What is __________ doing right now?" (smiling) "What do I have to add to this word to make it read that way?" (ING)

Before you add the ING, explain to the children that it is a spelling rule to take off the final silent E in words like this before adding the ING. Erase the E and write in ING.

Invite children to come to the front of the class and act out the following actions: write, ride (a horse). Drop the final E and add ING to each word following the same procedure as above.

Now write the following on the board: skating, shining, roping. Challenge the children to read the words, using the long sounds for the first vowels in each word.

Erase the ING from each word above and ask what you would need to add to form the words "skate," "shine," and "rope." (final silent E) Praise correct responses and write the words as directed.

You may also approach or supplement the decoding of these last words by reminding them of the syllabication rule for syllables which end in a vowel (the vowel is long). Have the children attempt to decode the above ING words by allowing the consonant following the first vowel to "stick to" the first syllable and using short sounds for the first vowel sounds. Ask if the words pronounced in this manner are meaningful (NO). Encourage them to move the consonant to the second syllable and then decode with the final vowel of the first syllable pronounced as a long vowel. They will recognize the words spoken in this manner.

Worksheet 73A: Read the instructions aloud. Have the children read each of the ING words aloud. Call particular attention to the word "smiling." Monitor as they respond as indicated.

Worksheet 73A
Reading
Name

INSTRUCTIONS:
Match the words on the left with the pictures on the right. There are more words than pictures.

crying
reading
falling
fishing
jumping
smiling
drumming
sleeping

219

ACTIVITY 2: SPELLING LIST 3

Write the words on Worksheets 73B/C on the board. Assist the children to decode and read each one. Circle letter pairs, backslash silent letters.

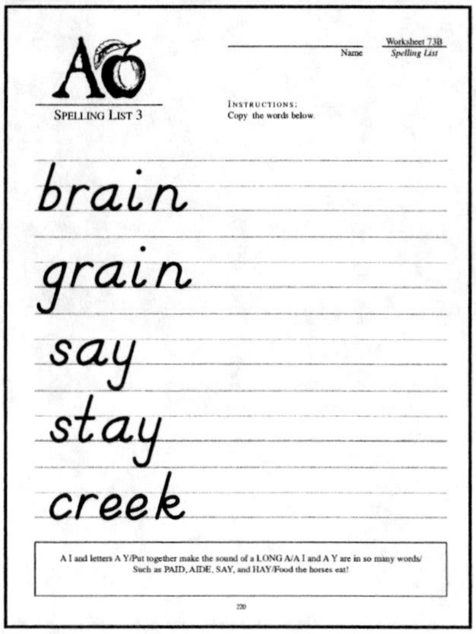

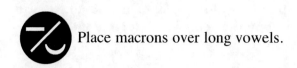

Place macrons over long vowels.

Invite children to the board to copy the words. Define them as necessary and use in original sentences. Remind them that they will be tested on these words in one week and they must review them daily until then.

Worksheets 73B/C: Read the instructions aloud. Monitor the students' progress as they work independently.

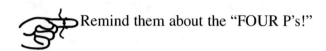

Remind them about the "FOUR P's!"

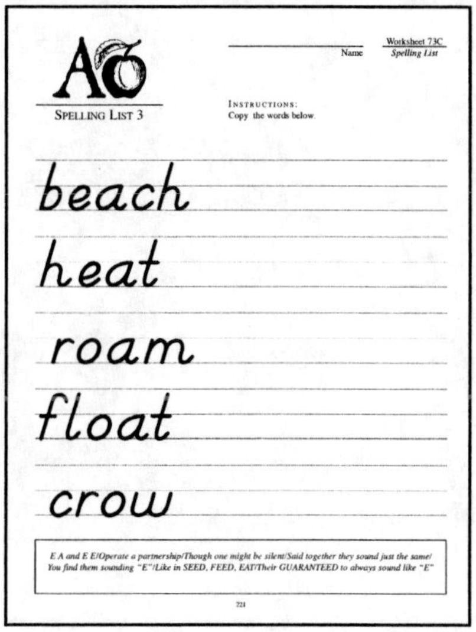

Lesson 74
Review and Final LY

Activity 1: Hearing and Writing Vowels

Tell the children they must be good listeners and lookers again today. You will read a word aloud, then write it on the board, without the vowel in it. They must determine what vowel is heard in the word and you will invite someone to write it in where it belongs.

Tell them this will be tricky—some of the words will have short vowels and some will have long vowels!

fat	cute	dim	hop	pet
cut	fate	hope	dime	Pete

Worksheets 74A/B: Read the instructions aloud. Monitor the students' progress as they work independently.

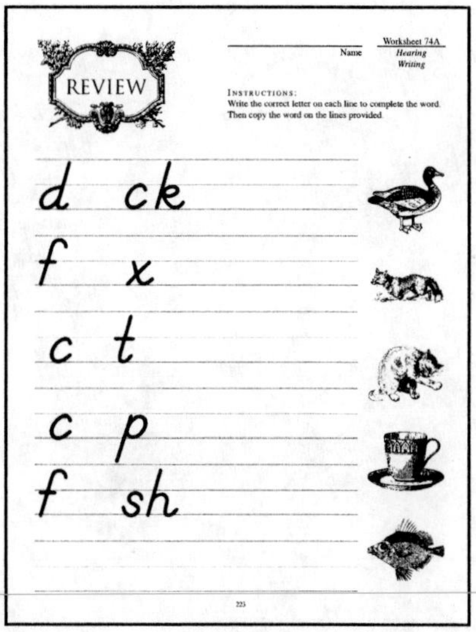

Worksheet 74C: Read the instructions aloud. Call on a student to read the sentence. Monitor as they copy the sentence independently.

Worksheet 74B
Name
Hearing
Writing
REVIEW
INSTRUCTIONS:
Write the correct letter on each line to complete the word. Then copy the word on the lines provided.
k te
b ll
fl te
d me
n se
224

ACTIVITY 2: FINAL LY

Write the following on the board: sad, glad. Allow the students to read the words aloud.

Call a student to the front of the room (preferably a child who is a good "actor!") Tell them privately to go out of the room and then return, walking as if he had just heard very sad news. You may want to go out with him and demonstrate: head bowed, walking slowly, no smile.

When he comes into the room in this manner, ask the children: Which of the words on the board describes him? (sad) Say the following: ____________ is walking SADLY into the room.

Now prompt the student privately to go back out of the room and come in, skipping, with a big smile. When he comes into the room in this manner, ask the children: Which of the words on the board describes him now? (glad) Say the following: ______________ is walking GLADLY into the room.

Worksheet 74C
Name
Writing
REVIEW
INSTRUCTIONS:
In your best handwriting copy the sentence below then color the picture.
The red plane flies in the air.
225

Repeat the words "sadly" and "gladly" and make appropriate expressions as you do so. Ask the children what they hear at the end of each of the words. (LY) Affirm correct responses. Tell the children that we write this as LY. Add LY to the words on the board.

When we have words like this which describe how someone does something, they are called ADVERBS. There are many, many words to which we can add LY to make adverbs. Write the following on the board as examples: badly, softly, safely, bravely, weakly, suddenly. Assist the children to decode and read each of these words.

Draw attention to the fact that in each one of these, the word without the LY is a word which describes a thing. Cover the LY, define each of the root words and use in sentences. Now reveal the LY again and explain that when LY is added, the word now describes an action. Use the new adverbs in sentences and point out how they tell HOW an action was done.

Lesson 75
Reading LEXI'S HOPE

ACTIVITY 1: SPECIAL EXHIBIT WORDS

Remind the children that sometimes they must be "word scientists" and experiment with the different sounds made by the letters in certain words. Remind them of the "wild words" which they have studied which use long sounds instead of short sounds.

Write "find," "most," and "Ruth" on the board. Ask the children if these words make any sense when pronounced with short vowel sounds. Demonstrate that they do not by reading them that way. Write a macron over each vowel in these words.

Challenge the children to read them using the long vowel sounds. Affirm that they are meaningful words now. Invite the children to make up original sentences using each word.

Tell them they will see each of these words in their next story.
Now tell them there are three new Special Exhibit words which they must learn to recognize for this story. Write the following on the board: ONLY, SAYS, LIVES (with a short I sound). Read each word and have the children echo them. Discuss how the sounds made by the O, AY, and I in each of these words is slightly different from what they would expect. Compare the word "lives" with the previous Special Exhibit "give."

In addition, inform them that there are two special names in this story which are pronounced in an unusual way. Write the following on the board: Lexi, Naomi. Read them aloud and have the children echo them after you. Affirm that the final I in each name makes the long E sound. Call to their attention that both the A and O in "Naomi" make long sounds.

Finally, write the word "husband" and "family" on the board. Guide them through decoding "husband," using the Z sound for the letter S and modifying the short A into the more familiar short I which is the common pronunciation in spontaneous speech. Guide them through decoding "family" using the short I sound instead of long I (which they may be more likely to do according to the pattern they have been taught).

Worksheet 75A: Read the instructions aloud. Use any of the previous techniques for eliciting student responses. Pay special attention to the new and unusual words. Define as needed and use in sentences to further reinforce meanings.

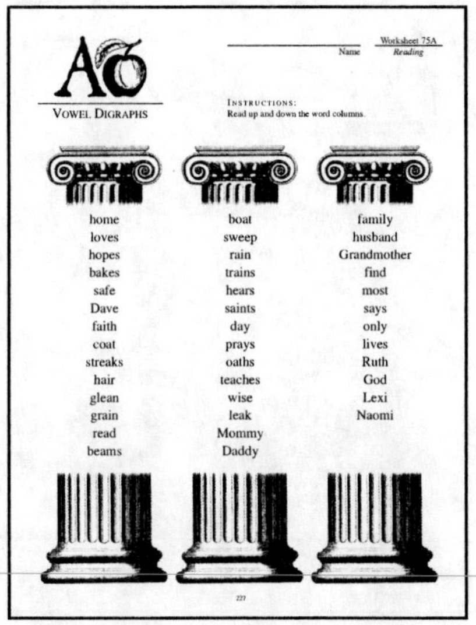
Worksheet 75A
Name ____ *Reading*

Vowel Digraphs

Instructions: Read up and down the word columns.

home	boat	family
loves	sweep	husband
hopes	rain	Grandmother
bakes	trains	find
safe	hears	most
Dave	saints	says
faith	day	only
coat	prays	lives
streaks	oaths	Ruth
hair	teaches	God
glean	wise	Lexi
grain	leak	Naomi
read	Mommy	
beams	Daddy	

ACTIVITY 2: READING LEXI'S HOPE

This is a fictional story about a young homeschooled girl, Lexi, and her parent's instruction on the faithfulness of God. The following vocabulary and expressions are used:

beam—to smile, respond with approval
print—write
wise—knowing what is right or true
sheaves—bundles
quaint—charming
finch—a kind of bird
braids—the dough was twisted into a special weave
steep—soak
mint green—pale green
feast—an abundant, delicious meal
oath—promise, covenant (see note below)
Word—Scripture
The Man in the Boat—Noah
Spies on the Wall—story of Rahab
Sam—Samuel
Joe—Joseph
streaks—lines, marks
sweep—to spread across
kin—family
trail of tears—sadness in their journey
glean—to take what is left over
wed—to marry

Call their attention to the words "leaves" and "sheaves." These are the plural forms of "leaf" and "sheaf." They have not yet learned this spelling rule, but should be instructed to recognize the meaning of the roots of each of these plural words.

You may want to expand slightly on the concept of "covenant" since it is so prominent in this story. Discuss the idea that covenants are promises or binding agreements and that God keeps all His promises all the time. Touch upon the concept of "signs of the covenant," especially with the rainbow and His promise never to bring about another flood like the one in Noah's time.

Westminster Larger Catechism, Question 30 "Doth God leave all mankind to perish in the estate of sin and misery?" Answer: "God doth not leave all men to perish in the estate of sin and misery, into which they fell by the breach of the first covenant, commonly called the Covenant of Works; but of his mere love and mercy delivereth his elect out of it, and bringeth them into an estate of salvation by the second covenant, commonly called the Covenant of Grace."

LEXI'S HOPE

Name

Worksheet 76A
Comprehension

INSTRUCTIONS:
Match the words on the left to the pictures on the right. There are more words than pictures.

bread
tea
pie
cake
butter
wheat
pear
beef
peach

229

Guide the students through the "round robin" reading of the story. Discuss the characters, events and ideas as they occur.

Some questions for discussion might include: What kinds of things do you do with your mother? father? grandparents? How did each of the saints in the stories Lexi reads show their faith? What does it mean to be "wise?"

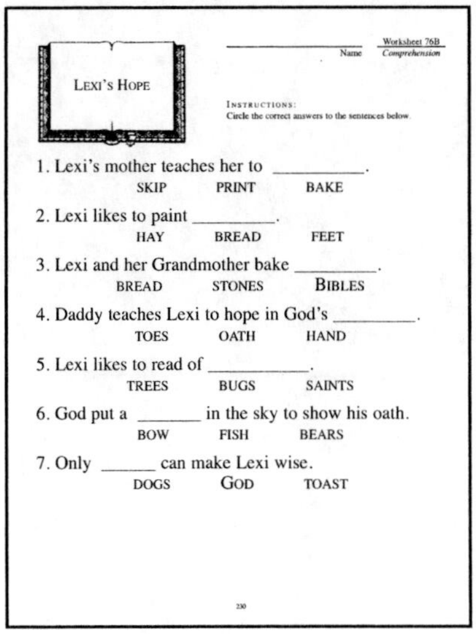

Worksheet 76B
Name
Comprehension

LEXI'S HOPE

INSTRUCTIONS:
Circle the correct answers to the sentences below.

1. Lexi's mother teaches her to ________.
   SKIP PRINT BAKE
2. Lexi likes to paint ________.
   HAY BREAD FEET
3. Lexi and her Grandmother bake ________.
   BREAD STONES BIBLES
4. Daddy teaches Lexi to hope in God's ________.
   TOES OATH HAND
5. Lexi likes to read of ________.
   TREES BUGS SAINTS
6. God put a ______ in the sky to show his oath.
   BOW FISH BEARS
7. Only ______ can make Lexi wise.
   DOGS GOD TOAST

230

LESSON 76
READING COMPREHENSION

ACTIVITY 1: READING WORDS

Briefly discuss yesterday's story. Review the main characters and ideas. Allow further discussion as time permits.

Worksheet 76A: Read the instructions aloud. Assist the children to decode as necessary. Monitor the students' progress as they work independently.

Worksheet 76C
Name
Comprehension

LEXI'S HOPE

INSTRUCTIONS:
In red crayon circle the things that Lexi painted, in a blue crayon the things she baked, and cross out in a green crayon things that were not in the story.

231

Worksheet 76B: Read the instructions aloud. Call on students to read the sentences, leaving out the word for the blank space. Call on other students to read the word choices. Monitor as they select the appropriate word for the blank and circle as indicated.

Worksheet 76C: Read the instructions aloud. Make sure the children realize that they will be putting a green X over items which were not mentioned in the story, as opposed to circling them. They will only make circles with red and blue. Monitor the students' progress as they work independently.

They may look through the book again if necessary to remind themselves of details. This is good practice in skimming for information.

Worksheet 76D: Read the instructions aloud and present an example of a finished painting of the rainbow. Prepare a table with the necessary paint and supplies. Assist as necessary to complete the project as described.

Worksheet 76D
Name
Art Activity

LEXI'S HOPE

INSTRUCTIONS:
Give students a large piece of finger painting paper and small amounts of finger paint. Have them paint the rainbow from the story, reminding them of its meaning.

232

LESSON 77
TARGET: THE TWO SOUNDS OF OO

Play The Alphabet Song for the children encouraging them to sing along.

ACTIVITY 1: HEARING AND SEEING

Write a large "boo" on the board. Chances are good that someone in your class will be able to tell you what this word is!

Challenge them to tell you what letters in this word are making the long U sound. (OO) Affirm that this is one of the two sounds made by this pair of twin O's. Circle the OO.

Draw a long macron over the OO and tell them that this will be the symbol to mean that this letter pair makes the sound of long U.

Write the following on the board in a vertical column under the "boo." zoo, soon, bloom, groom, moon. Invite students to the board to circle the OO they see in each word.

Using the long U sound to decode, read each of the words and have the children echo them after you. Affirm that the OO in each one sounds like long U.

Draw long macrons over each letter pair.

Now tell them that OO has another sound and this one is a little harder to hear and very different. Write the word "good" on the board and circle the OO. Read it aloud, emphasizing the unique OO sound in this word. Describe it as being "halfway" between a long U and a short U.

Draw a long, shallow breve over the OO in this word and tell them that this will be the symbol to mean the OO sound as in "good."

Write the following on the board in another vertical column under "good": hood, stood, wood, took, look. Invite children to the board to circle the OO in each word. Read them aloud and have the children echo them after you. Draw long, shallow breves over each letter pair.

Worksheet 77A

Name ____________ *Seeing*

OO

When O is doubled in a word it makes two different sounds as in *moon* and *good*.

INSTRUCTIONS:
Circle the double O in each word.

good	bloom	hood
cool	groom	stood
zoo	troop	wood
doom	look	wool
stool	took	moon
soon	brook	tool

There are twins who look exactly the same. They appear as OO, and Double O is their name. When they speak you hear a short or long U; The short one says good *and the long one says* zoo*.*

233

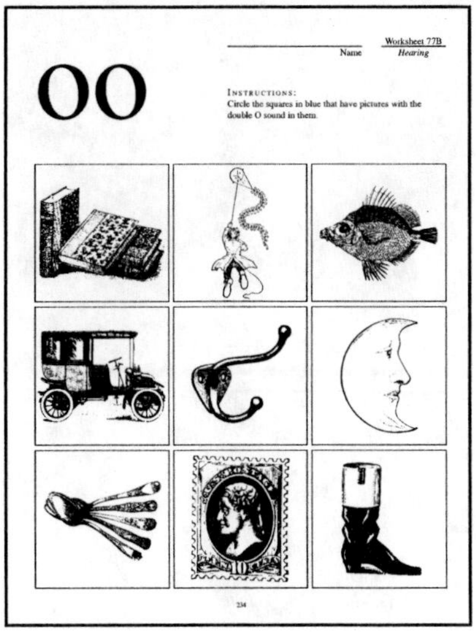
Worksheet 77B
Hearing
Name

OO

INSTRUCTIONS:
Circle the squares in blue that have pictures with the double O sound in them.

234

Affirm that all the words under "boo" use the OO sound as in "boo" and that all the words under "good" use the OO sound as in "good." Leave this on display as you present the worksheet.

There are twins who look exactly the same.
They appear as OO, and Double O is their name.
When they speak you hear a short or long U;
The short one says good and the long one says zoo.

Worksheet 77A: Read the instructions aloud. Allow the children to circle the OO in each word independently. Read the words aloud and ask if the word would be placed in the "boo" column or the "good" column. Affirm correct responses and have the children draw macrons or breves over the OO letter pair in each word according to the sound.

ACTIVITY 2: HEARING

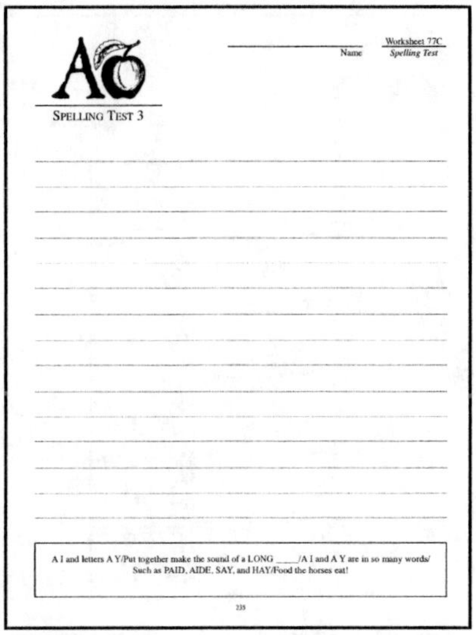
Worksheet 77C
Spelling Test
Name

SPELLING TEST 3

A I and letters A Y/Put together make the sound of a LONG ____/A I and A Y are in so many words/ Such as PAID, AIDE, SAY, and HAY/Food the horses eat!

235

Tell the children to put on their careful listening ears again! You will be reading a list of words. They will have to decide if it is a word which should go in the "boo" column, or the "good" column.

book	hook	moon	spoon	boot
room	loose	took	poodle	food
cook	moose	shook	wood	mood

Praise their "good" listening!

Worksheet 77B: Read the instructions aloud. Call on students to label the pictures and assist the children to determine if the label has either of the sounds of OO. Monitor their work.

ACTIVITY 3: SPELLING TEST 3

Worksheet 77C/D: Administer the test on Spelling List 3. Read each word once, use it in a sentence, then repeat it. Do not give any other sound or letter clues.

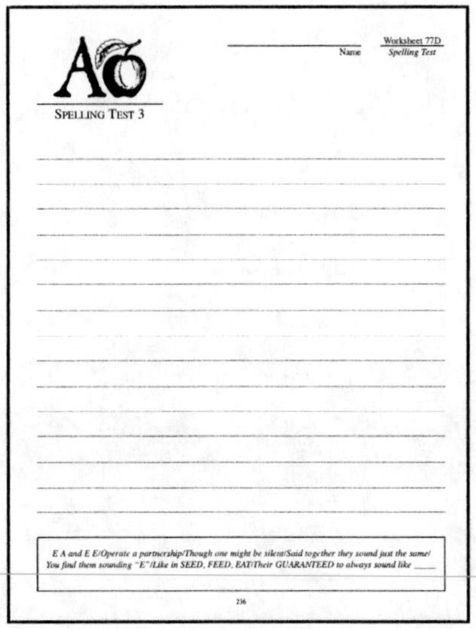
Worksheet 77D
Spelling Test
Name

SPELLING TEST 3

E A and E E/Operate a partnership/Though one might be silent/Said together they sound just the same/ You find them sounding "E"/Like in SEED, FEED, EAT/Their GUARANTEED to always sound like ____

236

Lesson 78
Target: OO

ACTIVITY 1: READING WORDS

Present the following puzzle pieces for: BR, CR, S, K, T, and OO. Read the following words and challenge students to link the proper puzzle pieces to form them: brook, crook, soot. Ask the students if these words use the twin O sound found in "boo" or "good." (good)

Now, present the following puzzle pieces: M, N and R. Read the following words and challenge students to link the proper puzzle pieces to form them: moon, broom, room.

Ask if these words use the twin O sound found in "boo" or "good." (BOO) Smile and tell them not to try to scare you like that!

Show the children the flashcard with the letters OO on it. Have them hear the sound of OO as in "book."

Worksheet 78A: Read the instructions aloud. Tell them the first three words use the OO in "good." Assist them to decode and read them aloud. Use them in original sentences. Tell them the last three words use the OO in "boo." Assist them to decode and read them aloud. Use them in original sentences.

Worksheet 78B: Read the instructions aloud. Tell the children that the first four words use the OO in "boo." The other four use the OO in "good." Assist them to decode each word and monitor as they respond as indicated.

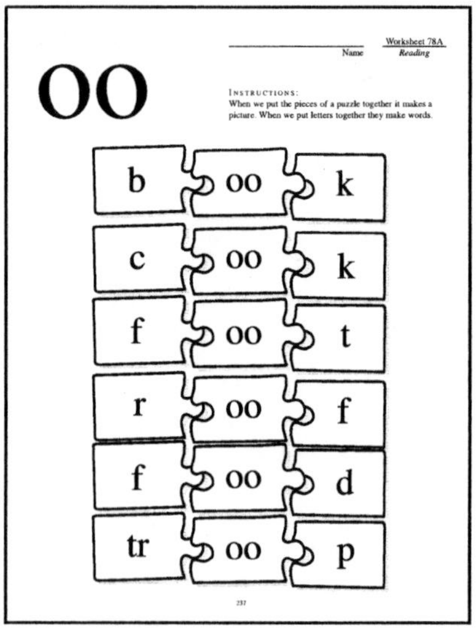

Worksheet 78A
Name
Reading

OO

INSTRUCTIONS:
When we put the pieces of a puzzle together it makes a picture. When we put letters together they make words.

b oo k
c oo k
f oo t
r oo f
f oo d
tr oo p

It takes a lot of time and experience, along with contextual clues, for children to decode these words with ease. Use of the macrons and breves is offered as an aid to children until they become more familiar with the words which utilize each sound. Since the short OO is more unique and difficult to remember, you will need to stimulate and model the use of this sound more frequently in the learning process.

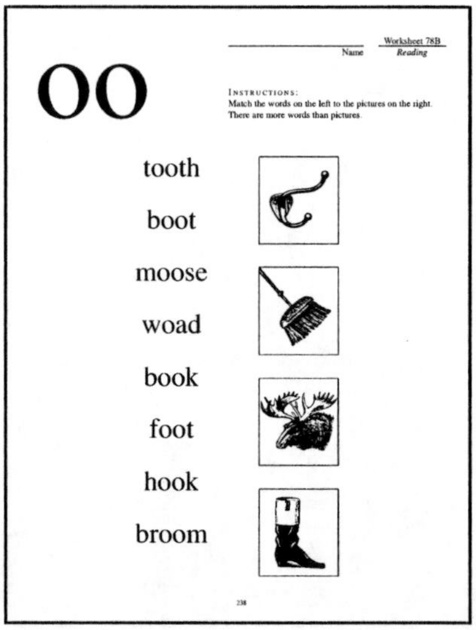

Worksheet 78B
Name
Reading

OO

INSTRUCTIONS:
Match the words on the left to the pictures on the right. There are more words than pictures.

tooth
boot
moose
woad
book
foot
hook
broom

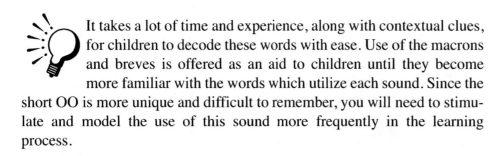

Give them their museum bag. Allow them time to go through the house and collect items that have the OO sound to make their own museum. If you are teaching in a school setting, instruct the children to take the bag home and bring in objects the following day.

Worksheet 78C
Name
Reading

OO

INSTRUCTIONS:
Read up and down the word columns.

took	spooky	loose
tools	looming	roof
boot	hood	nook
moon	too	good
scoop	hoop	mood
brook	shoot	
cool	loop	

ACTIVITY 3: READING MORE WORDS

Write the words found on Worksheet 78C on the board.

Invite students to the board to underline the OO in each word.

Encourage them to be "word detectives" again. Allow them to experiment with the two sounds of OO (you may prompt as necessary) to determine which sound yields a pronunciation which is meaningful. Affirm and define words which are less familiar and use them in original sentences.

Worksheet 78C: Read the instructions aloud. Assist them to read the words using any of the previous techniques for eliciting student response.

You may want to give the students the coloring page along with the flashcard. Read the information about the artist to your students before they color the picture.

LESSON 79
TARGET: UE/EW AS LONG U

ACTIVITY 1: SEEING AND HEARING UE AS LONG U

Write the following words on the board: pie, toe. Ask the children what letter they both have in common. (E)

Ask if the E in each of these words makes any sound. (NO) Which vowel is heard in the word "pie?" (long I) Which vowel is heard in the word "toe?" (long O) Circle the letter pairs in each word and a backslash through the silent E.

Place a macron over the long vowel.

Now write the word "Sue" on the board. Circle the UE, place a macron over the U, and backslash through the E. Ask them what sound is made by long U. Challenge them to decode this word. Praise correct reading!

Ask if anyone can tell you why this word has an upper case S. (it is a proper name) Erase the S and replace it with D. Call on a student to decode the new word according to the same sound pattern. Define it and use it in an original sentence.

Erase the D and replace it with the blend BL. Challenge a student to read this word aloud and use it in an original sentence.

Long U, long U do you have a friend?
Yes sir, E is with me to the end.
We cannot separate;
We stick together like glue.
You could search until you're blue
and never find a friend so true!

Worksheet 79A: Read the instructions aloud. Allow the children to circle the letter pair UE in each word independently. Assist them to decode each word shown. You may permit the addition of macrons and the backslashing of the E if desired to assist decoding.

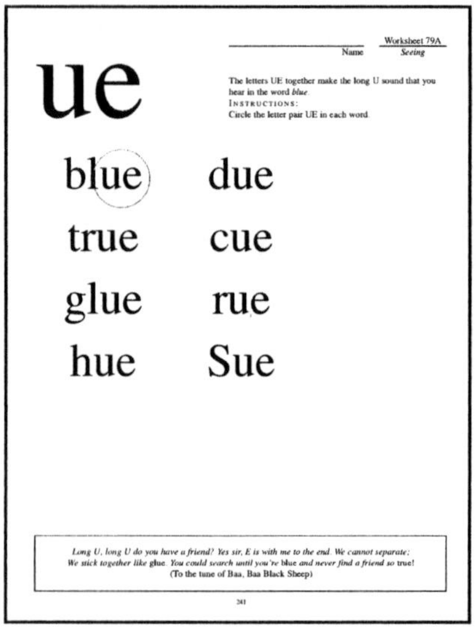

Name

Worksheet 79A
Seeing

ue

The letters UE together make the long U sound that you hear in the word *blue*.
INSTRUCTIONS:
Circle the letter pair UE in each word.

blue due
true cue
glue rue
hue Sue

Long U, long U do you have a friend? Yes sir, E is with me to the end. We cannot separate; We stick together like glue. *You could search until you're* blue *and never find a friend so* true!
(To the tune of Baa, Baa Black Sheep)

241

ACTIVITY 2: SEEING AND HEARING EW AS LONG U

Tell the children that there is another letter pair which also likes to make the long U sound. In fact, that is the only sound these two letters will make together.

Write the letter pair EW on the board. Tell them that this is the letter pair which is used in the word "mew"—the sound of a kitten! Allow the children to "mew" several times.

Under the word "mew" write the following: new, dew, few. Following the sound pattern for "mew," allow the children to read these words aloud.

Write the following sentences on the board using these words: There are a few new kittens in the dew. I can hear them "mew!" Read these sentences aloud and have the children echo them after you. Affirm that all the EW words rhyme.

Invite children to the board to circle the EW letter pair in each of the words.

E and W live very far apart;
So when they get together,
They catch up on the news.
While together, EW says long U
To make up words like grew and blew and stew.

Worksheet 79B: Read the instructions aloud. Allow the children to circle all the EW letter pairs independently. Assist them to read all the words aloud. Define any as necessary and use in original sentences.

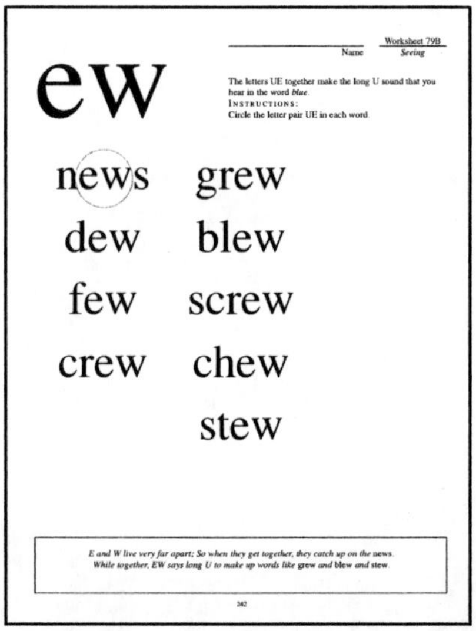

Name

Worksheet 79B
Seeing

ew

The letters UE together make the long U sound that you hear in the word *blue*.
INSTRUCTIONS:
Circle the letter pair UE in each word.

news grew
dew blew
few screw
crew chew
stew

E and W live very far apart; So when they get together, they catch up on the news.
While together, EW says long U to make up words like grew *and* blew *and* stew.

242

ACTIVITY 3: FORMING WORDS

Present the puzzle pieces necessary to form the following word pairs: blue/blew, flue/flew, due/dew.

Link the blend BL with the UE. Call on a student to decode and read it. Define it and use it in an original sentence. Write it on the board.

Now remove the UE puzzle piece and replace it with EW. Call on a student to decode and read it. Affirm that it sounds the same as the other "blue" on the board, but that it means something different when it is spelled this way. Define "blew" and use it in an original sentence. Write it on the board beside "blue."

Remind them that they have run into words like this before. They sound alike but mean different things depending on their spelling. They do not need to remember how to spell these right now, but should know how to recognize them when they see them in their reading.

Continue in the same manner with the other word pairs.

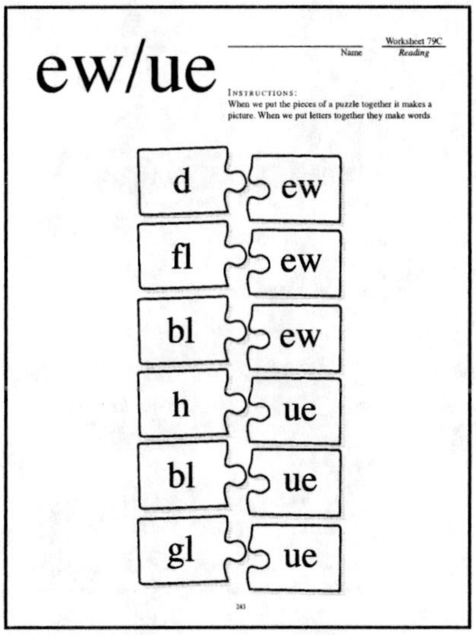

Worksheet 79C: Read the instructions aloud. Guide the children through the decoding and reading of each word, paying special attention to "blew" and "blue." Define any unfamiliar words and use them in original sentences.

Worksheet 79D: Test. This test is optional and is added to evaluate your students if you feel it is necessary at this time. The answers are worth 10 points each.

Lesson 80
Reading RED HOOD

ACTIVITY 1: SPECIAL EXHIBIT WORDS FOR READING RED HOOD

Sit down on the floor at the front of the room. Ask the children "Where am I sitting?" Affirm correct responses.

Go over and knock on the classroom door. Ask the children "What am I knocking on?" Affirm correct responses.

Say the two words "door" and "floor" several times. Affirm that they are rhyming words and that rhyming words always have the same ending sounds. What sound do they hear at the end of each of these words? (R)

Challenge them to tell you what OTHER sound they hear at the end of both words. (long O) Affirm that these words end in OR.

Call on a student to come to the board and write OR. Now ask the children what blend they hear at the beginning of "floor." (FL)

Call on a student to come to the board and direct him to write the letter pair FL to the left of and slightly apart from the OR.

Explain to the children that in words like "floor," the O takes its twin along. However, this time they both just say their name. They do not make the long U as in "boo" or the short OO as in "good." They just say OR.

Write another OR on the board. Ask the children what sound they hear at the beginning of the word "door." (D)

Ask them "Does this word sound like 'floor'?" Affirm that in this case it will also be spelled the same way.

Invite a student to the board to write the beginning letter D and the additional O.

Write this last word on the board: moor. Challenge the children to tell you how this word will be pronounced. Praise correct responses. Define this word (to tie up at a dock) and use it in an original sentence.

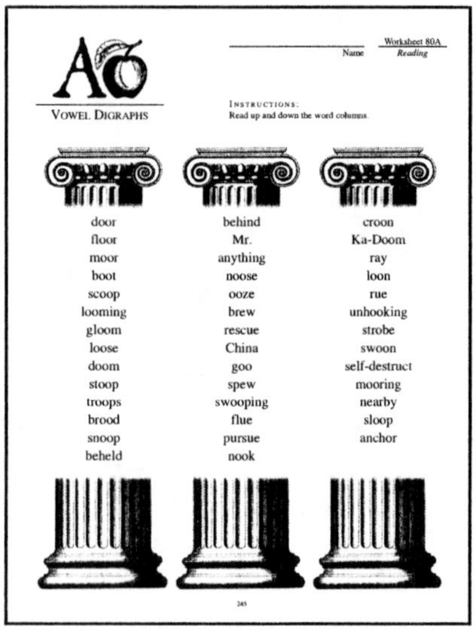

Worksheet 80A *Reading*
Name

Vowel Digraphs

Instructions: Read up and down the word columns.

door	behind	croon
floor	Mr.	Ka-Doom
moor	anything	ray
boot	noose	loon
scoop	ooze	rue
looming	brew	unhooking
gloom	rescue	strobe
loose	China	swoon
doom	goo	self-destruct
stoop	spew	mooring
troops	swooping	nearby
brood	flue	sloop
snoop	pursue	anchor
beheld	nook	

On the board, write the words found on Worksheet 80A. As you work through these words, call attention to the new compound words, the hyphenated words, the use of the prefix "un," and the special words "Mr.," "China," "beheld," "behind," and "anchor" (CH as K).

Worksheet 80A: Read the instructions aloud. Assist the children to properly decode each of the words. Use any of the previous techniques for eliciting student response. Define the words according to their use in the story (the vocabulary list with definitions follows).

ACTIVITY 2: READING RED HOOD

Yesterday the government of England recieved top secret information that a rogue element in the Russian army had established a secret hideout and developed a high-powered weapon that he was about to let loose on the world, enslaving the free, democratic countries. Time is running out! So the British send their best secret agent over to stop this fiend, armed with the latest in secret agent armaments! The following vocabulary and expressions are used in this story:

boot—trunk of the car
gleam—shine
scoop—outlet, exhaust pipe
cut across—flew across
brook—small stream of water
sped—ran quickly
spooky—frightful

looming in the gloom—standing in the dark
let loose doom—release a terrible event
stoop—crouch down
troops—army, henchmen
chew away—dissolve, corrode
brood—group
scooting—moving quickly
snuck—moved carefully so no one would see or hear
snoop—look
beheld—saw
shoo—leave, go away
cruel—mean, delighting in causing pain
noose—hanging loop
pool of ooze—liquid that would destroy them
brew—bubbling mixture
rescue—save from certain death
infiltrator—spy
drew—took out
goo—sticky, jelly-like substance
grate—a metal frame of crossed bars
spew—glob
cue—signal
swooping—flying low and wide
flue—conduit, vent
shaken—weak and trembling
stirring—able to move
pursue—follow, chase
nook—small, hidden area
croon—sing or speak slowly
loon—wild bird, crazy person
zooming—moving quickly
rook in a game of chess—attacking from a distance in a straight line (a metaphor)
rue—regret, be sorry for
strobe—blinking light
swoon—faint
self-destruct—destroy itself
mooring—docking, tied
sloop—a single-masted sailing boat
sprang—leaped suddenly
drew up—brought up

Guide the children through the "round robin" reading of the story. Assist with decoding as necessary, reminding them of the rules and patterns they have learned so far.

Discuss main ideas, characters, and events as they occur. Some questions for discussion may include: Would you like to try a flying backpack? Why or why not? If you could invent a spy gadget, what would it do?

Lesson 81
Reading Comprehension

ACTIVITY 1: REVIEWING RED HOOD

Lead the children of a brief review of yesterday's story. Outline the main events in order, discuss details.

Worksheet 81A
Name
Comprehension

Red Hood

Instructions:
Draw a line to connect the descriptions with the characters in the story.

From China

Had a Ka-Doom Ray

Set the Ka-Doom Ray to self-destruct

Used a hoop to trap his enemy

Used a strobe to blind his enemy

Did not escape on a boat

Put a pack by the stream to cool

247

Worksheet 81A: Read the instructions aloud. Assist the children to read the sentence fragments and identify the characters described.

Worksheet 81B: Read the instructions aloud. Demonstrate the use of the check to indicate responses. Monitor as they read the questions independently and respond as indicated.

Worksheet 81C: Read the instructions aloud. Tell the children you will read the sentences for them and they must choose the correct word to circle to finish the sentences appropriately. The last question they may do on their own.

Worksheet 81D: Read the instructions aloud. Present a finished example of the movie poster. Monitor as the children work independently.

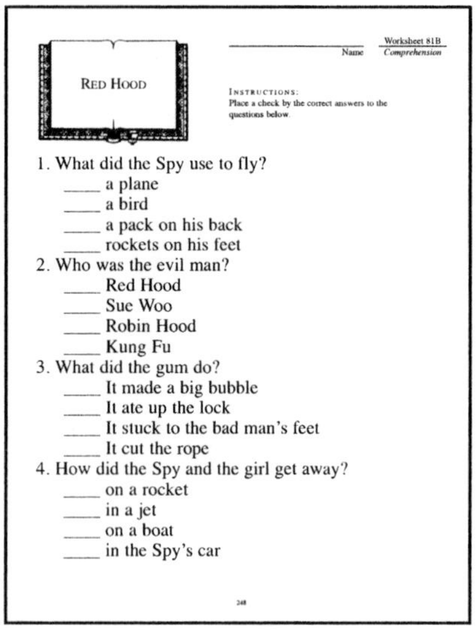

Worksheet 81B
Name
Comprehension

Red Hood

Instructions:
Place a check by the correct answers to the questions below.

1. What did the Spy use to fly?
   ____ a plane
   ____ a bird
   ____ a pack on his back
   ____ rockets on his feet
2. Who was the evil man?
   ____ Red Hood
   ____ Sue Woo
   ____ Robin Hood
   ____ Kung Fu
3. What did the gum do?
   ____ It made a big bubble
   ____ It ate up the lock
   ____ It stuck to the bad man's feet
   ____ It cut the rope
4. How did the Spy and the girl get away?
   ____ on a rocket
   ____ in a jet
   ____ on a boat
   ____ in the Spy's car

248

Lesson 82
Target: OI/OY

Play the Oysters song for the children encouraging them to sing.

ACTIVITY 1 : SEEING AND HEARING

Tell the children that today they will be learning another new letter pair. This pair is a blend of two vowel sounds.

Write a big "OINK" on the board. Tell the children that this is the sound made by a pig! Read the word aloud and allow the children to "oink" several times.

Underline the NK. Tell the children that they have had this letter pair before. Challenge them to tell you what the new letter pair is for today. (OI) Invite a child to come to the board and circle OI.

Make the sound several times. Have the children echo it after you. Affirm that it is a blend of the long O and the long E (not I!)

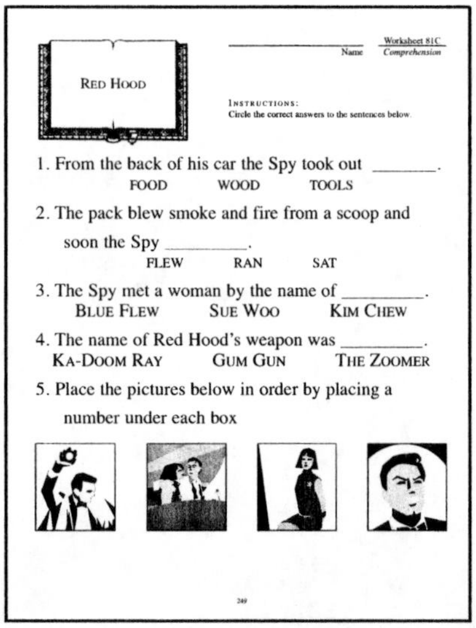

Worksheet 81C
Name
Comprehension

Red Hood

Instructions:
Circle the correct answers to the sentences below.

1. From the back of his car the Spy took out ________.
   FOOD WOOD TOOLS
2. The pack blew smoke and fire from a scoop and soon the Spy ________.
   FLEW RAN SAT
3. The Spy met a woman by the name of ________.
   BLUE FLEW SUE WOO KIM CHEW
4. The name of Red Hood's weapon was ________.
   KA-DOOM RAY GUM GUN THE ZOOMER
5. Place the pictures below in order by placing a number under each box

249

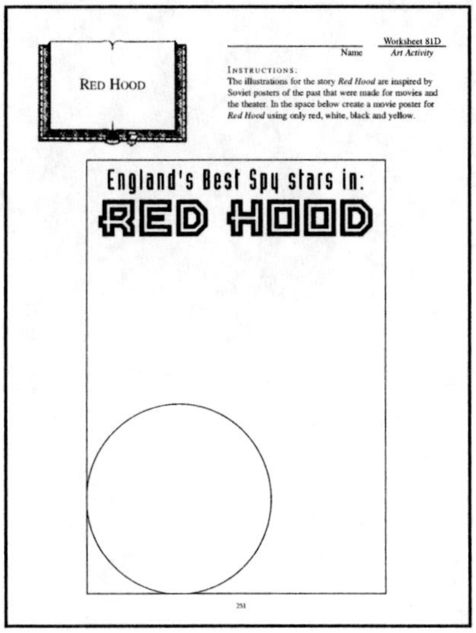

Worksheet 81D

Name — *Art Activity*

RED HOOD

INSTRUCTIONS: The illustrations for the story *Red Hood* are inspired by Soviet posters of the past that were made for movies and the theater. In the space below create a movie poster for *Red Hood* using only red, white, black and yellow.

England's Best Spy stars in:

RED HOOD

Write the following on the board: oil, soil, broil. Invite a child to the board and circle OI in each word. Read the word "oil." Tell the children that the other two words rhyme and call on children to decode "soil" and "broil." Define both words and use them in original sentences.

Now, explain that OI will only be found in the beginning or middle of words. However, the OI sound is heard at the end of words also. Read the following aloud: boy, toy, joy.

When the OI sound occurs at the end of words, it is spelled OY. Write this letter pair on the board.

Remind them how Y likes to make the long E sound sometimes at the end of words like "silly," "pretty," "lady." In the same way it makes the long E sound when paired with O in OY.

Write "boy," "toy," "joy" on the board and invite students to come up and circle the OY in each word.

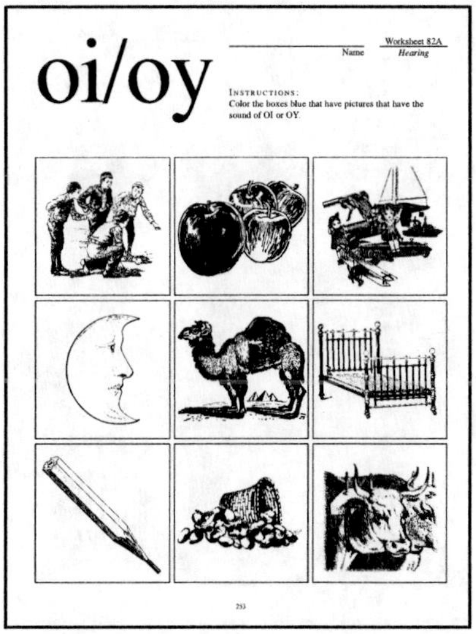

oi/oy

Worksheet 82A

Name — *Hearing*

INSTRUCTIONS: Color the boxes blue that have pictures that have the sound of OI or OY.

Now challenge them to listen carefully. You will be reading a list of words. When they hear OI, they are to push up the tips of their noses (like little piggy noses)!

coy	toe	baby	Roy	spoil	foil
spy	happy	noise	point	Sally	coin
annoy	joyful	joint	so	grew	gray

Show the children the flashcard with the letters OI/OY on it. Have them hear the sound of OI/OY as in "boy."

Give them their museum bag. Allow them time to go through the house and collect items that have the OY blend sound to make their own museum. If you are teaching in a school setting, instruct the children to take the bag home and bring in objects the following day.

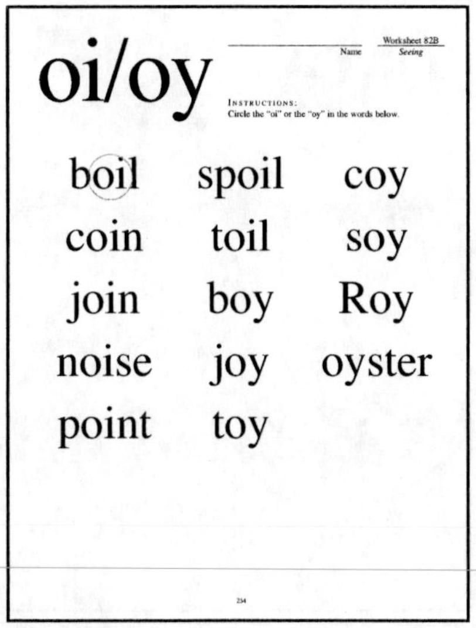

oi/oy

Worksheet 82B

Name — *Seeing*

INSTRUCTIONS: Circle the "oi" or the "oy" in the words below.

boil	spoil	coy
coin	toil	soy
join	boy	Roy
noise	joy	oyster
point	toy	

Worksheet 82A: Read the instructions aloud. Assist the children to label the pictures and color as indicated.

Row 1: boys, apples, toys
Row 2: moon, camel, bed
Row 3 pencil, oysters, oxen

Worksheet 82B: Read the instructions aloud. Monitor as they circle all the OI and OY letter pairs in the words. Assist to decode and read the words aloud. Define as necessary and use in original sentences.

You may want to give the students the coloring page along with the flashcard. Read the information about the artist to your students before they color the picture.

Percival's Pairs: Using ING, ANG, ONG, blends, long vowels Y as I, OA, OE OW, OO, and OI.

LESSON 83
TARGET: OI/OY

Play the Oysters song for the children encouraging them to sing.

ACTIVITY 1: READING

oi/oy

Name

Worksheet 83A

Reading

INSTRUCTIONS:

Read up and down the word columns

oil	join	soy
boil	foil	coy
toil	point	boys
soil	boy	toys
coin	toy	joys
coil	joy	oyster

Write a large OI on the left side of the board and a large OY on the right side.

Invite the children to brainstorm with you to come up with as many words containing the OI sound as possible.

As they offer words, write them in the proper column according to their correct spelling.

Invite children to come to the board and circle the OI or OY in each word.

Review the words with the children, having them come up with original sentences using each word.

Worksheet 83A: Read the instructions aloud. Use any of the previous techniques for eliciting student response.

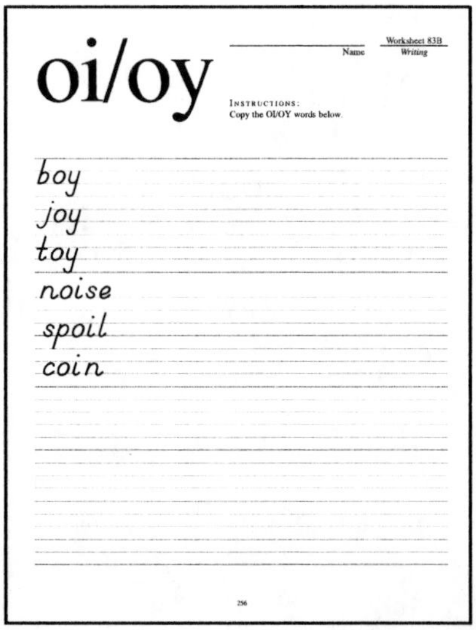
oi/oy

Name

Worksheet 83B

Writing

INSTRUCTIONS:

Copy the OI/OY words below

boy

joy

toy

noise

spoil

coin

Variations for prompting the reading of words on this sheet include: numbering the words and calling on students to read them by the designated number, verbal "fill-in-the-blanks," pointing to the written word on the board and having students point to the corresponding printed word on the sheet, riddle clues, categorizing on the basis of beginning sound or ending letter group, etc.

ACTIVITY 2: WRITING

Write the words found on Worksheet 83B on the board, along with lines. Invite children to the board to copy the words in their best handwriting.

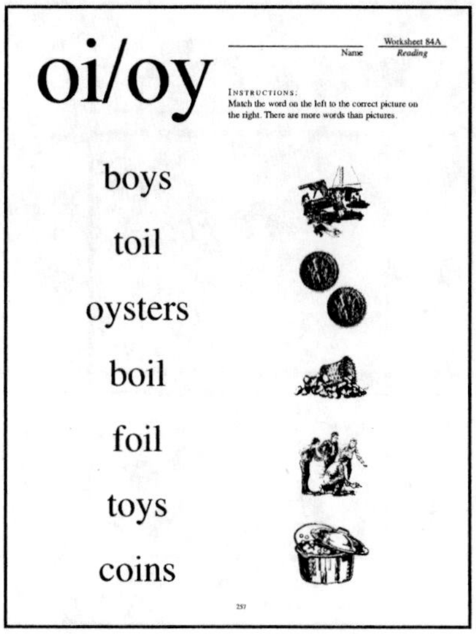

oi/oy

Name ______ Worksheet 84A *Reading*

INSTRUCTIONS: Match the word on the left to the correct picture on the right. There are more words than pictures.

boys
toil
oysters
boil
foil
toys
coins

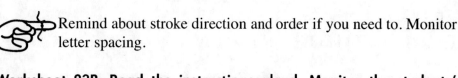

Remind about stroke direction and order if you need to. Monitor letter spacing.

Worksheet 83B: Read the instructions aloud. Monitor the students' progress as they work independently.

Lesson 84
Target: OI/OY

ACTIVITY 1: READING

Write the following on the board: MOIST, ENJOY, TOMBOY.

Invite children to the board to circle the OI/OY they see in each word. Have them decode and read each one.

Now play a brief game of verbal "fill-in-the-blanks." Make up a sentence which will use one of these words, but leave it out when you say the sentence. For example, say "My mother's chocolate cake is rich and ______________." Ask the children which of the words on the board would make sense in this sentence. (moist) Continue in the same manner for each of the words.

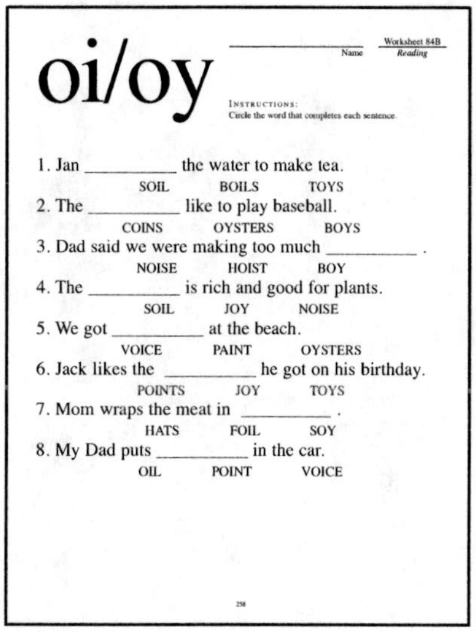

oi/oy

Name ______ Worksheet 84B *Reading*

INSTRUCTIONS: Circle the word that completes each sentence.

1. Jan __________ the water to make tea.
SOIL BOILS TOYS
2. The __________ like to play baseball.
COINS OYSTERS BOYS
3. Dad said we were making too much __________ .
NOISE HOIST BOY
4. The __________ is rich and good for plants.
SOIL JOY NOISE
5. We got __________ at the beach.
VOICE PAINT OYSTERS
6. Jack likes the __________ he got on his birthday.
POINTS JOY TOYS
7. Mom wraps the meat in __________ .
HATS FOIL SOY
8. My Dad puts __________ in the car.
OIL POINT VOICE

Write the following on the board: avoid, poison, coil. Follow the same procedure as above to draw attention to the OI letter pair and use the verbal fill-in-the-blanks to reinforce meaning.

Worksheets 84A/B: Read the instructions aloud. Assist as necessary to determine picture labels or decode, but encourage the children to work as independently as possible.

ACTIVITY 2: WRITING

Write the following on the board: Ahoy! Do you enjoy hoisting the sails or is it too much toil?

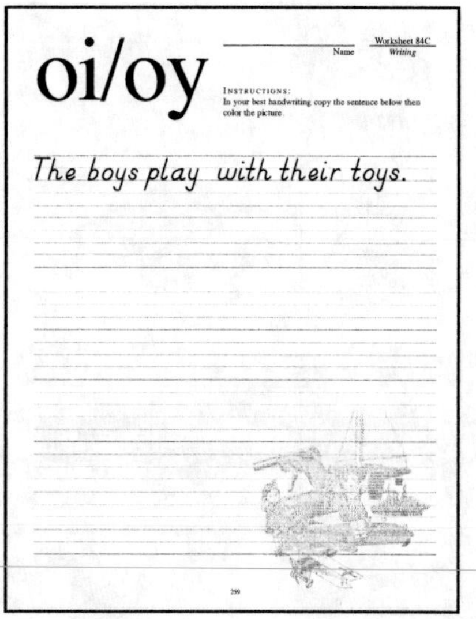

oi/oy

Name ______ Worksheet 84C *Writing*

INSTRUCTIONS: In your best handwriting copy the sentence below then color the picture.

The boys play with their toys.

Assist the children to decode and read the sentence aloud. Invite students to the board to copy the OI/OY words in the sentence.

Worksheet 84C: Read the instructions aloud. Monitor the students' progress as they work independently.

Lesson 85
Target: OI/OY, Review

ACTIVITY 1: ART ACTIVITY

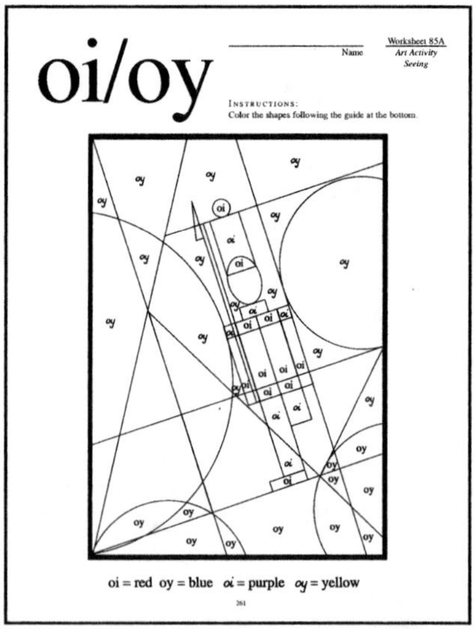
oi/oy

Name

Worksheet 85A
Art Activity
Seeing

Instructions:
Color the shapes following the guide at the bottom.

oi = red oy = blue *oi* = purple *oy* = yellow

261

Draw an artist's palette on the board and label the paint splotches according to the key at the bottom of Worksheet 85A.

Worksheet 85A: Read the instructions aloud. Monitor the students' progress as they work independently.

ACTIVITY 2: REVIEW OF BEGINNING BLENDS

Play the song Crash! Swing! Squash! for the children encouraging them to sing along.

Write the following letter pairs on the board: BL, FL, TR, GR, CR, FR, DR. Review the sounds made by each letter pair.

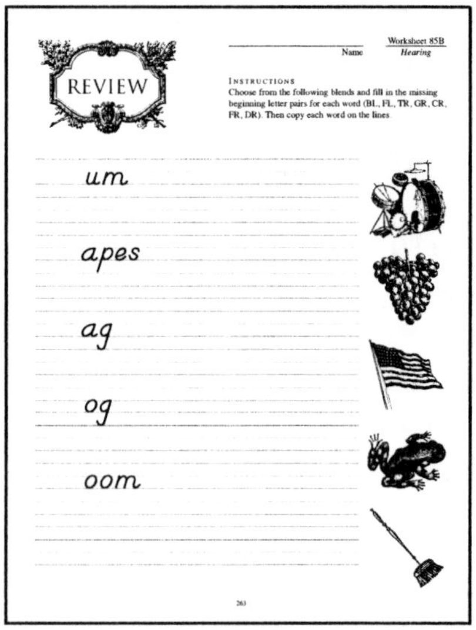
REVIEW

Name

Worksheet 85B
Hearing

Instructions
Choose from the following blends and fill in the missing beginning letter pairs for each word (BL, FL, TR, GR, CR, FR, DR). Then copy each word on the lines.

um

apes

ag

og

oom

263

Invite students to give you examples of words which begin with each of these blends. (Be careful with TR and DR, due to the similarity to CH and J!) Write these words on the board, leaving off the initial blend letters and allowing the child who offered that word to come to the board and fill in the needed letter pair to complete the word.

Continue until you have a word example for each of the blends.

Worksheet 85B: Read the instructions aloud. Monitor the students' progress as they work independently.

ACTIVITY 3: REVIEW OF ENDING SOUNDS

Play a modified riddle game this time. Tell the children you are thinking of a word which means a large boat. Start the word by saying the initial sounds SHI..., but leaving off the final sound.

Challenge the children to tell you what sound is needed to finish the word and answer the riddle. Write the word on the board, leaving off the final letter. Invite a student to the board to fill in the P and complete the word.

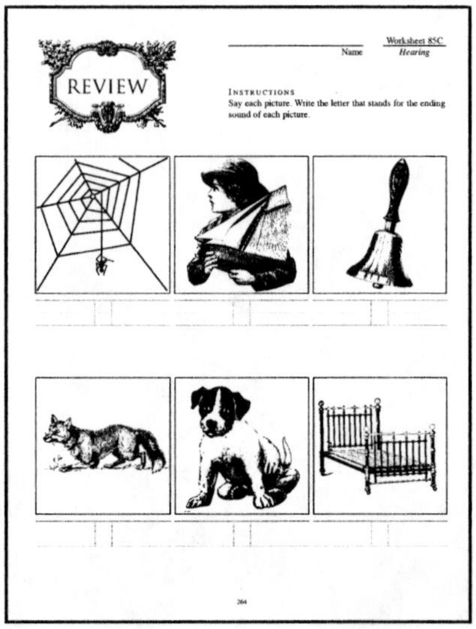
REVIEW

Name

Worksheet 85C
Hearing

Instructions
Say each picture. Write the letter that stands for the ending sound of each picture.

264

Continue in the same manner to elicit words ending in B, T, LL (assist with spelling here!), X, G, D. (Examples: crab, hat, pill, box, bag, food)

Worksheet 85C: Read the instructions aloud. Affirm label choices and Monitor the students' progress as they work independently.

Archives: Blends Edition.

Lesson 86
Target: OI/OY Reading and Spelling
List 4

ACTIVITY 1: READING WORDS

Write the words found on Worksheet 86A on the board. Invite students to decode and read each one, allow them to use them in original sentences.

Worksheet 86A: Read the instructions aloud. Use any of the previous variations or techniques for eliciting student responses.

Variations for prompting the reading of words on this sheet include: numbering the words and calling on students to read them by the designated number, verbal "fill-in-the-blanks," pointing to the written word on the board and having students point to the corresponding printed word on the sheet, riddle clues, categorizing on the basis of beginning sound, middle vowel, or ending letter group, spelling patterns, etc.

oi/oy

Worksheet 86A
Reading

Name

INSTRUCTIONS:
Read up and down the word columns. Circle those words that are OI/OY.

bake	pray	horn
boil	boil	coin
cake	toys	point
coil	hike	park
ride	boy	soil
rope	joy	join
dime	jump	

265

ACTIVITY 2: SPELLING LIST 4

Write the words found on Worksheets 86B on the board. Assist the children in decoding and reading each one.

Define as necessary and use in original sentences.

Invite students to the board to copy them in their best writing. Monitor their stroke direction and order.

Spell each word and have students echo the spelling after you. Alert them that this is their next spelling list and that they must study these words carefully over the next week!

Worksheets 86B: Read the instructions aloud. Monitor the students' progress as they work independently.

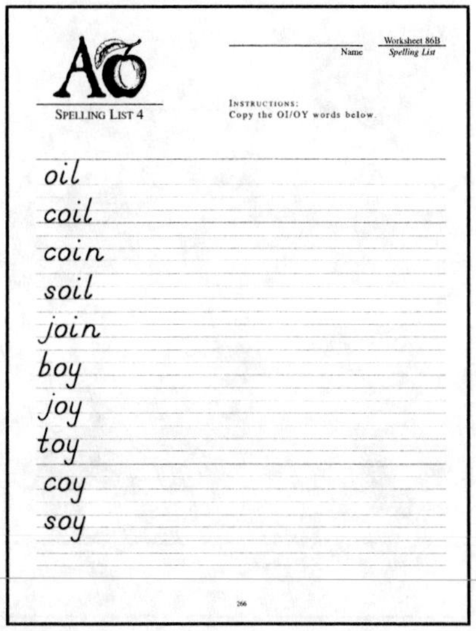

Worksheet 86B
Spelling List

Name

SPELLING LIST 4

INSTRUCTIONS:
Copy the OI/OY words below.

oil
coil
coin
soil
join
boy
joy
toy
coy
soy

266

Percival's Pairs: Using ING, ANG, ONG, blends, long vowels Y as I, OA, OE OW, OO, and OI.

LESSON 87
REVIEW: HEARING AND WRITING

ACTIVITY 1: HEARING IR

Write the word "bird" on the board. Call on a student to read it aloud.

Circle the IR in the middle of the word. Ask the children what sound is made by IR in this word.

Write the word "card" on the board. Call on a student to read it aloud.

Circle the AR in the middle of this word. Ask what sound is made by AR in this word.

Write the word "share" on the board. Call on a student to read it aloud.

Circle the AR in this word and ask what sound is made by this letter pair. Contrast this sound of AR with the previous one. Remind them that one uses the A as "ah" and the other uses A as short A.

Write the word "form" on the board. Call on a student to read it aloud.

Circle the OR in this words and ask what sound is made by this letter pair. Draw attention to the long O sound.

Tell the children you will be reading a list of words today which will contain each of these sounds. They are only to "wiggle their good listening rabbit ears" when they hear IR. Some of the words will also have AR (pronounced both ways as above) or OR, but they are ONLY to be listening for IR.

Caution them that this will be tricky so they must listen very carefully today.

Read the following words slowly and distinctly, giving time for student responses:

shirt	park	dare	bird	dirty	torn
horse	skirt	farm	careful	first	start
morning	fort	girl	pear	sir	stir

Continue with this activity as long as necessary to insure careful discrimination of the vowel + R blends.

Worksheet 87A: Read the instructions aloud. Call on students to label the pictures and monitor as they respond as indicated.

Row 1: horse, tent, shirt
Row 2: desk, bird, girl
Row 3 necklace, yo-yo, pear

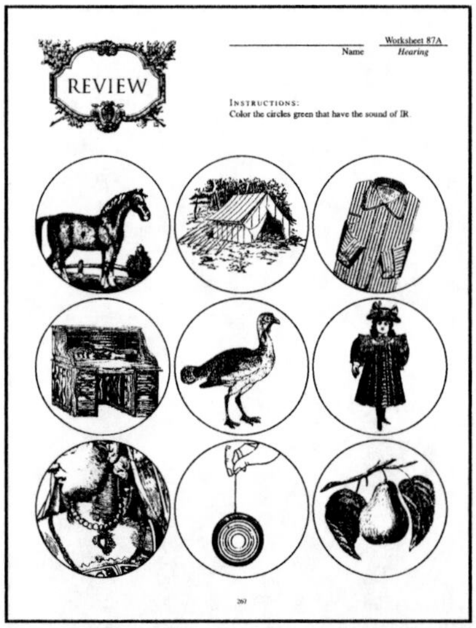

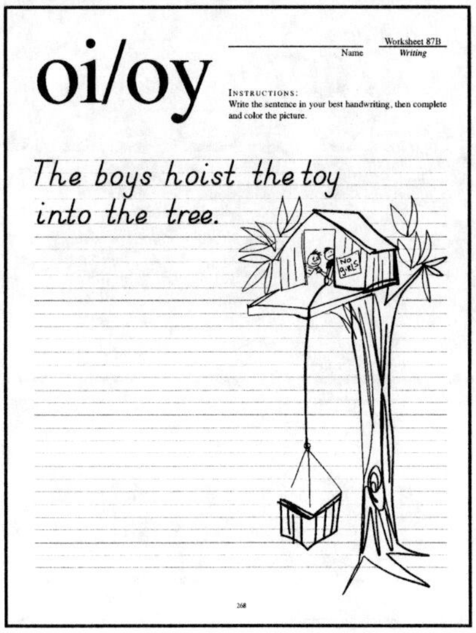
Worksheet 87B
Name
Writing

oi/oy

INSTRUCTIONS:
Write the sentence in your best handwriting, then complete and color the picture.

The boys hoist the toy into the tree.

268

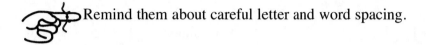

ACTIVITY 2: WRITING

Write the sentence found on Worksheet 87B on the board. Invite students one at a time to come and copy words of the sentence (each student to copy one word).

Invite the class to read the sentence aloud and in unison.

Worksheet 87B: Read the instructions aloud. Monitor as they copy the sentence.

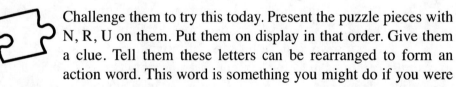

Remind them about careful letter and word spacing.

LESSON 88
SCRAMBLED WORDS AND VOCABULARY FOR A TALE OF SIR GALAHAD

ACTIVITY 1: SCRAMBLED WORDS

Tell the children that today they will learn a new game! Ask if anyone has ever played "Scrabble." Children who have may explain to the rest of the class how the game is played. Emphasize that the main idea is to figure out what words can be made from a group of mixed-up letters.

Challenge them to try this today. Present the puzzle pieces with N, R, U on them. Put them on display in that order. Give them a clue. Tell them these letters can be rearranged to form an action word. This word is something you might do if you were in a hurry.

Rearrange the letters at random. Attempt to sound out various incorrect combinations. Allow students to suggest letter order and, finally, assemble the word "run." Celebrate the correct answer with the children.

Continue in the same manner to form the words "pan," "fix," "rub," and any others you may choose. Stick to simple CVC words for now.

Worksheet 88A: Read the instructions aloud. Caution them that the mixed up words are not beside the right pictures! The pictures are clues for what the words will be when the letters are unscrambled. They should draw lines from the letter groups to the correct pictures, then reassemble the letters in order to form the word which labels that picture. You may want to do the first one for them to demonstrate how this is done.

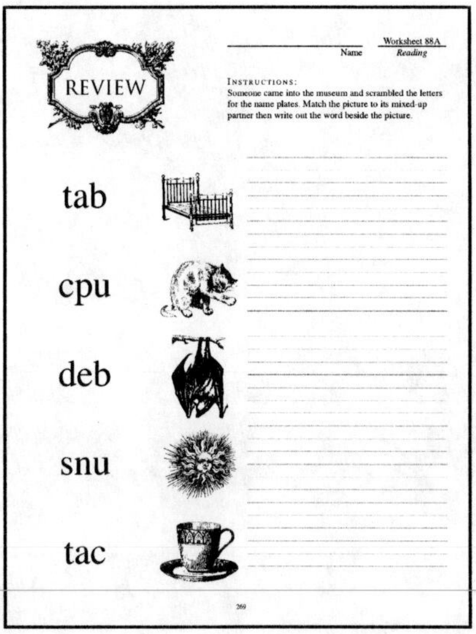
Worksheet 88A
Name
Reading

REVIEW

INSTRUCTIONS:
Someone came into the museum and scrambled the letters for the name plates. Match the picture to its mixed-up partner then write out the word beside the picture.

tab
cpu
deb
snu
tac

269

ACTIVITY 2: VOCABULARY AND SPECIAL WORDS FOR A TALE OF SIR GALAHAD

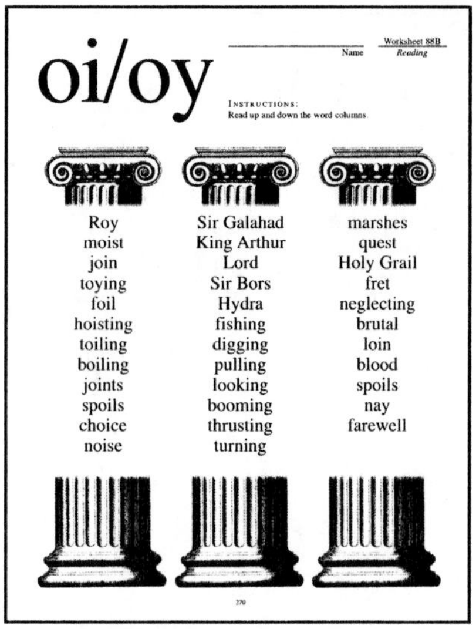
Worksheet 88B
Reading
Name

oi/oy

INSTRUCTIONS:
Read up and down the word columns

Roy	Sir Galahad	marshes
moist	King Arthur	quest
join	Lord	Holy Grail
toying	Sir Bors	fret
foil	Hydra	neglecting
hoisting	fishing	brutal
toiling	digging	loin
boiling	pulling	blood
joints	looking	spoils
spoils	booming	nay
choice	thrusting	farewell
noise	turning	

Write the words found on Worksheet 88B on the board. Guide the children through the decoding and reading of these words.

Define unfamiliar words and use in original sentences. The next lesson lists their meanings as they are used in the next story.

Worksheet 88B: Read the instructions aloud. Use any of the previous techniques for eliciting student response.

The word "blood" uses OO pronounced as short U. The only other common word in which this occurs is "flood." Describe it as an unusual sound for OO and that it is not used very often, so they need not experiment with it. You will remind them when they get to this word in the story. In addition, pay particular attention to "Hydra." A picture (from the next book) of this mythical beast would be helpful in defining and describing it.

LESSON 89
READING A TALE OF SIR GALAHAD

ACTIVITY 1: READING ALOUD

This story is based on the legends of King Arthur and the Knights of the Round Table and their search for the Holy Grail (cup of Christ's final Passover meal). Many regard Sir Thomas Malory's work on Arthur the definitive tale. The saga was built up over the centuries in Celtic lore and takes us from before Arthur's birth to the final demise of Camelot. The struggle with mythical beasts is a familiar theme in popular fairy tales, and Galahad is a classic fairy hero.

The following vocabulary and expressions are used:

oysters—clam-like shellfish
nets—meshed fabric used for catching fish
marshes—wetlands, generally by the sea
those of the Table—knights of the "Round Table"
tarry—stay, delay
quest—journey with a goal
Hydra—multi-headed beast
fret—worry
God has made me pure—cleansed from sin by faith in Christ
toying—cruelly played with
foil—spoil, thwart
hoisting—pulling

thrusting—pushing forcibly
toiling—working
boiling with anger—furious
neglecting—ignoring
fray—battle
brutal—harsh, difficult
throbbing—aching, severely
joints—shoulders, elbows, hips and knees
coiling—winding up
curb—slow down, stop
loin—stomach
oozing—flowing out slowly
in these parts—in this area of the country
spoils—plunder, items given or taken after battle
nay—no
coins—money
Prize—Holy Grail (upper case because of what it refers to)
farewell—goodbye, take care

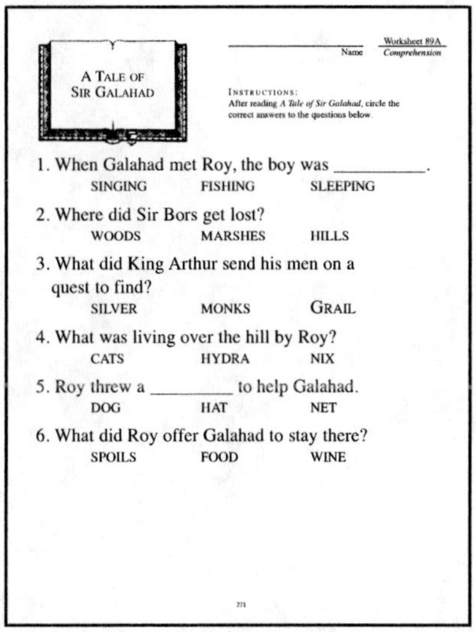
Worksheet 89A
Name
Comprehension

A TALE OF SIR GALAHAD

INSTRUCTIONS:
After reading *A Tale of Sir Galahad*, circle the correct answers to the questions below.

1. When Galahad met Roy, the boy was ___________.
   SINGING FISHING SLEEPING
2. Where did Sir Bors get lost?
   WOODS MARSHES HILLS
3. What did King Arthur send his men on a quest to find?
   SILVER MONKS GRAIL
4. What was living over the hill by Roy?
   CATS HYDRA NIX
5. Roy threw a _________ to help Galahad.
   DOG HAT NET
6. What did Roy offer Galahad to stay there?
   SPOILS FOOD WINE

271

Guide the children through the round robin reading of the story. Draw attention to main characters, ideas, and events as you proceed.

Some items for discussion may include: What gave Sir Galahad his courage? Why doesn't he want the "spoils"? Whose voice boomed from the sky?

ACTIVITY 2: READING COMPREHENSION

Worksheet 89A: Read the instructions aloud. Assist the children to respond as indicated. Monitor the students' progress as they work independently.

ACTIVITY 3: ART ACTIVITY

Worksheet 89B: Read the instructions aloud. Help the students as they work. Allow several days for the project to dry.

Worksheet 89B
Name
Art Activity

A TALE OF SIR GALAHAD

INSTRUCTIONS:
After reading *A Tale of Sir Galahad*, recreate some of the strange fish or perhaps even the hydra using the sand dough receipe below.

SUPPLIES:
Ingredients:
4 cups sand
2 cups cornstarch
1 tbl + 1 tsp Cream of Tartar
3 cups hot water

INSTRUCTIONS:
Mix sand, cornstarch and cream of tartar in large saucepan. Stir in hot water. Cook over medium heat, stirring constantly until water is absorbed and mixture is too stiff to stir. Cool until it can be handled.
Store in airtight container—air dries in a few days.

272

Lesson 90
Target: OU/OW

Play the Shout song for the children encouraging them to sing along.

ACTIVITY 1: HEARING

Tell the children it is time for a new sound!

Show the children the flashcard with the OU/OW on it. Have them hear the sound of OW as in "crown." Read the following aloud and challenge them to see if they can be good sound detectives and figure out what sound it is!

"The proud scout howled loudly when he found a brown cow eating flowers around the house down by the hay mow."

Read it several times if necessary until the children can tell you what sound is heard over and over in this sentence.

When they do, tease them slightly by asking "Where does it hurt? You keep saying "ow!"" Affirm that the sound today is OU/OW.

Tell them it can be spelled two different ways and write OU on the left side of the board and OW on the right side.

Now challenge the children to tell you which of these letter pairs they have seen before. (OW) Do they remember how it has been pronounced up to this point? (as long O) Affirm that OW is another one of those letter pairs which can make more than one sound. They will have to experiment with these two sounds when they see OW in words. However, for today, it will only make the sound like OU.

Challenge them to listen again for this sound in the following words. Tell them to watch out—it may be at the beginning, the middle, or the end of the word!

out	rug	round	song	sound	sour
down	now	load	fuel	growl	proud
rule	love	crowd	flour	color	town

Praise their terrific listening!

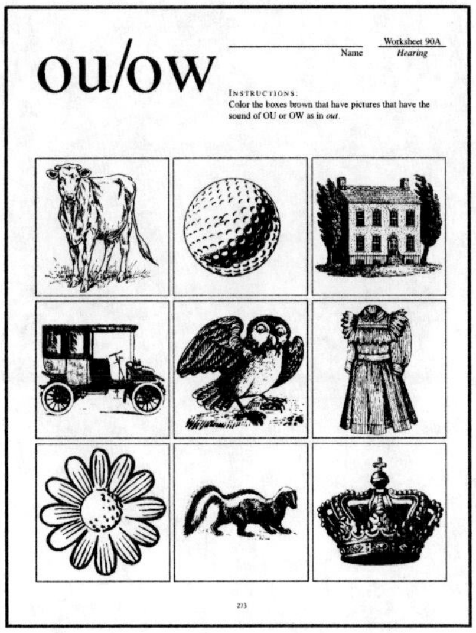

Worksheet 90A: Read the instructions aloud. Assist the children to label the pictures as necessary. Monitor their work.

Row 1: cow, ball, house
Row 2: car, owl, dress
Row 3 flower, skunk, crown

Give them their museum bag. Allow them time to go through the house and collect items that have the R blend sound to make their own museum. If you are teaching in a school setting, instruct the children to take the bag home and bring in objects the following day.

ACTIVITY 2: SEEING

On the left side of the board, under the OU, write the following: sound, around, bound, loud.

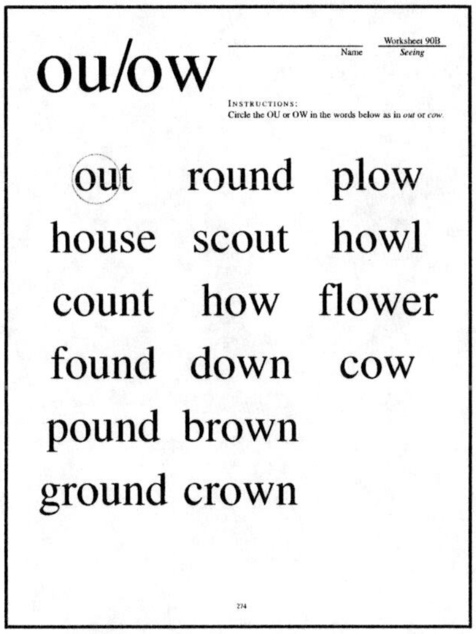

On the right side of the board, under the OW, write the following: now, town, gown, power. Assist the children to decode and read the words aloud. Define as necessary and use each word in an original sentence.

Invite children to the board to circle the OU or OW in each word.

Worksheet 90B: Read the instructions aloud. Monitor as the children respond as indicated. Assist them to read the words and use them in original sentences.

You may want to give the students the coloring page along with the flashcard. Read the information about the artist to your students before they color the picture.

LESSON 91
SPELLING TEST 4 AND VOCABULARY FOR HOWARD SAVES A HOUND

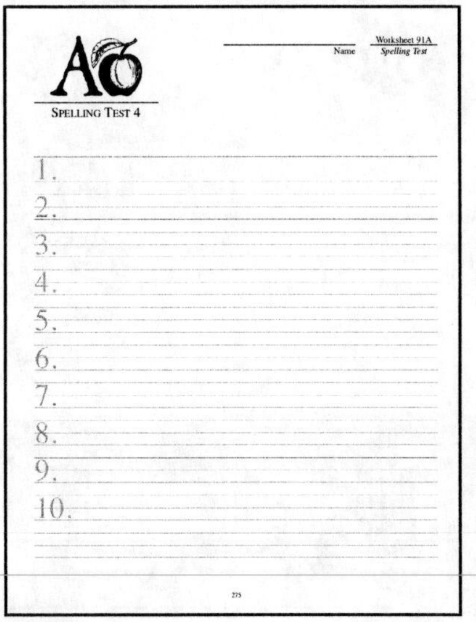

Play the Shout song for the children encouraging them to sing along.

ACTIVITY 1: SPELLING TEST 4

Worksheet 91A: Administer the test on Spelling List 4. Read each word once, use it in a sentence, then repeat it. Do not give any other sound or letter clues.

ACTIVITY 2: VOCABULARY FOR HOWARD SAVES A HOUND

Write the words found on Worksheet 91B on the board.

Make sure you write the words using OW as the OU sound in the same column or area and the words using OW as long O on another column or area.

Call students to the board to circle the OU/OW in each word. Remind them of the two sounds of OW—long O which they learned before, and the new sound of OU.

Draw attention to the list of words on the board which utilizes OW as long O. Ask if anyone remembers what we can do to this letter pair to help us know that it makes long O. If no one remembers, demonstrate this for them. Decode the word and read aloud. Use it in an original sentence. Tell them that all of the OW letter pairs in that area or column use the long O sound.

Invite students to the board to backslash each W and draw a macron over the O in each word.

Affirm that all the OW words in the column or area with the OU words make the same sound as OU.

There is no way to know which sound to use other than experience. The use of the symbols will help to remind them at this point in their reading.

Affirm that you will assist them to use the correct sound when they come to OW words in the next story. Also, for this exercise and story, the word "route" is pronounced with OU, not as long U. You may discuss differences in pronunciation with the children—people in different places say things differently!

In addition, the word "hour" utilizes silent H. Point this out to the children and assist them to pronounce it accordingly. You may want to compare and contrast it with the word "our," noting how the spelling affects the meaning. (They will be receiving formal instruction on silent H in Lesson 141.)

Assist the children to read the words on the board, define according to the meanings listed in the next lesson, use each word in original sentences.

Worksheet 91B: Read the instructions aloud. Use any of the previous variations for eliciting student response.

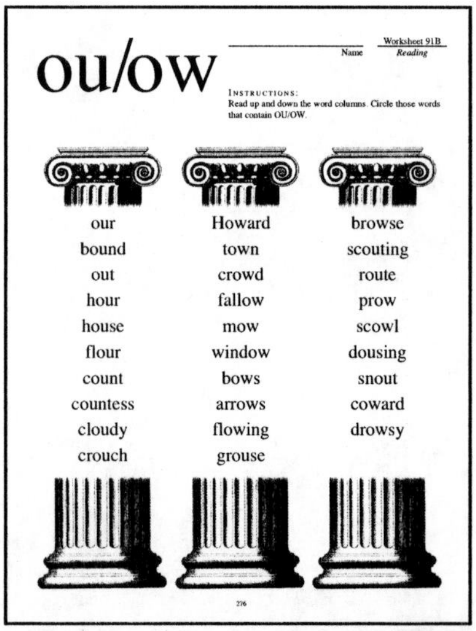
ou/ow

Name ______ Worksheet 91B *Reading*

INSTRUCTIONS: Read up and down the word columns. Circle those words that contain OU/OW.

our	Howard	browse
bound	town	scouting
out	crowd	route
hour	fallow	prow
house	mow	scowl
flour	window	dousing
count	bows	snout
countess	arrows	coward
cloudy	flowing	drowsy
crouch	grouse	

276

Lesson 92
Target: OU/OW and Spelling List 5

Play the Shout song for the children encouraging them to sing along.

ACTIVITY 1: READING OU/OW WORDS

Write the following on the board: town, round, loud. Do not decode or read them aloud.

Tell the children you will play the riddle game today. Give them a clue which will define one of the words above. For example: This is a place where many people live, but it's not as big as a city. What is it? (town)

Call on students to come to the board, point to the word which answers the riddle, and then read it aloud.
Continue in the same manner with the other two words. Present another group of three OU/OW words (all using the target sound OU, not OW as long O!) and repeat the activity.

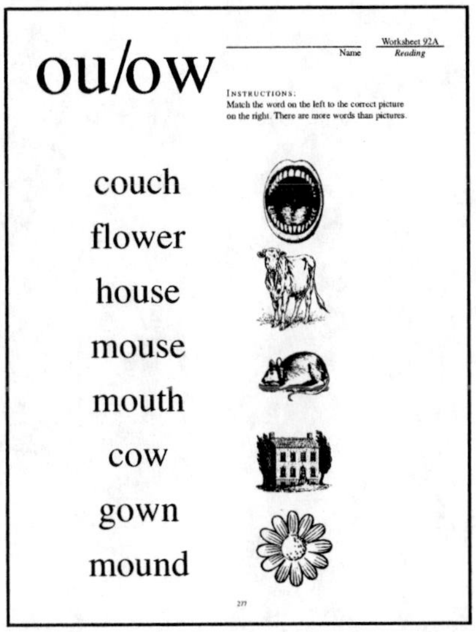

Worksheet 92A: Read the instructions aloud. Allow the children to work independently. Give clues to assist them to label the pictures, but do not give them the label words. Encourage them to read through the word list to find the best match for each picture.

ACTIVITY 2: SPELLING LIST 5

Write the words found on Worksheet 92B on the board, along with guidelines.

Invite children to the board to copy the words. Monitor their letter formation and spacing.

Decode and read the words aloud. Use in original sentences.

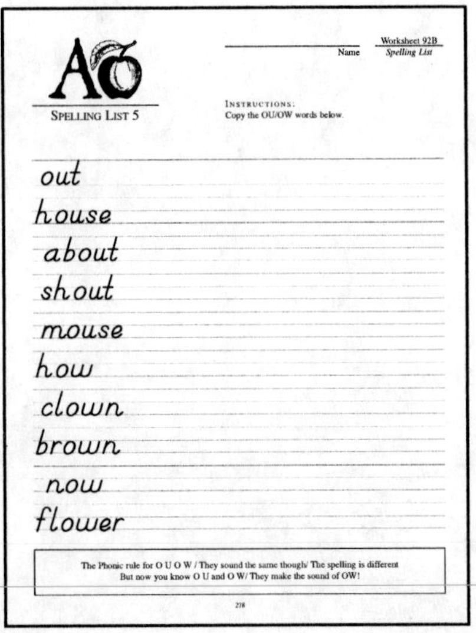

Worksheet 92B: Read the instructions aloud. Monitor the students' progress as they work independently.

Lesson 93
Reading HOWARD SAVES A HOUND

ACTIVITY 1: READING ALOUD

This story chronicles a young boy's first hunt during the Middle Ages and his act of bravery. The following vocabulary and expressions are used:

bound—jump
hour is near—it is time
estate—large property
Count/Countess—titles of landowners in the Middle Ages
kennels—caged areas for animals
run the hounds—manage the dogs during the hunt
huntsmen—hunters
grouse—wild game birds
fallow deer—broad antlered deer found in Europe
sleek—smooth and glossy
browse—graze
mount—to get up onto
howl—to cry out in a long, mournful way
scouting—searching
beaters—those who try to make the prey come out of hiding
prowl—hunt
thicket—many bushes grouped together
bowmen—archers
route—path
prow—front of a boat
scowl—deep frown
dousing—immersion in water
sputter—to spit explosively
spouts—flows out like a fountain
stroke—to pet
snout—nose
bravery—act of courage
coward—fearful person
crouch—sit in a curled up position
drowsy—sleepy
glowing—feeling proud and contented

In addition, the following compound words are used: outside, inside, huntsmen, rowboat, today.

This story also contains the word "poor," which uses the more unusual sound of long O for OO. Assist the children to decode this when they come to it.

Guide the children through the round robin reading of the story. Call attention to main characters, ideas, and events as they occur.

Assist especially with the decoding of the two sounds of OW.

Some questions for discussion may include: What kinds of abilities should a hunting dog have? Why were the beaters hitting the bushes? Howard was pleased with his father's praise. How do you feel when your parents are proud of you?

ACTIVITY 2: READING COMPREHENSION

Tell the children you will be doing the next two worksheets together.

Worksheet 93A: Read the instructions aloud. Call on students to read the questions to the class and each of the answer choices. Determine which is the best answer to each question and monitor as they respond as indicated.

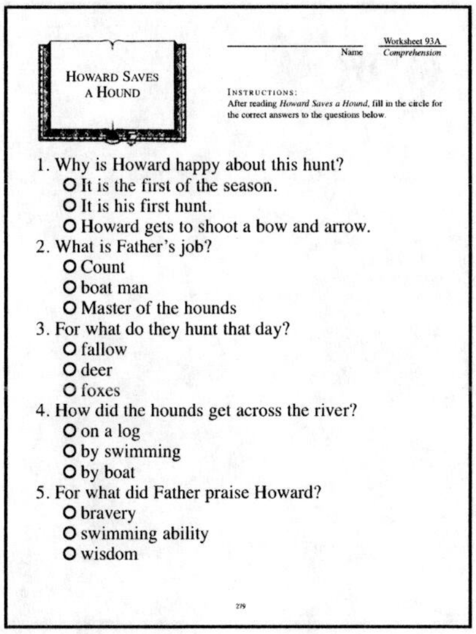

HOWARD SAVES A HOUND

Name

Worksheet 93A
Comprehension

INSTRUCTIONS:
After reading *Howard Saves a Hound*, fill in the circle for the correct answers to the questions below.

1. Why is Howard happy about this hunt?
   - O It is the first of the season.
   - O It is his first hunt.
   - O Howard gets to shoot a bow and arrow.
2. What is Father's job?
   - O Count
   - O boat man
   - O Master of the hounds
3. For what do they hunt that day?
   - O fallow
   - O deer
   - O foxes
4. How did the hounds get across the river?
   - O on a log
   - O by swimming
   - O by boat
5. For what did Father praise Howard?
   - O bravery
   - O swimming ability
   - O wisdom

LESSON 94
READING COMPREHENSION, WRITING, AND ART ACTIVITY

ACTIVITY 1: READING COMPREHENSION—CAUSE AND EFFECT

Briefly review the events from yesterday's story HOWARD SAVES A HOUND.

Explain to the children that some actions or event cause others to happen. Describe the following scene: A mouse creeps into the classroom. Some children, (and the teacher!), scream. Ask the children: "What made the children and the teacher scream?" (the presence of the mouse)

Explain that the mouse coming into the room would be the "cause" of the screaming. The screaming is the "effect" the mouse had on some of the people in the room. Other effects might be to stand on a chair, run away from it, or even try to chase or catch it.

In the story HOWARD SAVES A HOUND there are many "causes" which have "effects." Present Worksheet 94A and tell the children you will be working on this together today.

Worksheet 94A: Read the instructions aloud. Before cutting anything out, call on children to read through each of the cause and effect sentences. Then have the children cut out the entire strip of effect boxes. Go through the cause sentences one by one, choosing the effect sentence which answers each. Allow the children to cut out the effect sentence and glue it immediately beside the cause sentence it matches. Continue systematically in the same manner to complete the page.

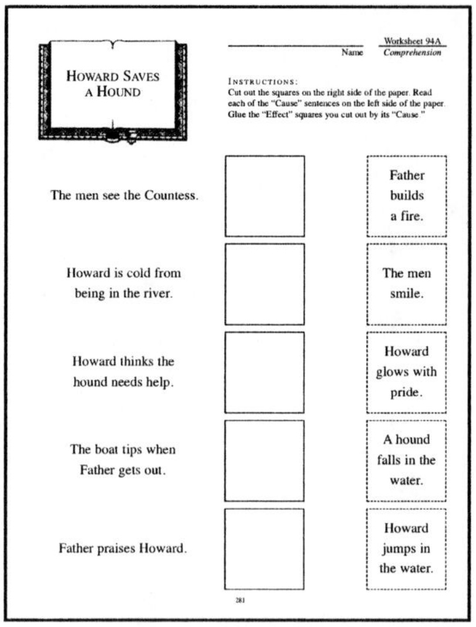
Worksheet 94A
Name
Comprehension

HOWARD SAVES A HOUND

INSTRUCTIONS:
Cut out the squares on the right side of the paper. Read each of the "Cause" sentences on the left side of the paper. Glue the "Effect" squares you cut out by its "Cause."

The men see the Countess.		Father builds a fire.
Howard is cold from being in the river.		The men smile.
Howard thinks the hound needs help.		Howard glows with pride.
The boat tips when Father gets out.		A hound falls in the water.
Father praises Howard.		Howard jumps in the water.

ACTIVITY 2: WRITING

Worksheet 94B: Present the worksheet and read the instructions aloud. Call on a student to read the sentence and monitor as the children copy the sentence in their best handwriting.

Remind about the "FOUR P's" if you haven't done so in a while!

ou/ow
Worksheet 94B
Name
Writing

INSTRUCTIONS:
Write the sentence in your best handwriting, and color the picture.

The brown mouse runs over the mound.

ACTIVITY 3: ART ACTIVITY

Present a finished example of the art activity described on Worksheet 94C. Prepare a table with the necessary materials and assist the children to create their own hunting hound pictures. Students press their forefinger to an ink pad and then place it horizontally on a piece of paper to make the head of a hound. Then put another fingerprint horizontally under the first to make the body. The body can be made longer by putting several fingerprints overlapping in a row. Using a fine tip marker, students can draw on whiskers, eyes, nose, legs, and tail. Let students make several hounds on their page, making some have short bodies and some have long bodies. Students can give their hounds names and write them underneath. They may also wish to decorate a background. Leaves on trees can be made with fingerprints and green ink.

Worksheet 94C: Monitor as they work on their pictures independently.

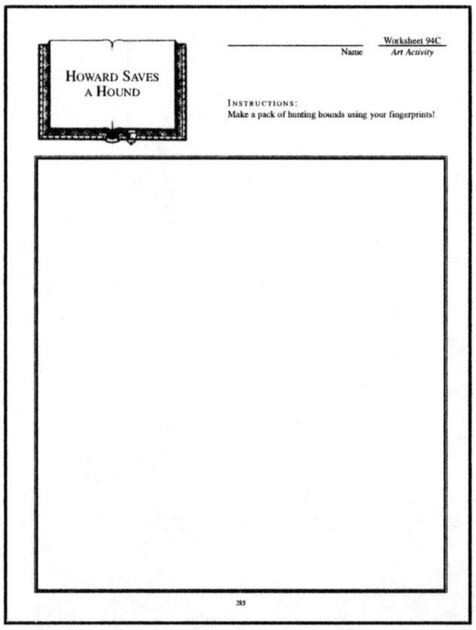
Worksheet 94C
Name
Art Activity

HOWARD SAVES A HOUND

INSTRUCTIONS:
Make a pack of hunting hounds using your fingerprints!

LESSON 95
TARGET: SOFT C (AS IN "LACE")

ACTIVITY 1: HEARING AND SEEING

Show the children the flashcard with the Soft C on it. Have them hear the sound of Soft C as in "lace."

Ask the children if any of them know the story "The Borrowers." Explain that the story is about a group of very tiny people who survive by "borrowing" items from big people (like us!). They often take things which are not very valuable and usually not noticed or missed—safety pins, old scraps of paper and fabric, stamps, etc.

Big people sometimes think they have lost or misplaced these things, but actually, they have been "borrowed" by the "borrowers!"

Tell them that the letter C is a "borrower." It doesn't really have a sound of its own. They have learned it so far as K, which is the sound of the letter K. Now they will learn its other "borrowed" sound. Write the following on the board: cent, center, cellar.

Now, tell them that if we were to use the K sound to decode these words, they wouldn't make any sense.

Explain that the other "borrowed" sound of C is S. Sometimes it is called Soft C. Read the words aloud, using the S sound for C. Ask the children if the words are now meaningful. Define them and use in original sentences.

Some students may think that the word "cent" is "sent" and try to define it that way. Explain that these are two different words because of their spelling, like others they have had. You may want to write "sent" on the board and define both words simultaneously to show the difference in meaning based on spelling.

Ask what other letter they see in all of these words, paired with the C. (E) Affirm that when C and E are together, the C will make the S sound.

Explain that this happens at the end of words also. Write the following on the board: FACE, GRACE, MICE.

Invite children to the board to circle the CE in each word. Remind them that the E will be silent at the end of these words. Ask them what that will do to the first vowel (make it long). Often when they see CE at the end of words, the C will make the S sound and the first vowel will be long and say its name.
Assist the children to decode each of the above words using this pattern. Define and use the words in original sentences.

Explain that there are times when the first vowel will not be long, however. This occurs when there is another letter between the vowel and CE.

Write the following on the board: PRINCE, FENCE, DANCE.

Ask the children what other letter they see between the first vowel and the CE. (N) Tell them that when this happens, the first vowel stays short.

Challenge the children to tell you what little symbol they have learned to mark a vowel which makes the short sound. (breve) If they cannot remember, remind them and place the breve over each of the first vowels in these words.

Decode them, read aloud, define, and use in original sentences. Now, tell them that C will make the S sound when it is paired with two other letters also. Write the following on the board: cinder, lacy, fancy.

What letters do they see after the C in these words? (I and Y) Affirm that in each word, C will make the S sound.

Assist them to decode and read the words accordingly. Draw attention to the long A in "lacy" and the short A in "fancy." Ask why the vowels make different sounds in these words (the final Y in "lacy" is making the first vowel long, the N in "fancy" goes with the first syllable and makes the first vowel short—or it comes between the vowel and the CY, making the vowel short).

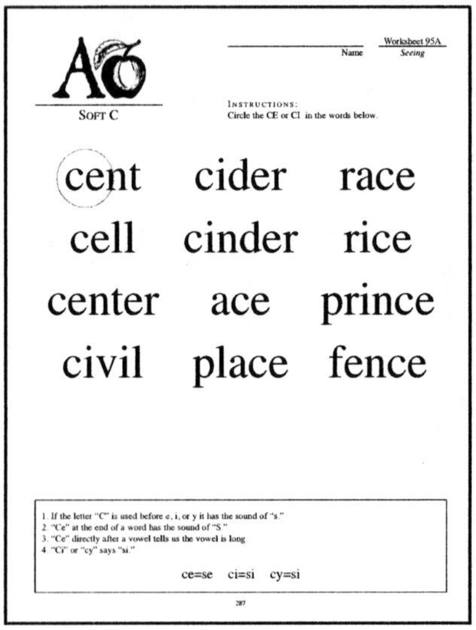

Worksheet 95A
Seeing

Name

SOFT C

INSTRUCTIONS:
Circle the CE or CI in the words below.

cent	cider	race
cell	cinder	rice
center	ace	prince
civil	place	fence

1. If the letter "C" is used before e, i, or y it has the sound of "s."
2. "Ce" at the end of a word has the sound of "S."
3. "Ce" directly after a vowel tells us the vowel is long
4. "Ci" or "cy" says "si."

ce=se ci=si cy=si

287

Give them their museum bag. Allow them time to go through the house and collect items that have the R blend sound to make their own museum. If you are teaching in a school setting, instruct the children to take the bag home and bring in objects the following day.

Worksheet 95A: Read the instructions aloud. Monitor as they respond as indicated. Assist them to decode and read the words. Define and use each in an original sentence.

Worksheet 95B: Read the instructions aloud. Remind the children that they are listening for "soft C" which is pronounced as S. When they hear S in these labels, it will be because that word is spelled with C. Allow the children to offer the labels for the pictures and monitor as they respond as indicated.

Row 1: lace, pencil, cigar
Row 2: hat, dice, cat
Row 3: yo-yo, box, mice

After doing this page, you may want to write the soft C word labels on the board so children can see that they are indeed spelled with C, not S.

You may want to give the students the coloring page along with the flashcard. Read the information about the artist to your students before they color the picture.

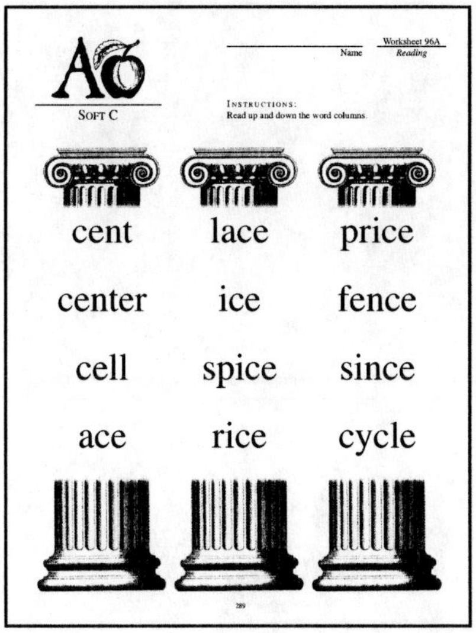

Worksheet 96A
Reading
Name

SOFT C

INSTRUCTIONS:
Read up and down the word columns.

cent	lace	price
center	ice	fence
cell	spice	since
ace	rice	cycle

LESSON 96
TARGET: SOFT C

ACTIVITY 1: READING WORDS

Write a big C on the board. Ask if anyone remembers what two sounds this letter "borrows." (K and S) Praise and affirm correct responses.

Ask if anyone remembers the letters which pair up with C to make it say S. (I, E, Y) Praise and affirm correct responses.

Write the words found on Worksheet 96A on the board. Invite students to come to the board and circle the C in each word.

Worksheet 96A: Read the instructions aloud. Assist the children to decode and read each one. Use any of the following variations to elicit student responses:

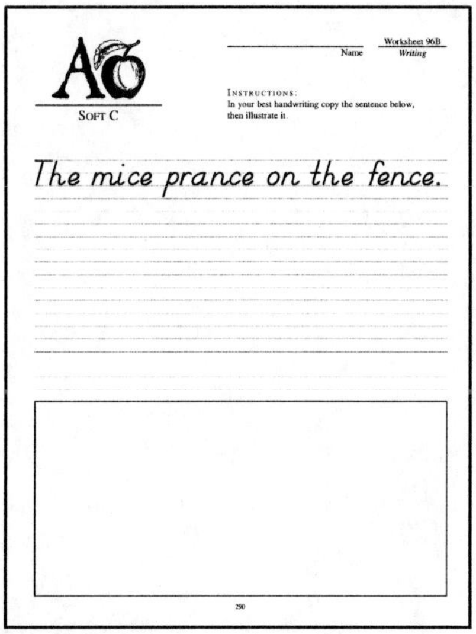

Worksheet 96B
Writing
Name

SOFT C

INSTRUCTIONS:
In your best handwriting copy the sentence below, then illustrate it.

The mice prance on the fence.

Variations for prompting the reading of words on this sheet include: numbering the words and calling on students to read them by the designated number, verbal "fill-in-the-blanks," pointing to the written word on the board and having students point to the corresponding printed word on the sheet, riddle clues, categorizing on the basis of vowel sounds or position of the target letter within the words.

ACTIVITY 2: WRITING

Worksheet 96B: Read the instructions aloud. Call on a student to read the sentence to the class. Monitor as they copy the sentence. Watch letter and word spacing carefully!

LESSON 97
MORE SOFT C WORDS AND SPELLING TEST 5

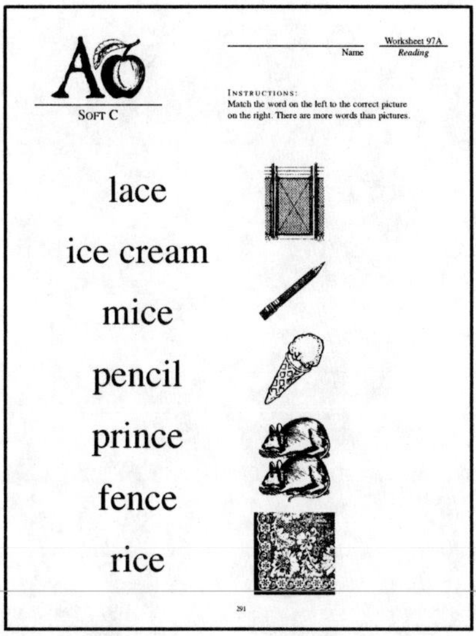

Worksheet 97A
Reading
Name

SOFT C

INSTRUCTIONS:
Match the word on the left to the correct picture on the right. There are more words than pictures.

lace
ice cream
mice
pencil
prince
fence
rice

ACTIVITY 1: READING SOFT C WORDS

Write the following on the board: race, center, dance. Play the riddle game by giving clues to define one of these words. Invite students to come to the board, point to the correct answer, and read it aloud.
Continue with each of the words above. Repeat the activity with the following words: December, cider, mercy. Draw attention to the use of ER in the word "mercy" and that the E is short.

Worksheet 97A: Read the instructions aloud. Assist the children to decode each of the choice words and then respond as indicated.

ACTIVITY 2: SPELLING TEST 5

Present Worksheet 97B: Administer the test on Spelling List 5. Read each word once, use it in a sentence, then repeat it. Do not give any other sound or letter clues.

Worksheet 97B
Spelling Test
Name

SPELLING TEST 5

1.
2.
3.
4.
5.
6.
7.
8.
9.
10.

The Phonic rule for O U O W / They sound the same though/ The spelling is different
But now you know O U and O W/ They make the sound of ____!

292

LESSON 98
TARGET: SOFT C AND SPELLING LIST 6

ACTIVITY 1: READING SENTENCES WITH SOFT C WORDS

Begin the lesson by playing a game of "verbal fill-in-the-blanks."

Write the following words on the board: fancy, trace, price. Read the following sentences to the children and invite them to determine which word best completes each sentence:

> Her dress for the ball was very ______________.
> I need to know the ______________ of that toy before I buy it.
> Can you ______________ the words on that page?

Allow them to circle the CE or CY in each of the above words. Discuss the reasons for the pronunciation of the vowel sounds in each word.

Write the following on the board: circus, peace, piece. Invite children to the board to circle the CE and CI in each word.

Call their attention to the CU in the word "circus." Ask what vowel comes after the C. (U) Ask if the C will be borrowing the S sound when it is paired with U. (NO) Affirm and praise correct responses.

Challenge them to tell you what sound C borrows when it is followed by U. (K)

Assist them to decode the word "circus" accordingly.

Underline the EA and IE in the other two words. Ask the children: "If the CE at the end will make the first vowels long, what sounds might each of these letter pairs make?" Affirm that EA could say long E or long A and IE could say long E or long I.

Give the children a hint. Tell them that these words sound exactly alike, although they are spelled differently. What sound can both EA and IE make which is the same sound? (long E)

Affirm and praise correct answers. Decode and read the words, using long

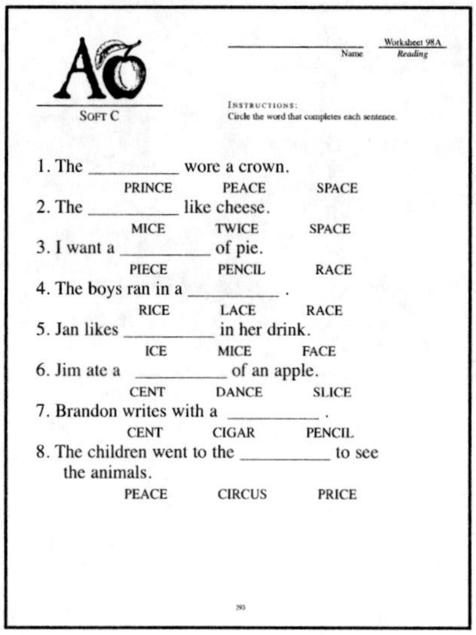

Worksheet 98A
Reading

Name

SOFT C

INSTRUCTIONS:
Circle the word that completes each sentence.

1. The __________ wore a crown.
   PRINCE PEACE SPACE
2. The __________ like cheese.
   MICE TWICE SPACE
3. I want a __________ of pie.
   PIECE PENCIL RACE
4. The boys ran in a __________ .
   RICE LACE RACE
5. Jan likes __________ in her drink.
   ICE MICE FACE
6. Jim ate a __________ of an apple.
   CENT DANCE SLICE
7. Brandon writes with a __________ .
   CENT CIGAR PENCIL
8. The children went to the __________ to see the animals.
   PEACE CIRCUS PRICE

293

E. They sound the same!

Again, tell them that the words mean different things, only because they are spelled differently. Define both words and use in original sentences.

Worksheet 98A: Read the instructions aloud. Call on students to read the questions and the answer choices. Monitor as they respond independently as indicated.

ACTIVITY 2: SPELLING LIST 6

Worksheet 98B: Spell each word and have students echo the spelling after you. Alert them that this is their next spelling list and that they must study these words carefully over the next week!

LESSON 99
ALPHABETICAL ORDER AND WRITING

Worksheet 98B
Spelling List

Name

SPELLING LIST 6

INSTRUCTIONS:
Copy the silent C words below

mice
race
cent
ice
face
nice
mince
space
dance
price

294

ACTIVITY 1: ALPHABETICAL ORDER

Write the following on index cards: PRINCE, PLACE, PACE.

For this activity homeschoolers should use pennies and the flashcards while in the school setting use children. Invite three students to the front of the class and give each of them a card. Have them decode and read the words aloud.

Tell them to find the flashcard which denotes the first letter of each word.

Affirm that it's crowded under the P!

Challenge the students to remember how we put words in alphabetical order if each of them begins with the same letter. (look at the second letter) Affirm and praise correct responses.

Now instruct the children with the cards to find the flashcards which depict the second letter of each of their words. Call the children's attention to the order of the words, based on the second letter of each word.
Reinforce that the only time we must go to the second letter to alphabetize words is when the first letters are the same.

Write the following on index cards: bounce, brace, lance. Proceed as above, alphabetizing by beginning letter only at first.

Now, tell the children that the two children whose words begin with B will still come before the child with the word "lance." However, they must stand side by side under the B according to the order of their SECOND letters.

Ask them which letter comes first in the alphabet: O or R. Affirm that O comes first. Arrange the two children under B to stand so that the child with the word "bounce" is to the left of the child with the word "brace" when viewed from the class.

Write each of the children's words on the board in a horizontal row in alphabetical order as they are standing: BOUNCE, BRACE, LANCE.

Affirm that this is the correct order for these three words. Write them again in a vertical column in order from top to bottom. Tell them that this is the way they would be written on a list.

Worksheet 99A: Read the instructions aloud. Allow the children to do the first and second lists independently. Remind them to number the words first, then copy them by number onto the lines provided. Assist them in the alphabetizing of the final set of words (with "pace" and "piece" on it).

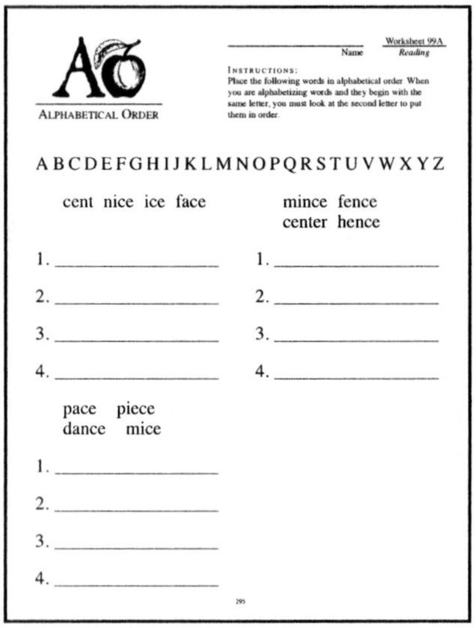
Worksheet 99A
Reading
Name
ALPHABETICAL ORDER
INSTRUCTIONS: Place the following words in alphabetical order. When you are alphabetizing words and they begin with the same letter, you must look at the second letter to put them in order.

A B C D E F G H I J K L M N O P Q R S T U V W X Y Z

cent nice ice face

1. ________
2. ________
3. ________
4. ________

mince fence
center hence

1. ________
2. ________
3. ________
4. ________

pace piece
dance mice

1. ________
2. ________
3. ________
4. ________

295

ACTIVITY 2: WRITING

Worksheet 99B: Read the instructions aloud. Assist the children to read the sentence. Discuss the use of the upper case for the word "France," find it on a map for them! Monitor as they copy the sentence independently.

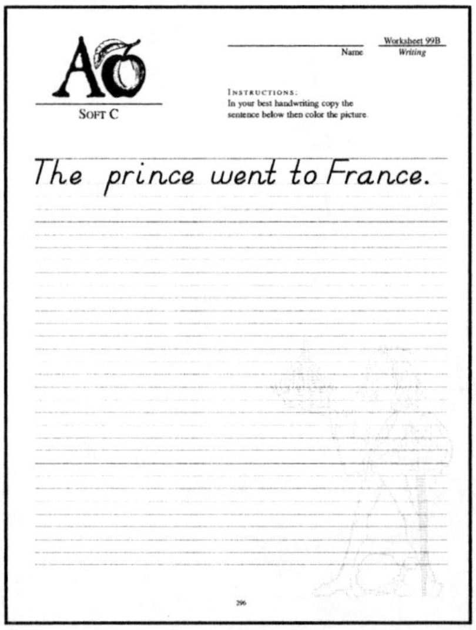
Worksheet 99B
Writing
Name
SOFT C
INSTRUCTIONS: In your best handwriting copy the sentence below then color the picture.

The prince went to France.

296

LESSON 100
TARGET: SOFT C AND REVIEW

ACTIVITY 1: SEEING AND READING

Write the following in a vertical column on the left side of the board: MERCY, CENTER, CINCH, PLACE.

Call students to the board to circle the CI, CE, or CY in each word. Assist them to decode and read the words. Define and use in original sentences. Now write the following in a vertical column down the right side of the board, in this order: CITRUS, CELLAR, RICE, FANCY.

Call on students to circle the CI, CE, or CY in each word. Assist them to decode and read the words. Define and use in original sentences.

Now challenge the children to draw a line to connect the words on the left with words on the right which have the same letter pairs in the same places. (For instance, "place" is a match with "rice," not "cellar," because the CE

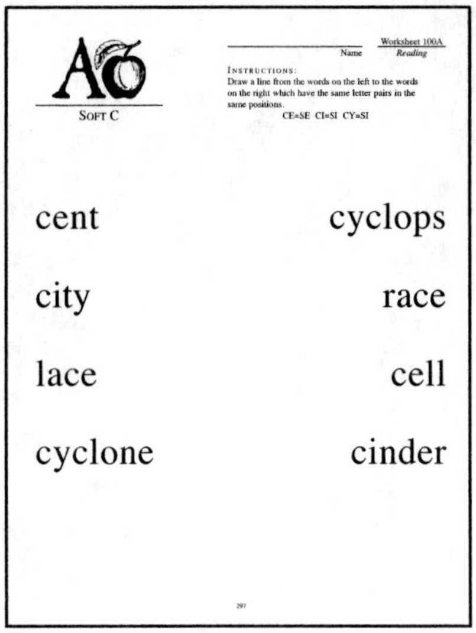

is at the END of these words.) Call on students to come to the board and draw lines to make matches accordingly.

Worksheet 100A
Reading
Name
Soft C
INSTRUCTIONS:
Draw a line from the words on the left to the words on the right which have the same letter pairs in the same positions.
CE=SE CI=SI CY=SI
cent
cyclops
city
race
lace
cell
cyclone
cinder

Worksheet 100A: Read the instructions aloud. Allow the children to circle or underline the CE, CI, or CY in each word and monitor as they respond as indicated. Call on students to read the words aloud, define, and use in sentences.

ACTIVITY 2: REVIEW

Play the How Many Sounds? song for the children encouraging them to sing along.

Review both the long and short sounds of each of the vowels.

Write them on the board with macrons and breves as you go over them.

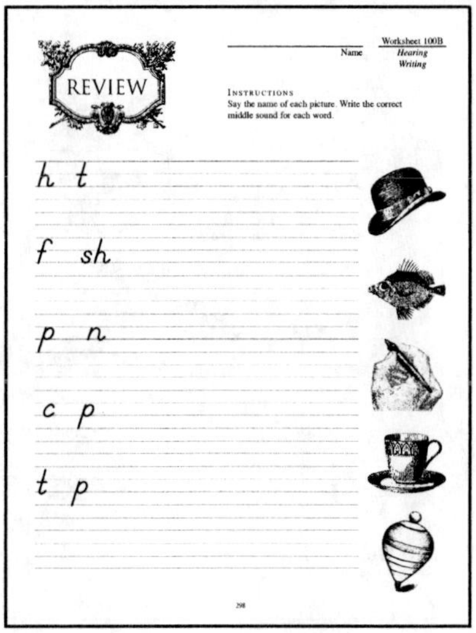

Brainstorm with the children to develop a list of three or four words which use the SHORT sound of each vowel. Write these on the board under or beside the appropriate vowel letter.

Worksheet 100B: Read the instructions aloud. Monitor the students' progress as they work independently.

Worksheet 100C: Test. This test is optional and is added to evaluate your students if you feel it is necessary at this time. The answers are worth 10 points each.

Lesson 101
Target: Soft C

ACTIVITY 1: HEARING AND SEEING

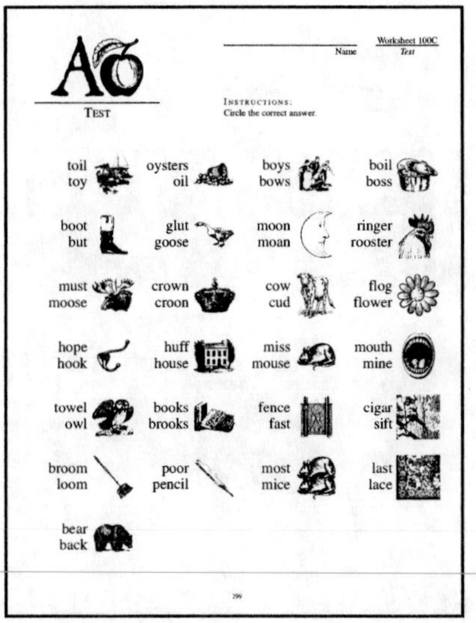

Write a large C in the center top of the board. Ask what two sounds are borrowed by the letter C. Write a lower case K in green marker or chalk on the left side of the board, slightly below the C, and a lower case S in orange marker or chalk on the right side of the board, slightly below the C.

Remind the children that the K sound of C is called its "hard" sound and the S sound of C is called its "soft" sound. They can remember this because "soft" starts with S.

Read the following words aloud and ask the children if they should be written under the K for the hard sound of C or the S for the soft sound, based on the beginning sound of each word:

candy cereal cookie celery cider cake

Write the words on the board under the correct "borrowed" sound of C as the children direct.

Read the words aloud again and challenge them to tell you to what category or group of things all of these words belong. (foods!) Call on students to give you sentences using each of the words.

Invite students to the board to circle the CA,CE,CO,CI in each word.

Draw attention to the fact that all the words under K start with CA or CO and all the words under S start with CE or CI. Remind them that this is how we can tell what sound is being "borrowed" by C in a new word—if it is followed by E, I, or Y, it will be using the S sound. If it is followed by any other vowel, or by another consonant, it will be using the K sound.

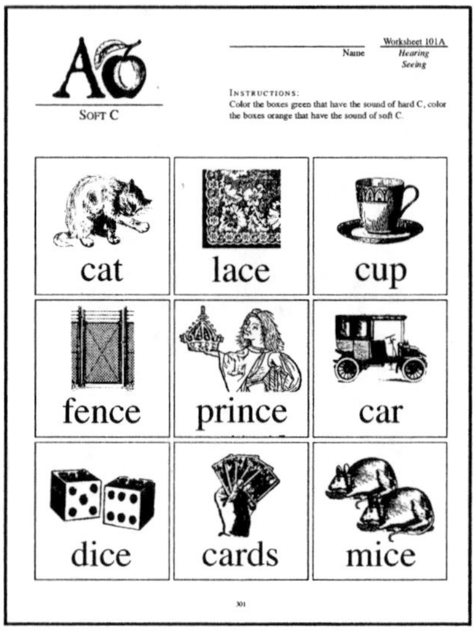

Worksheet 101A: Read the instructions aloud. Call their attention to the green K and the orange S on the board. This will help them remember which color to use for which "borrowed" sound. Monitor the students' progress as they work independently.

ACTIVITY 2: READING AND WRITING

Erase the board. Write the following: fence, ice, dice, dance, lace, mice, spaceship, pencil, cent.

Add lines and invite children to come to the board to write each of the words and use it in an original sentence.

Draw particular attention to the word "spaceship." Affirm that it is a compound word and assist the children to break it down into its two component words.

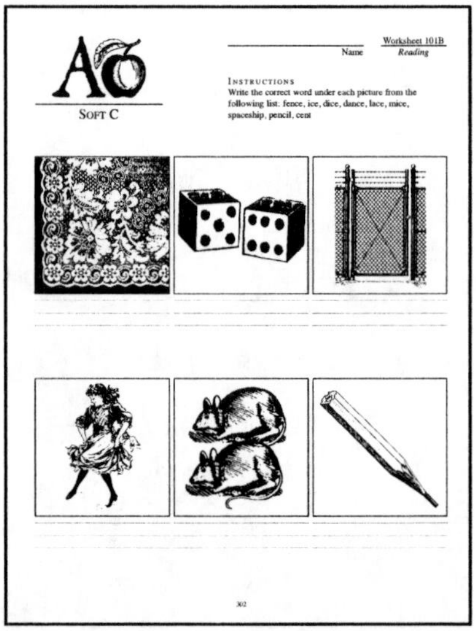

Worksheet 101B: Read the instructions aloud. Monitor the students' progress as they work independently.

Remind about letter spacing and the "FOUR P's!"

LESSON 102
TARGET: ADDING S AND ING TO FINAL CE WORDS AND REVIEW

ACTIVITY 1: HEARING AND SEEING S AND ING ENDINGS ON FINAL CE WORDS

Write the following on the board: RACE, BOUNCE, VOICE.

Call on students to decode and read each word. Define each word as a noun and use in that way in original sentences.

Now alter your sentences to use each word as a plural noun. After each sentence, ask "Now am I talking about one ____________ or more than one?" (more than one)

After all the sentences, ask what you will need to add to each of the words on the board to make them mean more than one. (S) Write an S after each word.

Now say them aloud. Clap out the syllables and ask how many are in each word. (2)

Remind them about other words which went from having one syllable to having two syllables when they were made to mean more than one: LUNCHES, BATCHES, RICHES, LASHES.

Explain that words which end with CE behave the same way.

Now, erase the S at the end of each word. Remind the children how words can do different jobs in sentences and that now these words will be action words. Use each word in a sentence as a verb.

Tell the children to listen carefully—you will now say the same sentences as if the action were taking place RIGHT NOW. Say the sentences again, using the ING form of each word.

Challenge the students to tell you what they hear at the end of each of the words in these new sentences. (ING)

Ask if anyone remembers what you must do to a word which ends with E before you add ING. (take off the E) If no one remembers this rule, state it for them and then erase all the E's at the end of the words. Write in the ING endings.

Read the words aloud. Draw attention to the fact that the sound of the first vowel stays the same (especially in the case of the word "race"). The sound of the C will still be S—after all, it is now followed by I instead of E!

The latter part of this activity serves as a review of the previously taught pattern for adding ING to final silent E words. If you like, you may want to add some additional board practice with this principle at this time.

Worksheet 102A: Read the instructions aloud. Assist as necessary and monitor their work.

ACTIVITY 2: HEARING: REVIEW OF THE SOUNDS OF E

Have the students take out one orange crayon and one yellow crayon.

Tell them that you will be reading a list of words. They are to hold up the yellow crayon when they hear the short sound of E ("yellow" has short E in it) and the orange crayon when they hear the long sound of E. Caution them to listen carefully—the sounds may come in any position of the word!

men	feel	ten	Deb	seat	deed
elephant	peas	dream	piece	end	rent
flea	tree	sense	friend	breeze	elk

Worksheet 102B: Read the instructions aloud. Tell them you will say the picture labels for them today.

Row 1: bed, seal, tent
Row 2: web, feet, read
Row 3: eggs, peacock, queen

LESSON 103
TARGET: OUL AS SHORT OO, VOCABULARY AND SPECIAL EXHIBIT WORDS FOR QUEEN OF THE SEA

ACTIVITY 1: SEEING AND HEARING OUL AS SHORT OO

Write the word "good" on the board. Call on a student to decode and read the word aloud, using the "short" sound of OO.

Tell the children you will be changing the beginning sound and they must read the rhyming words as you do so. Erase the G and replace it with H. Prompt the children to read "hood" in unison. Call on a student to make up an original sentence using this word.

Erase the H and replace it with W. Prompt the children to read "wood" in unison. Call on a student to make up an original sentence using this word also.

Now, tell the children you will be changing the vowels in the word "wood," but it will sound exactly the same. Erase the OO and replace it with OUL.

Explain that in this word the OU makes the short OO sound and the L does not say anything at all.

It has a different meaning from "wood" spelled with OO. This word "would" is a type of action word. Read the following sentences, as if two people were having a conversation: Would you help me carry that box? Yes, I would be happy to help you.

Tell the children that two other words are spelled this way in our language and have the same type of job in sentences. Under the word "would," write "could."

Ask the children what sound the C will "borrow" in this word. (K) Ask if they can tell you why. (because it is followed by O) Affirm correct responses and allow them to read the word in unison. Affirm that it rhymes with "would."

Read the following sentences, in the same manner as above: Could you help me carry that box? Yes, I could.

Discuss that in the first set of sentences using "would," the meaning is about being willing to help or not. In the second set of sentences, the meaning is about being able.

Although the children may not be able to grasp the full implications of this distinction at this time, a brief introduction to this subtlety is in order. This is similar to the basis for the differentiation between "may" and "can," which must be corrected frequently in the early years. "May" is a request for permission while "can" questions ability.

Now offer the final OUL word. Write "should" on the board. Assist the children to decode and read it. Read the following set of sentences: Should you help me carry that box? Yes, I should.

The word "should" in these sentences means that the action is something which ought to be done.

Invite students to come to the board and circle the OUL in each of these words. Backslash the L in each letter combination and write in a small OO with a breve over it above the OU to remind them of the sound which is used for this letter pair in these words.

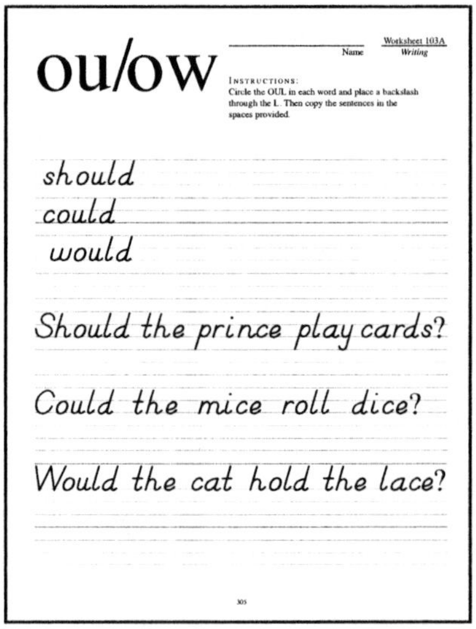
Worksheet 103A
Writing
Name

ou/ow

INSTRUCTIONS: Circle the OUL in each word and place a backslash through the L. Then copy the sentences in the spaces provided.

should
could
would

Should the prince play cards?

Could the mice roll dice?

Would the cat hold the lace?

305

Worksheet 103A: Read the instructions aloud. Monitor the students' progress as they work independently. Elicit sentences from the children which use each of these words appropriately.

ACTIVITY 2: VOCABULARY FOR QUEEN OF THE SEA

Write the words found on Worksheet 103B on the board in columns as shown.

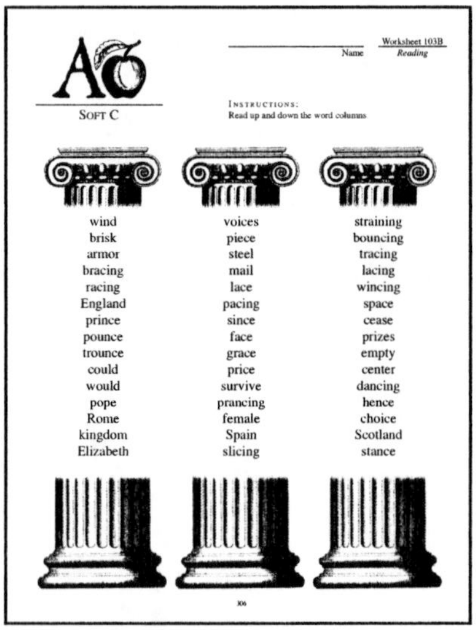
Worksheet 103B
Reading
Name

SOFT C

INSTRUCTIONS: Read up and down the word columns

wind	voices	straining
brisk	piece	bouncing
armor	steel	tracing
bracing	mail	lacing
racing	lace	wincing
England	pacing	space
prince	since	cease
pounce	face	prizes
trounce	grace	empty
could	price	center
would	survive	dancing
pope	prancing	hence
Rome	female	choice
kingdom	Spain	Scotland
Elizabeth	slicing	stance

306

Worksheet 103B: Read the instructions aloud. Use any of the previous variations or techniques for eliciting student response.

ACTIVITY 3: SPELLING TEST 6

Present Worksheet 103C: Administer the test on Spelling List 6. Read each word once, use it in a sentence, then repeat it. Do not give any other sound or letter clues.

ACTIVITY 4: ART ACTIVITY

Worksheet 103D: Before class, cut out pages from magazines that have soft C objects in them and place these pages in stacks on the table for the children to use. Read the instructions aloud. Help the students as they work.

LESSON 104
READING QUEEN OF THE SEA
AND COMPREHENSION

ACTIVITY 1: READING ALOUD

Worksheet 103C
Spelling Test
Name

SPELLING TEST 6

1.
2.
3.
4.
5.
6.
7.
8.
9.
10.

307

This story chronicles the unsuccessful invasion of England by the Spanish Armada in the 1588. The following vocabulary and expressions are used:

brisk—sharp and biting
men in armor—soldiers prepared for battle
bracing—waiting, preparing
serving as a fence—defending the coast
grief—sadness
fleet—a large group of ships
pounce—jump upon, take by surprise
trounce—defeat

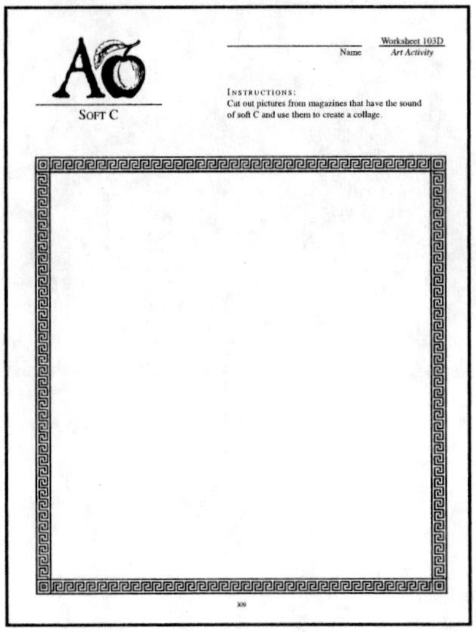
Worksheet 103D
Name — *Art Activity*

SOFT C

INSTRUCTIONS:
Cut out pictures from magazines that have the sound of soft C and use them to create a collage.

love the pope in Rome—be a Roman Catholic
steel mail—vest of interlocking metal links for protection
lance—spear
prancing—high stepping
slicing the waves—moving swiftly
razors—sharp-edged blades
straining—working hard
tracing and lacing—moving and weaving in and out
wincing—responding to a blow
cease—stop, break
dancing, roaring fire—the fire could easily spread to other ships
howling—despair
hence—therefore, as a result
sour—bitter and sad
stance—stand, firmly held position

Guide the children through the reading of the story, round robin style. Discuss main ideas, characters, and events as you proceed.

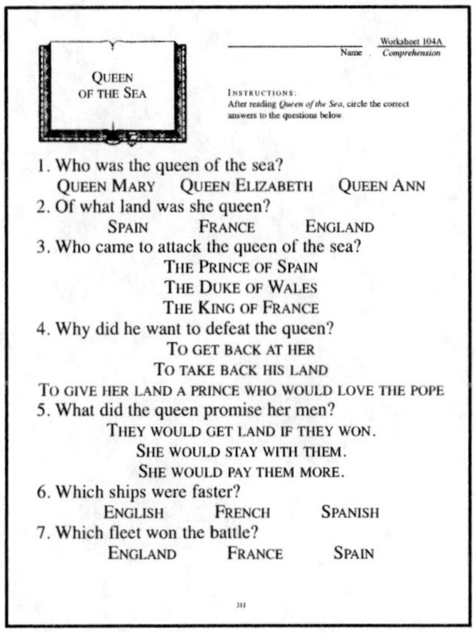
Worksheet 104A
Name — *Comprehension*

QUEEN OF THE SEA

INSTRUCTIONS:
After reading *Queen of the Sea*, circle the correct answers to the questions below.

1. Who was the queen of the sea?
QUEEN MARY QUEEN ELIZABETH QUEEN ANN
2. Of what land was she queen?
SPAIN FRANCE ENGLAND
3. Who came to attack the queen of the sea?
THE PRINCE OF SPAIN
THE DUKE OF WALES
THE KING OF FRANCE
4. Why did he want to defeat the queen?
TO GET BACK AT HER
TO TAKE BACK HIS LAND
TO GIVE HER LAND A PRINCE WHO WOULD LOVE THE POPE
5. What did the queen promise her men?
THEY WOULD GET LAND IF THEY WON.
SHE WOULD STAY WITH THEM.
SHE WOULD PAY THEM MORE.
6. Which ships were faster?
ENGLISH FRENCH SPANISH
7. Which fleet won the battle?
ENGLAND FRANCE SPAIN

You may want to do a limited map study in conjunction with this story.

Questions for discussion may include: What made the English nervous about the battle with the Spanish fleet? Why did Queen Elizabeth come to her men? Who won the battle and why? What route did the Spanish ships take to get back home and why?

ACTIVITY 2: READING COMPREHENSION

Worksheet 104A: Read the instructions aloud. Assist children to read each question and the answer choices. Allow them to answer independently as instructed.

ACTIVITY 3: ART ACTIVITY

Prepare an example of an English boat as directed on Worksheet 104B.

Organize all necessary art materials and supplies on a separate work table and assist the children to make their own boats according to the instructions on the sheet.

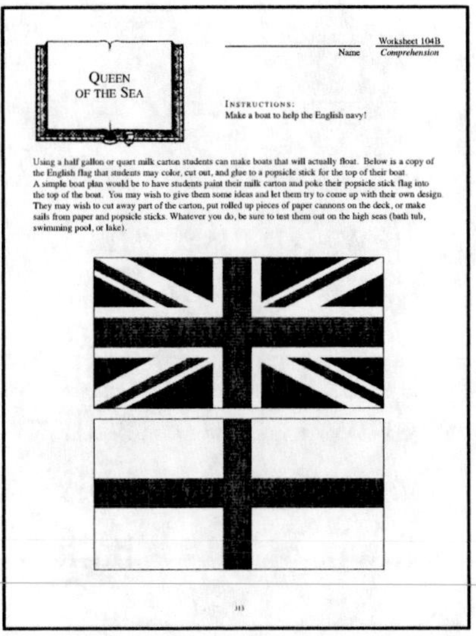
Worksheet 104B
Name — *Comprehension*

QUEEN OF THE SEA

INSTRUCTIONS:
Make a boat to help the English navy!

Using a half gallon or quart milk carton students can make boats that will actually float. Below is a copy of the English flag that students may color, cut out, and glue to a popsicle stick for the top of their boat. A simple boat plan would be to have students paint their milk carton and poke their popsicle stick flag into the top of the boat. You may wish to give them some ideas and let them try to come up with their own design. They may wish to cut away part of the carton, put rolled up pieces of paper cannons on the deck, or make sails from paper and popsicle sticks. Whatever you do, be sure to test them out on the high seas (bath tub, swimming pool, or lake).

Worksheet 104B: Read the instructions aloud. Assist as necessary.

LESSON 105
TARGET: AW/AU/AL
(AS IN "STRAW," "AUTO," AND "TALK")

Play The Broad-O Song for the children encouraging them to sing along.

Show the children the flashcard with AW/AU/AL on it. Have them hear the sound of AW as in "straw."

ACTIVITY 1: HEARING AND SEEING

Write the following previously taught Special Exhibits on the board: ALL, CALL, FALL, WALL.

Call on students to read each one. Say the words aloud slowly. Ask the children what sound is made by A in each of these words. (AH)

Explain that when AH is followed by L, both sounds change a little. Together they sound like AW.

Affirm that this is a completely new sound. It is much like the AH sound of A, but is pronounced with a more "rounded" mouth. Demonstrate the difference between the two sounds several times.

Explain that in words like "all," "fall," "call," etc., when the final letter pair is LL, the final L will be spoken. Circle only the middle AL in each of the words and draw attention to the final L. Read the words again, clearly pronouncing the final L in each one.

Write the following under the AL: talk, walk, chalk. Read the words aloud and have the children echo them. Affirm that the L does not make any sound in these words, but changes the AH into AW.

Invite children to the board to circle the AL in each word. Use each word in an original sentence.

Explain that the AW sound can be spelled in two other ways, just like OU/OW. Write the letter pair AW on the left side of the board and AU on the right side.

Write the following under the AW: saw, paw, yawn. Write the following under the AU: pause, haunt, launch. Invite children to the board to circle the AW or AU in each word. Assist them to decode the words using the AW sound. Define them and use in original sentences to reinforce meaning.

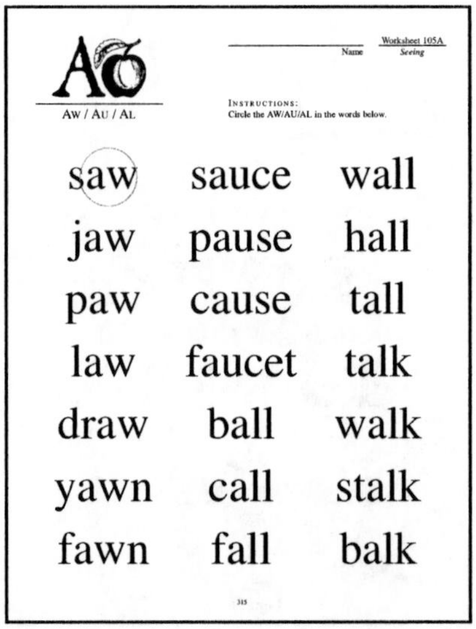
Worksheet 105A
Name
Seeing
AW / AU / AL
INSTRUCTIONS:
Circle the AW/AU/AL in the words below.

saw	sauce	wall
jaw	pause	hall
paw	cause	tall
law	faucet	talk
draw	ball	walk
yawn	call	stalk
fawn	fall	balk

315

Worksheet 105B
Name
Hearing
AW / AU / AL
INSTRUCTIONS:
Color the boxes blue where you hear the sound of AW. It may be spelled AU, AW or AL but you only have to listen for the sound AW.
316

Give them their museum bag. Allow them time to go through the house and collect items that have the AW/AU/AL sound to make their own museum. If you are teaching in a school setting, instruct the children to take the bag home and bring in objects the following day.

Worksheet 105A: Read the instructions aloud. Monitor as they respond as indicated. Assist them to decode and read the words aloud. Use them in original sentences.

Worksheet 105B: Read the instructions aloud. Label the pictures for the children as they respond as indicated.

Row 1: saw, bird, faucet
Row 2: wagon, crawl, sauce
Row 3: strawberry, fish, ball

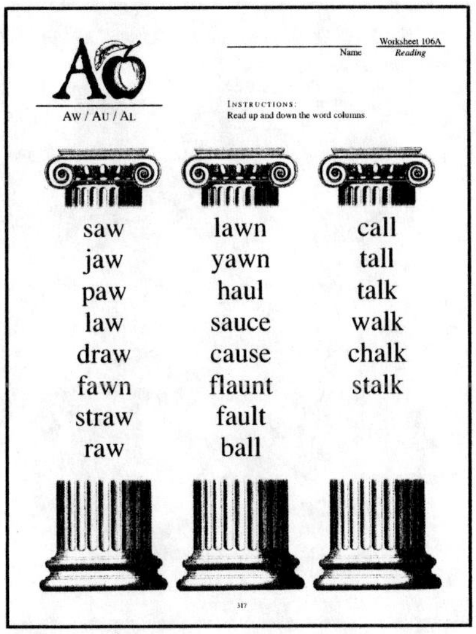
Worksheet 106A
Name
Reading
AW / AU / AL
INSTRUCTIONS:
Read up and down the word columns.

saw	lawn	call
jaw	yawn	tall
paw	haul	talk
law	sauce	walk
draw	cause	chalk
fawn	flaunt	stalk
straw	fault	
raw	ball	

317

You may want to give the students the coloring page along with the flashcard. Read the information about the artist to your students before they color the picture.

LESSON 106
TARGET: AW/AU/AL AND SPELLING LIST 7

Play The Broad-O Song for the children encouraging them to sing along.

ACTIVITY 1: READING

Write the words found on Worksheet 106A on the board in columns as shown.

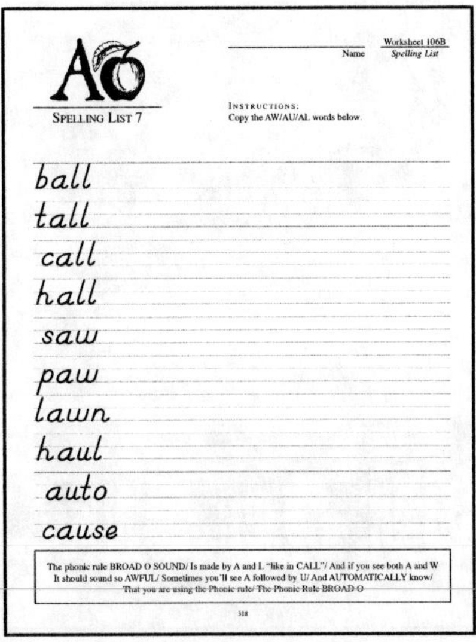
Worksheet 106B
Name
Spelling List
SPELLING LIST 7
INSTRUCTIONS:
Copy the AW/AU/AL words below.

ball
tall
call
hall
saw
paw
lawn
haul
auto
cause

The phonic rule BROAD O SOUND/ Is made by A and L "like in CALL"/ And if you see both A and W It should sound so AWFUL/ Sometimes you'll see A followed by U/ And AUTOMATICALLY know/ That you are using the Phonic rule/ The Phonic Rule BROAD O
318

Worksheet 106A: Read the instructions aloud. Allow the children to circle or underline the AW/AU/AL in each word. Use any of the previous variations or techniques for eliciting student response. Define all words and use in original sentences.

ACTIVITY 2: WRITING SPELLING LIST 7

Write the words found on Worksheet 106B on the board, along with lines. Call on students to read each word aloud and use it in a sentence. Invite children to the board to copy the words. Monitor letter formation and spacing.

Worksheet 106B: Read the instructions aloud. Monitor the students' progress as they work independently.

Lesson 107
Target: AW/AU/AL and Vocabulary for SERVING IN THE SHADOW OF DEATH

Play The Broad-O Song for the children encouraging them to sing along.

ACTIVITY 1: READING AND WRITING AW/AU/AL WORDS

This activity will also serve as a review of Spelling List 7. Write in large letters AW, AU, and AL at the top of the board.

Tell the children that you will be giving a definition of a word which will have AW, AU, or AL in it. Their job is to think of the word which fits the definition. You will call on students to come to the board and write the correct word under the letter pair which is contained in that word.

For instance, give the following definition: the foot of an animal. Ask if anyone can tell you the word that means this. (paw) Affirm correct responses. Now ask if this word is spelled with AW, AU, or AL. Allow them to consult the spelling list if necessary. Affirm that it is spelled with AW. Ask where it should be written on the board. (under the AW) Write it there. Continue in the same manner with the rest of the words on Spelling List 7.

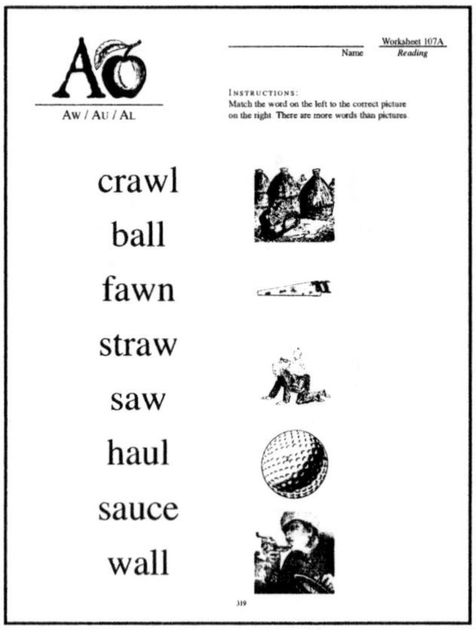

Worksheet 107A
Reading
Name
AW / AU / AL
INSTRUCTIONS: Match the word on the left to the correct picture on the right. There are more words than pictures.

crawl
ball
fawn
straw
saw
haul
sauce
wall

319

Worksheet 107A: Read the instructions aloud. Call on students to read each of the words aloud. Assist the children to determine which word best describes each picture. The picture labels are, from top to bottom, "straw," "saw," "crawl," "ball," "sauce."

ACTIVITY 2: VOCABULARY FOR SERVING IN THE SHADOW OF DEATH

Write the words found on Worksheet 107A on the board. Assist the children to decode and read the words. Define according to the meanings listed in the next lesson. Use each word in an original sentence.

Pay particular attention to the names "Aurelius" and "Claudius." These utilize the I as long E.

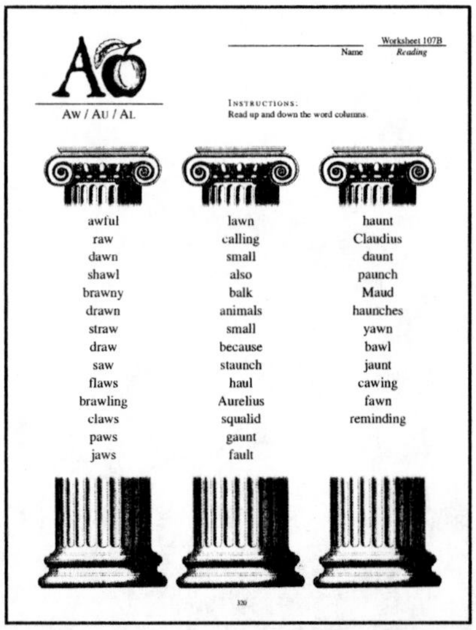

Worksheet 107B
Reading
Name
AW / AU / AL
INSTRUCTIONS: Read up and down the word columns.

awful	lawn	haunt
raw	calling	Claudius
dawn	small	daunt
shawl	also	paunch
brawny	balk	Maud
drawn	animals	haunches
straw	small	yawn
draw	because	bawl
saw	staunch	jaunt
flaws	haul	cawing
brawling	Aurelius	fawn
claws	squalid	reminding
paws	gaunt	
jaws	fault	

320

Worksheet 107B: Read the instructions aloud. Use any of the previous variations or techniques for eliciting student response.

The words "squalid" and "animals" contain the AL letter pair, but are not true AW words. "Squalid" is AH + L and "animals" is actually a schwa + L. Instruct the students accordingly when they decode these words.

Lesson 108
Reading SERVING IN THE SHADOW OF DEATH

ACTIVITY 1: READING ALOUD

This story chronicles the selfless act of service of a Christian mother and daughter during the time of the Black Death in Europe in the Middle Ages. The following vocabulary and expressions are used:

awful—very bad, horrible
fever—illness with a high temperature
raw—open, bleeding
bite—Gwen was hungry (a metaphor)
daunt—deter, discourage
dawn—when the sun is just coming up
shawl—garment that wraps around the shoulders and head
haul—pull
staunch—solid
brawny—muscled
squalid—dirty
gaunt—thin
drawn—tight with pain
paunch—stomach, front of torso
haunt—harass, go after
taunting—mocking, unkind teasing
mock—to ridicule
beggar—one who asks for aid but offers nothing in return
balk at—they did not let her affect them
flaws—sins
draw—bring
cawing—making a loud call
fawn—baby deer
burly—big in size, stout
brawling—fighting
clearing—an open area in the forest with no trees
haunches—strong legs and back
bawl—cry
cheering—heartening, pleasing
brisk jaunt—fast pace

Guide the children through the round robin reading of the story. Discuss main characters, ideas, and events as they occur.

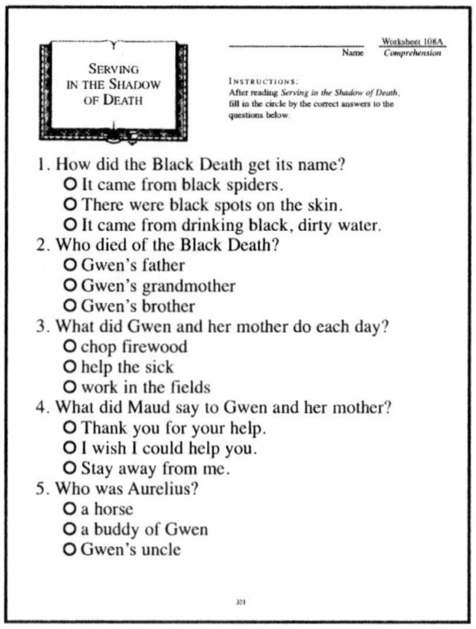
Worksheet 108A
Comprehension
Name

SERVING IN THE SHADOW OF DEATH

INSTRUCTIONS:
After reading *Serving in the Shadow of Death*, fill in the circle by the correct answers to the questions below.

1. How did the Black Death get its name?
   - O It came from black spiders.
   - O There were black spots on the skin.
   - O It came from drinking black, dirty water.
2. Who died of the Black Death?
   - O Gwen's father
   - O Gwen's grandmother
   - O Gwen's brother
3. What did Gwen and her mother do each day?
   - O chop firewood
   - O help the sick
   - O work in the fields
4. What did Maud say to Gwen and her mother?
   - O Thank you for your help.
   - O I wish I could help you.
   - O Stay away from me.
5. Who was Aurelius?
   - O a horse
   - O a buddy of Gwen
   - O Gwen's uncle

321

Some questions for discussion might include: What words would you use to describe Gwen and her mother? What kinds of things do we have today to assist those who are sick?

ACTIVITY 2: READING COMPREHENSION

Worksheets 108A/B: Present the worksheets one at a time. Read the instructions aloud. Call on students to read the questions and answers. Assist as necessary to respond as indicated.

Archives: Special Exhibit Edition

LESSON 109
TARGET: SILENT CONSONANTS

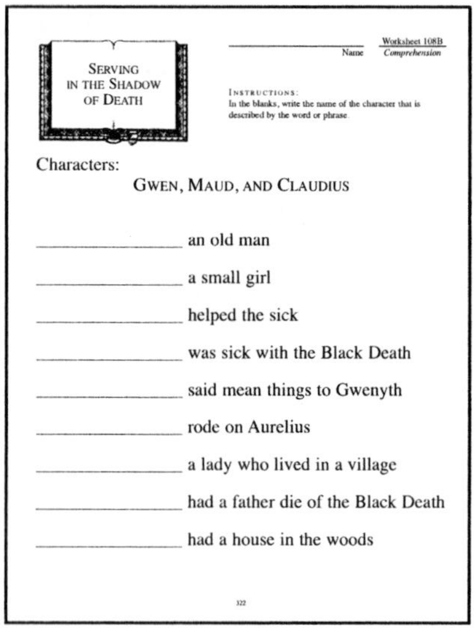
Worksheet 108B
Comprehension
Name

SERVING IN THE SHADOW OF DEATH

INSTRUCTIONS:
In the blanks, write the name of the character that is described by the word or phrase

Characters:
GWEN, MAUD, AND CLAUDIUS

______ an old man
______ a small girl
______ helped the sick
______ was sick with the Black Death
______ said mean things to Gwenyth
______ rode on Aurelius
______ a lady who lived in a village
______ had a father die of the Black Death
______ had a house in the woods

322

ACTIVITY 1: SEEING AND HEARING

Give a flashcard of the letter K and the letter N to two students in the school setting or the teacher and child if teaching at home. Tell the following story to the children:

Once upon a time a long while ago there was a frog that lived in a pool. The pool was cool and deep with lovely blossoming lily pads to sit on and was full of tasty bugs to eat. Since she was a tadpole, all that Katie the frog could remember was her lovely little pool.

One day she heard splashing above the wall. There was never sounds like that up there before. Above the wall of her pond was only ever sky. The splashing persisted then suddenly from over the top edge of the wall came flying a slick green creature with big eyes and a huge mouth.

"Who are you?' Katie inquired of the creature, "And what are you?"

"I am Nick and I am a frog like you." the other creature croaked. "Why don't you come up to the pool above—it is bigger than this one with more bugs."

"How could I get over the wall?" asked Katie.

"You are a frog, you just leap. That is what our large frog legs are for," said Nick. "Swimming is just one of the many great things frogs can do."

Katie was quite excited to learn of this new ability and the frogs played leap frog the rest of the afternoon in the pools above.

Now the students will play leap frog with the letters K and N. N will squat on the floor and the person with the K card would leap over the N person.

Worksheet 109A

Name Seeing

SILENT CONSONANTS

INSTRUCTIONS:
Circle the KN, GN or WR in the words below, then put a line through the silent partner.

knot gnaw wrong
knee write wretch
kneel wring knife
knit wren wreath
knob wreck wrench
knock wrist gnome
gnat wrote

In some words two consonants have one sound, just like the silent partners we already have studied. Look at the examples below.
kn as in *knot*—we only hear the sound of n
gn as in *gnat*—we only hear the sound of n
wr as in *write*—we only hear the sound of r

323

Repeat this with the letter pairs: W/R and G/N.

Worksheet 109A: Read the instructions aloud. Monitor as they work independently to circle each of the targeted letter pairs. Read through the list and have the children echo the words after you. Use any unfamiliar ones in original sentences.

Worksheet 109B: Read the instructions aloud. Tell the children that the label for each of the pictures is found on the last worksheet (109A). Assist the children to label the pictures and find the corresponding word on Worksheet 109A. They will then see what letter pair is used to spell each word and circle the correct pair in each box on Worksheet 109B. Monitor their work carefully.

Row 1: knees, gnat, wreath
Row 2: knot, wrench, knit
Row 3: knife, wrist, gnome

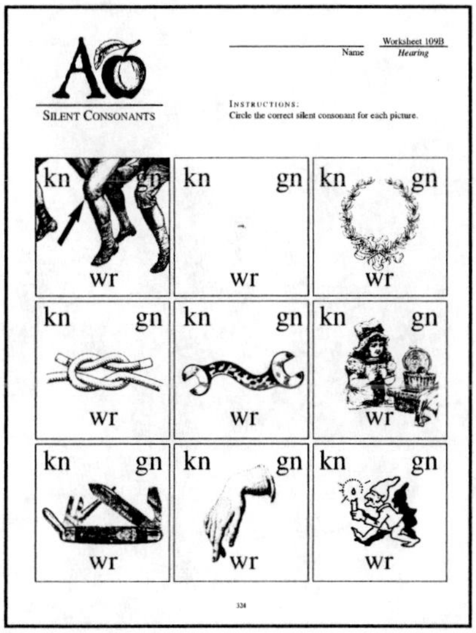
Worksheet 109B

Name Hearing

SILENT CONSONANTS

INSTRUCTIONS:
Circle the correct silent consonant for each picture.

324

LESSON 110
TARGET: SILENT CONSONANTS

ACTIVITY 1: SEEING AND HEARING

Write a large WR on the board. Ask if anyone remembers what sound is made by this letter pair. (R) Affirm correct answers. (This was taught in Lesson 11.)

Write the following words under the WR: write, wrote, wring, wrong. Call on students to decode and read each one.

Invite students to the board to circle the WR in each word. Ask which letter is silent in this letter pair. (W) Backslash through the W in each WR letter pair. Ask if the silent letter comes first or second. (first)

Explain that there are consonant letter pairs like this as well. Write the following on the board: KN, GN.

Challenge the children to tell you which letter they think will be silent in each of these pairs, based on the pattern of WR. (the first one) Affirm correct answers and backslash through the K and G.

Now ask the children: What sound is left? (N) So, both of these letter pairs will sound alike!

Write the following under the KN: KNOT, KNIT, KNEE.

Write the following under the GN: GNAT, GNAW, GNOME

Invite children to the board to circle the KN or GN in each word and backslash through the silent letter. Assist the children to decode and read each word.

Define any words which may be unfamiliar and use in original sentences to reinforce meaning. Tell the children that the next two worksheets will be used together and that you will be working on them as a group.

Worksheet 110A: Read the instructions aloud. Monitor the students' progress as they work independently.

ACTIVITY 2: READING

Write the following on the board: KNOT, KNEAD, KNOW

Assist the children to decode and read them aloud. Define and use in original sentences. Now, under each of these words, write the following: NOT, NEED, NO.

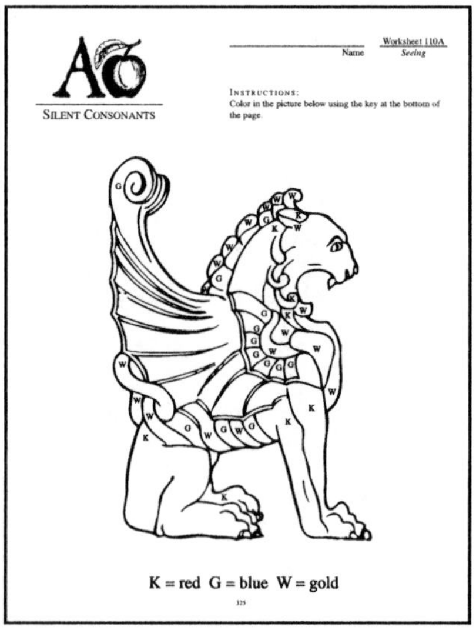

Call on children to read each of these words. Ask them if these words sound the same as the ones above them. (YES) Affirm that although they sound alike, they have different meanings. Define and use each of the second set of words in original sentences. Remind the children of previous lessons when there have been words which sound alike but are spelled differently and mean different things. The use of letter pairs with silent partners helps us identify the meanings when we are reading.

Write the following on the board: wring, wrung. Define and use in original sentences. Affirm that the words mean the same action, but it is happening at different times (present, past).

Erase the W in each word to form "ring" and "rung." Define and use in original sentences. Do these words sound the same as the first set? (YES) Yet their meaning is different. They still describe an action, however, which is happening at different times.

The above is not typical, but presents an interesting parallel within the lesson. Do not emphasize it, but merely mention it as an aside.

Worksheet 110B: Read the instructions aloud. Assist the children to read the words aloud. Define and use in sentences as necessary. Allow them to underline or circle the silent letter pairs in each word, backslash the silent partner, etc. Use any of the previous variations for eliciting student response.

Lesson 111
Target: Silent Consonants

Show the children the flashcard with the GH on it.

ACTIVITY 1: SEEING

Remind the children of the story about the frogs, Katie and Nick. When the played leap frog the began at the beginning of the words. Later in the day they leaped all over. In the same way, silent letters can come in other places besides the beginning of words. Now we will look at leap frog letters in other places in other words.

Tell the children you will doing the next two pages together as a class.

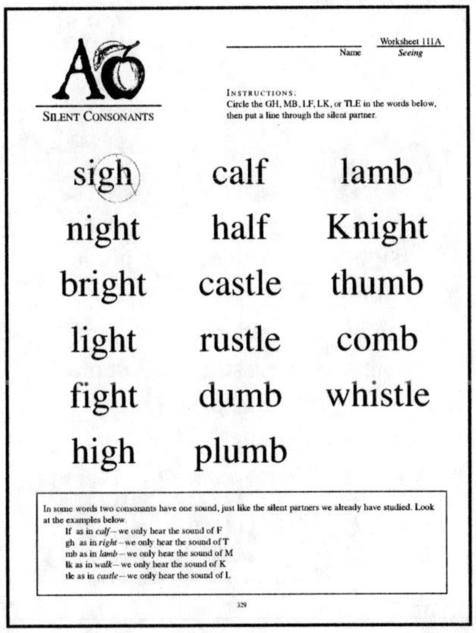

Worksheet 111A
Seeing

Name

SILENT CONSONANTS

INSTRUCTIONS:
Circle the GH, MB, LF, LK, or TLE in the words below, then put a line through the silent partner.

sigh	calf	lamb
night	half	Knight
bright	castle	thumb
light	rustle	comb
fight	dumb	whistle
high	plumb	

In some words two consonants have one sound, just like the silent partners we already have studied. Look at the examples below.
lf as in *calf*—we only hear the sound of F
gh as in *right*—we only hear the sound of T
mb as in *lamb*—we only hear the sound of M
lk as in *walk*—we only hear the sound of K
tle as in *castle*—we only hear the sound of L

329

Give them their museum bag. Allow them time to go through the house and collect items that have the silent consonants to make their own museum. If you are teaching in a school setting, instruct the children to take the bag home and bring in objects the following day.

Worksheet 111A: Read the instructions aloud. Monitor as they respond as indicated. Read the words aloud to the children and have them echo them after you. Affirm that the I in all of the GH words is pronounced as long. Tell them that this will always happen when the I is the only vowel before the GH. Call attention to the use of long O in "comb"—this is one of those "wild words!" Define and use the words in sentences as necessary.

Worksheet 111B: Read the instructions aloud. Assist the children to label the pictures, then locate that word on Worksheet 111A. Guide them to determine which silent letter group is seen in the stimulus word and then circle it on Worksheet 111A.

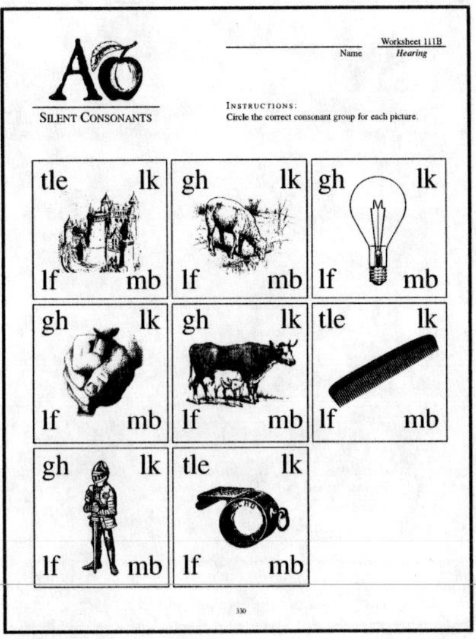

Worksheet 111B
Hearing

Name

SILENT CONSONANTS

INSTRUCTIONS:
Circle the correct consonant group for each picture.

tle lk lf mb | gh lk lf mb | gh lk lf mb
gh lk lf mb | gh lk lf mb | tle lk lf mb
gh lk lf mb | tle lk lf mb

330

Row 1: castle, lamb, light
Row 2: thumb, calf, comb
Row 3: knight, whistle

You may want to give the students the coloring page along with the flashcard. Read the information about the artist to your students before they color the picture.

Lesson 112
Target: Silent Consonants and Spelling Test 7

ACTIVITY 1: SEEING, HEARING, AND READING

Write the following on the board: WR, LF, MB, GN, KN, GH, TLE.

Call on students to come to the board and do the following:

point to the two letter pairs which make the same sound (GN,KN)
point to the letter group which makes the L sound
point to the letter pair which makes the F sound
point to the letter pair which makes the R sound
point to the letter pair which makes the M sound
point to the letter group which is completely silent

Allow the children to backslash through the silent partner(s) in each letter group. They must backslash through both letters in GH!

Worksheet 112A: Read the instructions aloud. Assist them to decode and read each of the word choices and then match as indicated.

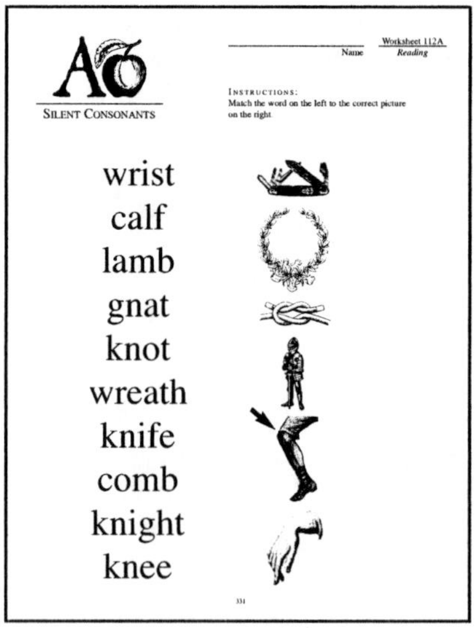
Worksheet 112A
Reading
Name
SILENT CONSONANTS
INSTRUCTIONS:
Match the word on the left to the correct picture on the right

wrist
calf
lamb
gnat
knot
wreath
knife
comb
knight
knee

ACTIVITY 2: READING WORDS

Write the words found on Worksheet 112B on the board.

Worksheet 112B: Read the instructions aloud. Assist the children to decode and read each word. Define as necessary and use in original sentences.

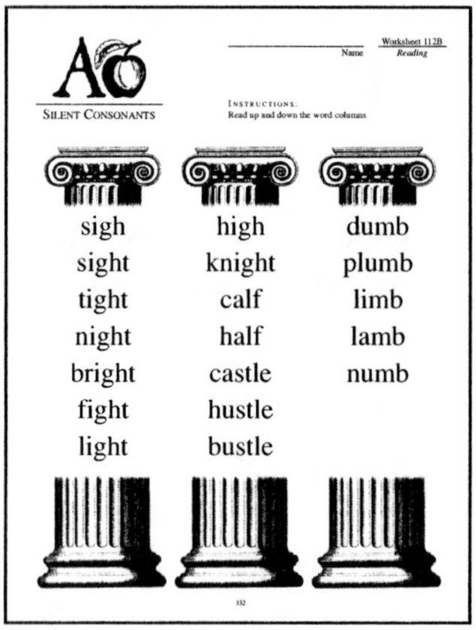
Worksheet 112B
Reading
Name
SILENT CONSONANTS
INSTRUCTIONS:
Read up and down the word columns

sigh	high	dumb
sight	knight	plumb
tight	calf	limb
night	half	lamb
bright	castle	numb
fight	hustle	
light	bustle	

ACTIVITY 3: SPELLING TEST 7

Worksheet 112C: Administer the test on Spelling List 7. Read each word once, use it in a sentence, then repeat it. Do not give any other sound or letter clues.

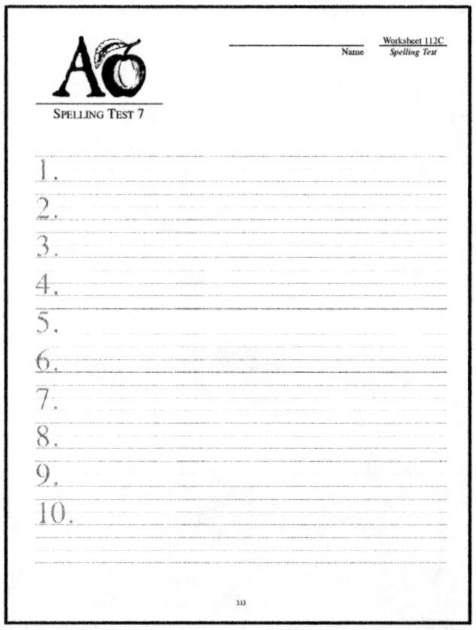
Worksheet 112C
Spelling Test
Name
SPELLING TEST 7

1.
2.
3.
4.
5.
6.
7.
8.
9.
10.

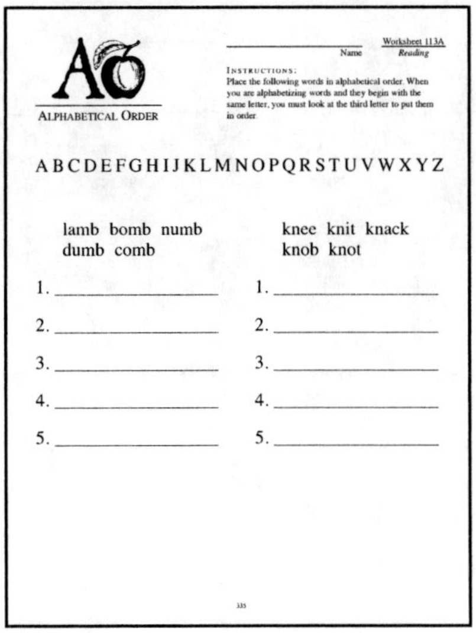

Worksheet 113A
Reading

Name

ALPHABETICAL ORDER

INSTRUCTIONS:
Place the following words in alphabetical order. When you are alphabetizing words and they begin with the same letter, you must look at the third letter to put them in order.

A B C D E F G H I J K L M N O P Q R S T U V W X Y Z

lamb bomb numb
dumb comb

1. ______
2. ______
3. ______
4. ______
5. ______

knee knit knack
knob knot

1. ______
2. ______
3. ______
4. ______
5. ______

335

LESSON 113
ALPHABETIZING AND SPELLING LIST 8

Play the Alphabet Song for the children encouraging them to sing along.

ACTIVITY 1: ALPHABETIZING

Explain to the students that we will be putting words into alphabetical order. Remind the students that if the words begin with the same letter, we must look to the next letter to get the words in order.

Worksheet 113A: Read the instructions aloud. Tell them to number the words first and then copy them onto the numbered lines accordingly. Monitor their work.

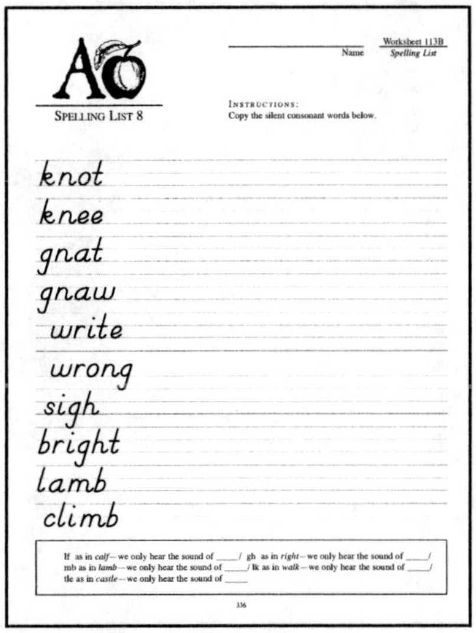

Worksheet 113B
Spelling List

Name

SPELLING LIST 8

INSTRUCTIONS:
Copy the silent consonant words below.

knot
knee
gnat
gnaw
write
wrong
sigh
bright
lamb
climb

lf as in *calf*—we only hear the sound of ____/ gh as in *right*—we only hear the sound of ____/
mb as in *lamb*—we only hear the sound of ____/ lk as in *walk*—we only hear the sound of ____/
tle as in *castle*—we only hear the sound of ____

336

ACTIVITY 2: SPELLING LIST 8

Write the words found on Worksheets 113B on the board, along with lines. Invite children to the board to copy each word, naming the letters in order as they write them. Read each word aloud. Define and use in original sentences.

Call attention to the long I in "climb"—it's another "wild word!"

Worksheets 113B: Read the instructions aloud. Monitor as they copy the words independently.

Remind about the "FOUR P's" if you haven't done so in a while!

Archives: Blends Edition.

LESSON 114
TARGET: SILENT CONSONANTS

ACTIVITY 1: READING

Play a game of verbal fill-in-the-blanks today. Tell the children you will be saying a sentence and leaving out the last word. They must choose from a list to determine which word best finishes the sentence.

Write the words of Spelling List 8 on the board. This activity will also serve as a review of their spelling!

Read the following: My brother fell and has a big bruise on his ____________.

Challenge the children to look over the list and decide which word should fill in the blank. (knee) Affirm correct answers.

Continue in the same manner with the rest of the words.

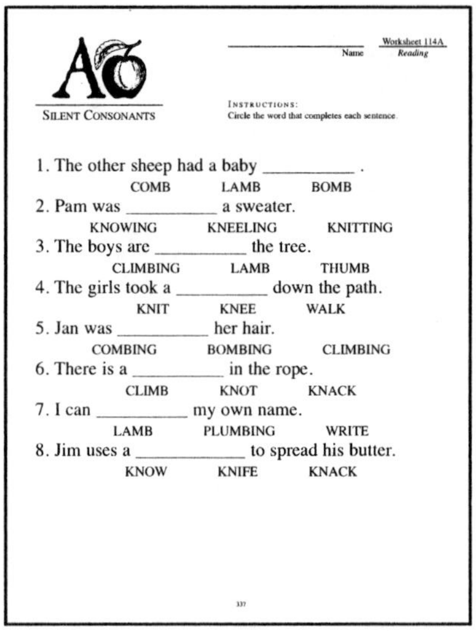

Worksheet 114A
Name
Reading

SILENT CONSONANTS

INSTRUCTIONS:
Circle the word that completes each sentence.

1. The other sheep had a baby __________ .
COMB LAMB BOMB
2. Pam was __________ a sweater.
KNOWING KNEELING KNITTING
3. The boys are __________ the tree.
CLIMBING LAMB THUMB
4. The girls took a __________ down the path.
KNIT KNEE WALK
5. Jan was __________ her hair.
COMBING BOMBING CLIMBING
6. There is a __________ in the rope.
CLIMB KNOT KNACK
7. I can __________ my own name.
LAMB PLUMBING WRITE
8. Jim uses a __________ to spread his butter.
KNOW KNIFE KNACK

Worksheet 114A: Read the instructions aloud. Call on students to read the sentences and the word choices. Pay particular attention to the words "comb" and "bomb" under Sentence 1—they look alike, but the O has a different sound in each! Define any words which may be unfamiliar. Monitor as they determine the correct word to complete each sentence and respond as indicated.

ACTIVITY 2: ART ACTIVITY

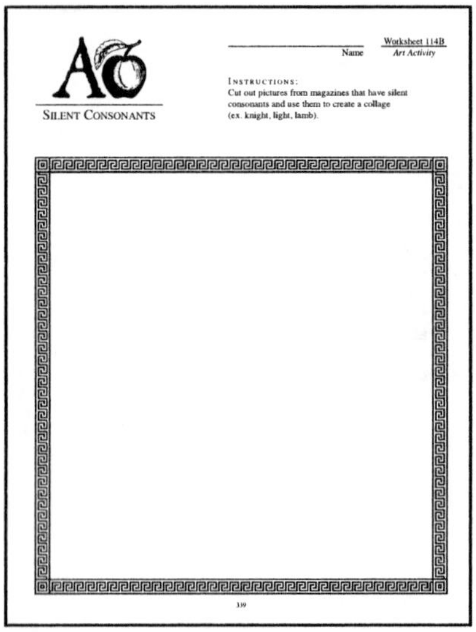

Worksheet 114B
Name
Art Activity

SILENT CONSONANTS

INSTRUCTIONS:
Cut out pictures from magazines that have silent consonants and use them to create a collage (ex. knight, light, lamb).

Worksheet 114B: Before class, go through magazines and rip out pages that have pictures from the following list. Read the instructions aloud. Assist the students in cutting and pasting the pictures together. There is no correct picture to create. This project reinforces the concept of silent consonants. Go through each magazine clipping and identify the target words for the students before cutting out the picture. Remind them of the frog story.

knife	knee	knot	knelt	knit
knocker	knight	knuckle	wreck	wrist
write	wreath	wrench	thumb	lamb
comb	climb	limb	night	fight
light	flight			

LESSON 115
TARGET: OU AS SHORT O AND VOCABULARY FOR BRIGHT NIGHT

ACTIVITY 1: OU AS SHORT O

Tell the children to listen carefully as you read the following sentence aloud: I ought to have brought the thing I bought.

Ask if they heard any rhyming words in that sentence. Read it a second time, emphasizing the words "ought," "brought," and "bought." As the children tell you the rhyming words, write them on the board.

Invite students to the board to circle the GH in each word.

Ask them if GH makes any sound in these words. (NO) Backslash through the G and H.

Now, write the five vowels on the board. Call on students to say the short vowel sounds of each of them.

Read the three words again, emphasizing the short O sound in each one.

Challenge the students to tell you which short vowel sound is heard in these words (O). Go through them again and compare with the sound in the words if necessary.

Affirm that the sound heard in these words is short O.

Ask if the U makes any sound. (NO) Backslash through the U.

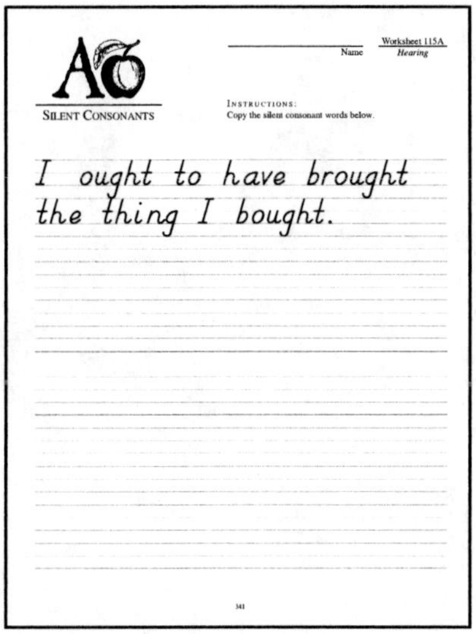
Worksheet 115A
Name
Hearing
SILENT CONSONANTS
INSTRUCTIONS:
Copy the silent consonant words below.

I ought to have brought the thing I bought.

Ask if anyone remembers how we show that a vowel has a short sound. (use a breve) Invite a child to the board to draw a breve over the O in each word.

Read the words again and have the children echo them.

Now write the following: sought, fought, thought. Call on students to come to the board, circle the GH; backslash through the G, H, and U.

Write a breve over the O.

Assist them to decode and read the words. Define them and use in original sentences.

Worksheet 115A: Read the instructions aloud. Monitor as the children work independently. Call on students to read each of the words aloud.

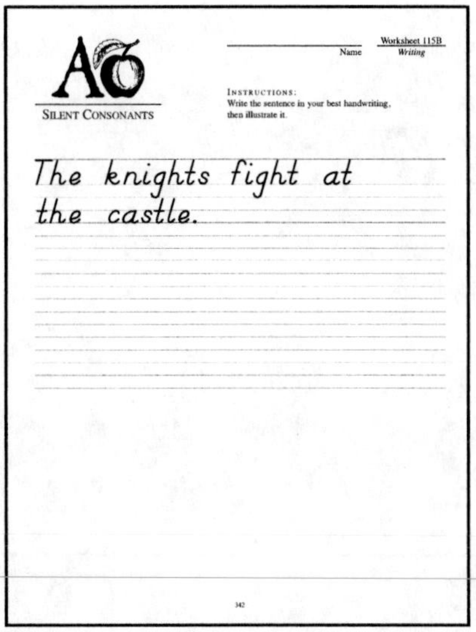
Worksheet 115B
Name
Writing
SILENT CONSONANTS
INSTRUCTIONS:
Write the sentence in your best handwriting, then illustrate it.

The knights fight at the castle.

ACTIVITY 2: WRITING

Write the sentence found on Worksheet 115B on the board, along with lines. Call on children to come to the board and copy each of the words in order on the lines. Have a student read the sentence aloud.

Worksheet 115B: Read the instructions aloud. Monitor the students' progress as they work independently. Remind about letter and word spacing.

ACTIVITY 3: VOCABULARY FOR BRIGHT NIGHT

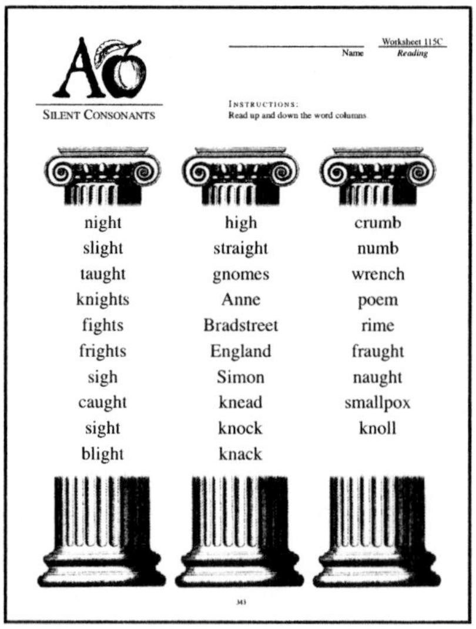
Name
Worksheet 115C
Reading
SILENT CONSONANTS
INSTRUCTIONS:
Read up and down the word columns

night	high	crumb
slight	straight	numb
taught	gnomes	wrench
knights	Anne	poem
fights	Bradstreet	rime
frights	England	fraught
sigh	Simon	naught
caught	knead	smallpox
sight	knock	knoll
blight	knack	

Write the words found on Worksheet 115C on the board.

Worksheet 115C: Read the instructions aloud. Use any of the previous techniques or variations for eliciting student response.

Call special attention to the pronunciation of the word "poem" (two syllables, O is long, E is short).

Variations for prompting the reading of words on this sheet include: numbering the words and calling on students to read them by the designated number, verbal "fill-in-the-blanks," pointing to the written word on the board and having students point to the corresponding printed word on the sheet, riddle clues, categorizing on the basis of silent letter group, rhyming words, etc.

LESSON 116
READING BRIGHT NIGHT

This story is about Anne Bradstreet, the Puritan poet. She was born in 1612, the daughter of the steward of the Puritan Earl of Lincoln, and was well educated. In 1628 she married Cambridge graduate Simon Bradstreet and emigrated to New England with John Winthrop's group in 1630. She bore eight children, managed a well-run household, and wrote poetry, some of which were eventually published under the title *The Tenth Muse Lately Sprung up in America*. One historian commented that her poetry showed that "the female Puritan . . . could be both a Puritan and a woman of great charm." (Above information condensed from Christian History Magazine, Issue 41, Vol. XIII, No.1.)

The art for this story is styled after American Primitive. At this time there were no art schools so any painting was done by self-taught artists. Perspective and anatomy are not used in a realistic fashion, and there is a great deal of repeated decorative patterns.

The following vocabulary and expressions are used:

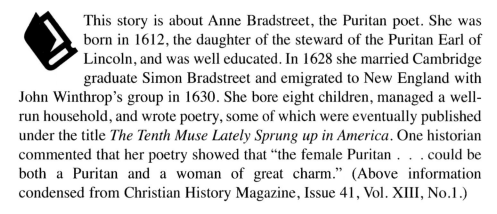

slight—slim
garden wren—a little bird
shining books—good literature
sought out—looked for
gnomes—tiny, old men in legends who live in the earth and guard its treasure
flights—stories about escaping from danger
frights—scary stories
knead bread—turn and press it to distribute the yeast

sigh—to exhale with weariness or desire
rimes—alternative spelling for *rhymes*
smallpox—a serious disease
half-numb—unable to feel anything
blight—illness
shone—glowed with light
harsh—stormy
roar and rage—had violent winds and waves
knock and wrench—toss about
wreck—crash to pieces
ought—should
knack—skill, talent
meek—humble
spin—make yarn from wool
swimming lakes—ponds used for swimming
gnat—small insect
naught—nothing
wreath of flames—the whole house was on fire
with all their might—as hard as they could
was no more—was completely destroyed
chest—storage trunk
wrung her hands—pressed them together in dismay
sobs—deep cries
wretches—poor, abandoned ones
wrath—anger
plight—difficult situation
speculate—to assume or be doubtful about
dependent—trusting, relying
fraught—full of
might—power
newborn—a baby recently born
dumb—so surprised she could not speak
coarse—not refined or well done

You may want to find some of her poetry to read to the children after the story to further enhance their understanding of her contribution to American literature. She is considered the first true American poet. Following are two poems by Anne you might read to your students:

Here Follows Some Verses
upon the Burning of Our House
July 10th, 1666

Copied Out of a Loose Paper

In silent night when rest I took
For sorrow near I did not look
I waked was with thund'ring noise
And piteous shrieks of dreadful voice.
That fearful sound of "Fire!" and "Fire!"

Let no man know is my desire.
I, starting up, the light did spy,
And to my God my heart did cry
To strengthen me in my distress
And not to leave me succorless.
Then, coming out, beheld a space
The flame consume my dwelling place.
And when I could no longer look,
I blest His name that gave and took,
That laid my goods now in the dust.
Yea, so it was, and so 'twas just.
It was His own, it was not mine,
Far be it that I should repine;
He might of all justly bereft
But yet sufficient for us left.
When by the ruins oft I past
My sorrowing eyes aside did cast,
And here and there the places spy
Where oft I sat and long did lie:
Here stood that trunk, and there that chest,
There lay that store I counted best.
My pleasant things in ashes lie,
And them behold no more shall I.
Under thy roof no guest shall sit,
Nor at thy table eat a bit.
No pleasant tale shall e'er be told,
Nor things recounted done of old.
No candle e'er shall shine in thee,
Nor bridegroom's voice e'er heard shall be.
In silence ever shall thou lie,
Adieu, Adieu, all's vanity.
Then straight I 'gin my heart to chide,
And did thy wealth on earth abide?
Didst fix thy hope on mold'ring dust?
The arm of flesh didst make thy trust?
Raise up thy thoughts above the sky
That dunghill mists away may fly.
Thou hast an house on high erect,
Framed by that mighty Architect,
With glory richly furnished,
Stands permanent though this be fled.
It's purchased and paid for too
By Him who hath enough to do.
A price so vast as is unknown
Yet by His gift is made thine own;
There's wealth enough, I need no more,
Farewell, my pelf, farewell my store.
The world no longer let me love,
My hope and treasure lies above.

In Reference to Her Children, 23 June, 1659

I had eight birds hatched in one nest,
Four cocks there were, and hens the rest.
I nursed them up with pain and care,
Nor cost, nor labour did I spare,
Till at the last they felt their wing,
Mounted the trees, and learned to sing;
Chief of the brood then took his flight
To regions far and left me quite.
My mournful chirps I after send,
Till he return, or I do end:
Leave not thy nest, thy dam and sire,
Fly back and sing amidst this choir.

[THIS POEM IS AN EXCERPT FROM A MUCH LONGER WORK]

Guide the children through the round robin reading of the story. Call attention to the main characters, ideas, and events as they occur.

Some possible questions for discussion include: What kind of stories would be about "knights and gnomes, fights, flights, and frights?" Why would she "sigh when she caught sight of ink and pen?" Discuss the things that happened to her which the Lord used to strengthen her faith.

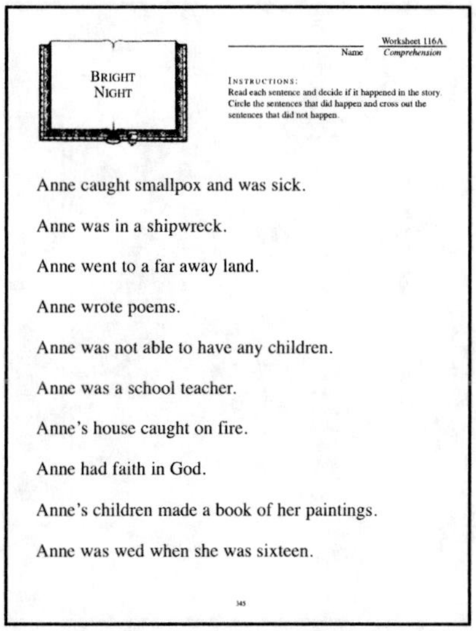

BRIGHT NIGHT

Name ______ Worksheet 116A *Comprehension*

INSTRUCTIONS:
Read each sentence and decide if it happened in the story. Circle the sentences that did happen and cross out the sentences that did not happen.

Anne caught smallpox and was sick.

Anne was in a shipwreck.

Anne went to a far away land.

Anne wrote poems.

Anne was not able to have any children.

Anne was a school teacher.

Anne's house caught on fire.

Anne had faith in God.

Anne's children made a book of her paintings.

Anne was wed when she was sixteen.

Worksheet 116A: Read the instructions aloud. Call on students to read each of the sentences and decide together if it happened or not. Monitor as they respond as indicated.

LESSON 117
READING COMPREHENSION

ACTIVITY 1: COMPREHENSION

Briefly review yesterday's story. Continue the discussion on the questions as necessary.

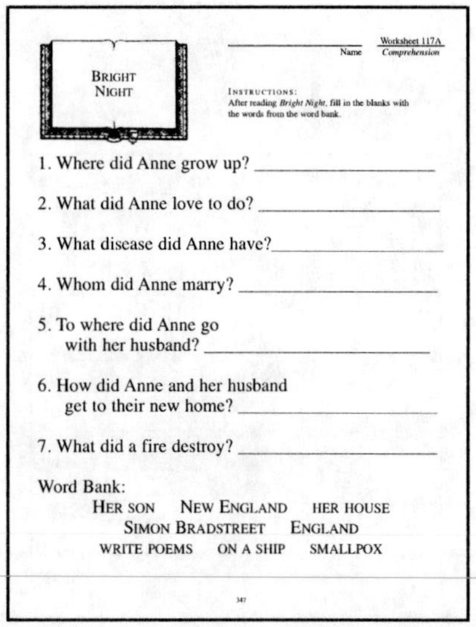

BRIGHT NIGHT

Name ______ Worksheet 117A *Comprehension*

INSTRUCTIONS:
After reading *Bright Night*, fill in the blanks with the words from the word bank.

1. Where did Anne grow up? ______
2. What did Anne love to do? ______
3. What disease did Anne have? ______
4. Whom did Anne marry? ______
5. To where did Anne go with her husband? ______
6. How did Anne and her husband get to their new home? ______
7. What did a fire destroy? ______

Word Bank:
HER SON NEW ENGLAND HER HOUSE
SIMON BRADSTREET ENGLAND
WRITE POEMS ON A SHIP SMALLPOX

Worksheet 117A : Read the instructions aloud. Call on students to read the questions aloud. Assist them to determine the best answer from the word bank. Monitor as they write their answers on the lines provided.

ACTIVITY 2: WRITING

Write the sentence found on Worksheet 117B on the board, along with lines. Have a student read it aloud.

Call on students to come to the board and copy the words of the sentence in order on the lines provided.

Worksheet 117B: Read the instructions aloud and Monitor the students' progress as they work independently.

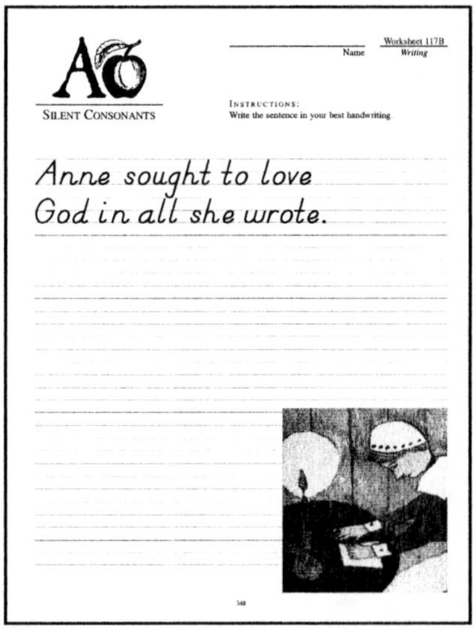
Worksheet 117B
Writing
Name
SILENT CONSONANTS
INSTRUCTIONS:
Write the sentence in your best handwriting.
Anne sought to love
God in all she wrote.
348

ACTIVITY 3: ART ACTIVITY

Worksheet 117C: Have the students color in the border using colors similar to those in the book BRIGHT NIGHT. Read the poem on the worksheet and have the students fill in the blanks with words they choose. You may need to assist with spelling.

Worksheet 117C
Art Activity
Name

The sun is shining,
The birds are singing
And my eyes are waking.
I think of things I'll do today.
There will be
□ running and ________.
□ laughter and ________.
□ books and ________.

The sun is high,
My friends are here
And I am ________.
We plan our day's adventures.
We will
□ talk and ________.
□ make and ________.
□ eat and ________.

The moon is high,
The stars are shining
My family is giving thanks.
I thank thee good Lord
For
□ playmates and ________.
□ food and ________.
□ books and ________.
And for your Presence always with me.

349

LESSON 118
REVIEW AND SPELLING TEST 8

ACTIVITY 1: REVIEW OF L BLENDS

Write the following across the top of the board: FL, BL, PL, CL.

Brainstorm with the children to come up with as many words as they can which begin with the blends shown. Write them on the board as they are offered.

Invite the children to make up sentences which use some of the words shown. Allow them to think up riddles which can be answered by some of the words.

Find all the action words (verbs). Find all the "things" (nouns). Locate any words which describe (adjectives).

Worksheet 118A: Read the instructions aloud. Assist the children to label the pictures as necessary. Monitor their work.

Row 1: flower, clock, sled
Row 2: plug, glove, flag
Row 3: blade, globe, clothespin

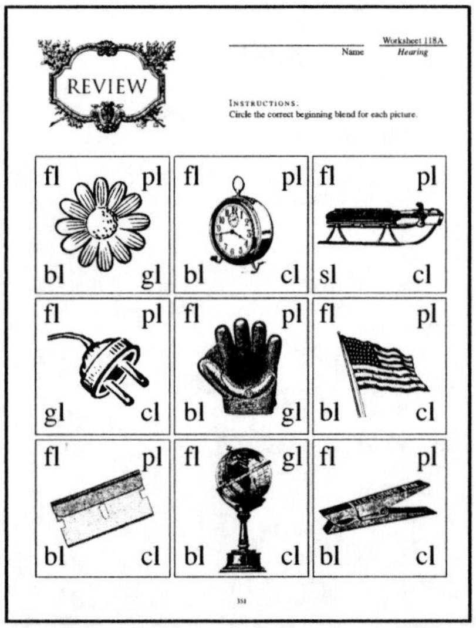
Worksheet 118A
Hearing
Name
REVIEW
INSTRUCTIONS:
Circle the correct beginning blend for each picture.

fl pl bl gl	fl pl bl cl	fl pl sl cl
fl pl gl cl	fl pl bl gl	fl pl bl cl
fl pl bl cl	fl gl bl cl	fl pl bl cl

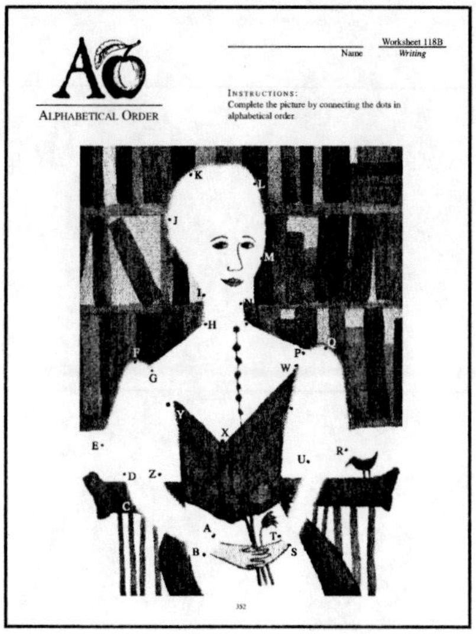

Worksheet 118B
Writing
Name

AB

ALPHABETICAL ORDER

INSTRUCTIONS:
Complete the picture by connecting the dots in alphabetical order.

352

ACTIVITY 2: ALPHABETICAL ORDER

Worksheet 118B: Read the instructions aloud. Allow them to work independently. Remind them who is depicted in this picture!

ACTIVITY 3: SPELLING TEST 8

Worksheet 118C: Administer the test on Spelling List 8. Read each word once, use it in a sentence, then repeat it. Do not give any other sound or letter clues.

Worksheet 118C
Spelling Test
Name

AB

SPELLING TEST 8

1.
2.
3.
4.
5.
6.
7.
8.
9.
10.

lf as in *calf* – we only hear the sound of ____/ gh as in *right* – we only hear the sound of ____/
mb as in *lamb* – we only hear the sound of ____/ lk as in *walk* – we only hear the sound of ____/
tle as in *castle* – we only hear the sound of ____

353

LESSON 119
TARGET: FINAL GE/DGE

ACTIVITY 1: HEARING AND SEEING

Tell the children they must be good "sound detectives" today. You will read a list of words and they must tell you what ending sound they all have in common.

Read the following list:

cage   edge   judge   huge   bridge

Ask what the ending sound is of each word. (J) Affirm correct answers. Write a large J on the board.

Explain to the children that even though that is the sound they hear, the letter J is never found at the end of words in our language. Instead, we use something else.

Write GE under the J and slightly to the left and write DGE under the J slightly to the right.

Explain that when we pair G with E, the G makes a J sound which we call "soft G."

Write the following under the GE: age, page, huge.

Write the following under the DGE: ledge, nudge, bridge.

Read the words aloud and have the children echo them after you. Affirm that the E at the end of each word is not heard and is a silent partner to G. It affects the G however, by turning it into a J sound.

Circle the GE in "age" and backslash through the final E. Invite students to the board to do the same with "page" and "huge."

Affirm that the final silent E in these words makes the first vowel say its name or make the long sound. Write macrons over the first vowels. Call on students to decode and read each one again.

Circle the DGE in "ledge." Backslash through the final E. Explain that in words where DGE is used, the first vowel is short.

Draw breves over each of the vowels in these words.

Call on students to decode and read the words again. Define as necessary and use in original sentences.

Show the children the flashcard with the DGE on it. Have them hear the sound J as in "bridge."

Give them their museum bag. Allow them time to go through the house and collect items that have the J sound to make their own museum. If you are teaching in a school setting, instruct the children to take the bag home and bring in objects the following day.

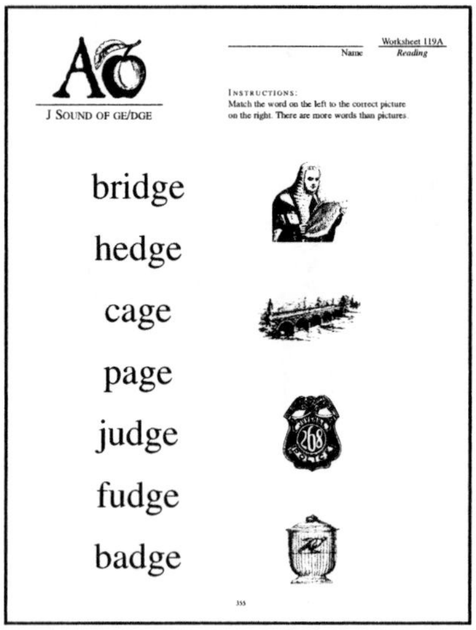

Worksheet 119A: Read the instructions aloud. Monitor as they respond as indicated. Read the words and have the children echo them after you. Define any unfamiliar words and use in sentences.

Worksheet 119B: Read the instructions aloud. Label the pictures for the children and monitor as they respond as indicated.

Row 1: judge, toes, badge
Row 2: girl, bridge, boys
Row 3: bench, star, cage

You may want to give the students the coloring page along with the flashcard. Read the information about the artist to your students before they color the picture.

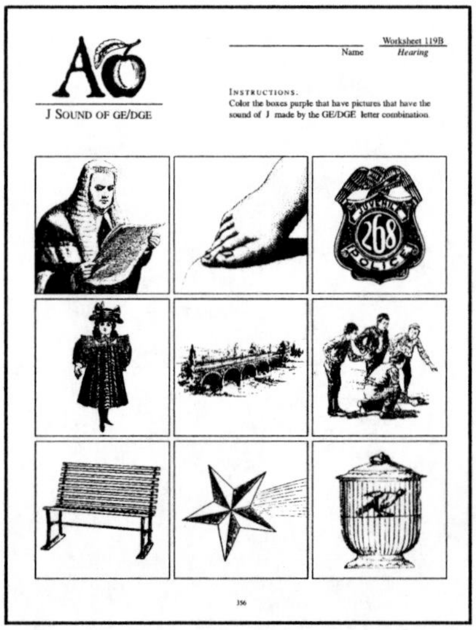

LESSON 120
TARGET: FINAL GE/DGE/NGE

ACTIVITY 1: HEARING, SEEING AND READING

Read the following words to the children: BINGE, HINGE, RANGE, CHANGE.

Ask them what sound is heard at the end of each word. (J) Ask if anyone remembers how we spell words with the J sound at the end. (GE) Affirm correct answers and remind them that this is called "soft G."

Write the above words on the board, placing "binge" and "hinge" together and "range" and "change" together. Invite students to come to the board and underline the GE in each word.

Draw attention to the fact that each word also contains an N which comes before the GE. Say the words again, emphasizing the N.

Explain that in words like these, sometimes the first vowel will be long and sometimes it will be short. Ask if the vowel I in "binge" and "hinge" is short or long. (short)

Invite a child to the board to write a breve over the I in each word.

Ask if the vowel in "range" and "change" is short or long. (LONG)

Invite a child to the board to write a macron over the A in each word.

Tell them that there is really no way to know which sound the vowel will be making, so they need to be "sound scientists" and experiment sometimes to see which sound will make the word meaningful.

Worksheet 120A: Read the instructions aloud. Use any of the previous techniques and variations to elicit student response. Define any unfamiliar words and use in sentences.

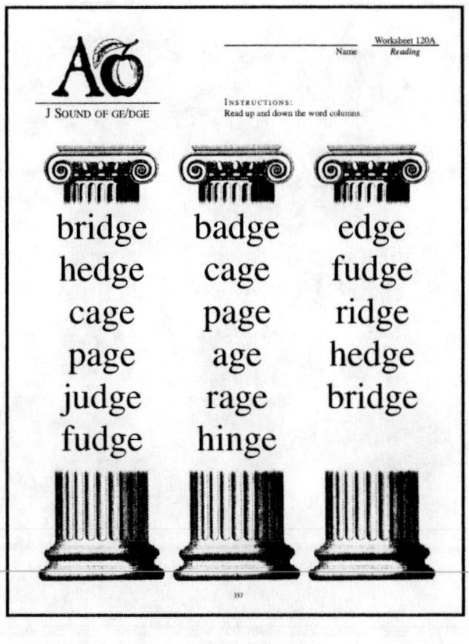

Worksheet 120A
Reading

Name

J SOUND OF GE/DGE

INSTRUCTIONS:
Read up and down the word columns.

bridge	badge	edge
hedge	cage	fudge
cage	page	ridge
page	age	hedge
judge	rage	bridge
fudge	hinge	

Variations for prompting the reading of words on this sheet include: numbering the words and calling on students to read them by the designated number, verbal "fill-in-the-blanks," pointing to the written word on the board and having students point to the corresponding printed word on the sheet, riddle clues, categorizing on the basis of vowel sounds or ending letter groups, etc.

ACTIVITY 2: WRITING

Worksheet 120B: Read the instructions aloud and Monitor the students' progress as they work independently.

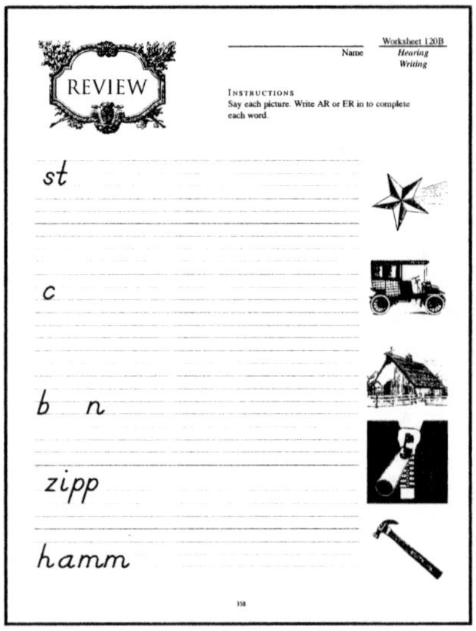
Worksheet 120B
Name
Hearing
Writing
REVIEW
INSTRUCTIONS
Say each picture. Write AR or ER in to complete each word.
st
c
b n
zipp
hamm

Worksheet 120C: Test. This test is optional and is added to evaluate your students if you feel it is necessary at this time. The answers are worth 10 points each.

Archives: Special Exhibit Edition.

LESSON 121
TARGET: FINAL GE/DGE/NGE

ACTIVITY 1: READING

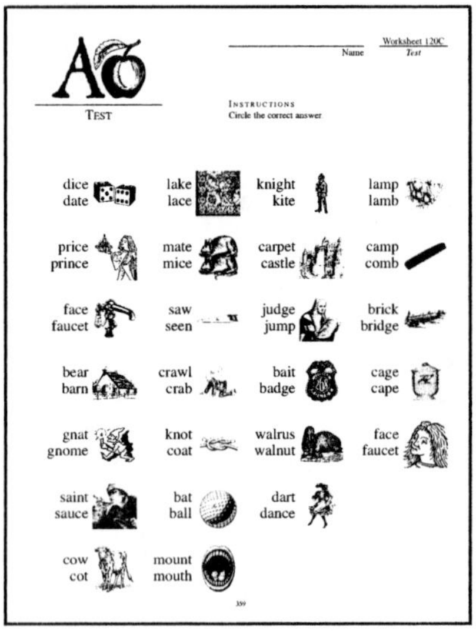
Worksheet 120C
Name
Test
TEST
INSTRUCTIONS
Circle the correct answer

dice / date	lake / lace	knight / kite	lamp / lamb
price / prince	mate / mice	carpet / castle	camp / comb
face / faucet	saw / seen	judge / jump	brick / bridge
bear / barn	crawl / crab	bait / badge	cage / cape
gnat / gnome	knot / coat	walrus / walnut	face / faucet
saint / sauce	bat / ball	dart / dance	
cow / cot	mount / mouth		

Play the riddle game today. Write the following words on the board: HEDGE, FUDGE, PAGE.

Tell the children you will give them clues about one of the words on the board. They must determine which word best answers the riddle.

Read the following: I am sweet and tasty. Most people think of me as chocolate, but I can be flavored vanilla, peanut butter, or even butterscotch. What am I? (FUDGE)

Call on students to come to the board, point to the word which answers the riddle and read it aloud. Continue with the other two words.

Worksheet 121A: Read the instructions aloud. Allow the children to decode and read the words independently and respond as indicated.

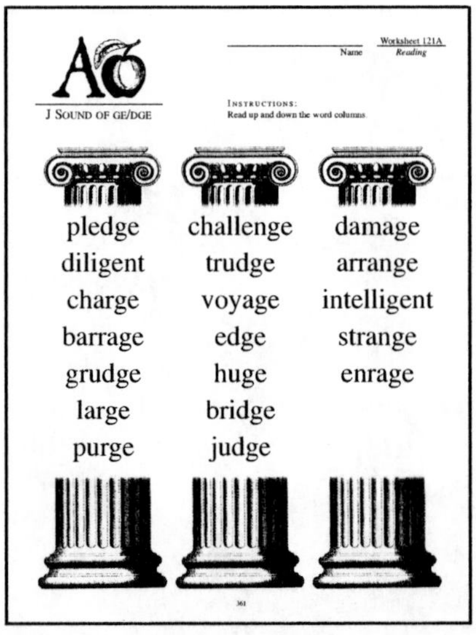
Worksheet 121A
Name
Reading
J SOUND OF GE/DGE
INSTRUCTIONS:
Read up and down the word columns.

pledge	challenge	damage
diligent	trudge	arrange
charge	voyage	intelligent
barrage	edge	strange
grudge	huge	enrage
large	bridge	
purge	judge	

ACTIVITY 2: REVIEW

Write the following on the board: AR, ER. Call on students to tell the class what sound is made by each of these letter pairs.

Remind them that AR can be pronounced with an AH sound, or with short A, if followed by final silent E.

Write the following letter groups on the board with the blank spaces underlined: f_ _ m, moth _ _, st _ _ e, f _ _ n.

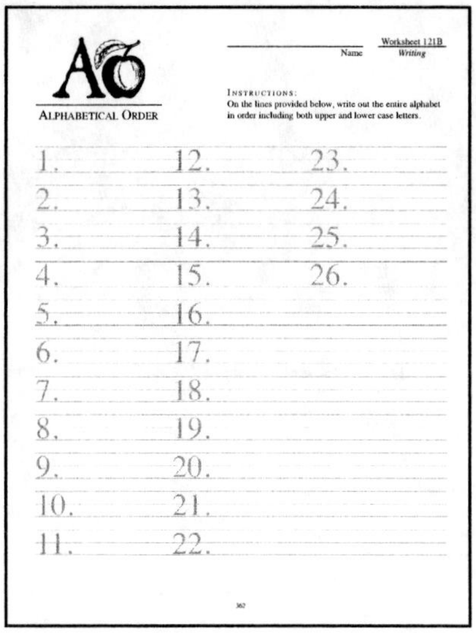
Worksheet 121B
Writing
Name
ALPHABETICAL ORDER
INSTRUCTIONS:
On the lines provided below, write out the entire alphabet in order including both upper and lower case letters.

1.	12.	23.
2.	13.	24.
3.	14.	25.
4.	15.	26.
5.	16.	
6.	17.	
7.	18.	
8.	19.	
9.	20.	
10.	21.	
11.	22.	

Ask the children which letter pair, AR or ER, should be written into the blanks in the first word to mean "a place where crops are grown." (AR) Call on a student to come to the board and fill in the missing letter pair.

Continue in the same manner with the other three words (mother, stare, fern) Draw attention to the sound change for the vowel A.

Worksheet 121B: Read the instructions aloud. Monitor the students' progress as they work independently.

Lesson 122

Target: Final GE/DGE/NGE and Alphabetical Order

ACTIVITY 1: READING

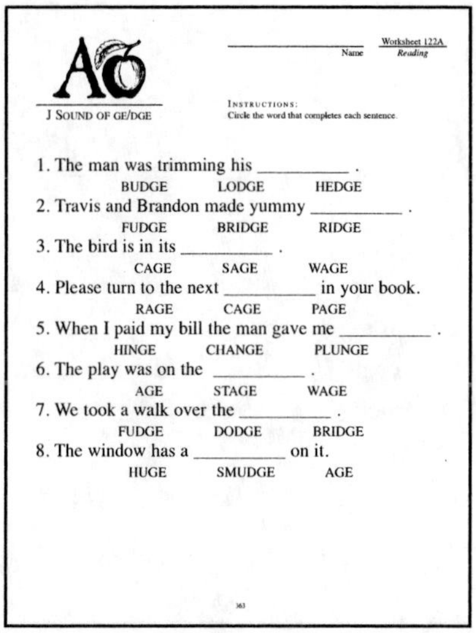
Worksheet 122A
Reading
Name
J SOUND OF GE/DGE
INSTRUCTIONS:
Circle the word that completes each sentence.

1. The man was trimming his __________ .
BUDGE LODGE HEDGE
2. Travis and Brandon made yummy __________ .
FUDGE BRIDGE RIDGE
3. The bird is in its __________ .
CAGE SAGE WAGE
4. Please turn to the next __________ in your book.
RAGE CAGE PAGE
5. When I paid my bill the man gave me __________ .
HINGE CHANGE PLUNGE
6. The play was on the __________ .
AGE STAGE WAGE
7. We took a walk over the __________ .
FUDGE DODGE BRIDGE
8. The window has a __________ on it.
HUGE SMUDGE AGE

Write the words found as answer choices on Worksheet 122A on the board.

Assist the children to decode and read them aloud. Define unfamiliar words and use in sentences.

Worksheet 122A: Read the instructions aloud. Call on children to read the sentences and the answer choices. Assist them to determine which word best completes the sentence and circle it as directed.

ACTIVITY 2: ALPHABETICAL ORDER

Sing the Alphabet Song with enthusiasm today, especially if you haven't done so in a while!

Invite children one at a time to come to the board and write one of the letters of the alphabet, in order, both upper and lower cases, in whatever color they choose.

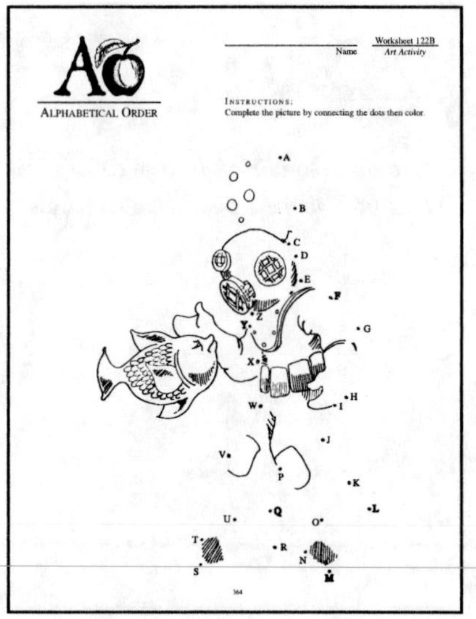
Worksheet 122B
Art Activity
Name
ALPHABETICAL ORDER
INSTRUCTIONS:
Complete the picture by connecting the dots then color.

Affirm correct stroke direction and order, especially for those who may be persisting in error with certain letters.

Worksheet 122B: Read the instructions aloud and Monitor the students' progress as they work independently.

Lesson 123
Review and Writing Practice

Play the song How Many Sounds? for the children encouraging them to sing.

ACTIVITY 1: HEARING AND SEEING

Write the following on the board: pea, feed, soak, goes.

Invite students to the board to circle the vowel letter pairs in each word.

Call on students to read each of the words aloud and tell the class what vowel sound is heard in each one.

Allow students to backslash through the silent partner in each vowel letter pair.

Place a macron over the long vowel.

Leave the words on display as examples while you present Worksheet 123A.

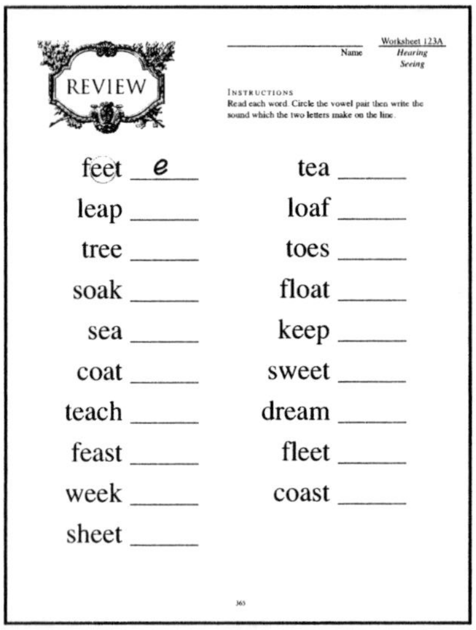
Worksheet 123A
Hearing
Seeing

Name

REVIEW

INSTRUCTIONS
Read each word. Circle the vowel pair then write the sound which the two letters make on the line.

feet e	tea ____
leap ____	loaf ____
tree ____	toes ____
soak ____	float ____
sea ____	keep ____
coat ____	sweet ____
teach ____	dream ____
feast ____	fleet ____
week ____	coast ____
sheet ____	

Worksheet 123A: Read the instructions aloud. Monitor carefully as they work independently. After the children have completed the sheet, read all the words aloud as a group and call on children to make up original sentences with each one.

ACTIVITY 2: WRITING PRACTICE

Write the sentence found on Worksheet 123B on the board, along with lines. Invite children to come to the board and copy the words of the sentence in order on the lines.

Call on a student to read the sentence aloud.

Worksheet 123B
Writing

Name

J SOUND OF GE/DGE

INSTRUCTIONS:
Write the sentence in your best handwriting.

The cat does not budge when the boy jumps over the hedge.

Worksheet 123B: Read the instructions aloud. Monitor as they copy the sentence from Worksheet B onto the lines on Worksheet C independently. Remind them about letter and word spacing.

Percival's Pairs: Using ING, ANG, ONG, blends, long vowels Y as I, EE, EA, OA, OE OW, OO, OY, OU, OW, SOFT C, AW

Lesson 124
Target: GE/GI in Initial and Medial Positions

ACTIVITY 1: HEARING AND SEEING

Read the following words aloud: gem, gel, gentle. Ask the children what sound is heard at the beginning of each of these words. (J)

Explain that sometimes the J sound at the beginning of words is spelled with GE, just like at the end of words. Write the above words on the board.

Underline the GE in each word. Affirm that the E is not silent in these words, it makes its short vowel sound. The G is the "soft G" sound of J.

Now read the following: urgent, diligent, intelligent. Ask if they hear the J sound in the middle of these words.

Worksheet 124A
Seeing
Name

J Sound of GE/DGE

Instructions:
Circle the GE or GI in the words below, then read them aloud.

gem germ margin
gee gin tragic
gel ginger urgent
gentle magic

Write them on the board and underline the GE in the middle of each one. Read them again, emphasizing the J sound. Again, demonstrate that the J is spelled with the GE letter pair in these words and that the E makes its short sound.

Point out that we often pronounce this short E as short I when we say these words. In fact, sometimes short I will follow the soft G in some words.

Write the following on the board: gin, ginger, magic, margin. Read each word aloud, underline the GI in each one (and the GE in "ginger!"). Have the children echo them after you. Define them and use in original sentences.

Worksheet 124A: Read the instructions aloud. Monitor as they respond as instructed. Assist the children to read through the words. Define any which are unfamiliar and use in original sentences.

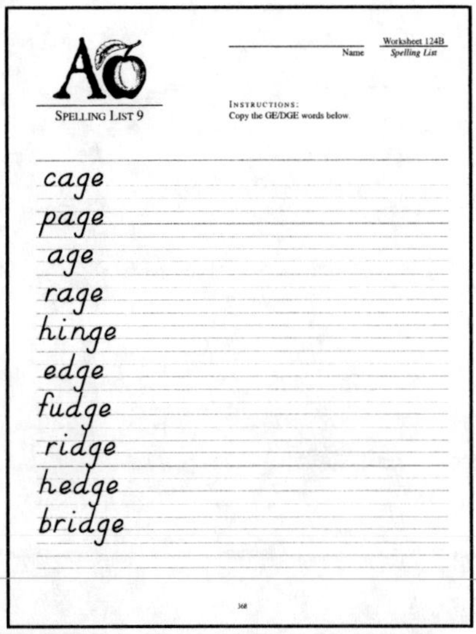
Worksheet 124B
Spelling List
Name

Spelling List 9

Instructions:
Copy the GE/DGE words below.

cage
page
age
rage
hinge
edge
fudge
ridge
hedge
bridge

ACTIVITY 2: SPELLING LIST 9

Write the words found on Worksheet 124B on the board, along with lines.

Invite students to the board to copy the words, naming the letters in order as they do so and reading each word aloud.

Worksheets 124B: Read the instructions aloud. Monitor the students' progress as they work independently.

Lesson 125
Review, Vocabulary and Special Words for CYRUS THE ARCHER

ACTIVITY 1: REVIEW

Tell the children we will be playing a fill-in-the-blank game again today.

Write the following on the board: _ ite. Ask the children what letter they would need to complete a word which means "a toy which you fly in the sky on a string." Affirm correct answers and invite a child to come to the board and fill in the blank with the letter K.

Continue in the same manner with the following words, leaving out one of the consonant letters of your choice: mask, drum, barn, lips, desk.

Worksheet 125A: Read the instructions aloud. Assist the children to use the pictures in order to determine what the completed words should be. Then monitor as they write in the necessary letters to complete the words accordingly.

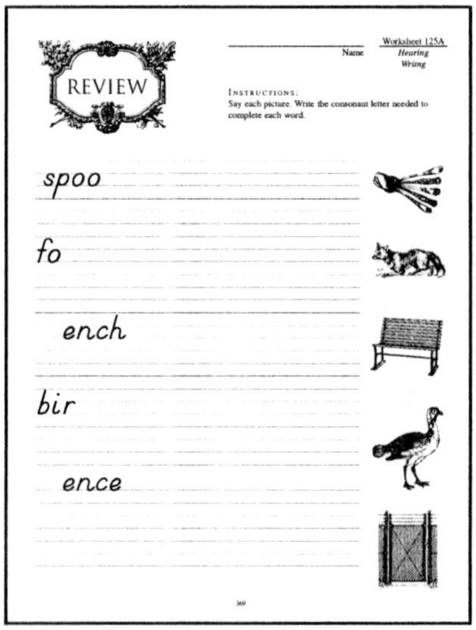

ACTIVITY 2: VOCABULARY AND SPECIAL EXHIBIT WORDS FOR CYRUS THE ARCHER

Write the words found on Worksheet 125B on the board, but do not include the Special Exhibits.

Assist the children to decode and read the words. Define any unfamiliar terms according to the meanings listed in the next lesson. Use the words in original sentences to reinforce meaning.

Pay special attention to the name "Cyrus" and the use of Y as long I at the end of the first syllable, and to the word "genius" and the use of I as long E (similar to the former names "Aurelius" and "Claudius" in SERVING IN THE SHADOW OF DEATH).

After they have read all the regular vocabulary and special words, write the four new Special Exhibits on the board: very, body, build, two.

Explain that in some words with VC and Y, the first vowel may be short.

Draw breves over the E in "very" and the O in "body."

Read the words aloud and have the children echo them. Now pronounce them with long E and long O for contrast. Affirm that the words pronounced with the long vowel sounds are meaningless. Remind them that sometimes they must be "sound scientists" to determine how words sound and what they mean!

Draw attention to the word "build." In this word, the U is a silent partner. Draw a backslash through the U.

Write a breve over the I. Challenge the students to decode and read this word. Affirm correct responses. Use the word in a sentence.

Finally, point to the word "two." Tell them that there is a silent partner in this word also.

Hold up two fingers or point to the number 2 somewhere in the room. Tell them this is the meaning of this word. Allow them to respond with the word "two."

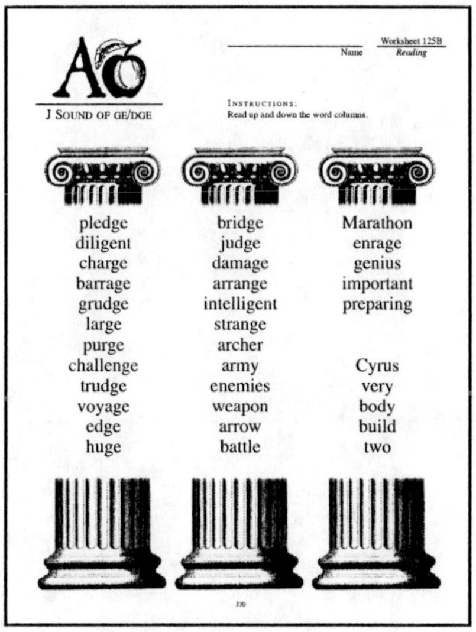
Worksheet 125B
Name
Reading

J Sound of GE/DGE

Instructions:
Read up and down the word columns.

pledge	bridge	Marathon
diligent	judge	enrage
charge	damage	genius
barrage	arrange	important
grudge	intelligent	preparing
large	strange	
purge	archer	
challenge	army	Cyrus
trudge	enemies	very
voyage	weapon	body
edge	arrow	build
huge	battle	two

Ask them what letter in the word on the board is not heard when they say "two." (W) Backslash through the W. Affirm that the O in this word makes the long U sound. Write the Special Exhibit "to" on the board. Affirm that this word sounds the same. The spelling makes the difference in meaning. Use both words in original sentences.

Worksheet 125B: Read the instructions aloud. Use any of the previous techniques or variations for eliciting student responses.

Lesson 126
Reading CYRUS THE ARCHER

ACTIVITY 1: READING ALOUD

This story chronicles the invasion of Greece by the Persian Army (from the East) in the early 400's B.C. The building of the bridge of boats and the counting of troops in "cages" is historical fact.

Before reading the story, you may want to look for Persia and Greece on a map of the ancient world and trace the probable route of the Persian Army.

The following vocabulary and expressions are used:

archer—one who is skilled at shooting a bow
Army of (from) the East—Persian army
King of the East—Darius I
diligent—hard-working, applied
master archer—one of the best archers
enrage—make angry
grudge—bitterness toward

Battle of Marathon—major defeat of the Persian army at the hands of the Greeks
purge—get rid of
trudge—march
East to West—Asia to Europe
barge—a boat used for transporting freight
planks—long, flat pieces of wood
wedge—push in between
rig up sails—the sails were tied up on either side of the walkway
twinge—small, sharp pain; a pang
nudge—push or prod
budge—move
sage—clever, wise
corral—fenced-in area
intelligent—smart
troops—soldiers
range of hills—chain of mountains
climbing up from the sea—the mountains rise steeply from the shoreline
fringe of clouds—a feathery wisp of clouds
inhale—breathe in
pass—cut-out area through a mountain range
arrangement—formation, lines
combat—fight
genius—very intelligent

In addition, you will need to assist the children with the numbers in this story.

Guide the children in the round robin reading of the story. Discuss main characters, ideas, and events as they occur.

Some questions for discussion may include: What would make a bow and arrow more effective than a spear? Why do they need to hide the view of the sea from the animals? What do you think of the idea of counting large numbers in "cages" or "groups"? Do we do anything like this when we count by two's or three's?

ACTIVITY 2: WRITING

Write the sentence found on Worksheet 126A on the board, along with lines. Invite students to the board to copy the words of the sentence in order on the lines. Monitor letter and word spacing carefully.

Worksheet 126A: Read the instructions aloud. Monitor as they copy the sentence independently.

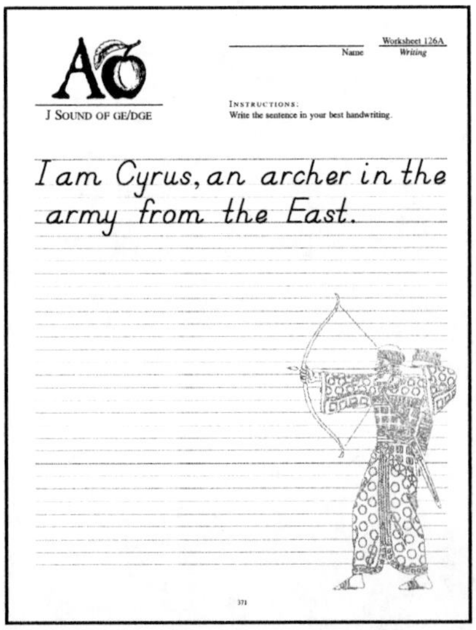
Worksheet 126A
Name
Writing
J Sound of GE/DGE
Instructions:
Write the sentence in your best handwriting.
I am Cyrus, an archer in the army from the East.

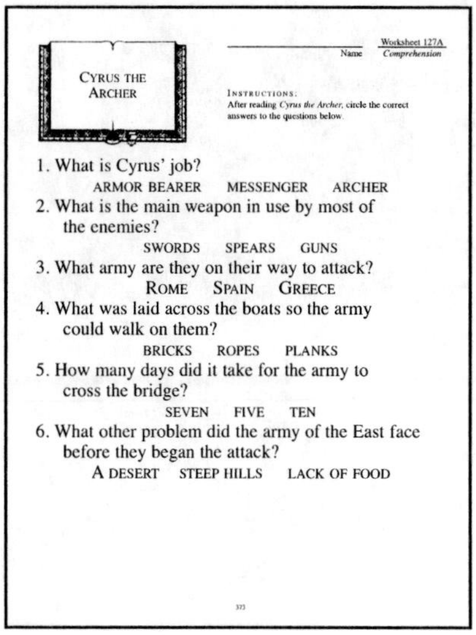
Worksheet 127A
Comprehension
Name

CYRUS THE ARCHER

INSTRUCTIONS:
After reading *Cyrus the Archer*, circle the correct answers to the questions below.

1. What is Cyrus' job?
ARMOR BEARER MESSENGER ARCHER
2. What is the main weapon in use by most of the enemies?
SWORDS SPEARS GUNS
3. What army are they on their way to attack?
ROME SPAIN GREECE
4. What was laid across the boats so the army could walk on them?
BRICKS ROPES PLANKS
5. How many days did it take for the army to cross the bridge?
SEVEN FIVE TEN
6. What other problem did the army of the East face before they began the attack?
A DESERT STEEP HILLS LACK OF FOOD

373

LESSON 127
READING COMPREHENSION

ACTIVITY 1: COMPREHENSION

Briefly review the story CYRUS THE ARCHER.

Worksheet 127A: Read the instructions aloud. Call on students to read the questions and the answer choices. Allow children to make their choices independently and circle the answers as indicated.

ACTIVITY 2: ART ACTIVITY

Worksheet 127B: Build a bridge!

LESSON 128
REVIEW

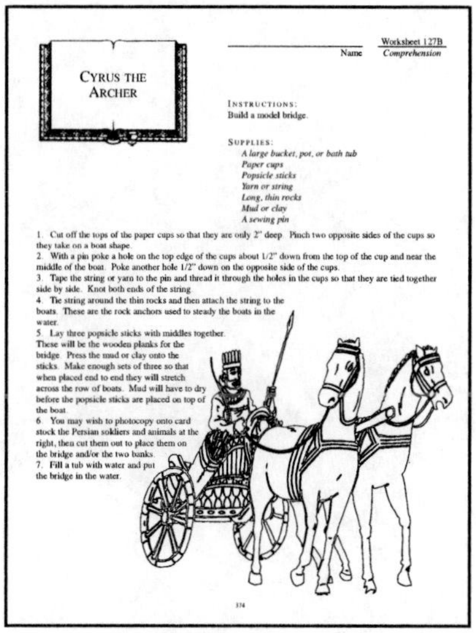
Worksheet 127B
Comprehension
Name

CYRUS THE ARCHER

INSTRUCTIONS:
Build a model bridge.

SUPPLIES:
A large bucket, pot, or bath tub
Paper cups
Popsicle sticks
Yarn or string
Long, thin rocks
Mud or clay
A sewing pin

1. Cut off the tops of the paper cups so that they are only 2" deep. Pinch two opposite sides of the cups so they take on a boat shape.
2. With a pin poke a hole on the top edge of the cups about 1/2" down from the top of the cup and near the middle of the boat. Poke another hole 1/2" down on the opposite side of the cups.
3. Tape the string or yarn to the pin and thread it through the holes in the cups so that they are tied together side by side. Knot both ends of the string.
4. Tie string around the thin rocks and then attach the string to the boats. These are the rock anchors used to steady the boats in the water.
5. Lay three popsicle sticks with middles together. These will be the wooden planks for the bridge. Press the mud or clay onto the sticks. Make enough sets of three so that when placed end to end they will stretch across the row of boats. Mud will have to dry before the popsicle sticks are placed on top of the boat.
6. You may wish to photocopy onto card stock the Persian soldiers and animals at the right, then cut them out to place them on the bridge and/or the two banks.
7. Fill a tub with water and put the bridge in the water.

374

Play the song How Many Sounds? for the children encouraging them to sing.

ACTIVITY 1: HEARING

Read the following list and have the children raise their hands to answer whether the words have short or long vowels.

pen	hat	pine	top	cat	boat
not	tub	bead	bed	pig	tote
pea	hate	note	tube	box	cake

Praise their careful listening!

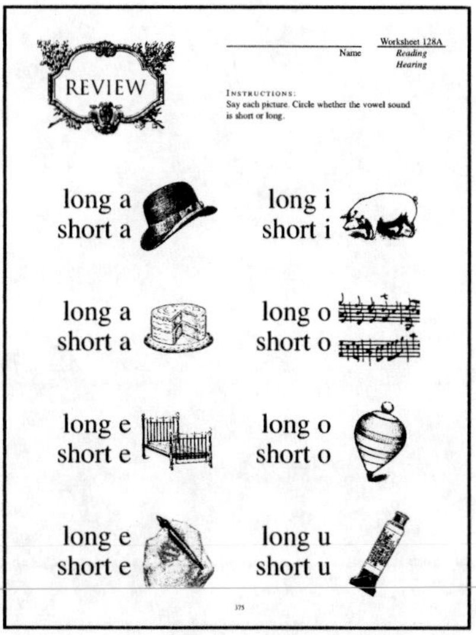
Worksheet 128A
Reading
Hearing
Name

REVIEW

INSTRUCTIONS:
Say each picture. Circle whether the vowel sound is short or long.

long a / short a — long i / short i
long a / short a — long o / short o
long e / short e — long o / short o
long e / short e — long u / short u

375

Worksheet 128A: Read the instructions aloud. Tell the children to say the words quietly to themselves, determine if the word has a short or long vowel sound, and circle the correct answer. Assist with labeling as necessary.

Row 1: hat, pig
Row 2: cake, notes
Row 3: bed, top
Row 4: pen, tube

ACTIVITY 2: HEARING AND WRITING

Call students to the board to write the following: CH, SH, TH, WH. Ask them to tell the class what sound is made by each of these letter pairs and to give an example of a word which starts with each one.

Write their word examples on the board. Circle the targeted letter pair in each one.

Worksheet 128B: Read the instructions aloud. Remind them that the pictures at the end of the guidelines will be the clue to the word at the beginning of the guidelines. Assist as necessary to complete the words correctly.

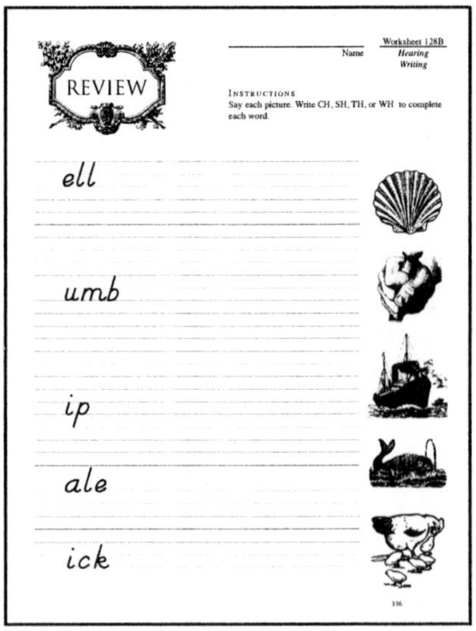

Tomorrow is the Spelling Test on List 9. You may want to do a spelling bee today to review and prepare!

Archives: Long Vowel Edition

LESSON 129
TARGET: TION/SION AND SPELLING TEST 9

Play the Mission to the Moon song for the children encouraging them to sing along.

Show the children the flashcard with TION/SION on it. Have them hear the sound of SHUN in "adoration."

ACTIVITY 1: HEARING AND SEEING TION/SION

Make the SH sound several times to start the class today. Encourage the children to echo it after you and "shush" one another.

Invite a child to come to the board and write the letter pair which makes the SH sound.

Now explain that other letter pairs in our language will make this sound as well. Write TI and SI on the board.

When TI and SI make the SH sound, they take along two other buddy letters. Write ON after each letter pair, forming TION and SION. These four letters will make their own syllable which sounds like this: SHUN.

Tell them that we use words which use the TION or SION syllables all the time. Say the following, exaggerating the SHUN sound in each word: action, mission, question, mansion.

Write the above words on the board, under the letter pair which is contained in each.

Invite students to the board to circle the TI or SI in each word and then underline the entire TION or SION syllable.

Now, have the children experiment a little with you. Have them say SH several times, then add their voices to make ZH. You may want them to place their hands on their throats to reinforce the feel of the vibration of the vocal cords.

Tell them that sometimes the SION will sound like ZHUN. Assure them that you will assist them when they come to words which use this voiced sound.

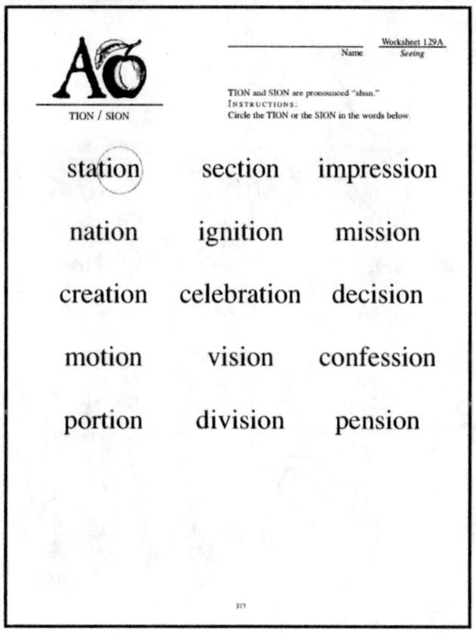
Worksheet 129A
Name
Seeing
TION / SION
TION and SION are pronounced "shun."
INSTRUCTIONS:
Circle the TION or the SION in the words below.

station	section	impression
nation	ignition	mission
creation	celebration	decision
motion	vision	confession
portion	division	pension

377

Worksheet 129A: Read the instructions aloud. Monitor as they respond as indicated. Read the words aloud and have the children echo after you. Pay special attention to the word "creation"—both of the vowels are long and form separate syllables. Also, the words "vision," "division" and "decision" all use the SI as ZH!

Give them their museum bag. Allow them time to go through the house and collect items that have the TION/SION blend sound to make their own museum. If you are teaching in a school setting, instruct the children to take the bag home and bring in objects the following day.

ACTIVITY 2: SPELLING TEST 9

Worksheet 129B
Name
Spelling Test
SPELLING TEST 9
1.
2.
3.
4.
5.
6.
7.
8.
9.
10.

378

Worksheet 129B: Administer the test on Spelling List 9. Read each word once, use it in a sentence, then repeat it. Do not give any other sound or letter clues.

You may want to give the students the coloring page along with the flashcard. Read the information about the artist to your students before they color the picture.

Lesson 130
Target: TION/SION

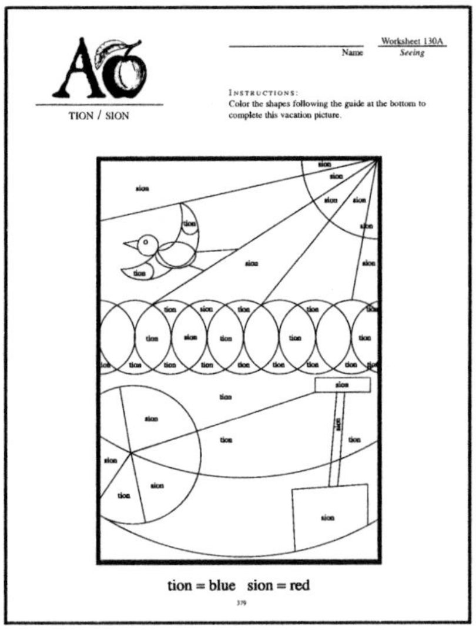

Play the Mission to the Moon song for the children encouraging them to sing along.

ACTIVITY 1: SEEING

Draw an artist's palette on the board, labeling the paint splotches according to the key on Worksheet 130A.

Worksheet 130A: Read the instructions aloud. Allow the children to work independently, following the coloring key as shown on the board.

ACTIVITY 2: READING

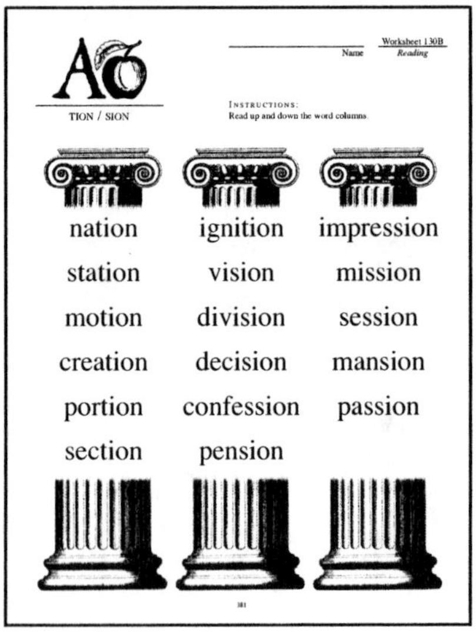
Worksheet 130B
Name
Reading
TION / SION
INSTRUCTIONS:
Read up and down the word columns.

nation	ignition	impression
station	vision	mission
motion	division	session
creation	decision	mansion
portion	confession	passion
section	pension	

Invite a child to the board to write the two letter groups which say SHUN. (TION and SION). Have them write one on the left side of the board and the other on the right side.

Write the words found on Worksheet 130B on the board, placing them under or around the appropriate letter group according to spelling.

Read the words aloud and have the child echo them after you. Define any unfamiliar words and use them in sentences.

Call attention to the words which use SI as ZH: mission, division, decision.

Worksheet 130B: Read the instructions aloud. Use any of the previous variations or techniques to elicit student response.

Percival's Pairs: Using ING, ANG, ONG, blends, long vowels Y as I, EE, EA, OA, OE OW, OO, OY, OU, OW, SOFT C, and AW

Lesson 131
Target: TION/SION

Play the Mission to the Moon song for the children encouraging them to sing along.

ACTIVITY 1: READING

Write the words found on Worksheet 131A on the board.

Read each one aloud, have the children echo them after you, define unfamiliar terms and use in original sentences.

Many of these are multisyllablic words. It may be a good idea to clap out the syllables and do a little syllabication review at this time to assist in decoding. Remind them about the long sound of vowels in syllables which end in vowels and the short sounds of vowels when they are "closed in" by consonants. Explain again that long words are just made up of "pieces of syllables," which can be read separately and then put together.

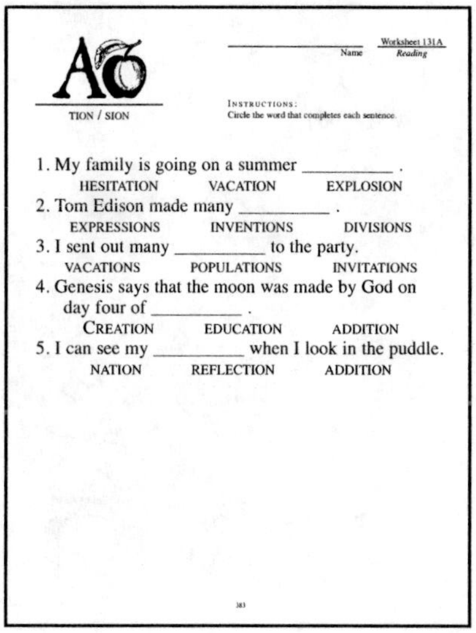
Worksheet 131A
Reading
Name ____________
TION / SION
Instructions: Circle the word that completes each sentence.

1. My family is going on a summer ________ .
   HESITATION VACATION EXPLOSION
2. Tom Edison made many ________ .
   EXPRESSIONS INVENTIONS DIVISIONS
3. I sent out many ________ to the party.
   VACATIONS POPULATIONS INVITATIONS
4. Genesis says that the moon was made by God on day four of ________ .
   CREATION EDUCATION ADDITION
5. I can see my ________ when I look in the puddle.
   NATION REFLECTION ADDITION

Worksheet 131A: Read the instructions aloud. Call on students to read the sentences and the word choices. Assist them to decode the word "fourth" in sentence 4 since it uses OU as long O (relate it to their Special Exhibit "your"). Monitor as they select the best word to finish each sentence and circle it as indicated.

ACTIVITY 2: WRITING

Write the sentence found on Worksheet 131B on the board, along with lines. Read the sentence aloud and have the children read it in unison with you.

Call on students to come to the board and copy the words of the sentence in order on the lines.

Monitor letter formation and spacing.

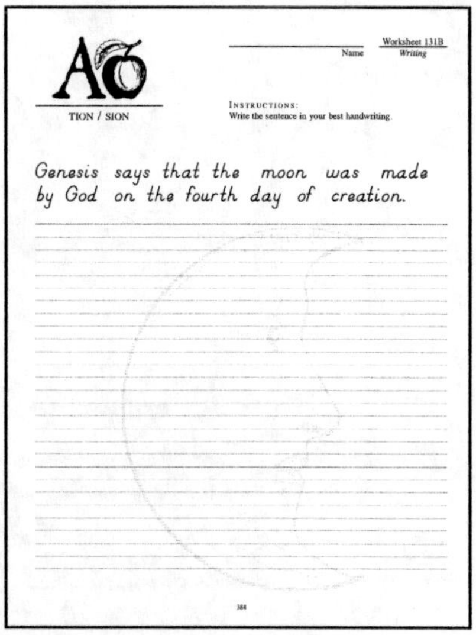
Worksheet 131B
Writing
Name ____________
TION / SION
Instructions: Write the sentence in your best handwriting.

Genesis says that the moon was made by God on the fourth day of creation.

Worksheet 131B: Read the instructions aloud. Monitor as they copy the sentence independently.

Some children may have more difficulty than others with the new size of the print and the length of the sentence. Assist them as necessary.

Lesson 132
Review

Play the Mission to the Moon song for the children encouraging them to sing along.

ACTIVITY 1: HEARING

Tell the children to be "sound detectives" today and discover what today's review sound is. Read the following, exaggerating the long U sounds:

Do you have a broom in the room?
You are doomed if you do not use a broom to groom the room!

Affirm that the sound they were listening for is long U.

Remind them that long U can be spelled in a number of ways. They have learned two so far: the letter U (especially when final silent E is at the end of the word) and the letter pair OO.

Today we will be concentrating on long U spelled as OO. Write OO on the board. Underneath and slightly to the left, write the following: BROOM, ROOM, DOOM, GROOM.

Call on students to read each of the words. Allow them to make up their own sentences using each one.

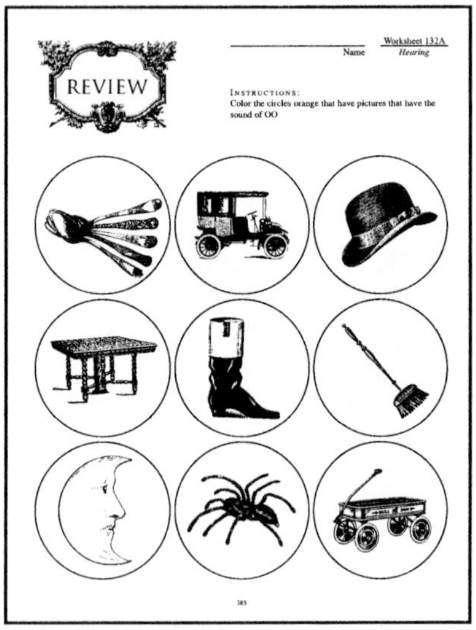

Worksheet 132A: Read the instructions aloud. Assist as necessary to label the pictures, but encourage independent work as much as possible.

Row 1: spoons, car, hat
Row 2: table, boot, broom
Row 3: moon, spider, wagon

ACTIVITY 2: HEARING, READING, AND WRITING

Now, ask if any of them remember the OTHER sound which is made by OO. (short OO as in "book") Remind them if necessary and affirm correct responses.

Write the following under the OO on the board and slightly to the right: LOOK, GOOD, HOOD, BROOK. Call on students to read each one and use in original sentences.

Remind them that we call this "short OO" and draw a breve over the OO in each of these words.

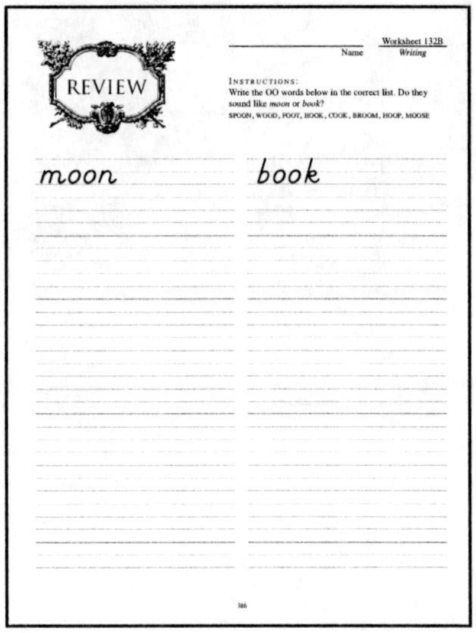
Worksheet 132B
Name
Writing

REVIEW

INSTRUCTIONS:
Write the OO words below in the correct list. Do they sound like *moon* or *book*?
SPOON, WOOD, FOOT, HOOK, COOK, BROOM, HOOF, MOOSE

moon	book

Worksheet 132B: Read the instructions aloud. Call on students to read each of the words on the list under the instructions. They may "experiment" with both of the sound of OO in order to determine how each is pronounced with meaning. They may then write the words in the proper columns as they have marked them.

Tell the children to draw a long breve over the OO in the word "book." Instruct them to draw breves over those words which have the short OO sounds.

Lesson 133
Review and Alphabetical Order

Play the Alphabet Song and Crash! Swing! Squash! for the children encouraging them to sing along.

ACTIVITY 1: REVIEW OF L AND R BLENDS

Write the following on index cards: FL, BL, CL, TR, BR, GR, DR, FR.

In the school setting, play "Around the World" today with these blend cards. One student rises and stands beside the desk of another. Present one of the blend cards to them and let them race to think of and say a word which begins with that blend. The child who does this correctly first proceeds to stand beside the next child in the next desk, while the "losing" child sits in the first desk (even though it may not be theirs). Proceed "Around the World (Room)" in this manner, using all the blends several times.

If teaching in the home, write the blends on the board then play a game of associations. The teacher calls out a word using the first blend then the child calls back with another word using that blend and so on until one can't think of a word using that blend and moves onto the next blend. This continues until all the blends are used.

Worksheet 133A
Name
Reading
Hearing

REVIEW

INSTRUCTIONS:
Match the blend on the left to the correct picture on the right. There are more blends than pictures.

bl
fl
cl
tr
br
gr
dr
fr

Worksheet 133A: Read the instructions aloud. Monitor the students' progress as they work independently.

ACTIVITY 2: ALPHABETICAL ORDER

Write the following words on the board: mansion, mission, action, ration.

Review with the children aloud, how to put them in alphabetical order, numbering the words from 1-4.

Worksheet 133B: Read the instructions aloud. Remind them to number the words first, then copy them onto the lists accordingly. Assist with the alphabetizing of "addition" and "affection" on the second list as necessary.

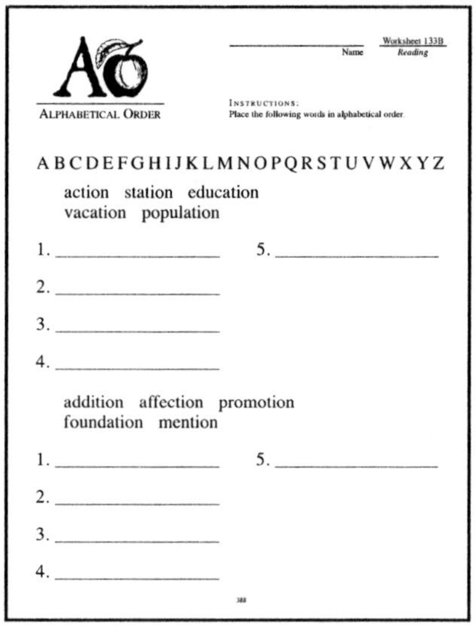
Worksheet 133B
Reading
Name

ALPHABETICAL ORDER

INSTRUCTIONS:
Place the following words in alphabetical order.

A B C D E F G H I J K L M N O P Q R S T U V W X Y Z

action station education
vacation population

1. ______ 5. ______
2. ______
3. ______
4. ______

addition affection promotion
foundation mention

1. ______ 5. ______
2. ______
3. ______
4. ______

388

ACTIVITY 3: WRITING

Write the sentence found on Worksheet 133C on the board, along with lines. Read the sentence aloud and have the children echo it after you.

Invite students to the board to copy the words of the sentence in order on the lines. Monitor letter and word spacing carefully.

Worksheet 133C: Read the instructions aloud. Monitor as they copy it independently.

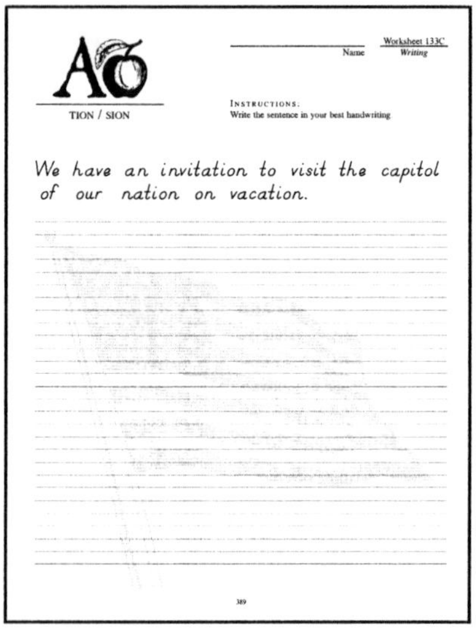
Worksheet 133C
Writing
Name

TION / SION

INSTRUCTIONS:
Write the sentence in your best handwriting.

We have an invitation to visit the capitol of our nation on vacation.

389

LESSON 134
TARGET: TION/SION

Play the Mission to the Moon song for the children encouraging them to sing along.

ACTIVITY 1: SPELLING LIST 10

Write the words found on Worksheet 134A on the board. As you write them, say the letter names in order as an oral spelling activity.

Assist the children to decode and read each one. Use them in original sentences.

Worksheets 134A: Read the instructions aloud. Monitor the students' progress as they work independently.

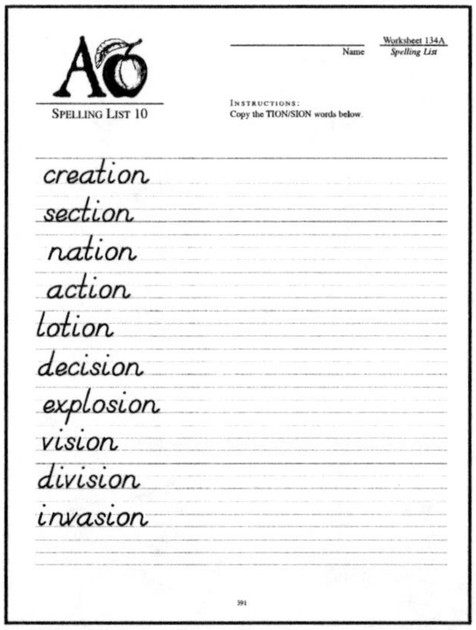
Worksheet 134A
Spelling List
Name

SPELLING LIST 10

INSTRUCTIONS:
Copy the TION/SION words below.

creation
section
nation
action
lotion
decision
explosion
vision
division
invasion

391

Encourage neatness and accuracy in spelling! Recommend that they silently read the letter names as they copy the words to assist in putting all the letters in the right order.

Archives: Special Exhibit Edition.

Lesson 135
Review of OU

Play the Shout song for the children encouraging them to sing along.

ACTIVITY 1: HEARING AND WRITING

Remind the children of the two sounds of OU: OU as in the Special Exhibit "our" and as long O as in the Special Exhibits "your." Write these two Special Exhibits on the board, "our" on the top left and "your" on the top right.

Write a macron over the O in "your" to help them remember how this OU is pronounced.

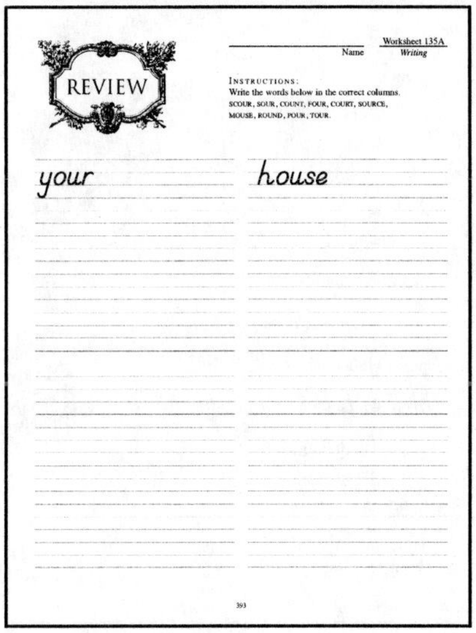
Worksheet 135A
Writing
Name
REVIEW
INSTRUCTIONS:
Write the words below in the correct columns.
SCOUR, SOUR, COUNT, FOUR, COURT, SOURCE, MOUSE, ROUND, POUR, TOUR.

your	house

393

Tell the children you will be reading a list of words, and they are to raise their left hands if the sound of OU is the same as that in "our," and their right hands if the sound is the same as in "your." Read the following, watching carefully for accurate responses:

sour	mouse	pour	four	count
bounce	scour	tour	round	court
pound	source			

Praise their careful listening!

Worksheet 135A: Read the instructions aloud. Assist them to decode and read the words as necessary. Allow them to write macrons over the O in the words which use long O and then transfer the words to the proper lists. Monitor as they write them in the correct columns.

ACTIVITY 2: WRITING

Worksheet 135B
Writing
Name
TION / SION
INSTRUCTIONS:
Write the sentence in your best handwriting.

The mouse ran in the house to pounce on the snout of the hound.

394

Write the sentence found on Worksheet 135B on the board, along with lines. Invite students to the board to copy the words of the sentence in order on the lines.

Monitor letter and word spacing carefully.

Worksheet 135B: Read the instructions aloud. Monitor the students' progress as they work independently.

Lesson 136
Review

Play the song How Many Sounds? for the children encouraging them to sing.

ACTIVITY 1: HEARING AND READING

If teaching in a school setting, divide the class into two halves, the "Short Vowel Team" and the "Long Vowel Team."

Tell the children that one person from each team will come to the front of the room. You will show them a vowel letter flashcard. They must come up with a word which has either the short or long sound of that letter in it, according to what team they are on. The first person to give a real word with their team's sound will get a point.

For instance, when you show the E, the short vowel team must come up with a word using the short E sound (in any position) before the long vowel team comes up with one using long E (or vice versa) in order to get the point for that round.

Keep a tally of the points on the board for each team.

In the home setting, use the puzzle pieces to have the child create words that have short or long vowels. Keep a list of the words made to see if the students come up with more short or long vowel words.

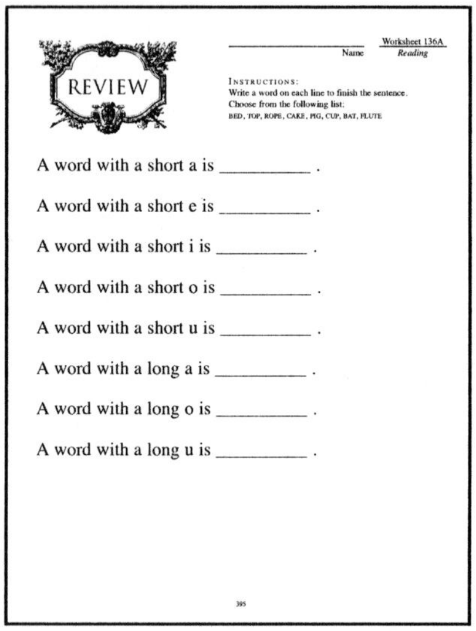

REVIEW

_______________ Name

Worksheet 136A
Reading

INSTRUCTIONS:
Write a word on each line to finish the sentence.
Choose from the following list:
BED, TOP, ROPE, CAKE, PIG, CUP, BAT, FLUTE

A word with a short a is ________ .

A word with a short e is ________ .

A word with a short i is ________ .

A word with a short o is ________ .

A word with a short u is ________ .

A word with a long a is ________ .

A word with a long o is ________ .

A word with a long u is ________ .

Worksheet 136A: Read the instructions aloud. Monitor their work.

Worksheet 136B: Read the instructions aloud. Allow the children to read the sentences describing the colors to be used for which objects. Monitor carefully as they complete the page as directed.

REVIEW

_______________ Name

Worksheet 136B
Reading

INSTRUCTIONS:
The animal friends have gone sailing! Color in the picture following the instructions below.

Color the cat orange.
Color the pig pink.
Color the horse brown.
Color the frog green.
Color the butterfly purple.

Lesson 137
Vocabulary and Special Words for MOON MISSION

ACTIVITY 1: TION/SION VOCABULARY WORDS

Tell the children that today they will be decoding some long words which they will need to know in order to read their next story. All of them will end with TION or SION, so they already know one part of each of them!

Review with the children of how we link letters and the sounds they make together to make words. In long words, the letters can be grouped into pieces which we have called "syllables." Each syllable will have a "beat" and will always contain a vowel sound.

Write the following on the board: BED, STORY, STARVATION. Read each word and clap out the syllables along with the children. Ask how many syllables are heard in each word.

Write a number 1 over the E in the word "bed" since it has one syllable. Tell them that you place the number over the vowel because it is the sound which "makes" the syllable. Draw a slash between the O and R in the word "story." Explain that this is where we divide the two syllables in this word. Write a 1 over the O in the syllable "sto" and a 2 over Y in the syllable "ry." Remind them that when syllables end in vowels, the vowel sound is usually long.

Now, clap out "starvation" again. Affirm that it has 3 syllables. Say the first syllable "star." Invite a child to come to the board and write a 1 over the A in this syllable.

Now, say the second syllable "va." The A makes the long sound. Where will the second syllable end? (with the vowel A) Invite a child to come to the board and write a 2 over the A in "va."

Draw attention to the syllable which is left. It is TION. Remind them that they have learned that TION and SION make their own syllables. Underline the TION in this word and write a 3 over the O. Explain that since the I doesn't really make any sound and "goes with" the T to make the SH sound, it isn't the vowel in this syllable.

Say the word again, in separate syllables and then fluently as a word. Define the word and use it in an original sentence.

Now, explain that some words may have even more beats. Assure them that if they are able to break the word down into syllables, they will be able to read words that look very long!

Write the following on the board: HESITATION, GENERATION, INNOVATION.

First, ask the children what they see at the end of each word. (TION) So, they already know one of the syllables. Underline the TION in each word.

Now, guide them to break the words into syllables by reading the first syllable of the word "hesitation" ("hes") Sound it out by using short E and S as Z. Write a 1 over the E. Point to the letter I. Tell them that the I makes the short sound in this word and is a syllable all by itself. Write a 2 over the I. Now, draw attention to the fact that there are only two letters left between the I and the T (in TION). These two letters are another syllable. Ask the children how the A will be pronounced, since it is coming at the end of the syllable. (as long A) Write a 3 over the A in "ta." Ask them what should be written over the O in TION. (4) Affirm correct answers and write in the number.

Guide the children through the sounding out of the word, syllable by syllable, with greater and greater fluency until the word "hesitation" is spoken. Tell the children that this word means "to pause" or "stop briefly." When we read, we try to do it without "hesitation!"

Affirm that it is a long word, but praise and encourage them that they are able to read it by breaking it down into smaller syllables.

Continue in the same manner with "generation" and "innovation." The syllabication patterns are as follows:

gen/er/a/tion in/no/va/tion

Make sure you write the syllable numbers over the vowels to reinforce the vowel/syllable connection.

Define each word and use in an original sentence.

Write the words found on Worksheet 137 on the board for a stimulus display and demonstration for the next worksheet.

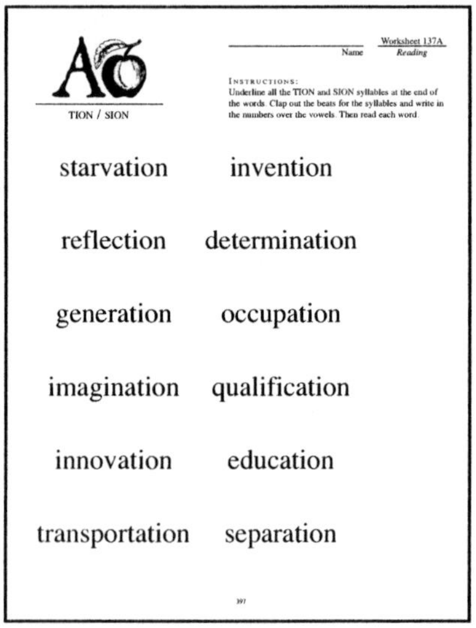
TION / SION

Name

Worksheet 137A
Reading

INSTRUCTIONS:
Underline all the TION and SION syllables at the end of the words. Clap out the beats for the syllables and write in the numbers over the vowels. Then read each word.

starvation invention

reflection determination

generation occupation

imagination qualification

innovation education

transportation separation

Worksheet 137A: Read the instructions aloud. Monitor as they underline all the TION/SION endings. Read them aloud, have them echo and clap out the syllables. Demonstrate on the board how to number above the vowels in each word and monitor as they do so on their own papers. Finally, elicit student reading of the words as independently as possible.

ACTIVITY 2: MORE SYLLABICATION

Write the word "creation" on the board. Remind the children that the E and A both make long sounds in this word. Read the word aloud, slowly breaking it into syllables. Ask the children how many syllables they hear. (3) Invite a child to the board to write in the numbers over the vowels for each syllable.

Draw attention to the fact that in this word the EA does not go together. Each vowel goes with a different syllable.

Tell the children that there are other words which are broken into syllables between their vowels like this one. Write the following on the board: giant, fuel, coordination. Underline the IA in "giant," the UE in "fuel," and the OO in "coordination."

Explain that in these words, the first vowel goes with the first syllable and the second vowel goes with the second syllable. Write a 1 over the first vowel in each word and a 2 over the second vowel.

Ask the children what sound the first vowel will make in these words, since it is at the end of the first syllable. (long)

Remind them that the G will be "soft" since it comes before I. Call on a student to decode the first syllable "gi" .

Call on a student to decode the second syllable "ant." Say the word several times, with greater and greater fluency until the word "giant" is spoken. Ask the children to define this word—they should all know!

The short A sound in this word is generally spoken as short E or short I. You may allow your students to pronounce it in this way after they have decoded it according to the above pattern.

Continue in the same manner with the other two words. Define and use in sentences as necessary.

The word "fuel" is often slurred into one syllable in spontaneous speech, although some still pronounce it with an unstressed schwa in the second syllable. Again, you may allow your students to pronounce it in this way after they have decoded it according to the above pattern.

Now write the word "scientist" on the board. Tell them that this is another example of a word in which the vowel pair splits into two syllables. Write a 1 over the I, a 2 over the E, and a 3 over the second I.

Remind them that since the first I comes at the end of the syllable, it will be long.

Read the word aloud, first in separate syllables, then fluently into the word "scientist." Tell them there is something else which is unusual about this word. Circle the SC at the beginning. Ask the children how we usually say the letter pair SC (as a blend as in the word "scout"). Say the word "scientist" again. Ask if they hear the hard C (K) sound at the beginning. (NO) Affirm that in this word, the SC make the same S sound. Remind them that we already know how C can make the S sound. In this word it just remains silent and lets the S do it!

You may want to backslash through the C to symbolize that it is silent. This could be a good lead in for the next part of the lesson.

Now, tell them that there are two more words which they will need to know for this next story. Write the word "people" on the board.

Tell them this is another Special Exhibit word. The O is silent and the E is long. Backslash through the O.

Draw a macron over the E.

Challenge the children to decode it according to your markings.

Write the word "special" on the board. Tell them that this word really is SPECIAL! Circle the CI. Explain that in this word the CI makes the SH sound just like TI and SI.

Worksheet 137B: Read the instructions aloud. Repeat the above activity, instructing the children to do the same with the words on their papers. Elicit student reading of the words and use in original sentences.

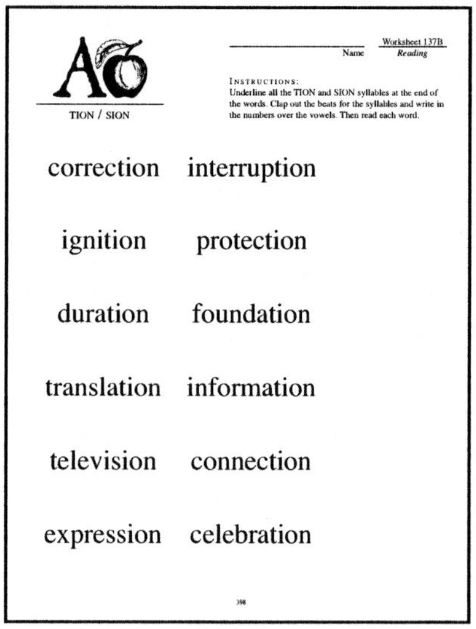
TION / SION

Name

Worksheet 137B
Reading

INSTRUCTIONS:
Underline all the TION and SION syllables at the end of the words. Clap out the beats for the syllables and write in the numbers over the vowels. Then read each word.

correction interruption

ignition protection

duration foundation

translation information

television connection

expression celebration

Lesson 138
Reading MOON MISSION

This story describes the early space program and the first landing on the moon in 1969. It contains many proper names/titles which the children may need assistance to read. The following is a list of these.

United States	John F. Kennedy
American	Alan Shepard
July	Apollo
Michael Collins	Lunar Module
Neil Armstrong	Edwin Aldrin

In addition, the following vocabulary is used:

Genesis—the first book of the Bible
starvation—lack of food
reflection—return of light waves from a surface
generations—ancestors/descendants
imagination—creativity
innovation—development of new ideas
transportation—mode of travel
invention—development and building of new ideas/machines/etc.
explosion—blast
research—exploring, study
mission—trip with a goal
vision—dream
determination—desire to succeed
occupation—job

qualifications—abilities
education—studying to gain knowledge
tension—stress
capsule—a compact compartment
separation—disconnection, taking apart
section—part
fuel—gas
portion—part
gravity—force of attraction which draws us to earth
(assist to decode with short I as in "family")
hesitation—a concerned pause
corrections—repairs
ignition—start up
duration—length
division—split
motion—movement
coordination—working together, team effort
translation—changing from one language to another
millions—many thousands
(assist to decode with I as long E, as in "genius")
commander—captain
expression—emotion
interruptions—breaks
protection—watchful care
foundation—solid base
traction—ability to grip
connection—hook-up, link
celebration—party

In addition, the word "mirror" is used in this story. While it may be decoded using the short I sound, permit students to modify the pronunciation of this word into its more familiar form (utilizing I as long E) when it has been recognized. The students will also need assistance with the dates and numbers in this story.

Guide the children through the round robin reading of the story. Call attention to main characters, ideas, and events as they occur.

Hyphens are used in one of the early sentences to set a phrase apart. Tell the children that this only means that one should pause briefly.

Some questions for discussion may include: Would you like to go into space? Why or why not? What kinds of things are difficult in a place with little or no gravity? Why do men need special gear in space or on the moon?

Lesson 139
Reading Comprehension

Play the Mission to the Moon song for the children encouraging them to sing along.

ACTIVITY 1: WRITING

Briefly review the story MOON MISSION. Tell the children that you will be doing the next worksheet together to go over the events of the story.

Worksheet 139A: Read the instructions aloud. Call on students to read each sentence in the paragraph, leaving out the blanks when they are encountered. Assist them to determine which word in the Word Bank best completes each sentence and copy it into the appropriate blank. They will need some help with some of the Word Bank words.

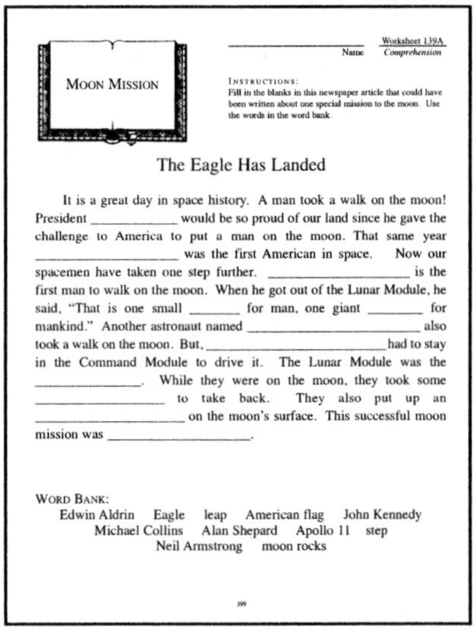

Moon Mission

Name ____________ Worksheet 139A *Comprehension*

INSTRUCTIONS:
Fill in the blanks in this newspaper article that could have been written about one special mission to the moon. Use the words in the word bank.

The Eagle Has Landed

It is a great day in space history. A man took a walk on the moon! President ____________ would be so proud of our land since he gave the challenge to America to put a man on the moon. That same year ____________ was the first American in space. Now our spacemen have taken one step further. ____________ is the first man to walk on the moon. When he got out of the Lunar Module, he said, "That is one small _______ for man, one giant _______ for mankind." Another astronaut named ____________ also took a walk on the moon. But, ____________ had to stay in the Command Module to drive it. The Lunar Module was the ____________. While they were on the moon, they took some ____________ to take back. They also put up an ____________ on the moon's surface. This successful moon mission was ____________.

WORD BANK:
Edwin Aldrin Eagle leap American flag John Kennedy
Michael Collins Alan Shepard Apollo 11 step
Neil Armstrong moon rocks

399

Worksheet 139B: Test. This test is optional and is added to evaluate your students if you feel it is necessary at this time. The answers are worth 10 points each.

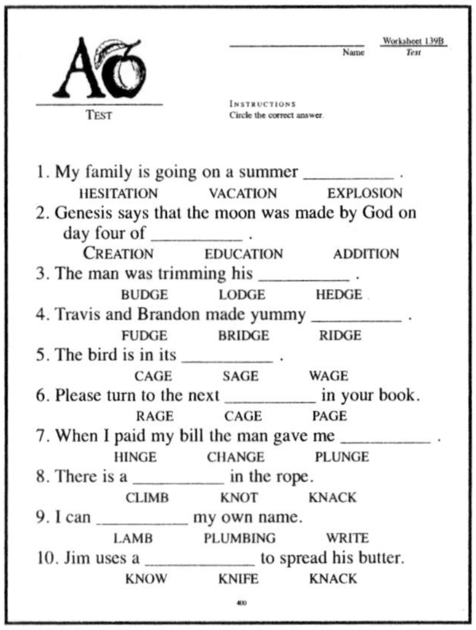

TEST

Name ____________ Worksheet 139B *Test*

INSTRUCTIONS
Circle the correct answer.

1. My family is going on a summer ____________ .
HESITATION VACATION EXPLOSION
2. Genesis says that the moon was made by God on day four of ____________ .
CREATION EDUCATION ADDITION
3. The man was trimming his ____________ .
BUDGE LODGE HEDGE
4. Travis and Brandon made yummy ____________ .
FUDGE BRIDGE RIDGE
5. The bird is in its ____________ .
CAGE SAGE WAGE
6. Please turn to the next ____________ in your book.
RAGE CAGE PAGE
7. When I paid my bill the man gave me ____________ .
HINGE CHANGE PLUNGE
8. There is a ____________ in the rope.
CLIMB KNOT KNACK
9. I can ____________ my own name.
LAMB PLUMBING WRITE
10. Jim uses a ____________ to spread his butter.
KNOW KNIFE KNACK

400

ACTIVITY 2: ART ACTIVITY

Prepare a display model of the rocket on Worksheet 139C.

Worksheet 139C: Copy the templates onto thick, colored paper and have the children cut them out. Use markers to decorate a paper towel roll and the templates BEFORE any gluing is done. Overlap A/B on the cone piece and glue the edge. Attach side pieces and cone piece to the paper towel roll.

Students may also make tissue paper flames for under their rockets!

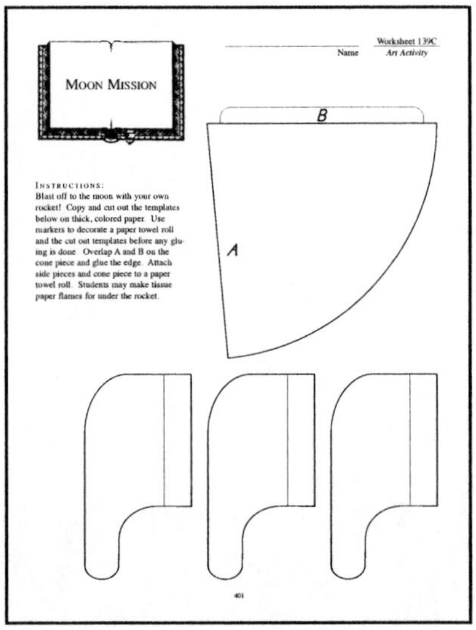

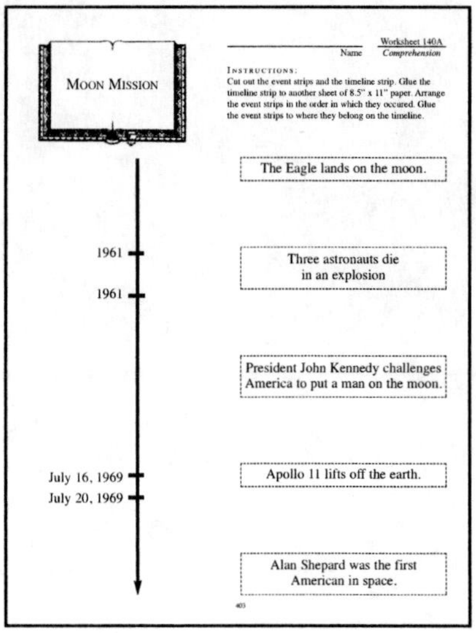

Worksheet 140A
Name ____________ *Comprehension*

MOON MISSION

INSTRUCTIONS:
Cut out the event strips and the timeline strip. Glue the timeline strip to another sheet of 8.5" x 11" paper. Arrange the event strips in the order in which they occured. Glue the event strips to where they belong on the timeline.

1961
1961
July 16, 1969
July 20, 1969

The Eagle lands on the moon.

Three astronauts die in an explosion

President John Kennedy challenges America to put a man on the moon.

Apollo 11 lifts off the earth.

Alan Shepard was the first American in space.

LESSON 140
READING COMPREHENSION AND SPELLING TEST

ACTIVITY 1: MAKING A TIMELINE

Worksheet 140A: Prepare a timeline strip (without the events) according to the directions on Worksheet 140A. Assist the children to assemble timelines of their own.

As a class, determine where the events belong on the line, according to the information in MOON MISSION.

The explosion is not dated, but students should be prompted to place it on the line between 1961 and 1969.

Worksheet 140B
Name ____________ *Spelling Test*

SPELLING TEST 10

1.
2.
3.
4.
5.
6.
7.
8.
9.
10.

ACTIVITY 2: SPELLING TEST 10

Worksheet 140B: Administer the test on Spelling List 10. Read each word once, use it in a sentence, then repeat it. Do not give any other sound or letter clues.

LESSON 141
TARGET: PH AS F AND SILENT FINAL H

ACTIVITY 1: SEEING AND HEARING

Show the children the flashcard with the PH on it. Have them hear the sound of F as in "pharaoh." Initiate a discussion about the pharaoh in the picture.

Explain that a pharaoh was a king in ancient Egypt. They were very mighty and powerful for Egypt was a great and mighty nation at one time.

Briefly discuss the Bible story of Joseph and his service under the Egyptian pharaoh at that time. Describe how Joseph's family came to live with him in Egypt and that many, many years later, they became slaves under another pharaoh. It was then that God called on Moses to bring His people out of Egypt and into the Promised Land. Tell them they will read a story about this in a few weeks.

Give them their museum bag. Allow them time to go through the house and collect items that have the PH sound to make their own museum. If you are teaching in a school setting, instruct the children to take the bag home and bring in objects the following day.

What they must learn now, however, is that the word "pharaoh" is spelled very differently.

Say the word "pharaoh" several times and ask the children what sound they hear at the beginning of this word. (F) Affirm correct responses. Draw attention to the PH on the card. Tell them that "pharaoh" spells his name with a PH making the F sound.

Write the word "pharaoh" on the board. Draw their attention to the AO. Tell them that in this word the A is silent and the O is long. Point to the H. Explain that in this word, the H is silent also.

Now, explain that there are other words in our language which use PH as F also. Write the following on the board: phone, phase, gopher, alphabet, Philip, Ralph. Invite children to the board to circle the PH in each word.

Assist them to decode and read each one. Ask if they know anyone with those proper names. Use each one in an original sentence.

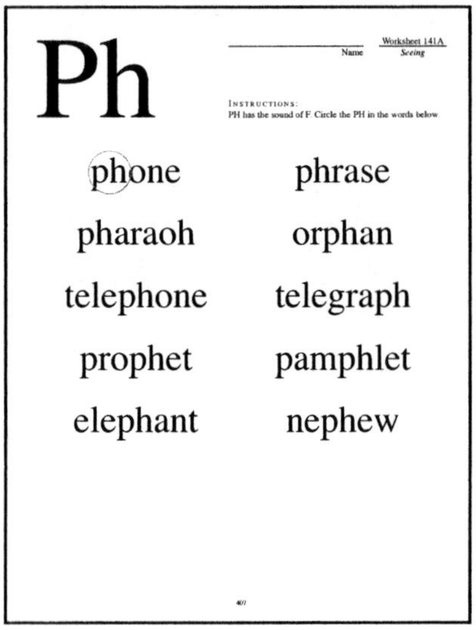

Worksheet 141A: Read the instructions aloud. Monitor as they circle the PH letter pairs. Assist them to decode each word. Use them in original sentences to reinforce meaning.

Worksheet 141B: Read the instructions aloud. Say each of the labels for the children and have them respond as indicated if they hear the F sound in any word. Tell them that if they hear F, that means it is spelled with PH in that word.

Row 1: telephone, ship, cake
Row 2: rabbit, elephant, horse
Row 3: trophy, chair, photograph (there are two PH's in this one!)

ACTIVITY 2: SILENT H

Write the word "pharaoh" on the board again. Circle the final H.

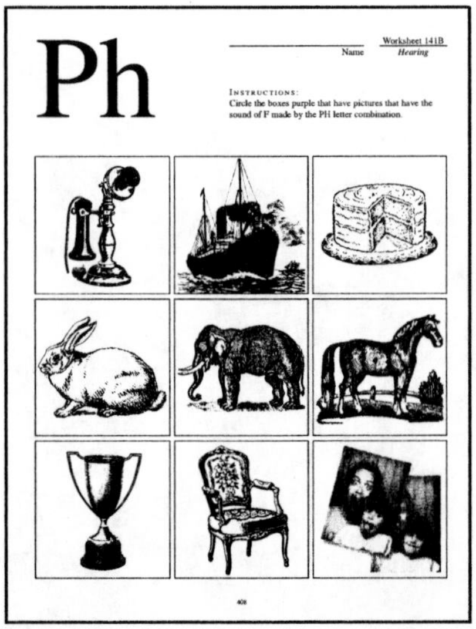

Ask the children what sound is made by this letter in this word. (none) Affirm that it is silent.

Write the following on the board, with exclamation points after each one: AH!, OH!, HURRAH!, YEAH!, HALLELUJAH!

Read each word aloud with ENTHUSIASM! Invite a child to the board to underline the H at the end of each word.

Ask if these final H letters make any sound. (NO) Explain that in our language we do not pronounce H at the end of words.

Call their attention to the exclamation points at the end of the words and explain that often these words are used to show great emotion. Have the children read them again, with GUSTO!

Now tell them that sometimes H likes to be silent at the beginning or middle of words also. Write the following on the board: HOUR, HONEST, HERB, JOHN, SHEPHERD.

Invite a child to the board to circle H in each word. Read them aloud for the children, one at a time, and ask if they can hear the H. (NO) Each time, draw a backslash through the H.

Read them again and have the children echo them after you. Use in original sentences to reinforce meaning.

Remind them that "hour" sounds the same as "our," which they have already discussed in Lesson 91. Again, the spelling makes the difference in meaning!

You may want to give the students the coloring page along with the flashcard. Read the information about the artist to your students before they color the picture.

LESSON 142
TARGET: PH AS F, CI AS SH

Play The Alphabet Chase for the children encouraging them to sing along.

ACTIVITY 1: READING

Write a large PH at the top of the board. Ask who can remember the sound that this letter pair makes. (F) Affirm correct responses.

Remind the children that there is no way to really know when the F sound is being spelled with PH, but when they see PH in words it is usually pronounced as F.

Write the following on the board: PHONICS, DOLPHIN, GRAPH. Invite a student to the board to circle the PH in each word.

Assist the children to decode the words. Define them and use in original sentences. Call to their attention that they are learning to read using PHONICS!

Write the words found on Worksheet 142A on the board. Invite students to come to the board and circle the PH in each word.

Assist them to decode and read each one. Define them and use in original sentences.

Some of these words represent quite advanced vocabulary. Simplify the meanings as much as possible, using more basic synonyms. It is not necessary for the children to fully understand or remember the meanings of them at this time, however, they should be able to decode them accurately.

Please note that the Y in "physical" is pronounced as short I, which will not be formally taught in this program. Explain briefly that sometimes Y will make the short I sound and that you will assist them when this happens.

Worksheet 142A: Read the instructions aloud. Read the words to the children and have them echo after you. Encourage them to read them independently, using the rules for decoding and syllabication patterns which have already been taught.

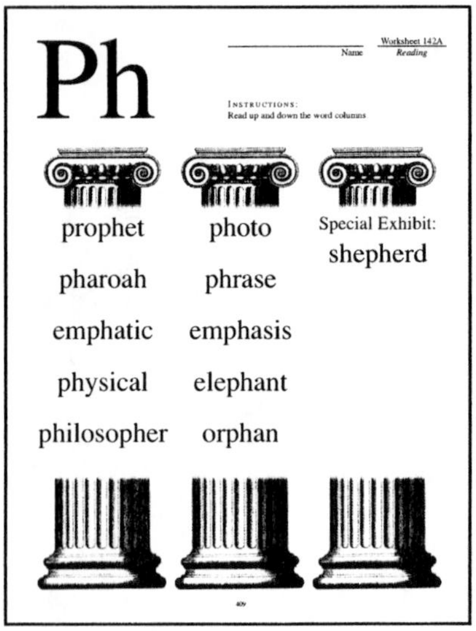

Ph

Name ______ Worksheet 142A Reading

INSTRUCTIONS: Read up and down the word columns

prophet
pharoah
emphatic
physical
philosopher

photo
phrase
emphasis
elephant
orphan

Special Exhibit:
shepherd

ACTIVITY 2: CI AS SH

Write the following on the board: special. Remind the children that they read this word in the story MOON MISSION.

Circle the CI. Remind them that just like TI and SI, this letter pair can make the sound SH.

Assist them to read the word aloud. Use it in an original sentence.

Now, write the following on the board: ancient, social, glacier.

Invite children to the board to circle the CI in each word. Assist them to decode and read the words. Use them in original sentences.

Finally, write the word "physician." Alert them that the Y will make the short I sound in this word. Invite a student to come to the board and circle the CI. Assist them to decode and use the word in a sentence.

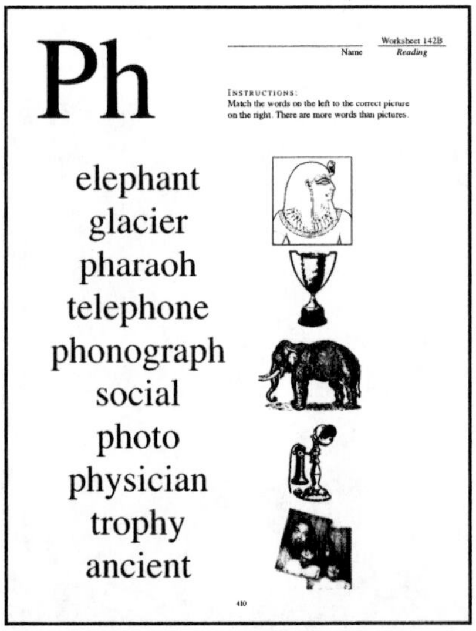

Ph

Name ______ Worksheet 142B Reading

INSTRUCTIONS: Match the words on the left to the correct picture on the right. There are more words than pictures.

elephant
glacier
pharaoh
telephone
phonograph
social
photo
physician
trophy
ancient

Worksheet 142B: Read the instructions aloud. Assist to decode and read the words, matching them to the pictures as instructed.

Lesson 143
Target: Final ED for Past Tense

Show the children the flashcard with the ED on it. Have them hear the sound of ED as in "seated."

ACTIVITY 1: SEEING AND HEARING FINAL ED AS A SEPARATE SYLLABLE

Tell the children it is time to be good "sound detectives" again. You will be reading a list of words and their job is to figure out what is the same about all of them.

Read the following aloud:

started wanted folded acted painted

Affirm correct responses that they all have the D or ED sound at the end.

Write the root words on the board: start, want, fold, act, paint.

Call on students to read each word. Use them in the following sentences:

I start my car.

We want to go to the store.

You fold the paper in half.

I act in the school play.

We paint pictures in class.

Explain that all of these sentences describe action which is taking place right now. However, if we want to tell someone that these actions have already happened, we can add ED to each of the words.

Read the sentences again, using the ED past tense form of each verb.

You may prompt the past tense visually by using your hand to "wave" back over your shoulder. Hold your hand, palm facing you, at shoulder height and then bring the hand toward you and above that shoulder. Each time the children see that gesture, they will know you mean "past."

Write ED after each of the words on the board.

Invite students to come and circle the ED in each one. Allow them to decode and read them independently.

Ask them how many syllables they hear in these words and clap them out. Explain that in words that end in a T or D sound, the ED is a separate syllable.

Put a 1 over the first vowel (or letter pair which makes a single vowel sound) and a 2 over the E in ED for each word.

Now write the following: taste, trade.

Call on students to read them aloud. Ask the children how you would say these words if the action happened in the past. (tasted, traded) Use sentence prompts if necessary.

Draw attention to the fact that these words already have an E at the end. Do we hear the E at the end? (NO) Why not? (it is a final silent E) So what sound is the final sound in each of these words? (D or T)

What will we need to add to make ED. (only a D) Write the D at the end of each word.

How many syllables does each word have? Clap them out. Now the E is part of the second syllable ED!

Invite a student to come to the board and write a 1 over the first vowel and a 2 over the E in each word.

Final ED sounds like ED after final T or D (including if the root ends in D or T plus silent E) and is a separate syllable. Final ED sounds like D after any voiced consonant or a vowel, except D.

Give them their museum bag. Allow them time to go through the house and collect items that have the ED sound to make their own museum. If you are teaching in a school setting, instruct the children to take the bag home and bring in objects the following day.

Worksheet 143A: Read the instructions aloud. Monitor as they respond as indicated. Call on students to read each word aloud and use in an original sentence. As additional reinforcement, have them underline the present tense form in each word, including the final silent E if necessary.

ed

Name

Worksheet 143A
Seeing

INSTRUCTIONS:
Circle the ED in the words below.

tasted	acted
seated	sounded
started	folded
wanted	added
painted	wasted
listed	blasted

If ED is added to a word that ends in D or T the ED sound is heard. If the word ends in silent E preceded by a D or T the sound of ED is heard. Otherwise ED at the end of a word says D

411

ACTIVITY 2: FINAL ED AS D

Erase the board and write the following: BANG, TURN, JOIN.

Call on a student to read each one and use in an original sentence.

Now, challenge them to tell you how we would say these words if the actions took place in the past. Affirm correct responses. Use the past tense forms in original sentences.

Ask the children what we need to add to each word to show that the action already happened. (ED) Write final ED at the end of each word.

Say the words again aloud. Have the children clap out the syllables. Watch out! Affirm that the words still only have ONE syllable.

Explain that when action words do not end with a D or T sound, the ED just sounds like D. The E does not make any sound. It does not make another syllable.

Draw a backslash through the E in each word. Write a 1 over the first vowel. Say the words again and have the children echo to affirm the single syllable.

Tell them that this can happen with any action word which does not end with the D or T sound. Write the following on the board: name, save. What do they see at the end of each of these words? (E) Does it make any sound? (NO) Affirm that it is final silent E.

Ask what the final sound is in each of these words. (M and V) Call their attention to the fact that the final sound heard is not D or T.

Use them in sentences as present tense and again as past tense.

Add D to the end of each one to form the past tense. Explain that you only need to add D because the E is already there.

Have the children clap out the syllables with you. Affirm that there is still only one syllable in each word. Backslash through the E and write a 1 over the first vowel (or letter pair which makes the single vowel sound).

Say the words again and have the children echo them to affirm that there is only one syllable.

Now write the following: SHOW, PLAY, STRAY.

Call on students to read the words aloud. Use in original sentences to reinforce meaning.

Challenge them to tell you how the word would be pronounced if the action occurred in the past. Invite a child to come to the board and add the ED to each word.

Clap out the syllables. Does the E in the ED ending make any sound? (NO) Backslash through the E, put a 1 over the first vowel in each group. Call attention to the fact that the vowel sound in each word is spelled with a letter pair (OW or AY). Even though the words end in consonants, the last sound heard is the vowel sound.

Worksheet 143B: Read the instructions aloud. Call on students to read the words. Allow them to use them in original sentences. Ask if the action is happening now or already happened. Affirm the number of syllables in each word and number them if you like.

You may want to give the students the coloring page along with the flashcard. Read the information about the artist to your students before they color the picture.

ed

Name

Worksheet 143B
Reading

INSTRUCTIONS:
Read up and down the word columns

ED sound	D sound
Words that end in D or T or a silent E preceeded by a D or T	
seat	name
seated	named
end	play
ended	played
trade	turn
traded	turned
sound	save
sounded	saved
start	join
started	joined

LESSON 144
TARGET: FINAL ED

ACTIVITY 1: READING

Tell the children they will each get a puzzle card (photocopy Appendix 14 onto card stock and cut apart. If you are teaching at home, mix up the puzzle cards on the desk and have the child locate and assemble). Some will have final ED on the words and some will not. Their job is to find the child whose card matches theirs, either with or without the ED. For instance, if they get a card with the ED form on it, they need to find the child whose card has the word without the ED. If their card does not have the ED form, they are to find the child whose card does have the ED form.

Mix them up and allow the children to pick out cards at random. When everyone has a card (you may need to add extra words if you have a very large class), tell the children to move about the room and find their match.

When all the matches are made, have the children come to the front of the room in pairs, read their words, use them in sentences, tell whether the action is taking place now or has already happened, and how many syllables are in their words.

Worksheet 144A: Read the instructions aloud. Monitor the students' progress as they work independently. Have children read the words aloud and use in sentences.

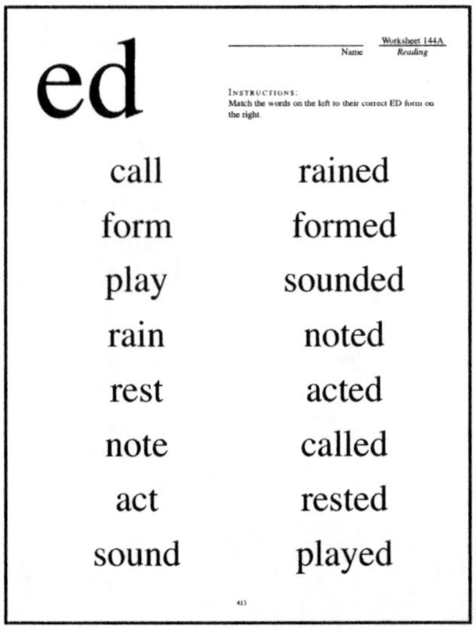
ed

Name

Worksheet 144A
Reading

INSTRUCTIONS:
Match the words on the left to their correct ED form on the right

call	rained
form	formed
play	sounded
rain	noted
rest	acted
note	called
act	rested
sound	played

ACTIVITY 2: FINAL ED AS T

Write the following on the board: bump, mash, lock. Call on children to read each one and use in a sentence as an action word.

Ask what sound they hear at the end of each of these words. (P, SH, K)

Now ask them how we would say these words if the action happened in the past. Affirm correct responses and repeat them, emphasizing the final ED which is pronounced as T.

Challenge the children to tell you what sound they hear at the end of these words. (T) Praise correct responses.

Affirm that in words like these, the final ED sounds like T. Write ED at the end of each of the words. Repeat them and have the children echo them.

Ask how many syllables are heard in each one and clap it out. Ask if the E makes any sound. (NO) Backslash through it. Write a 1 over the first vowel in each word.

Now write the following: ROPE, FAKE, RACE. Allow children to read each word and use it in a sentence as an action word.

Ask what sound is heard at the end of each word. (P, K, S) Affirm that the final E is silent.

Ask what we will need to add to each word to show that the action has already happened. Guide them to realize that they only need to add D since the E is already there.

Read the new past tense words aloud and have the children echo them. What sound do they hear at the end of each word? (T) Praise correct responses.

How many syllables do they hear? (1) Does the E make any sound? (NO) Backslash through it and put a 1 over the first vowel in each word.

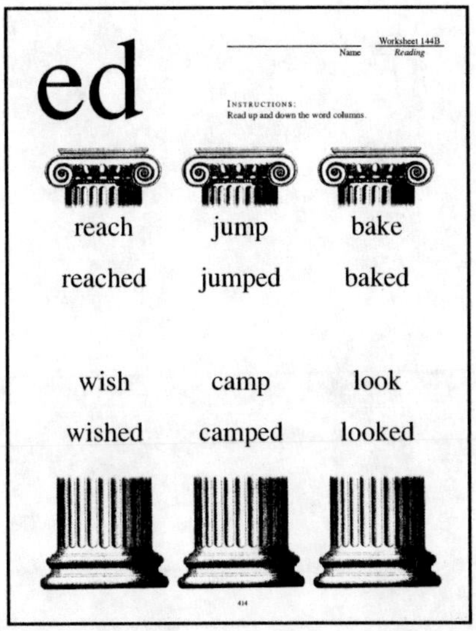
ed

Name

Worksheet 144B
Reading

INSTRUCTIONS:
Read up and down the word columns.

reach	jump	bake
reached	jumped	baked
wish	camp	look
wished	camped	looked

Final ED sounds like T after any unvoiced consonant, except T.

Worksheet 144B: Read the instructions aloud. Call on students to read each word pair. Call attention to the pronunciation of ED as T and the single syllable of each past tense form. Use the words in sentences to reinforce tense meaning.

Lesson 145
Target: Final ED

ACTIVITY 1: FINAL ED ADJECTIVES

Remind the children that we have only put ED on the end of action words up to this point. Review that this means that the action happened in the past. Explain that ED may also be added to "thing" words. When we do that, it will form a word which describes.

Write the following on the board: BEARD.

Read the following sentence pair:

He has a beard. He is bearded.

Say the word "bearded" again. Emphasize the ED syllable at the end. Ask the children what they hear at the end of this word. (ED) Write it at the end of the word "beard."

Read the following sentence pair:

His clothes are like rags. He is ragged.

Before you invite a child to come to the board to write ED after this word, add a second G to the end of "rag." Remind them how you had to do this to some words when you added ING. Assure them they do not need to know how or when to do this right now, but they should recognize that the two G's together will still only make one G sound.

Allow a child to write the ED at the end of "ragg." Explain to the children that this may be pronounced two ways. Say the word with one syllable, according to the previously taught rule and with two syllables. Tell them that with this word the second pronunciation is the most common. Have the children clap out the two syllables. Write a 1 over the first vowel (or letter pair representing the vowel sound) in each word and a 2 over the E in ED.

Ask the children: What does "bearded" mean? (having a beard) What does "ragged" mean? (dressed in rags)

Now write the following on the board: CURSE

Call on a student to read it aloud and use it in an original sentence.

Ask the children what you will need to add to this word to make it mean "one who is under a curse." (ED) Praise correct responses. Ask them if you need to add both an E and a D. (no, only a D, because the word already

ends in E)
Now, read the word aloud, pronouncing it with only one syllable and the T sound at the end. Explain that this is the way it is usually pronounced, which would be according to the decoding rules they have already learned.

However, explain that sometimes this word is pronounced with two syllables, like "ragged," especially in poetry or ancient literature.
Read the word as two syllables, emphasizing the ED.

Affirm that the meaning does not change, no matter how it is pronounced. Assure them you will let them know if a word like this comes up in their reading and will assist them to pronounce it correctly.

Worksheet 145A: Read the instructions aloud. Assist the children to decode and read the words. Define as necessary and use the root forms in sentences as nouns and the ED forms in sentences as adjectives.

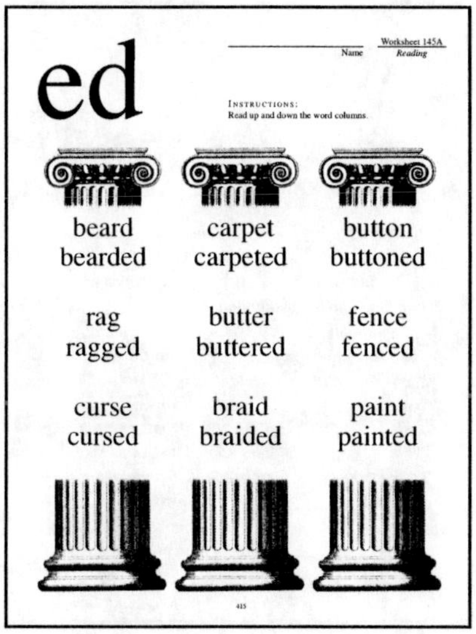
ed

Worksheet 145A
Name
Reading

INSTRUCTIONS:
Read up and down the word columns.

beard bearded	carpet carpeted	button buttoned
rag ragged	butter buttered	fence fenced
curse cursed	braid braided	paint painted

ACTIVITY 2: WRITING

Write the sentence found on Worksheet 145B on the board, along with lines.

Call on a student to read the sentence aloud. Draw attention to the PH as F sounds and the final ED as T in "photographed."

Invite students to the board to copy the words of the sentence in order on the lines.

Monitor letter and word spacing carefully.

Worksheet 145B: Read the instructions aloud. Monitor the students' progress as they work independently. Encourage them to take their time to copy accurately and neatly.

ed

Worksheet 145B
Name
Writing

INSTRUCTIONS:
Write the sentence in your best handwriting.

The pharaoh photographed the elephant.

LESSON 146
TARGET: PH WORDS, FINAL ED, AND SPELLING LIST 11

ACTIVITY 1: READING

Play a game of verbal fill-in-the-blanks today.

Write the following three words on the board: phone, Ralph, dolphin.

Read the following sentence: I called him on the ______________.

Invite a child to come to the board, point to and read the word which best completes the sentence.

Continue in the same manner to use the other two words.

Write the following on the board: started, placed, banged.

Read the following sentence: He ______________ the plate on the table.

Invite a child to come to the board, point to and read the word which best completes this sentence. (Affirm that "banged" is not an acceptable answer for this one!)

Continue in the same manner to use the other two words.

Worksheet 146A: Read the instructions aloud. Call on students to read each sentence and the word choices under it. You will need to assist with the word "Egypt"—the Y is short I. Monitor as they circle the appropriate word for each sentence.

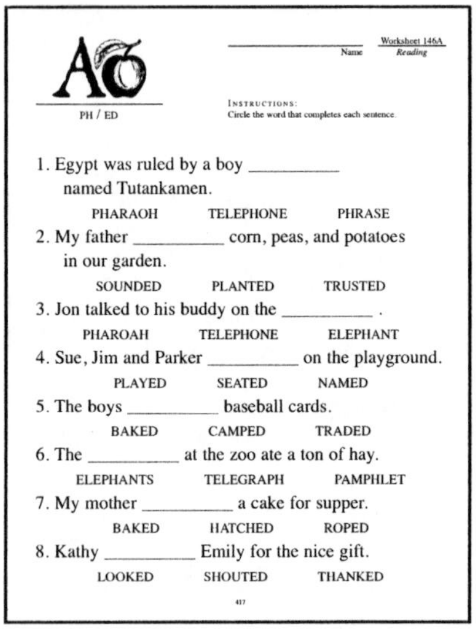

PH / ED

Name ____________ Worksheet 146A *Reading*

INSTRUCTIONS:
Circle the word that completes each sentence.

1. Egypt was ruled by a boy __________ named Tutankamen.
   PHARAOH TELEPHONE PHRASE
2. My father __________ corn, peas, and potatoes in our garden.
   SOUNDED PLANTED TRUSTED
3. Jon talked to his buddy on the __________ .
   PHAROAH TELEPHONE ELEPHANT
4. Sue, Jim and Parker __________ on the playground.
   PLAYED SEATED NAMED
5. The boys __________ baseball cards.
   BAKED CAMPED TRADED
6. The __________ at the zoo ate a ton of hay.
   ELEPHANTS TELEGRAPH PAMPHLET
7. My mother __________ a cake for supper.
   BAKED HATCHED ROPED
8. Kathy __________ Emily for the nice gift.
   LOOKED SHOUTED THANKED

ACTIVITY 2: SPELLING LIST 11

Write the words found on Worksheet 146B on the board, along with lines.

As you write the words, name the letters in order to reinforce spelling patterns.

Call on students to come to the board and copy the words, naming the letters as they do so.

Discuss meanings as necessary and use in original sentences.

Worksheets 146B: Read the instructions aloud. Monitor the students' progress as they work independently. Encourage neatness and accuracy!

Remind about the "FOUR P's" if you haven't done so in a while!

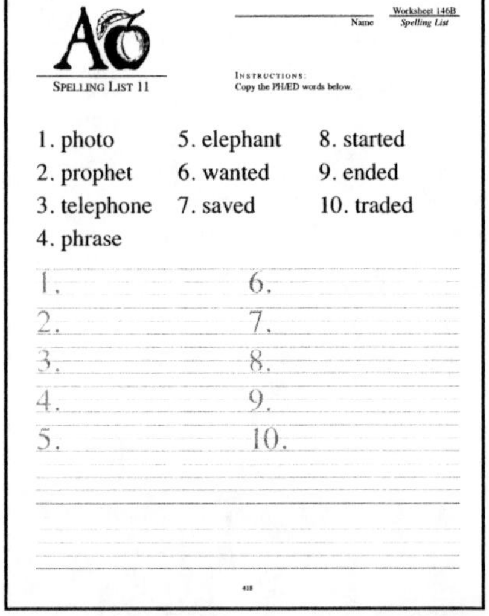

SPELLING LIST 11

Name ____________ Worksheet 146B *Spelling List*

INSTRUCTIONS:
Copy the PH/ED words below.

1. photo	5. elephant	8. started
2. prophet	6. wanted	9. ended
3. telephone	7. saved	10. traded
4. phrase		

1. 6.
2. 7.
3. 8.
4. 9.
5. 10.

LESSON 147
VOCABULARY, SIGHT AND SPECIAL WORDS FOR QUOTHE THE PROPHET

ACTIVITY 1: READING SIGHT AND SPECIAL WORDS

Remind the children that in our language there are words which do not like to obey the phonics rules. They are displayed in the Special Exhibit section of the Phonics Museum.

Some of these words are very much like each other, however, and we can learn them in groups because of this.

Write the following on the board: SOME, LOVE, GIVE, HAVE.

Ask the children how these words would be pronounced if they obeyed the final silent E rule. Affirm that they are meaningless when pronounced with long vowels. We have learned that the first vowel is short in these words.

Call on students to read them again correctly.

Under the word "some," write "come." Point to it and tell the children that this is another word which breaks the final silent E rule and, in fact, rhymes with "some." Allow the children to read it aloud, using the same pronunciation pattern as in "some."

Now, under the word "love," write the word "done." Explain that in this word, the O borrows the short U sound, just like in "love." Read it aloud and have the children echo it after you. Use it in an original sentence.

Under the word "give" write the word "live." Remind them that they have read this word before as a plural. Call on a student to read it aloud after the pattern of "give."

Circle this entire group of words. Call to their attention that the spelling patterns are the same in each one, and they all break the same rule. (The vowel before the final silent E is not always long.)

Inform the children that they will begin to encounter more and more words like this as they become better readers. Remind them that good readers are often "sound scientists," experimenting with different pronunciations and looking at how the word is used in the sentence in order to decode.

On another part of the board, write the following: one. Call on a student to read it aloud.

Affirm that in the pronunciation of this word, we actually add a W sound to the beginning. Write the word "won" beside it and point out that the two words are pronounced exactly the same way. The way they are spelled changes their meanings. Use each in sentences.

Erase the word "won." Under the word "one" write the word "once." Ask what is different between this word and the one above it. ("once" has a C in it). Challenge the children to tell you how this word will be pronounced. Tell them the ON will sound just like the ON in "one." Point out that the C is followed by an E, which changes the C sound.

Praise and affirm correct reading. Define "once" and use in a sentence.

Finally, write the following on the board: PLAGUE, GUESS.

Circle the GU in each of these words. Tell the children that the U does not make any sound in these words, but it does tell us that the G will be hard G. Backslash through the U in each word.

Now, call attention to the E at the end of "plague." Explain that this is a final silent E. Ask if it will make any sound of its own. (NO) Ask what it will do to the first vowel in the word. (make it long) Affirm that this does not mean the U, which is silent also, but the A.

Draw a macron over the A.

Read the word aloud according to the pronunciation symbols. Define it and use in an original sentence. (preferably pertaining to Moses and the Ten Plagues on Egypt!)

Now turn their attention to the word "guess." Affirm again that the U is silent. Ask what the next vowel sound is. (E) Will it be short or long? (short). Draw a breve over the E.

Read the word aloud according to the pronunciation symbols. Use it in a sentence.

Now write the following on the board: IRON.

Read the word aloud for the children according to the decoding rules they have already learned. It will sound like I—RON. Challenge the children to think what this word should be and how it should be pronounced. Give them clues if necessary (this is a very strong metal, or, something your mother uses to make your clothes smooth).

Praise correct responses. Pronounce the word both ways several times for contrast. Then affirm the correct pronunciation.

Worksheet 147A: Assist the children to decode and read the words. Define and use in sentences.

The following words on the above list will need some assistance in pronunciation: stature, decipher, precious. Note that the TU in "stature" is generally slurred into a CH, the I in "decipher" is long due its position at the end of the syllable, and the O in "precious" is silent.

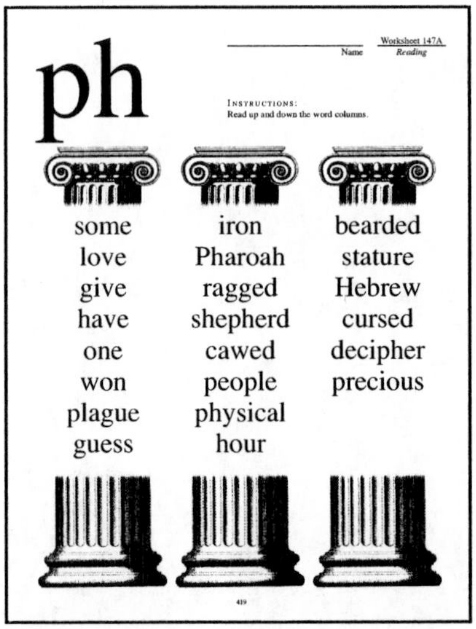
ph

Worksheet 147A
Name
Reading

INSTRUCTIONS:
Read up and down the word columns.

some	iron	bearded
love	Pharoah	stature
give	ragged	Hebrew
have	shepherd	cursed
one	cawed	decipher
won	people	precious
plague	physical	
guess	hour	

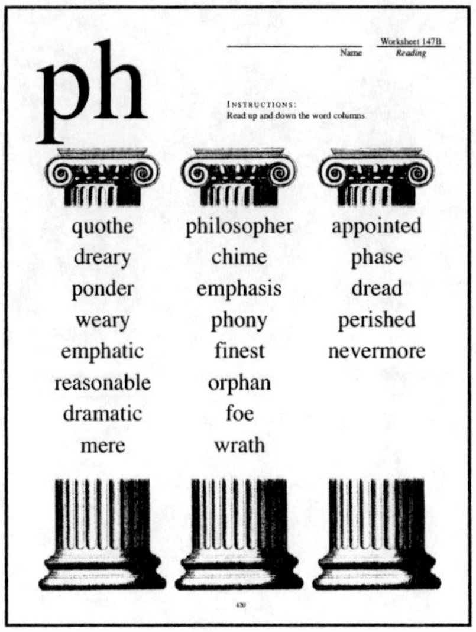
ph

Name ______ Worksheet 147B Reading

INSTRUCTIONS:
Read up and down the word columns.

quothe	philosopher	appointed
dreary	chime	phase
ponder	emphasis	dread
weary	phony	perished
emphatic	finest	nevermore
reasonable	orphan	
dramatic	foe	
mere	wrath	

ACTIVITY 2: VOCABULARY FOR QUOTHE THE PROPHET

Write the words found on Worksheet 147B on the board.

Worksheet 147B: Read the instructions aloud. Assist the children to decode and read each word. Define and use in original sentences.

LESSON 148
READING QUOTHE THE PROPHET

Activity 1: Reading Aloud

QUOTHE THE PROPHET is written entirely in rhyming verse (patterned after Edgar Allan Poe's "The Raven") and chronicles the story of the Exodus from Pharaoh's perspective.

Before reading the story, review the story of the Exodus with the children to make certain they are familiar with the main elements: Moses' calling (the burning bush manifestation), the slavery of the Hebrews, the plagues, the Passover and its foreshadowing of the death and resurrection of Christ, and the final victory of the Lord when He comes again.

The following are the phrases and expressions which will need further explanation as the children read through the text:

quothe—said
dreary—miserable
Pharaoh—a king in ancient Egypt
pondered—considered, thought
weary—tired
ragged—humbly dressed
shepherd—person who cares for sheep
cawed—spoke
emphatic—forceful
reasonable—level-headed
dramatic—acting like it is worse than it is
physical work—manual labor
burning bush—the bush seen by Moses that was on fire but not consumed
perhaps—it may be, possibly
prophet—one who speaks God's truth
philosopher—someone who thinks about the meaning of life
rod—a long staff used to prod sheep
chime—the sound a clock makes; loud and clear
emphasis—force; importance
phony—fake prophet

my finest hour—a time of triumph
attack—strife, show aggression
flee—run away
make an orphan of your son—cause your death
decipher—decode; make sense out of
foe—enemy
stature seemed to grow—he seemed to grow larger
life was well within my hand—Pharaoh has the power to let Moses live or die
wrath—anger
strayed—wandered from
his appointed path—the course and purpose given to him by God
lacking brains—stupid
just a phase—only a temporary thing, soon to go away
pass—go away
take another tack—try another method
stayed firm—would not back down
prophet-bird—Moses, who did not stop speaking God's words
wore me down—made me tired
drove me bats—irritated me
boils—oozing sores on the skin
lice—tiny insects which bite and suck blood
locusts—insects like grasshoppers
perished—died
catch my breath—get ready
plagued—caused to happen
Hebrew—God's chosen people, descended from Abraham
cursed—hated
crow—cry
Son—Jesus Christ
all the slaves to give release—free all believers from the power of death and sin
bear an iron rod—sign of Christ from Psalm 2—"You will rule them with an iron scepter"

Assist the children to read the story round robin style. Demonstrate the fluency of the rhythm and cadence of the phrases after the children have decoded the words. Call attention to the rhyming words, main characters, ideas, and events as they occur.

Questions for discussion may include: Pharaoh compares Moses to a crow—an annoying bird! Why? Why does Pharaoh consider himself as an elephant's back and Moses as a mouse? What gives Moses such confidence in Pharaoh's presence? What was the final plague which made Pharaoh change his mind? How did the Hebrews escape this plague? How is the Passover lamb like Jesus? How does Jesus "set His people free," now and in the future?

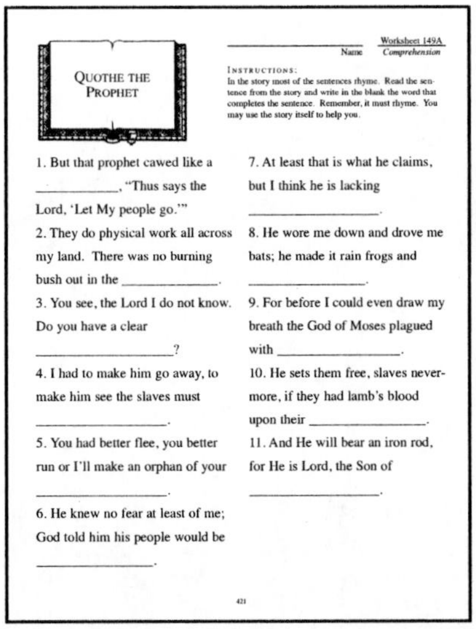
QUOTHE THE PROPHET

_______________ Name

Worksheet 149A
Comprehension

INSTRUCTIONS:
In the story most of the sentences rhyme. Read the sentence from the story and write in the blank the word that completes the sentence. Remember, it must rhyme. You may use the story itself to help you.

1. But that prophet cawed like a ___________, "Thus says the Lord, 'Let My people go.'"
2. They do physical work all across my land. There was no burning bush out in the ___________.
3. You see, the Lord I do not know. Do you have a clear ___________?
4. I had to make him go away, to make him see the slaves must ___________.
5. You had better flee, you better run or I'll make an orphan of your ___________.
6. He knew no fear at least of me; God told him his people would be ___________.
7. At least that is what he claims, but I think he is lacking ___________.
8. He wore me down and drove me bats; he made it rain frogs and ___________.
9. For before I could even draw my breath the God of Moses plagued with ___________.
10. He sets them free, slaves nevermore, if they had lamb's blood upon their ___________.
11. And He will bear an iron rod, for He is Lord, the Son of ___________.

421

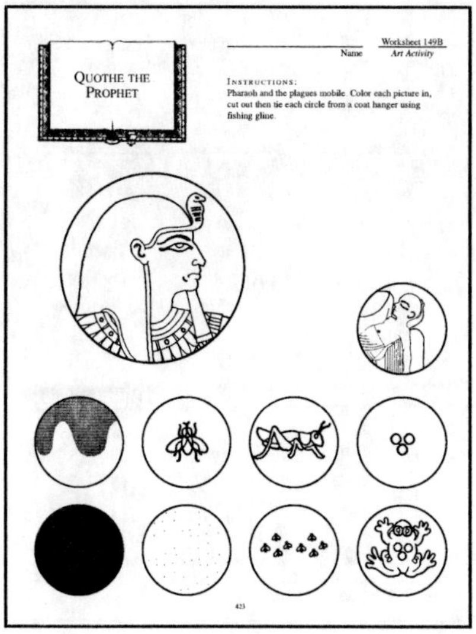

LESSON 149
READING COMPREHENSION

ACTIVITY 1: COMPREHENSION

Briefly review yesterday's story and continue any discussion as necessary.

Worksheet 149A: Read the instructions aloud. Work on this sheet as a class. Call attention to the words which will rhyme with the ones needed in the blanks in order to assist with word choice. Allow children to consult the text as needed, especially for spelling.

Worksheet 149B: Prepare a display model of the mobile as described on the worksheet. Present all materials needed for its completion and monitor and assist as necessary.

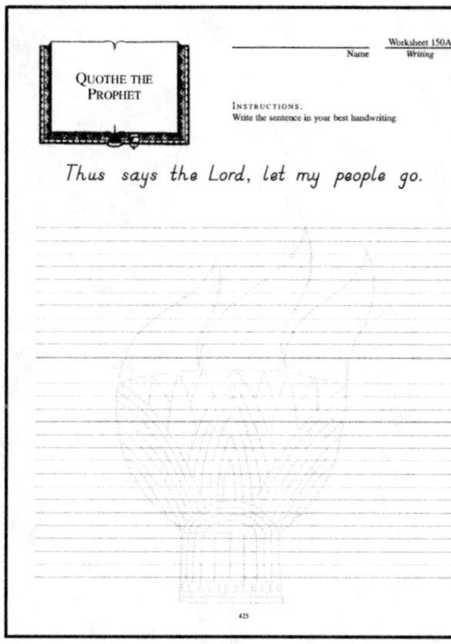

LESSON 150
READING COMPREHENSION

ACTIVITY 1: WRITING

Write the sentence found on Worksheet 150A on the board, along with lines. Call on a student to read the sentence aloud.

Invite students to the board to copy the words of the sentence in order on the lines. Monitor letter and word spacing carefully.

Worksheet 150A: Read the instructions aloud. Monitor the students' progress as they work independently.

ACTIVITY 2: COMPREHENSION

Worksheet 150B: Read the instructions aloud. Call on students to read the questions and the answer choices. They may need some help decoding and understanding the words "athletic" and "sacrificed." Assist the children to choose the correct answers and circle as indicated.

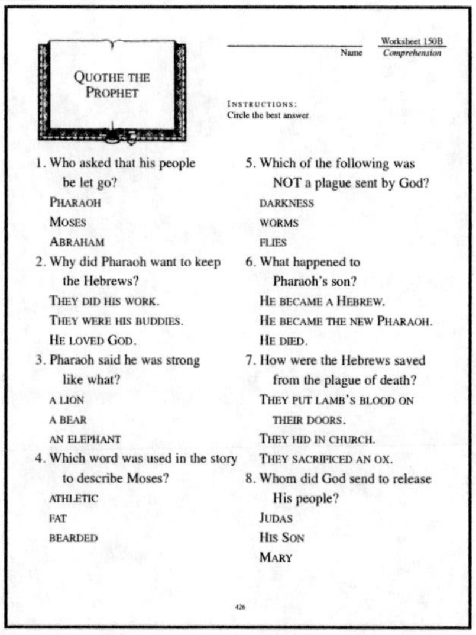

Worksheet 150B
Name
Comprehension

QUOTHE THE PROPHET

INSTRUCTIONS:
Circle the best answer

1. Who asked that his people be let go?
   PHARAOH
   MOSES
   ABRAHAM
2. Why did Pharaoh want to keep the Hebrews?
   THEY DID HIS WORK.
   THEY WERE HIS BUDDIES.
   HE LOVED GOD.
3. Pharaoh said he was strong like what?
   A LION
   A BEAR
   AN ELEPHANT
4. Which word was used in the story to describe Moses?
   ATHLETIC
   FAT
   BEARDED
5. Which of the following was NOT a plague sent by God?
   DARKNESS
   WORMS
   FLIES
6. What happened to Pharaoh's son?
   HE BECAME A HEBREW.
   HE BECAME THE NEW PHARAOH.
   HE DIED.
7. How were the Hebrews saved from the plague of death?
   THEY PUT LAMB'S BLOOD ON THEIR DOORS.
   THEY HID IN CHURCH.
   THEY SACRIFICED AN OX.
8. Whom did God send to release His people?
   JUDAS
   HIS SON
   MARY

426

LESSON 151
VOCABULARY AND READING THE SWORD OF ROB ROY

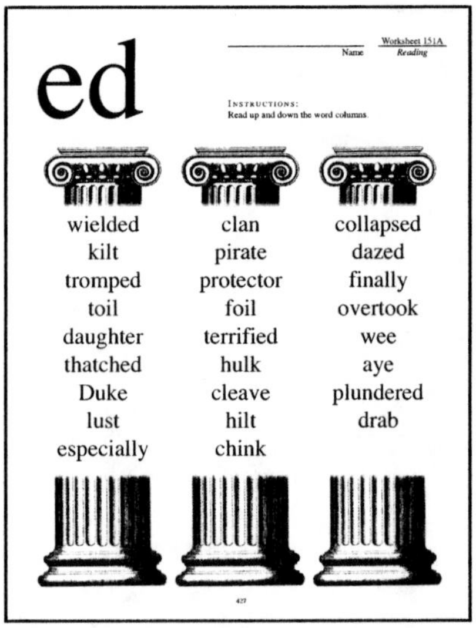
ed

Name Worksheet 151A *Reading*

INSTRUCTIONS:
Read up and down the word columns.

wielded	clan	collapsed
kilt	pirate	dazed
tromped	protector	finally
toil	foil	overtook
daughter	terrified	wee
thatched	hulk	aye
Duke	cleave	plundered
lust	hilt	drab
especially	chink	

ACTIVITY 1: READING NEW VOCABULARY WORDS

Write the words found on Worksheet 151A on the board.

Worksheet 151A: Read the instructions aloud. Use any of the previous variations or techniques for eliciting student response. Define unfamiliar terms according to the definitions in the following activity and use in original sentences.

Variations for prompting the reading of words on this sheet include: numbering the words and calling on students to read them by the designated number, verbal "fill-in-the-blanks," pointing to the written word on the board and having students point to the corresponding printed word on the sheet, riddle clues, determining the root word of words with ED endings, saying the words aloud and having the students point to the corresponding word on the worksheet.

ACTIVITY 2: READING THE SWORD OF ROB ROY

This story is about the Scottish folk hero Rob Roy, (real name: Robert MacGregor) who lived in the late 1600's and early 1700's. He is sometimes called Robert the Red, because of his red hair, or the Scottish Robin Hood, because of his lifestyle. He fell into debt to the Duke of Montrose who confiscated his lands, which lead him to coordinate various uprisings until coming under the protection of the Duke of Argyll and taking the name of Campbell. He is the protagonist in Sir Walter Scott's popular novel *Rob Roy*.

The following vocabulary and expressions are used:

hovered—hung in the air
wielded—held and used skillfully
when the castles breathed—when people lived in them
kilts—skirt-like garment worn by Scottish men
tromped—walked purposefully, marched
driving the herd—making the cattle go a certain way
toil—work
thatched—made of interlocked grass used for roofing
Duke—title of landowner
lust—greatly desire
especially—particularly
mind was full—thoughts of
lost freedom—no longer was independent, but imprisoned
sneaked—escaped without being seen

clan—extended family group
resist—oppose, fight against
thieving—taking something that is not yours
enraged—greatly angered
gathering—coming together
plotting—planning
men in armor—knights, bodyguards
band—group of followers
pirates—criminals
riches from wickedness profit nothing—the consequences of doing evil are worthless
goodness delivers from death—doing right keeps one from harm
protectors—ones who defend
their noses high and their chests puffed out—they were arrogant
terrified—greatly afraid
cast—threw
dim—dark
clashing—banging, hitting
clanged—hit against
hail—shower
hulk—large form
cleave—split apart
whistled—passed quickly
hilt—handle of a sword
thrust—pushed hard
chink—opening
collapsed—fell
dazed—astonished
overtook—came over, overwhelmed
roared—yelled
wee lot—a very small group
aye—term for "yes!"
raided—attacked
plundered—taken by force or unlawfully
in vain—without effect or result
spoiled—ruined
rejoice—be glad
drab—dull, tarnished, faded

Guide the children through the round robin reading of the story. Draw attention to main characters, ideas, and events as they occur.

Some questions for discussion might include: Is the Duke a character you admire? Why or why not? Is Rob Roy a character you admire? Why or why not? What kind of a life did Rob Roy and his followers lead in the forest? What other story is like this one? (Robin Hood)

Lesson 152
Reading Comprehension

ACTIVITY 1: REVIEWING THE STORY

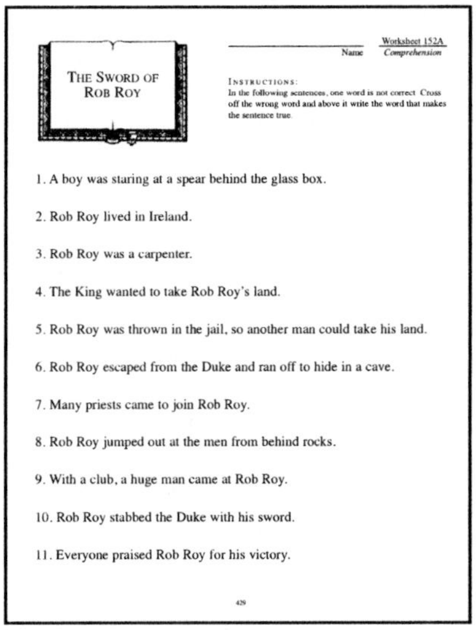
Worksheet 152A
Comprehension
Name
THE SWORD OF ROB ROY
INSTRUCTIONS:
In the following sentences, one word is not correct. Cross off the wrong word and above it write the word that makes the sentence true.

1. A boy was staring at a spear behind the glass box.
2. Rob Roy lived in Ireland.
3. Rob Roy was a carpenter.
4. The King wanted to take Rob Roy's land.
5. Rob Roy was thrown in the jail, so another man could take his land.
6. Rob Roy escaped from the Duke and ran off to hide in a cave.
7. Many priests came to join Rob Roy.
8. Rob Roy jumped out at the men from behind rocks.
9. With a club, a huge man came at Rob Roy.
10. Rob Roy stabbed the Duke with his sword.
11. Everyone praised Rob Roy for his victory.

429

Briefly review the main elements of yesterday's story, THE SWORD OF ROB ROY. Continue any discussion as necessary.

Worksheet 152A: Read the instructions aloud. Call on students to read the sentences aloud. Determine together what is wrong with each sentence and what is needed to make it right. Assist the children to write in the corrections.

ACTIVITY 2: ART ACTIVITY

Worksheet 152B: Trace the handle on the worksheet onto a piece of cardboard. Draw a blade on the cardboard to the length you desire. Color the handle with paint or markers. Cut out the sword and wrap the blade in tin foil.

Before doing the next worksheet, you may want to make an overhead of it to project on the whiteboard or chalkboard. That way, you can do the puzzle with them and assist them to place the letters in the correct boxes.

Worksheet 152C: Read the instructions aloud. Call on students to read the clues and determine the correct answers for the spaces provided in the crossword puzzle.

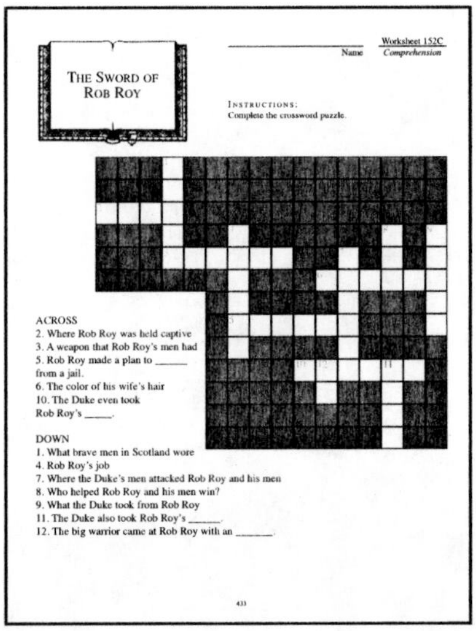
Worksheet 152C
Comprehension
Name
THE SWORD OF ROB ROY
INSTRUCTIONS:
Complete the crossword puzzle.

ACROSS
2. Where Rob Roy was held captive
3. A weapon that Rob Roy's men had
5. Rob Roy made a plan to ______ from a jail.
6. The color of his wife's hair
10. The Duke even took Rob Roy's _____.

DOWN
1. What brave men in Scotland wore
4. Rob Roy's job
7. Where the Duke's men attacked Rob Roy and his men
8. Who helped Rob Roy and his men win?
9. What the Duke took from Rob Roy
11. The Duke also took Rob Roy's ______.
12. The big warrior came at Rob Roy with an ______.

433

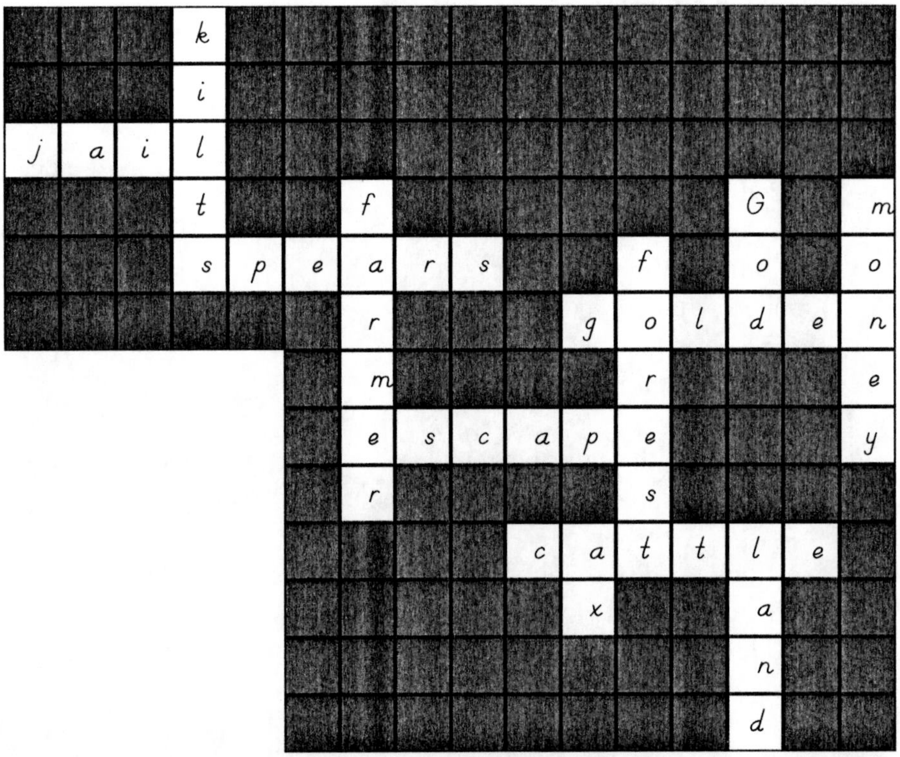

Remind the children about their spelling test tomorrow!

Lesson 153
Review and Spelling Test 11

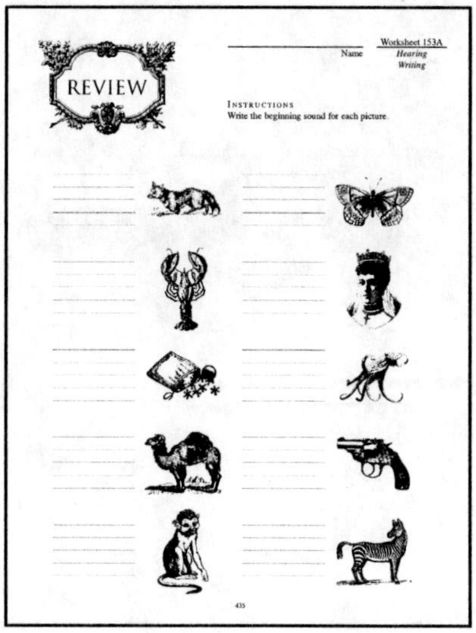

ACTIVITY 1: REVIEW

Little to no instruction should be needed for the students to complete the following worksheets.

Worksheet 153A: Read the instructions aloud. Monitor the students' progress as they work independently.

Row 1: fox, butterfly
Row 2: lobster, queen
Row 3: jacks, octopus
Row 4: camel, gun
Row 5: monkey, zebra

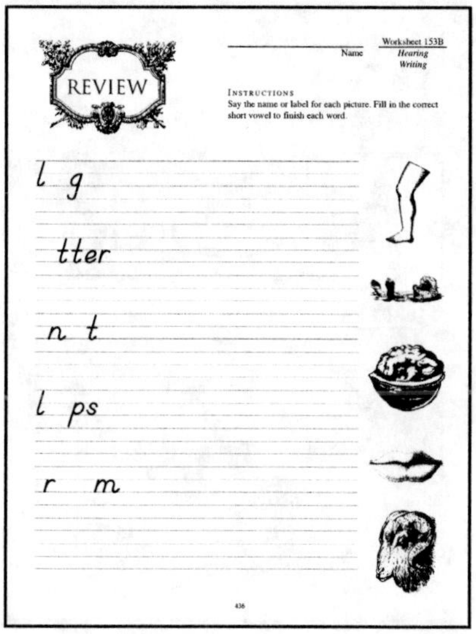

Worksheet 153B: Read the instructions aloud. Monitor the students' progress as they work independently.

ACTIVITY 2: SPELLING TEST ON LIST 11

Worksheet 153C. Administer the test on Spelling List 11. Read each word once, use it in a sentence, then repeat it. Do not give any other sound or letter clues.

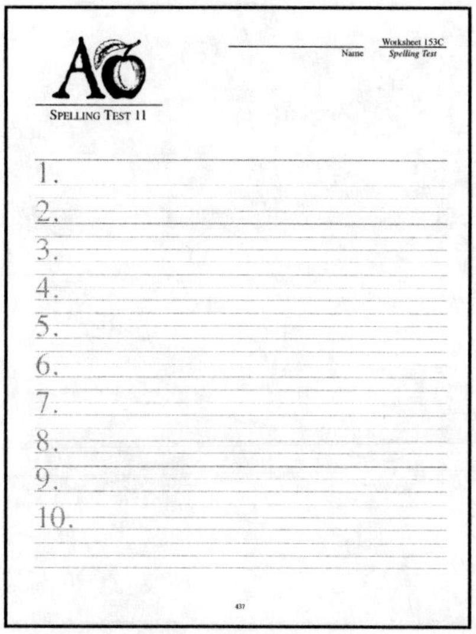

Lesson 154
Review

ACTIVITY 1: HEARING AND WRITING LETTER PAIRS AND GROUPS

Little to no instruction should be necessary to complete the following worksheets. Present each, read the instructions aloud, and Monitor the students' progress as they work independently.

Worksheets 154A–D: Assist as necessary to complete the worksheet as instructed.

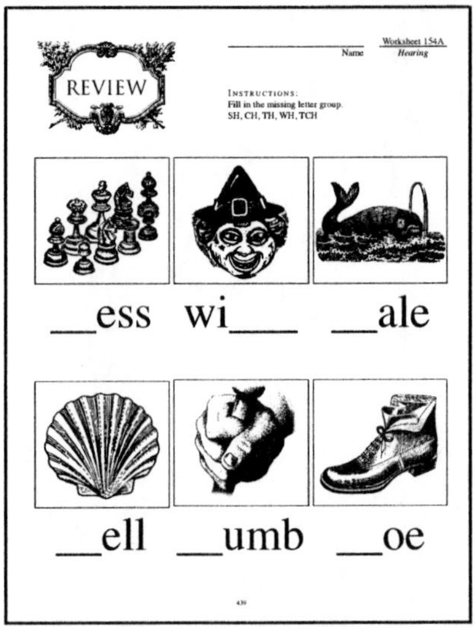

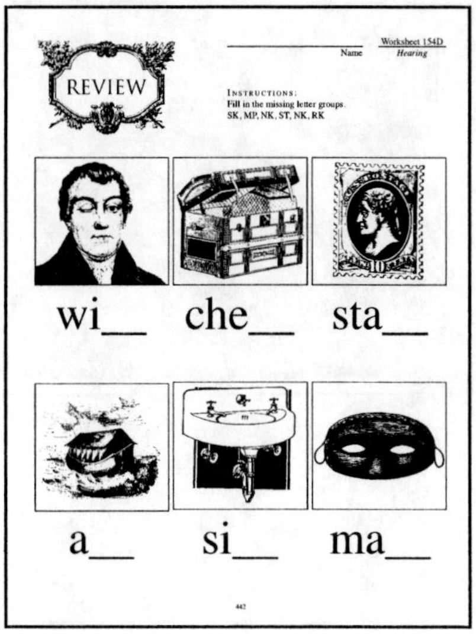
Name
Worksheet 154D
Hearing

REVIEW

INSTRUCTIONS:
Fill in the missing letter groups
SK, MP, NK, ST, NK, RK

wi__ che__ sta__

a__ si__ ma__

442

LESSON 155
READING CAUGHT IN SMILES

ACTIVITY 1: SPECIAL EXHIBIT WORDS

Write the following on the board: France, Catherine, Jeanne, Paris, Christian.

Assist the children to decode and read each word. Find France and Paris on a map of Europe.

ACTIVITY 2: READING ALOUD

This story chronicles the early life of Henry IV, the first Bourbon king of France, son of Anthony of Bourbon and Jeanne D'Albret, queen of Navarre.

The following vocabulary and expressions are used:

Queen Mother—mother of the present monarch
spray—the pieces fell like rain
spoil—fail to discipline, give too many gifts to
wretch—person in great need
in line—next
twisted—evil
fawning—doting, devoted
beaming—smiling with pride
loading—giving to excess
robes—royal clothes
plush—costly and luxurious
flaunting—prideful
sport with—play with
coy—flirtatious, clever
blushing—having reddened cheeks
chide—correct, rebuke
work of her hands—what she did
those who loved God's grace—the Huguenots
idols—false gods, worshipped images
raining—giving liberally
phony—fake
poured—gave to excess
sick with fear—scared and worried
all smiles—overly cheerful
rude—without manners
trapped—kept against their will
tricky—clever
sporting hunt—recreational hunting
flight—travel to escape or get away
steaming—very angry

Guide the children through the round robin reading of the story. Discuss main characters, ideas, and events as they occur.

Some questions for discussion might include: Why didn't Catherine want Henry to be a strong king? How would the things she did weaken him?

Lesson 156
Reading Comprehension

ACTIVITY 1: MAIN IDEAS

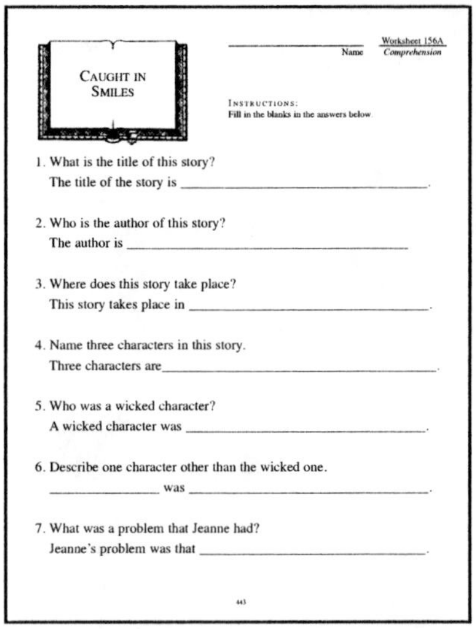

Worksheet 156A
Comprehension
Name

CAUGHT IN SMILES

INSTRUCTIONS:
Fill in the blanks in the answers below

1. What is the title of this story?
The title of the story is ______.

2. Who is the author of this story?
The author is ______

3. Where does this story take place?
This story takes place in ______.

4. Name three characters in this story.
Three characters are ______.

5. Who was a wicked character?
A wicked character was ______.

6. Describe one character other than the wicked one.
______ was ______.

7. What was a problem that Jeanne had?
Jeanne's problem was that ______.

Review briefly the main characters and events of yesterday's story. Continue any discussion as necessary.

Worksheet 156A: Read the instructions aloud. Tell the children you will be doing this sheet together. Call on students to read the questions aloud. Assist in decoding any unfamiliar words. Decide on the appropriate answers to use to fill in the blanks. Write these answers on the board for the children to copy.

Draw attention to the fact that they are completing full sentences. Explain that this is the way we should frame answers to questions.

ACTIVITY 2: ORDER OF EVENTS

Worksheet 156B: Read the instructions aloud. Discuss the events of the story and determine the correct order of the pictures shown. Have the children number them before cutting out to glue in the correct order.

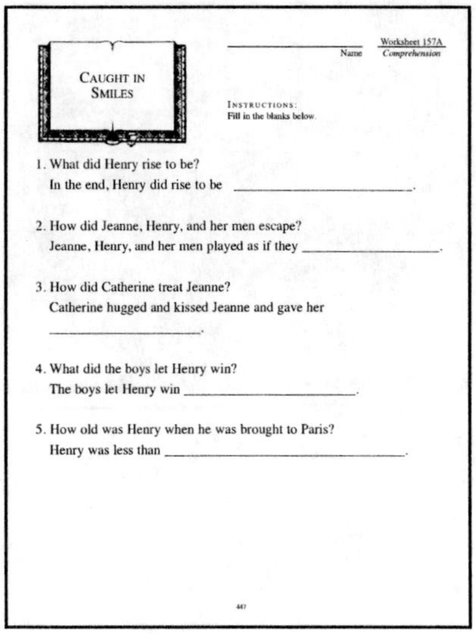

Worksheet 157A
Comprehension

Name ____________

Caught in Smiles

Instructions:
Fill in the blanks below.

1. What did Henry rise to be?
In the end, Henry did rise to be ____________.

2. How did Jeanne, Henry, and her men escape?
Jeanne, Henry, and her men played as if they ____________.

3. How did Catherine treat Jeanne?
Catherine hugged and kissed Jeanne and gave her ____________.

4. What did the boys let Henry win?
The boys let Henry win ____________.

5. How old was Henry when he was brought to Paris?
Henry was less than ____________.

447

Lesson 157
Reading Comprehension

ACTIVITY 1: MAIN IDEAS

Tell the children you will be working on the next worksheet together.

Worksheet 157A: Call on students to read the questions aloud. Determine the best answers to write in the blanks for each answer sentence. Write these answers on the board for the children to copy.

Remind them once again that these are complete sentences and the proper way to answer questions.

Worksheet 157B: Read the instructions aloud. Assist the children to frame complete sentences to answer the questions. Write the sentences on the board and monitor as the children copy them onto their papers. Encourage them to take their time and write neatly and carefully.

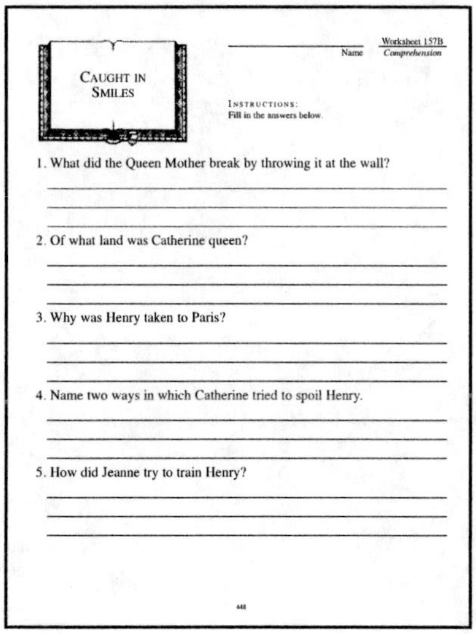

Worksheet 157B
Comprehension

Name ____________

Caught in Smiles

Instructions:
Fill in the answers below.

1. What did the Queen Mother break by throwing it at the wall?

2. Of what land was Catherine queen?

3. Why was Henry taken to Paris?

4. Name two ways in which Catherine tried to spoil Henry.

5. How did Jeanne try to train Henry?

448

Lesson 158
Art Activity and Writing Review

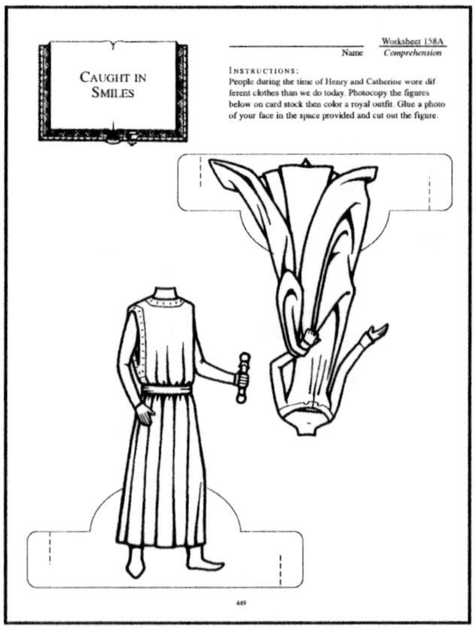

ACTIVITY 1: ART ACTIVITY

Worksheet 158A: Read the instructions aloud. Monitor the students' progress as they work independently. Encourage the use of color and creative design. Then let the students walk their creations through the museum!

ACTIVITY 2: WRITING THE ALPHABET

Worksheet 158B: Read the instructions aloud. Monitor the students' progress as they work independently. Remind about the "FOUR P's" and letter spacing.

Lesson 159
Review

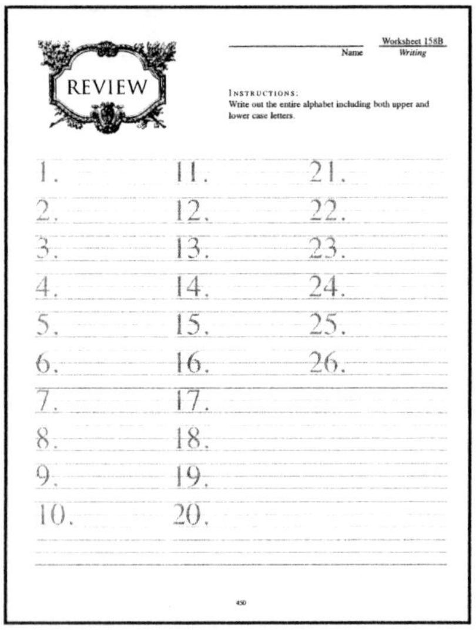

ACTIVITY 1: HEARING

The following worksheets should need little to no instruction to complete.

Worksheet 159A: Read the instructions aloud. Assist to label as necessary. Monitor the students' progress as they work independently.

> Row 1: alligator, owl, map
> Row 2: cow, zebra, crown
> Row 3: mouse, house, notes

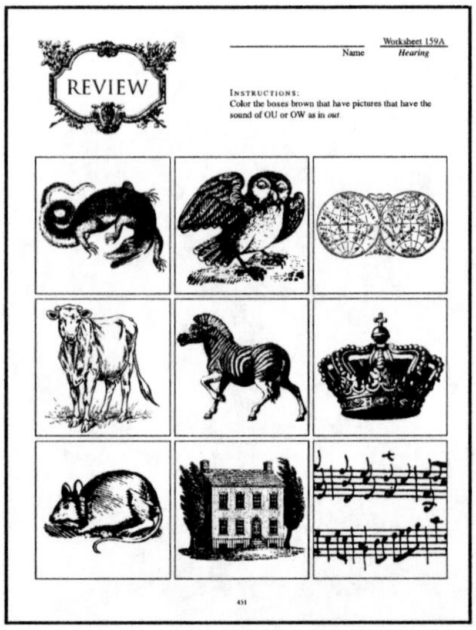

Worksheet 159B/C: Read the instructions aloud. Allow the children to work independently. Remind them that not every word will have a matching picture!

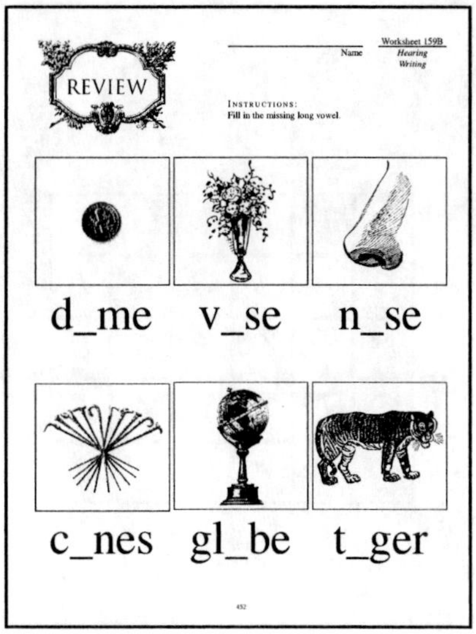

Lesson 160
Review

ACTIVITY 1: HEARING AND SEEING

The following worksheets should need little to no instruction.

Worksheet 160A: Read the instructions aloud. Monitor the students' progress as they work independently.

Row 1: moon, moose, broom
Row 2: spoons, goose, toes
Row 3: books, hook, rooster

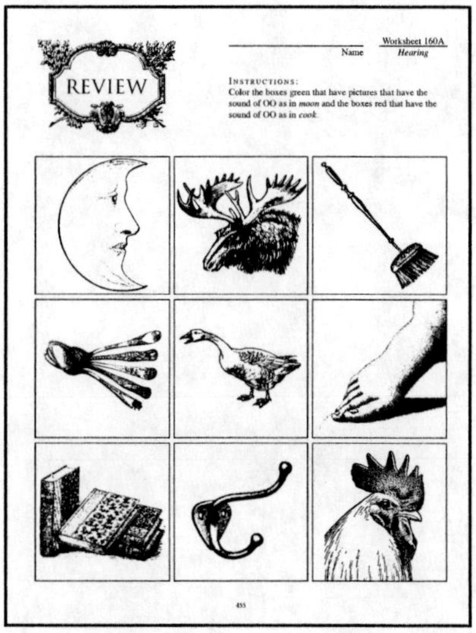

Worksheet 160B: Read the instructions aloud. Monitor the students' progress as they work independently. Caution them that one word has TWO silent letters in it!

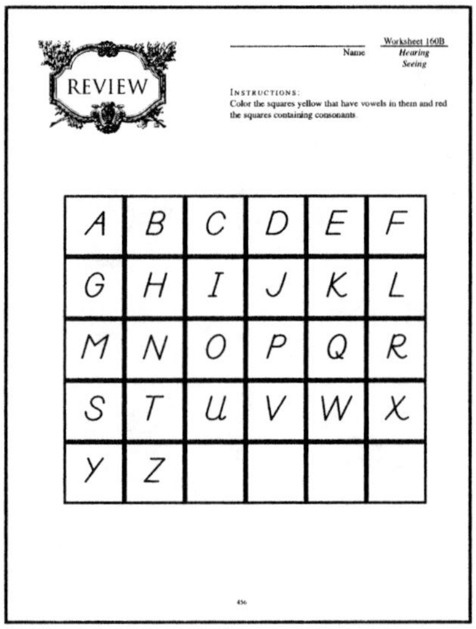

Worksheet 160C: Read the instructions aloud. Monitor the students' progress as they work independently.

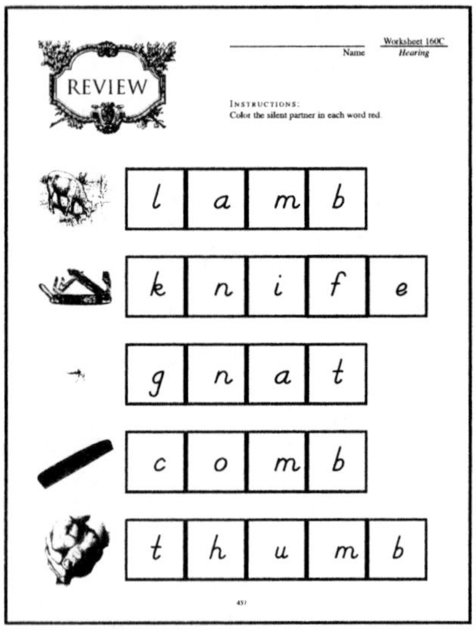

LESSON 161
READING FATHERS' FAITH

ACTIVITY 1: SPECIAL WORDS

Write the following on the board: Augustine, Boniface, Cyprian, Chrysostom.

Assist the children to decode and read each one. Explain that these are proper names of people they will learn about in the next story.

Write the following on the board: idea, quietly. Explain that these are words where the syllables are divided between the vowel letter pairs, like "giant" and "fuel" which they have had before.

Draw a slash between the E and A in "idea" and the I and E in "quietly." Remind them that the vowel to the left of each slash will be long because it ends that syllable and the vowel to the right of each slash will be short (or "ah" in the case of "idea"). Write macrons over the E and the I. Decode and read as indicated.

ACTIVITY 2: READING FATHERS' FAITH

This story is about a young boy receiving his father's instruction about great men of the faith.

The following vocabulary is used:

allowed—permitted
determined—concluded, decided
eager—enthusiastic
pagan—unbeliever
continued—kept on telling the story
convinced—persuaded
imagining—seeing in his mind's eye
woodsman—a lumberman or a man used to living in the woods
dent—a significant mark to cut it down
chuckled—laughed
preached—share the Gospel
powerful—strong, mighty
scoffed—laughed at, ridiculed

tremble—shake
quake—shake in fear
crackling—the noise of the wood burning
sizzling—the sound the fish made in the pan as it was cooking
observed—noticed
wondered—questioned
remarked—said
sermons—talks about the Bible
exclaimed—cried out
royal family—a family ruling over a kingdom
emperor—a great king
fend off—repel, push away
stern—serious
gigantic—huge, grand
festival—party, celebration
harshly—cruelly, severely
inquired—asked
repent—be sorry for sin and turn from it
thundered—spoke loudly
swooped—flew down
stillness—quietness, peacefulness
broken—ended

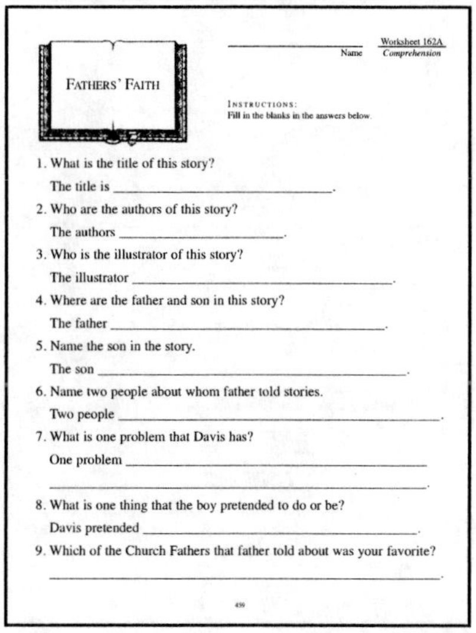

Worksheet 162A
Comprehension

Name ____________

FATHERS' FAITH

INSTRUCTIONS:
Fill in the blanks in the answers below.

1. What is the title of this story?
   The title is ____________.
2. Who are the authors of this story?
   The authors ____________.
3. Who is the illustrator of this story?
   The illustrator ____________.
4. Where are the father and son in this story?
   The father ____________.
5. Name the son in the story.
   The son ____________.
6. Name two people about whom father told stories.
   Two people ____________.
7. What is one problem that Davis has?
   One problem ____________
   ____________.
8. What is one thing that the boy pretended to do or be?
   Davis pretended ____________.
9. Which of the Church Fathers that father told about was your favorite?
   ____________.

459

Guide the children through the round robin reading of the story. Discuss main characters, ideas, and events as they occur.

Some questions for discussion may include: How did Augustine's mother Monica show her faith? Who was really responsible for the felling of the oak tree? Why did they call Chrysostom "Golden Mouth?" How did Ambrose show his faith?

Lesson 162
Reading Comprehension

ACTIVITY 1: MAIN IDEAS

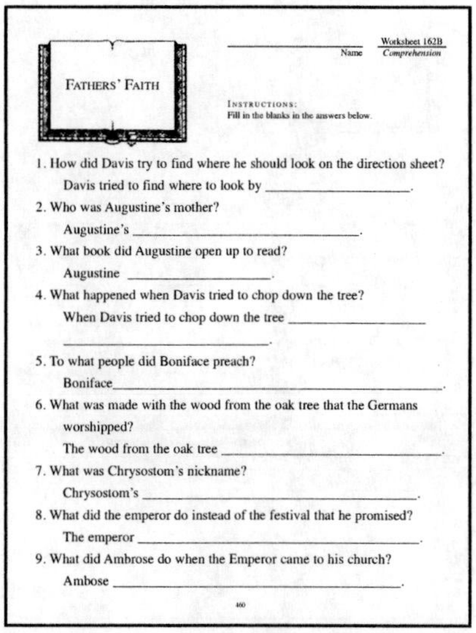

Worksheet 162B
Comprehension

Name ____________

FATHERS' FAITH

INSTRUCTIONS:
Fill in the blanks in the answers below.

1. How did Davis try to find where he should look on the direction sheet?
   Davis tried to find where to look by ____________.
2. Who was Augustine's mother?
   Augustine's ____________.
3. What book did Augustine open up to read?
   Augustine ____________.
4. What happened when Davis tried to chop down the tree?
   When Davis tried to chop down the tree ____________
   ____________.
5. To what people did Boniface preach?
   Boniface____________.
6. What was made with the wood from the oak tree that the Germans worshipped?
   The wood from the oak tree ____________.
7. What was Chrysostom's nickname?
   Chrysostom's ____________.
8. What did the emperor do instead of the festival that he promised?
   The emperor ____________.
9. What did Ambrose do when the Emperor came to his church?
   Ambose ____________.

460

Briefly review yesterday's story. Continue any discussion as needed.

Tell the children you will be working on the following worksheets together.

Worksheet 162A: Read the instructions aloud. Assist the children to read the questions aloud and determine the best answer for the blanks. Write these answers on the board and monitor as they copy them on their papers.

Worksheet 162B: Read the instructions aloud. Proceed as above.

LESSON 163
READING COMPREHENSION

ACTIVITY 1: CHARACTERS AND EVENTS

Prepare an example of the pockets to be made according to the directions on Worksheet 163A.

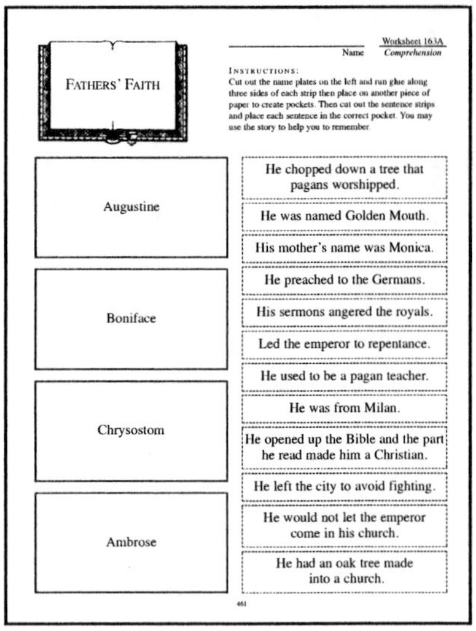
Worksheet 163A
Name
Comprehension

FATHERS' FAITH

INSTRUCTIONS:
Cut out the name plates on the left and run glue along three sides of each strip then place on another piece of paper to create pockets. Then cut out the sentence strips and place each sentence in the correct pocket. You may use the story to help you to remember.

Augustine

Boniface

Chrysostom

Ambrose

He chopped down a tree that pagans worshipped.

He was named Golden Mouth.

His mother's name was Monica.

He preached to the Germans.

His sermons angered the royals.

Led the emperor to repentance.

He used to be a pagan teacher.

He was from Milan.

He opened up the Bible and the part he read made him a Christian.

He left the city to avoid fighting.

He would not let the emperor come in his church.

He had an oak tree made into a church.

461

Worksheet 163A: Read the instructions aloud. Assist the children to prepare the pockets as directed. Guide them to determine which character is best described by the sentences and place the sentences in the proper character pocket.

Worksheet 163B/C: Read the instructions aloud. Assist the children to frame complete sentences in answer to each question. Write these sentences on the board and monitor as the children copy them onto their own papers.

Encourage neatness and accuracy!

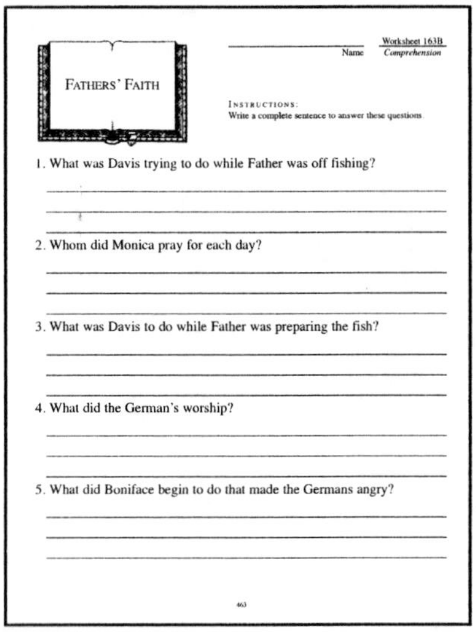
Worksheet 163B
Name
Comprehension

FATHERS' FAITH

INSTRUCTIONS:
Write a complete sentence to answer these questions.

1. What was Davis trying to do while Father was off fishing?

2. Whom did Monica pray for each day?

3. What was Davis to do while Father was preparing the fish?

4. What did the German's worship?

5. What did Boniface begin to do that made the Germans angry?

463

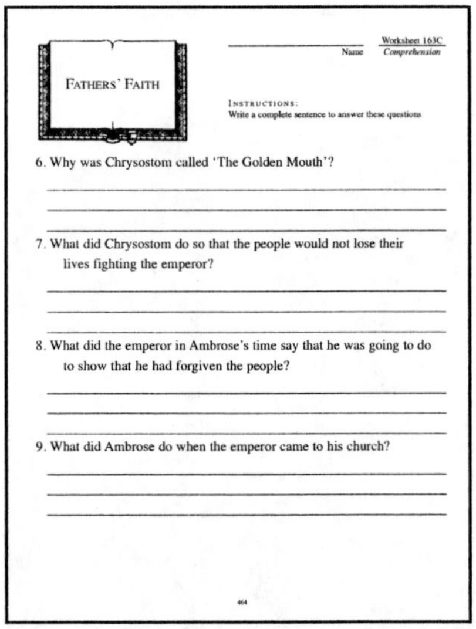
Worksheet 163C
Name
Comprehension

FATHERS' FAITH

INSTRUCTIONS:
Write a complete sentence to answer these questions.

6. Why was Chrysostom called 'The Golden Mouth'?

7. What did Chrysostom do so that the people would not lose their lives fighting the emperor?

8. What did the emperor in Ambrose's time say that he was going to do to show that he had forgiven the people?

9. What did Ambrose do when the emperor came to his church?

464

Lesson 164
Art Activity and Review

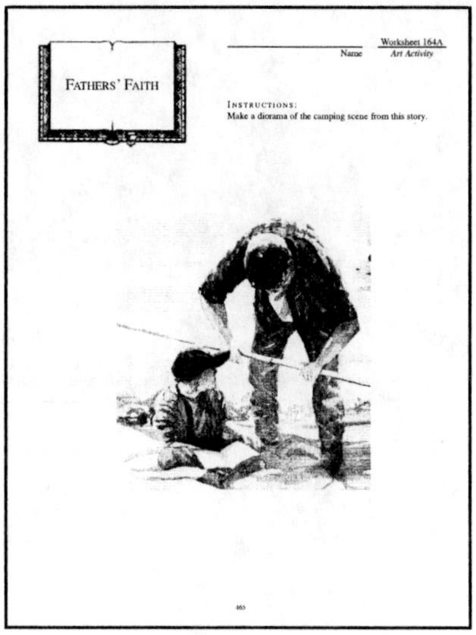
Worksheet 164A
Art Activity
Name
FATHERS' FAITH
INSTRUCTIONS:
Make a diorama of the camping scene from this story.
465

ACTIVITY 1: ART ACTIVITY

Worksheet 164A: Prepare an example of a diorama showing the setting of this story.

Each student will need a box, shoe box size or larger.

Make a diorama showing the setting of this story. Each student will need a shoe box (or a larger box). Take students on an excursion outside to gather twigs, moss, small plants, mud, etc to create a small outdoor world inside of their shoe box. A shallow cup or dish filled with water can become a fishing pond. Fold a square of construction paper in half to make a tent. Students may cut out the models of Davis and his father to put in their scene. Allow students the opportunity to be creative.

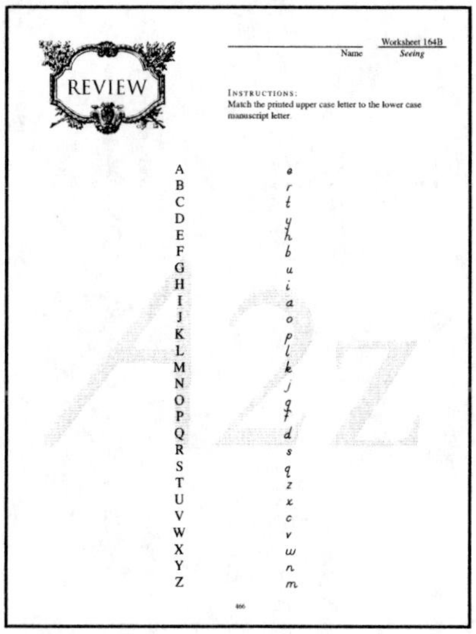
Worksheet 164B
Seeing
Name
REVIEW
INSTRUCTIONS:
Match the printed upper case letter to the lower case manuscript letter.

A	e
B	r
C	t
D	y
E	h
F	b
G	u
H	i
I	a
J	o
K	p
L	l
M	k
N	j
O	g
P	f
Q	d
R	s
S	q
T	z
U	x
V	c
W	v
X	w
Y	n
Z	m

466

ACTIVITY 2: REVIEW

Worksheet 164B: Read the instructions aloud. Monitor the students' progress as they work independently.

Worksheet 164C/D: Test. This test is optional and is added to evaluate your students if you feel it is necessary at this time. The answers are worth 10 points each.

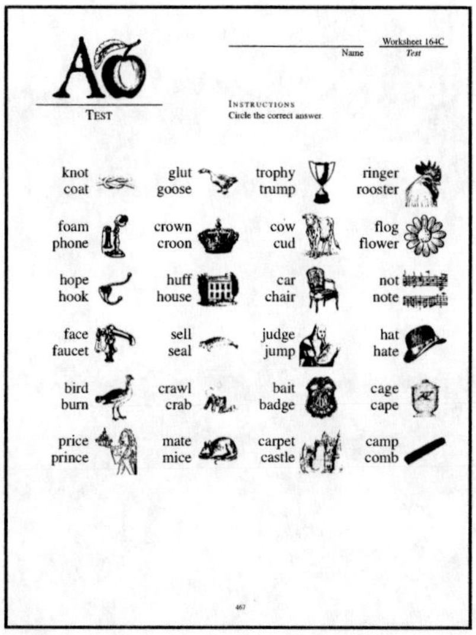
Worksheet 164C
Test
Name
TEST
INSTRUCTIONS
Circle the correct answer.

knot / coat	glut / goose	trophy / trump	ringer / rooster
foam / phone	crown / croon	cow / cud	flog / flower
hope / hook	huff / house	car / chair	not / note
face / faucet	sell / seal	judge / jump	hat / hate
bird / burn	crawl / crab	bait / badge	cage / cape
price / prince	mate / mice	carpet / castle	camp / comb

467

Dear Parents,

This week we will be studying the letter __________, as in ______________. Please have your child fill their Museum Bag with at least one item that begins with this letter sound. We will be using these items to build our own class museum. Each child will have a turn during "Show and Tell" to tell the rest of the class about their special item.

When you are looking for these objects help your child to look through the house by asking questions such as, Look there is a cup, what sound does that begin with? /c/, that's right—cup begins with the letter C. Remember the reason for doing this is to help your child learn the sounds of the letters in the alphabet.

Please come and visit our classroom and see the items in our museum. The children always love to show their parents their work.

Thank you,

Veritas Press
PHONICS MUSEUM

Dear Parents,

This week we will be studying the letter __________, as in ______________. Please have your child fill their Museum Bag with at least one item that begins with this letter sound. We will be using these items to build our own class museum. Each child will have a turn during "Show and Tell" to tell the rest of the class about their special item.

When you are looking for these objects help your child to look through the house by asking questions such as, Look there is a cup, what sound does that begin with? /c/, that's right—cup begins with the letter C. Remember the reason for doing this is to help your child learn the sounds of the letters in the alphabet.

Please come and visit our classroom and see the items in our museum. The children always love to show their parents their work.

Thank you,

Veritas Press
PHONICS MUSEUM

ABOUT THE AUTHOR:

Veritas Press
PHONICS MUSEUM

NK POEMS

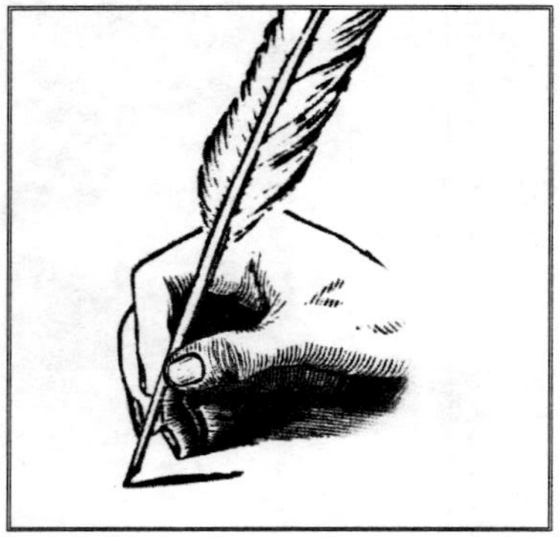

Bingo

You will need:

1 game board

25 game pieces per student

Object of the Game:

The winner is the first student to fill a row vertically, horizontally or diagonally and yell "Bingo!"

Set Up:

Photocopy this game board so each student gets a copy. Fill in the squares with the letters you have studied. Give each student enough game pieces to cover all the squares. Call out letters at random until there is a winner.

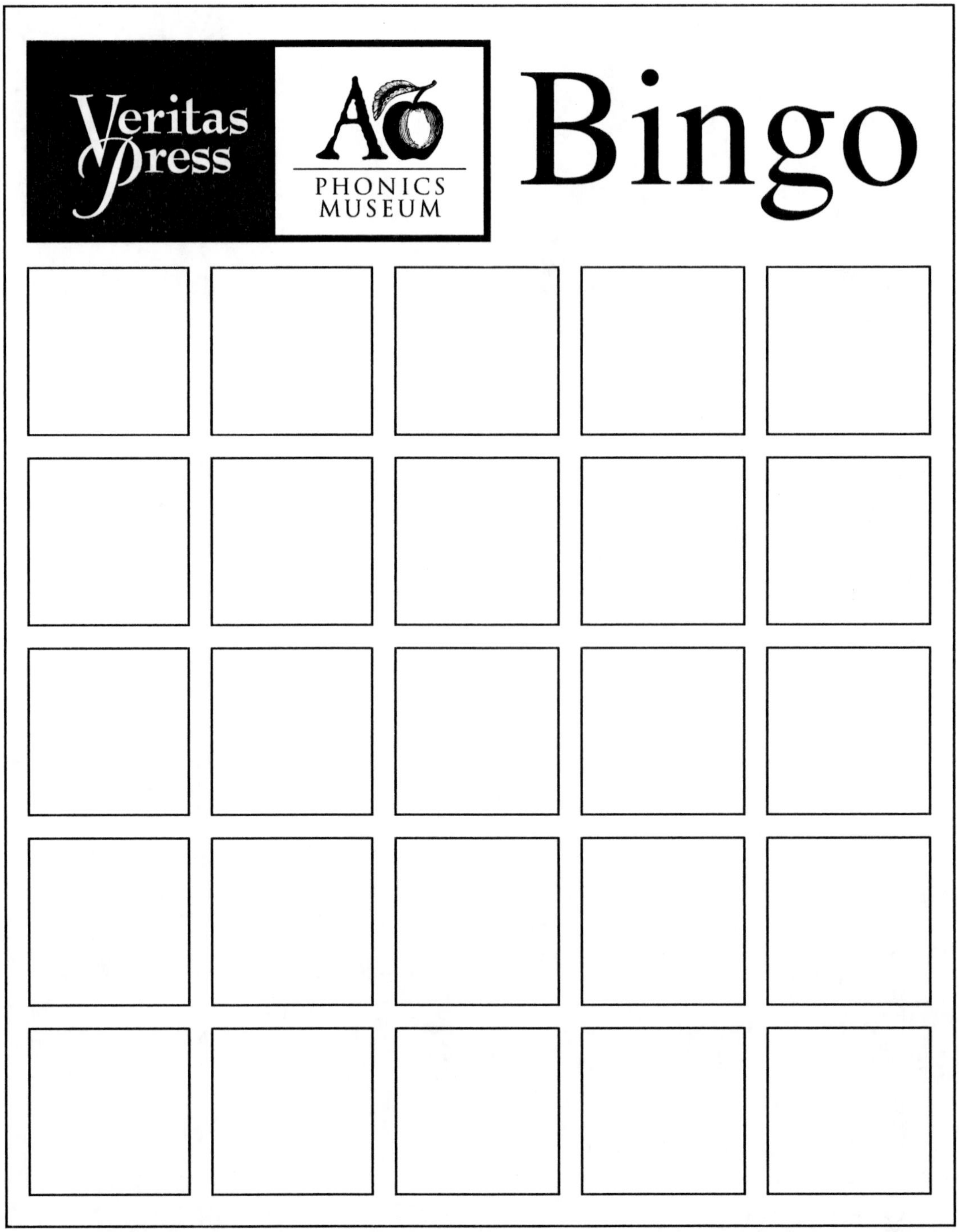

SPECIAL EXHIBIT LISTS

Book 11:
Ella Sings Jazz
swing
like
bebop

Book 12:
Alfred the King
North
love
do
push
who
we

Book 13:
My Clara
she
bush
her

Book 16:
Up in the Sky
some
many
also

Book 19:
Lexi's Hope
says
only
lives

Book 26:
Cyrus the Archer
very
body
build
two

Book 28:
Quothe the Prophet
come
once
done

Phonics Museum Answer Key

1A
Row 1:
d g t
Row 2:
r u h

1B
Row 1:
f i q
Row 2:
b x j

2A
Row 1:
d j
Row 2:
a k
Row 3:
u e
Row 4:
n v

2B
Row 1:
h w
Row 2:
c q
Row 3:
b t
Row 4:
s g

3A
Row 1:
u a e
Row 2:
a o i

4A
Row 1:
wh sh ch
Row 2:
wh th ch
Row 3:
sh ch th

8B
Row 1:
sh ch th
Row 2:
sh ch wh
Row 3:
wh th sh

10A
Chick
Jazz Pop
Top

11A
Row 1:
crab
dragon
Row 2:
drum
Row 3:
tricycle
frog

13A
Row 1:
crab
crown
Row 2:
drum
dress
Row 3:
frame
frog
Row 4:
train
trophy
tricycle

14A
Row 1:
train
Row 2:
frog
grapes
crayon
Row 3:
brush

16A
Row 1:
glasses
Row 2:
clothespin
Row 3:
sled globe

18A
Row 1:
gl gl sl
Row 2:
fl pl cl
Row 3:
gl sl cl

20C
Row 1:
n c r
Row 2:
e m g

20D
Row 1:
gl gl sl
Row 2:
fl pl cl
Row 3:
br sl
Row 4:
cr cr

22A
Row 1:
skate
Row 2:
smoke
Row 3:
snake
Row 4:
swing

24A
Row 1:
sc sk sm
sn
Row 2:
sl sw sk st

26A
Row 1:
blade
Row 2:
glasses
Row 3:
cross
crayon
Row 4:
dragon
dress

26B
Row 1:
frame
Row 2:
train
Row 3:
scale
Row 4:
skunk

27B
Row 1:
frog drum
Row 2:
dress crab
Row 3:
clock sled
Row 4:
crib plug

29A
1.sleeping
2.singing
3.ring
4.Clara,
my Clara
5.lass

30A
Row 1:
o (dog)
e (leg)
Row 2:
a (man)
e (web)
Row 3:
u (jug)
a (ram)
Row 4:
u (nut)
i (pin)

32A
Row 1:
sk st st
Row 2:
st st sk

33A
Row 1:
mp nt mp
Row 2:
nk nk nd

35A
1. slack
2. bun
3. hat
4. stilt
5. hat

37C
Row 1:
star car
Row 2:
fork bird
Row 3:
corn horn
Row 4:
barn
hammer

38A
Row 1:
girl star
zipper
Row 2:
bird corn
fork

40B
1. cutter
2. skull
3. cannon
balls
4. silver
5. pastor

41A
Row 1:
ride
Row 2:
hate bade
Row 3:
kite
Row 4:
tube tone
Row 5:
dime pipe
Row 6:
note

41B
Row 1:
vase skate
Row 2:
snake
Row 3:
scale cake

42A
Row 1:
dive
Row 2:
slide kite
Row 3:
bike

43A
Row 1:
nose
Row 2:
globe
Row 3:
rose

43B
Row 1:
note pan
Row 2:
cane kite
Row 3:
tube tape
Row 4:
hat dime

44A
Row 1:
tube
Row 2:
mule flute

Phonics Museum Answer Key

45A
Row 1:
long i,
long i
Row 2:
long e,
long e
Row 3:
long e,
long e

46A
Row 1:
1. bat 2.
cat 3. hat
1. duck 2.
fan 3. tag
Row 2:
1. dog 2.
fish 3. rug
1. bus 2.
cake 3.
flute

49B
1. wing
2. airplane
3. bicycle
4. God

51A
1. monk
2. Bible
3. Jesus
4. brave
5. hare

53A
Row 1:
sk st st
Row 2:
nk nk nd

55B
Row 1:
ch sh wh
Row 2:
ch sh wh

56C
Row 1:
train feet
seal
Row 2:
deer ear
queen

56D
Column 1:
long i
note
cane
read
chair
Column 2:
long e
pan
kite
seal
hay
Column 3:
long e
hat
tube
star
fork
Column 4:
long i
dime
tape
car
bird

59A
Row 1:
soap toes
Row 2:
window
bowl
Row 3:
goat boat

59B
1. blow 2.
coat 3.
hoe 4.
load 5.
row
1. boat 2.
fellow 3.
Joe 4.
road 5.
yellow

60A
1. coat
2. boat
3. road

60B
4. snow
5. toad
6. crow

61A
Row 1:
toad
Row 2:
crow
Row 3:
pillow
Row 4:
toes

62A
Row 1:
ch ch sh
Row 2:
sh sh ch
Row 3:
wh ch wh

66B
1. monk
2. Christ
3. land
4. skins
5. sheep
6. whale
7. Christ

68A
Blue:
cake, cane
Red: nose,
toes, hoe,
note
Yellow:
hive, kite,
pipe

69A
Row 1:
br dr tr
Row 2:
fr br fr
Row 3:
tr dr tr

71A
Row 1:
1. bat 2.
bed 3. big
1. set 2.
sin 3. sun
Row 2:
1. tan 2.
ten 3. top
1. pan 2.
peg 3. pig

71B
1. beach
2. bread
3. green
4. foal
5. sleep
6. bear
7. deer
8. jeep

76B
1. print
2. hay
3. bread
4. oath
5. saints
6. bow
7. God

76C
Red: boat,
hay
Blue:
bread
Green:
pizza

77B
Row 1:
books
Row 2:
hook
moon
Row 3:
spoon
boot

79D
soap
toes
hat
dime
window
bowl
tube
tape
goat
boat
star
car
moon
moose
fork
bird
books
boot
hook
screw

81B
1. a pack
on his
back
2. Red
Hood
3. It ate
up the
lock
4. on a
boat

81C
1. tools
2. flew
3. Sue
Woo
4. Ka-
Doom
Ray
5. 3 4 2 1

83B
Row 1:
boys toys
Row 3:
oysters

84B
1. boils
2. boys
3. noise
4. soil
5. oysters
6. toys
7. foil
8. oil

85C
Row 1: r t l
Row 2: x g
d

87A
shirt
bird
girl

89A
1. fishing
2. marshes
3. Grail
4. hydra
5. net
6. spoils

90A
Row 1:
cow house
Row 2:
owl
Row 3:
flower
crown

93A
1. It is his
first hunt
2. Master
of the
hounds
3. deer
4. by boat
5. bravery

Phonics Museum Answer Key

95B
Row 1:
lace pencil
cigar
Row 2:
dice
Row 3:
mice

98A
1. prince
2. mice
3. piece
4. race
5. ice
6. slice
7. pencil
8. circus

99A
Row 1:
1. cent
2. face
3. ice
4. nice
1. center
2. fence
3. hence
4. mince
Row 2:
1. dance
2. mice
3. pace
4. piece

100C
Row 1:
toy
oysters
boys boil
Row 2:
boot
goose
moon
rooster
Row 3:
moose
crown
cow
flower
Row 4:
hook
house
mouse
mouth
Row 5:
owl books
Row 6:
broom
pencil

101A
green:
cat cup
car cards
orange:
lace fence
prince
dice mice

101B
Row 1:
lace dice
fence
Row 2:
dance
mice
pencil

102B
orange:
bed tent
web eggs
yellow:
seal feet
read
peacock
queen

104A
1. Queen Elizabeth
2.England
3. The Prince of Spain
4. To give her land a prince who would love the pope
5. She would stay with them
6. English
7.England

105B
Row 1:
saw faucet
Row 2:
crawl
sauce
Row 3:
strawberry
ball

108A
1. There were black spots on the skin.
2. Gwen's father
3. help the sick
4. Stay away from me.
5. a horse

108B
Claudius
Gwen
Gwen
Claudius
Maud
Gwen
Maud
Gwen
Claudius

109B
Row 1:
kn gn wr
Row 2:
kn wr kn
Row 3:
kn wr gn

111B
Row 1:
tle mb gh
Row 2:
mb lf mb
Row 3:
gh tle

113A
1. bomb 2. comb 3. dumb 4. lamb 5. numb
1. knack
2. knee 3. knit 4. knob 5. knot

114A
1. lamb
2. knitting
3.climbing
4. walk
5.combing
6. knot
7. write
8. knife

117A
1.England
2. write poems
3.smallpox
4. Simon Bradstreet
5. New England
6. on a ship
7. her house

118A
Row 1:
fl cl sl
Row 2:
pl gl fl
Row 3:
bl gl cl

119B
Row 1:
judge
badge
Row 2:
bridge
Row 3:
cage

120C
dice
lace
knight
lamb
prince
mice
castle
comb
faucet
saw
judge
bridge
barn
crawl
badge
cage
gnome
knot

122A
1. hedge
2. fudge
3. cage
4. page
5. change
6. stage
7. bridge
8. smudge

1123A
Column 1:
e e e o e o
e e e e
Column 2:
e o o o e e
e e o

125A
n x b d f

127A
1. archer
2. swords
3. Greece
4. planks
5. seven
6. steep hills

128A
Row 1:
short a, short i
Row 2:
long a, long o
Row 3:
short e, long u

131A
1.vacation
2.inven-tions
3.invita-tions
4.Creation
5.reflec-tion

132A
spoon
boot
broom
moon

132B
moon:
spoon
broom
hoop
moose
book:
wood foot
hook cook

133B
1. action
2. educa-tion
3. popula-tion
4. station
5.vacation

1. addition
2. affec-tion
3. founda-tion
4. mention
5. promo-tion

Phonics Museum Answer Key

135A
your:
four court
source
pour tour
house:
scour sour
count
mouse
round

136A
1. bat 2. bed 3. pig 4. top 5. cup 6. cake 7. rope 8. flute

139A
John Kennedy
Alan Shepard
Neil Armstrong
step
leap
Edwin Aldrin
Michael Collins
Eagle
moon
rocks
American flag
Apollo 11

141B
Row 1: telephone
Row 2: elephant
Row 3: trophy photograph

146A
1. pharaoh
2. planted
3. telephone
4. played
5. traded
6. elephants
7. baked
8. thanked

149A
1. crow
2. sand
3. photo
4. stay
5. son
6. free
7. brains
8. gnats
9. death
10. door
11. God

150B
1. Moses
2. They did his work.
3. elephant
4. bearded
5. worms
6. He died.
7. They put lamb's blood on their doors.
8. His Son

152A
1. sword
2. Scotland
3. farmer
4. Duke
5. cattle
6. hills
7. men
8. trees
9. ax
10. huge man
11. wise men

153A
Column 1: f l j c m
Column 2: b q o g z

153B
e o u i a

154A
Row 1: ch tch wh
Row 2: sh th sh

154B
Row 1: ang ing ong
Row 2: ong ing ing

154C
Row 1: fr cr sl
Row 2: fl tr dr

154D
Row 1: nk st mp
Row 2: rk nk sk

156A
1. Caught in Smiles
2.Douglas Jones
3. France
4. Henry, Jeanne, Catherine
5. Catherine
6. Father was a wretch.
7. unable to leave

157B
1. vase
2. France
3. study
4. gifts and lack of discipline
5. good and godly men

159A
owl cow
crown
mouse
house

159B
Row 1: i a o
Row 2: a o i

160A
green:
moon
moose
broom
spoon
goose
rooster
red:
foot book
hook

160C
b k g b b

162A
1. Fathers' Faith
2. Ty & Emily Fischer
3. Todd Ream
4.camping
5. Davis
6. Boniface, Chrysostom, Augustine, Ambrose
7. tent, tree
8. emperor

162B
1. chance
2. Monica
3.Romans
4.he failed
5.German pagans
6. was made into a church.
7. nickname was golden mouth.
8. murdered guests
9. stopped him

163B
Augustine: opened Bible/ Monica/ pagan teacher/
Chysostom: Golden Mouth/ angered royals/ left to avoid fighting
Ambrose: led emperor to repent/ from Milan/ not let emperor in church/
Boniface: oak tree into church/ chopped down tree/ preached to Germans

163B
1.set up tent
2.Augustine
3.chopping wood
4.trees
5.chop tree

163C
6.speaking ability
7.left city
8.feast
9.stopped him

164C
knot
goose
trophy
rooster
phone
crown
cow
flower
hook
house
chair
note
faucet
seal
judge
hat
bird
crawl
badge
cage
prnce
mice
castle
comb

Archives Game

You will need:
Game board
Die
Game cards

Object of the Game:
To reach the stack of paintings at the end of the path. The first player to reach the stack of paintings wins.

Set Up:
Each player chooses a game piece and places it on the first space. Place the game card deck on the card pile space on the game board.

Special Spaces on the board:
Roll Again:
If a player lands on one of these spaces, he rolls again and moves ahead that many spaces.
+3/-2:
If a player lands on one of these spaces, he moves forward or backward that many spaces.

Directions for game play:
Players roll the die and the player with the highest number goes first.

The first player draws a card from the card pile and reads it out loud.

BLENDS EDITION
The purple cards contain initial blend words and the red cards contain final blend words. This game is played in three variations: initial blend words only, final blend words only, or with a combined deck of initial and final blend words. If the student reads the blend correctly, he rolls the die and moves ahead that many spaces. After landing on the space, he must follow any direction printed there.

LONG VOWEL EDITION
These cards are blue. If the student identifies the beginning letter sound correctly, he rolls the die and moves ahead that many spaces. After landing on the space, he must follow any direction printed there.

SPECIAL EXHIBIT EDITION
These cards are green. If the student identifies the beginning letter sound correctly, he rolls the die and moves ahead that many spaces. After landing on the space, he must follow any direction printed there.

Percival's Pairs

You will need:
Playing card deck
(using only letters prescribed in teacher's manual)

Object of the Game:
Collect the highest number pairs.

Set Up:
This game is best for 3-6 players, but it is possible for 2 to play. The dealer deals 5 cards to each player (7 each for 2 players). The remaining cards are placed face down to form a stock.

The player to dealer's left starts. A turn consists of asking a specific player for a specific letter. For example, if it is my turn I might say:
'Parker, would you please give me a letter F card?'. The player who asks must already hold at least one cards requested. If the player who was asked (Parker) has the card requested, he must give it to the player who asked for them. That player then gets another turn and may again ask any player for any other letter card already held by the asker.

If the person asked does not have any cards of the named, they say 'Pick a card'. The asker must then draw the top card of the undealt stock. If the drawn card is the letter asked for, the asker shows it and gets another turn. If the drawn card is not the rank asked for, the asker keeps it, but the turn now passes to the player who said 'Pick a card'.

The game continues until either someone has no cards left in their hand or the deck runs out. The winner is the player who then has the most pairs.

VARIATION: Instead of asking for a card by letter, the players request cards using the letter sounds.

[1] The Alphabet Song *2:54*

[2] The Museum Song *2:21*

[3] The Alphabet Chase *2:09*

[4] Short Vowels Song *1:09*

[5] Chickens & Sheep
(Consonant Digraphs) *1:36*

[6] The Ing Ang Song *1:07*

[7] Crash! Swing! Squash!
(Beginning Consonant Blends) *3:07*

[8] Act Like a Clown
(Final Consonant Blends) *2:09*

[9] Funny Butterfly (sounds of y) *1:01*

[10] The E Partnership (ea/ee) *0:49*

[11] Play Everyday (ai/ay) *0:53*

[12] The South Sea (oa/ow) *0:47*

[13] Oysters (oi/oy) *0:54*

[14] Shout (ou/ow) *1:00*

[15] The Broad-O Song (au/aw/al) *1:27*

[16] Mission to the Moon (sion/tion) *1:15*

[17] How Many Sounds? (a/e/i/o/u/y) *3:40*

Tracks 18-34 are the previous songs without vocals. [18] *2:54* [19] *2:20* [20] *2:05* [21] *1:00* [22] *1:35* [23] *0:58* [24] *3:07* [25] *2:09* [26] *0:51* [27] *0:40* [28] *0:44* [29] *0:39* [30] *0:47* [31] *0:52* [32] *1:19* [33] *1:05* [34] *3:37*

The Museum Song

Percival a knight in shining armor
And a boy who came to see the art
In a museum
They passed their time away
Looking at the paintings
Playing alphabetic games

Phonic sounds are simple
See the picture say the word
Just say it with a stutter and the phonic rule is heard
And with a little practice you'll be nimble you'll be quick
To say the sound of each that you have picked

A A Apples then M M Mummy B B Bull and
P P Pig then T T Table D D Dancer N N Nuts and G G Goat

S S Sun and F F Fan R R Rabbit and E E Egg
I I Indian and O O Ox U U Umbrella and L L Lion

CHORUS

H H Hat and C C Cow K K Kangaroo and J J Jar
Z Z Zebra then Y Y Yellow
Four more letters we will learn
So say them with each picture

W W Wind mill and Q Q Queen V V Vi o lin and X X Boxing
Twenty six letters in all Perhaps you'll try again
When you go to a museum
Try and play this phonic game

THE MUSEUM SONG

Veritas Press
Copyright 2000 Steve Scheffler

15
say the sound of each that you have picked A A Ap ples then
19
M M Mum my B B Bull and P P Pig then T T Ta ble
23
D D Dan cer N N Nuts and G G Goat S S Sun and F F
29
Fan R R Rab bit and E E Egg I I In di an and O O Ox U U Um
34
brel la and L L Lion Pho nic sounds are
36
sim ple See the pic ture say the word Just say it with a
38
stut ter and the pho nic rule its heard And with a lit tle
40
prac tice you'll be nim ble you'll be quick To say the sound of

42
each that you have picked
H H Hat and C ´ C
46
Cow K K Kan ga roo and J J Jar Z Z Ze bra then Y Y Yel low Four more let ters
51
we will learn So say them with each pic ture
W W Wind mill and
55
Q Q Queen V V Vi o lin and X X Box ing Twen ty six let ters in all Per
59
haps you'll try a gain When you go to a mu se um Try and play this pho nic game

The Alphabet Song

The words we speak they come together
By using alphabetic letters;
And in this song we are going to teach you
The alphabet your gonna use.

Like a puzzle picture each jigsaw piece
Is like the letters in a word
And when they're put together in proper order
Then the sounds of each are heard.

Speak each letter they form the words
You can really do it if you try!

ABCDEFGHIJKLMNOPQRSTUVWXY and Z

Repeat

The Alphabet Song

Veritas Press

Joyful

The words we speak they
come to ge ther by us ing al pha be tic let ters; And
in this song we are
going to teach you the al pha bet your
gon na use. Like a puz zle pic ture each
jig zaw piece is like the let ters in a word;

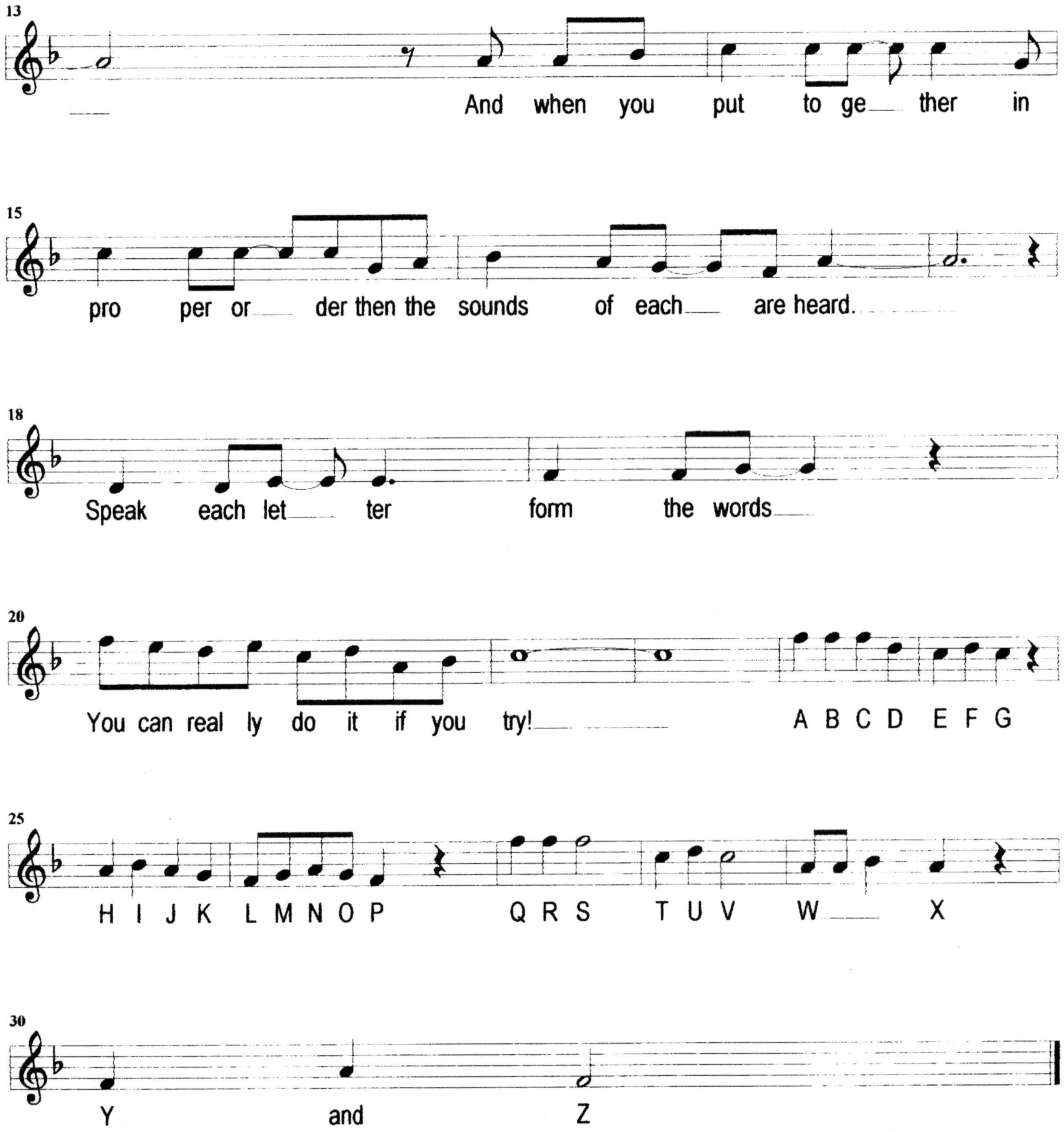
13
And when you put to ge ther in
15
pro per or der then the sounds of each are heard.
18
Speak each let ter form the words
20
You can real ly do it if you try!
A B C D E F G
25
H I J K L M N O P Q R S T U V W X
30
Y and Z

Short Vowels Song

A as in APPLE
E as in EGG
You can even say IT
Standing on your HEAD
And IF you were AN INDIAN
Short I is what you'd use
Just like using O in OX
Short O is what you'd choose

And finally now we introduce the one and only U
The SOUND when short comes OUT like the
UMBRELLA that we use in a rainstorm

A as in APPLE
E as in EGG
I as in INDIAN
And O as in OX
U as in UMBRELLA
There are five short vowels
They are A E I O U

SHORT VOWELS SONG

Veritas Press

Lullabye

1
A as in AP PLE E as in EGG
4
You can e ven say IT Stand ing on your HEAD And
6
IF you were AN IN DI AN Short I is what you'd use
8
Just like us ing O in OX Short O is what you'd choose And
10
fi nally now we in tro duce the one and on ly U The
12
SOUND when short comes OUT like the UM BREL LA that we use in a

14
rain storm A as in AP PLE E as in EGG I as in IN DI AN
18
O as in OX U as in UM BREL LA
20
There are five short vowels They are A E I O U

Chickens & Sheep

(Consonant Digraphs)

Consonant Digraphs there are five of them
C H S H are the first two
Then there is two of the same T H letters
Yet one is voiced and the other is not
And finally the letters W - - H
Concludes this list of these consonant sounds

C H is used in words like CHICKEN
CHURCH and CHALK and CHIMPANZEE
S H is used in SHEEP SHELL SHOWBOAT
and W - - H in WHITE WHIPPO'WILL

Now the T H sound that is VOICED and heard
Is found in words like THIN THICK THANK

And don't forget at times that T H isn't voiced
As in words like THIS and THAT

Consonant Digraphs there are five of them
C H S H are the first two
Then there are two of the same T H letters
Yet one is voiced and the other is not

CHICKENS & SHEEP

Veritas Press

Sing Song with Talk

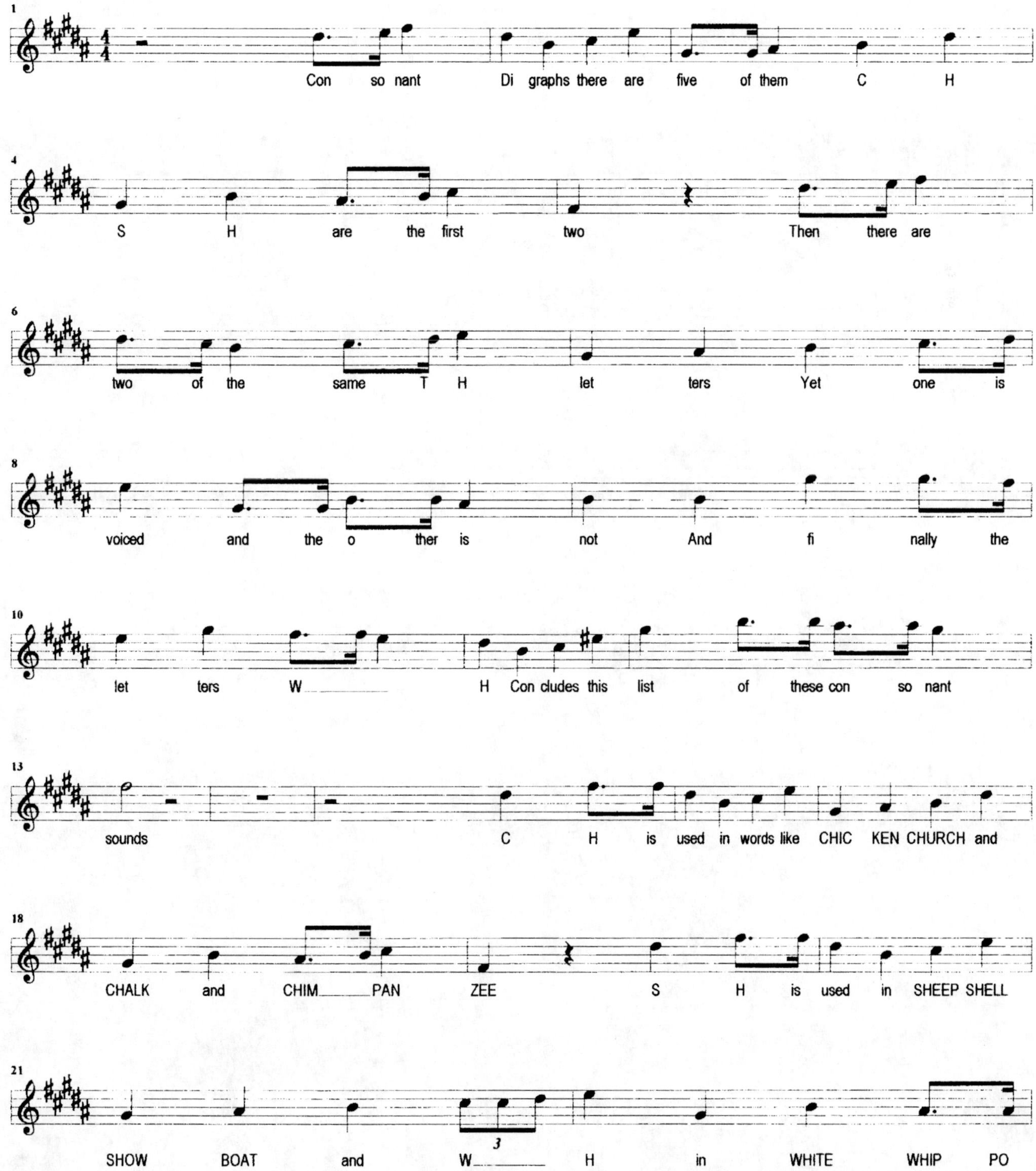

23
WIL Now the T H sound that is VOICED and heard Is found in
26
words like THIN THICK THANK And don't for get at times that T H is n't
29
voiced As in words like THIS and THAT Con so nant
34
Di graphs there are five of them C H S H are the first
37
two Then there are two of the same T H
39
let ters Yet one is voiced and the o ther is not

The ING ANG ONG Song

There are many songs that have no rhyme or reason to sing em
So we change those sounds as we go a long
The same is said about times and the seasons
Describing them requires a different sound

Sing can be Sang and Sang can be Sung
Ring can be Rang and Rang can be Rung

ING ANG And ONG is just a way you may say it
When explaining the time it might have occurred

THE ING ANG ONG SONG

Veritas Press

Jazz

17
sound Sing can be Sang
19
and Sang can be Song Ring can
22
be Rang and Rang can be Rung
25
ING ANG And ONG is just
27
a way you may say
29
it When ex plain ing the time it might have oc
31
curred

CRASH! SWING! SQUASH!

Beginning Consonant Blends

Those consonant blends oh those consonant blends
Some have a family still some have none
But we will learn beginning consonant blends
Five categories each to attend

First the R family there's eight in the list
I'll teach you the blend a word I'll suggest
And then you will know the R family
Here we go do them accurately

B R as in BROKE
C R as in CRASH
D R as in DRAG
F R as in FRANK
G R as in GREAT
P R as in PRUNE
T R as in TRAIN
W R as in WRECK

Let's talk about that L family
Its really quite simple and easy you'll see
There's only the six that we have to know
Join with me and go with the flow

B L as in BLUE
C L as in CLAM
F L as in FLOOD
G L as in GLAD
P L as in PLANS
S L as in SLOUSH

And for the letter the letter called S
No family here just seven on that list
Get yourself ready to repeat them out loud
Here we go again and I'll show you how

S C as in SCAT
S K as in SKATE
S M as in SMITTEN
S N as in SNAKE
S P as in SPOILED
S T as in STOP
S W as in SWING

And believe it or not S has a family too
Seven members make up this family and crew
Keep in the beat and you will learn all them well
Don't be afraid you are doing just swell

S C R for SCREAM
S Q U for SQUASHED
S T R for STRIK ING
S P R for SPRING ING
S P L for SPLIT TING
And S H R for SHRIEKED
And S C H for SCHOOL

Finally there's one that has no family all
Its members are three, the list is quite small
But here is the list called the orphan Blends
Just three more till we come to the end

D W like in DWELL
T W like in TWIN KLE
T H R as in THREE

Well that's all of them
Surely the best of them
Those Beginning Consonant Blends

Crash! Swing! Squash!

Veritas Press

Broadway Musical

29
real ly quite sim ple and eas y you'll see There's on ly the six that we have to know
33
Join with me and go with the flow B L as in BLUE C L as in CLAM F
37
L as in FLOOD G L as in GLAD P L as in PLANS S
40
L as in SLOUSH And for the let ter the let ter called S
44
No fami ly here just se ven on the list Get your self rea dy to re
47
peat them out loud Here we go a gain and I'll show you how S
50
C as in SCAT S K as in SKATE S M as in SMIT TEN S
53
N as in SNAKE S P as in SPOIL ED S T as in STOP S
56
W 3 as in SWING Be lieve it or not S has a

59
fa mi ly too
Se ven mem bers make up this fami ly and crew
62
Keep in the beat and you will learn all them well
Don't be a fraid you are
65
do ing just swell
S C R for SCREAM
S Q U for SQUASHED
68
S T R for STRIK ING
S P R for SPRING ING
70
S P L for SPLIT TING and
S H R for SHRIEKED
72
S C H for SCHOOL
Fin al ly there's one that has
no fa mi ly Its
76
small and its short its
mem bers are three
Here is the list of
79
these or phan Blends
Just three more to go
till we come to the end D
82
W like in DWELL
T W like in TWIN KLE
T H R

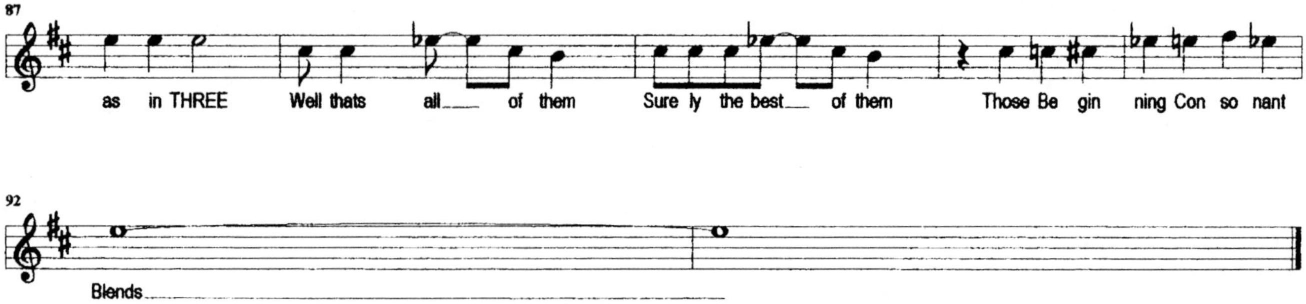
87
as in THREE Well thats all of them Sure ly the best of them Those Be gin ning Con so nant
92
Blends

Act Like a Clown

(Final Consonant Blends)

Final Consonant Blends we will try to attend
So come on say them out loud show everyone you know how

C T in ACT like a clown
F T in LIFT up your frown
L D as OLD as the hills
L T in SALT for the meal

Those Final Consonant Blends when said right they can make you grin
And if you say them out loud you'll make the teacher quite proud

M P in JUMP up and down
N C in SINCE we're a round
N D AND don't you forget
N K don't get INK on your pants

Final Consonant Blend's three more that we must attend
So that we can learn to say these Consonants Perfectly

N T in ANTS at the picnic
P T in KEPT them a way
Still I find it's not so easy
R D in HARD you might say

Final Consonant Blends we have one more list to attend
Join with me to say them out loud show everyone that you know how

R K in DARK as the night
R T in ART painted bright
S T in LEAST of them all
S K in RISK if you fall

These are the Consonant Blends that you will find in the end
Of words like the ones we just used say them again if you choose

ACT LIKE A CLOWN

Veritas Press

29
we're a round N D AND don't you for get
32
N K don't get INK on___ your pants
35
Fi nal Con so nant Blends Three more we will at tend So
39
that we can learn to say These Con so nants per fec tly
43
N T in ANTS at the pic nic P T in KEPT them a way
47
Still I find its not so ea sy R D in HARD you might say
51
Fi nal Con so nant Blends We have one more list to at
55
tend Join with me to say them out loud And show eve

58
ry one that you know how R K in DARK as the night
62
A T in ART paint ed bright S T in LEAST of them all
66
S K in RISK if you fall These are the Con so nant Blends
70
That you will find in the end Of words like the ones we just used
74
Say them a gain if you choose

Funny Butterfly

(Two Y Sounds)

There are two sounds that the Y makes
Though its still the letter Y
Sometimes Y will sound like long E
Other times will sound like I

Words like SUNNY FUNNY PONY and the like
End with Y sounding like E
And in words like CRY TRY BUTTERFLY it is true
That the Y comes out sounding like I

There are two sounds that the Y makes
Though its still the letter Y
Sometimes Y will sound like long E
Other times will sound like I

FUNNY BUTTERFLY

Veritas Press

Joyful

The E Partnership

(Phonics Rule EA & EE)

E A and E E
Operate a partnership
Though one might be silent
Said together they sound just the same
You find them sounding "E"
Like in SEED, FEED, EAT
Their GUARANTEED to always sound like "E"

So E A and E E
Operate their partnership
Though one might be silent
They always sound like "E"

THE E PARTNERSHIP

Veritas Press

With Expression

8
FEED, EAT Their GUAR EN
9
TEED to al ways sound like "E"
10
So E A and E E Op er
12
ate their part ner ship Though one might
13
be si lent They al ways sound like "E"

Play Everyday

(ai/ay)

A I and letters A Y
Put together make the sound of a LONG A
A I and A Y are in so many words
Such as PAID, AIDE, SAY, and HAY
Food the horses eat!

A I and also A Y when they're said correctly they say A
A I used in words such as RAIN, BRAIN, MAID
And A Y in some other words like DAY, WAY, PAY
And do not think it hard in words like RAID, PLAY, EVERYDAY
The Phonic rule for A I and A Y

Play Everyday

Veritas Press
Veritas Press

Joyful

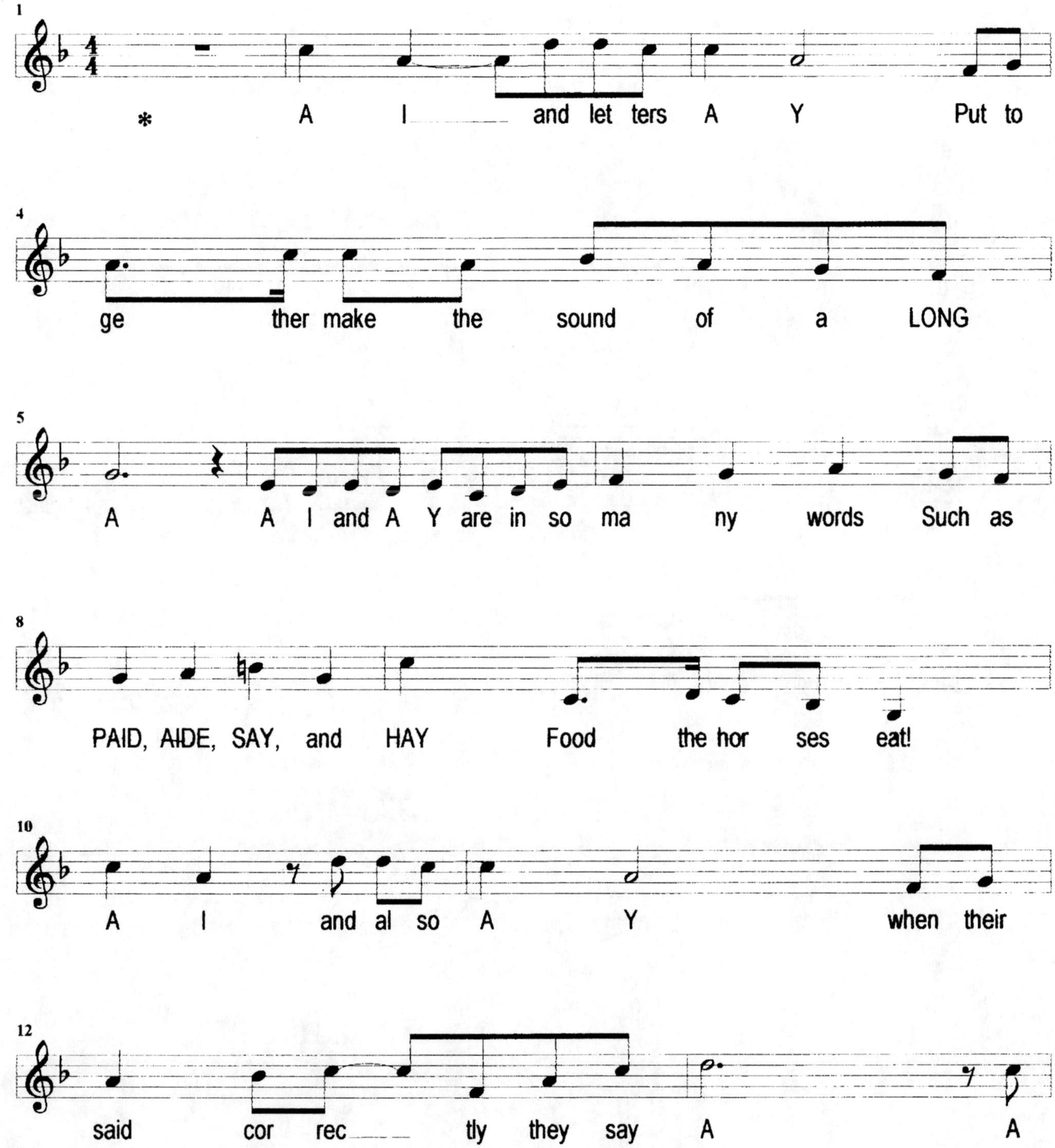

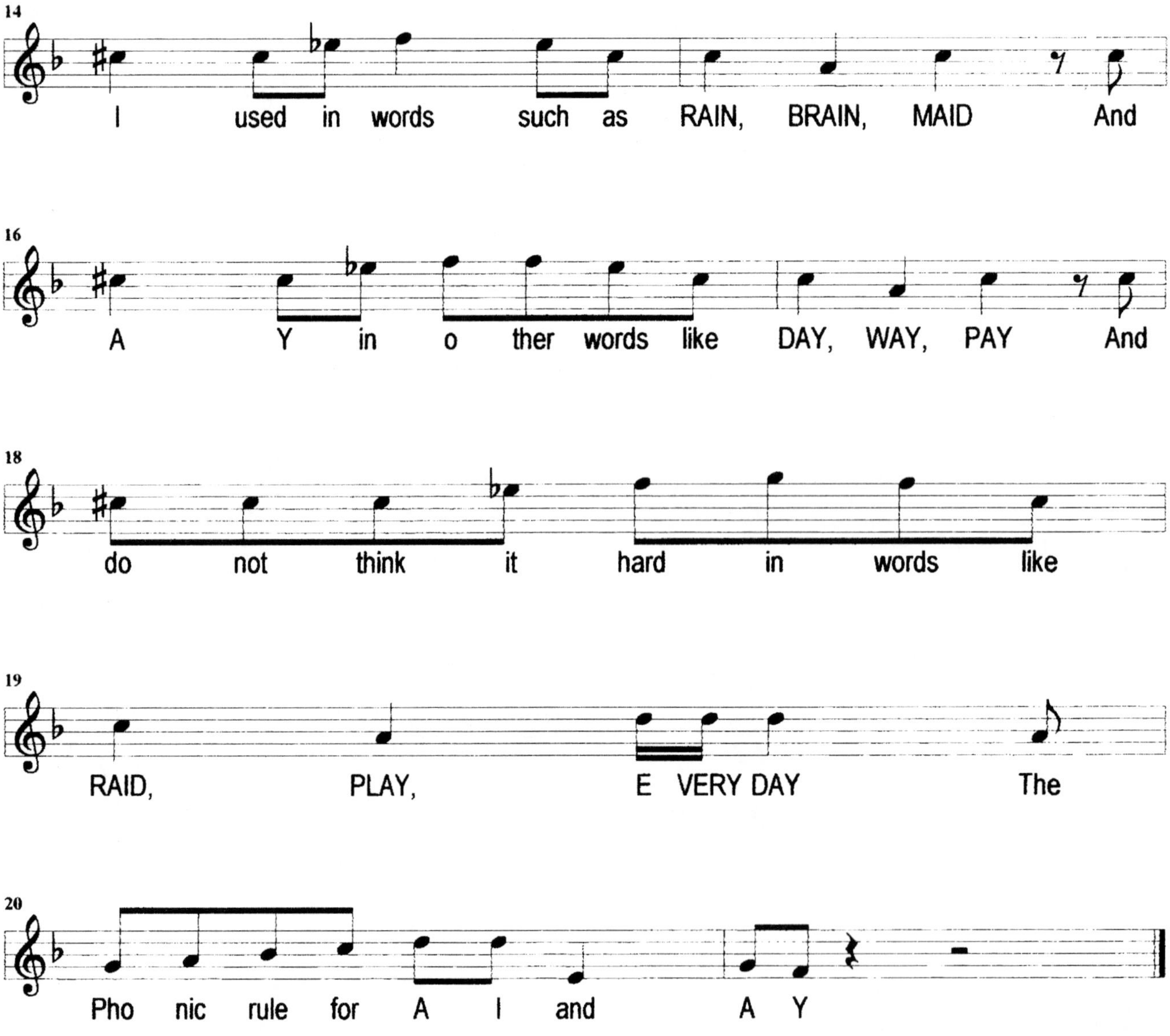
14
I used in words such as RAIN, BRAIN, MAID And
16
A Y in o ther words like DAY, WAY, PAY And
18
do not think it hard in words like
19
RAID, PLAY, E VERY DAY The
20
Pho nic rule for A I and A Y

The South Sea
(oa/ow)

Off an island in the south sea
(Underneath men sing throughout entire song) O - A   O - W
On a BOAT in a nice breeze
We all do KNOW -
Where the south wind BLOWS — —

When we hear the sounds GROANING
We KNOW the letters O A
And O W - - -
Make the sound of "O"

The South Sea

Veritas Press

Hawaii Style

10
GROAN ING
11
We KNOW the let ters
12
O A And O W
14
15
Make the sound of "O"

Oysters

(oi/oy)

I knew a BOY who loved to eat OYSTERS
He'd TOIL all day in the SOIL and then
He'd bring em home with JOY and excitement
Sit down to eat em then go diggin' again

And then one day while diggin' up OYSTERS
He swallowed one whole and his VOICE went a way
So when they asked him what was the trouble
OI OY OI OY was all he could say

Phonic rule O I
Phonic rule O Y
OI OY OI OY was all he could say

OYSTERS

Veritas Press

Jazz

13
So when they asked him
14
what was the trou ble OI OY OI OY was
16
all he could say Pho nic rule O I
18
Pho nic rule O Y
21
OI OY OI OY was all he could say

Shout
(ou/ow)

The Phonic rule for O U O W
They sound the same though
The spelling is different

Come sing with me and I will show you how
This Phonic rule applies

O U in words like out pout house snout and here about
When you see a mouse you shout

O W in how now brown cow let him pull the plow he likes it anyhow

The Phonic rule for O U O W
They sound the same though
The spelling is different

But now you know O U and O W
They make the sound of OW!

Shout

Veritas Press

Bouncy

11
and here a bout When you see a mouse you shout
13
O W in how now brown cow
15
let him pull the plow he likes it a ny how
17
The Pho nic rule for O
20
U O W
21
They sound the same though The
22
spel ling is dif fe rent But now you know O U
24
and O W

25
They make the sound of OW!

The Broad-O Song

Ah
Ah
Ah
AH
The phonic rule BROAD O SOUND
Is made by A and L "like in CALL"
And if you see both A and W
It should sound so AWFUL

Sometimes you'll see A followed by U
And AUTOMATICALLY know
That you are using the Phonic rule
The Phonic Rule BROAD O

A W
A W
A U
A U
A I
A I

Ah
Ah
Ah
Ah
The phonic rule BROAD O SOUND
Is made by A and L "like in CALL"
And if you see both A and W
It should sound so AWFUL

Some times you'll see A followed by U
And AUTOMATICALLY know
That you are using the Phonic rule
The Phonic Rule BROAD O

THE BROAD-O SONG

Veritas Press

Up Beat

23
A W A U A U A I A I Ah Ah Ah
30
AH The pho nic rule BROAD O SOUND
33
Is made by A and L "like in CALL"
35
And if you see both A and W
37
It should sound so AW FUL
39
Some times you'll see A fol lowed by U
41
An AU TO MA TIC ALLY know That you are u sing the
44
Pho nic rule The Pho nic Rule BROAD O

Mission to the Moon

(sion/tion)

A MISSION to the moon we all will take some ACTION
A NATION to the moon we'll build a real space STATION
And when we get all through we'll have the world's ATTENTION
The Phonic rule for S I O N is the same for T I O N
They may sound the same but still their spelling is quite different
They both sound like SHUN

A MISSION to the moon we all will take some ACTION
A NATION to the moon we'll build a real space STATION
And when we get all through we'll have the world's ATTENTION
The Phonic rule for S I O N is the same for T I O N
They may sound the same but still their spelling is quite different
They both sound like SHUN

MISSION TO THE MOON

Veritas Press
Copyright Veritas Press

Militant

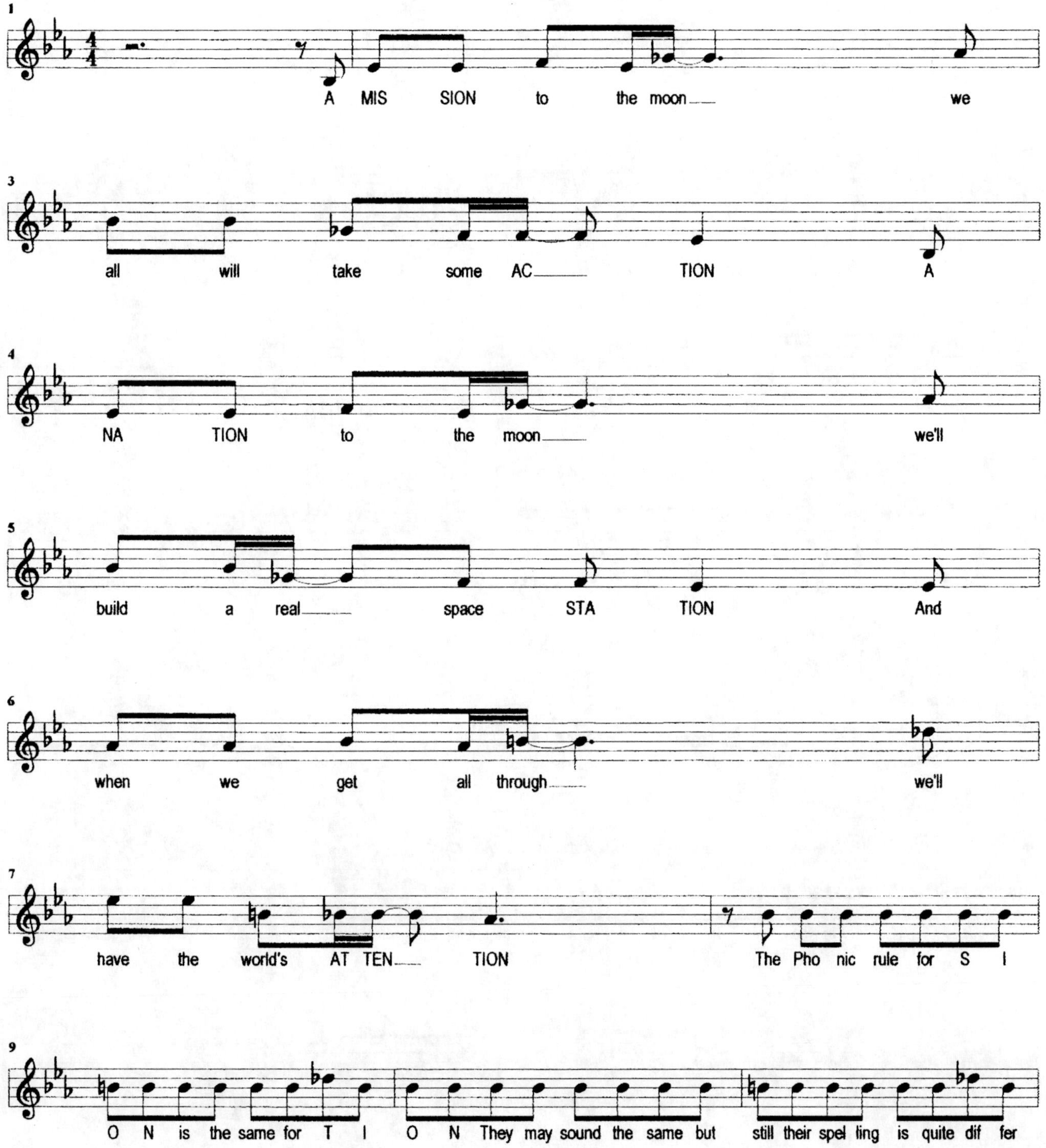

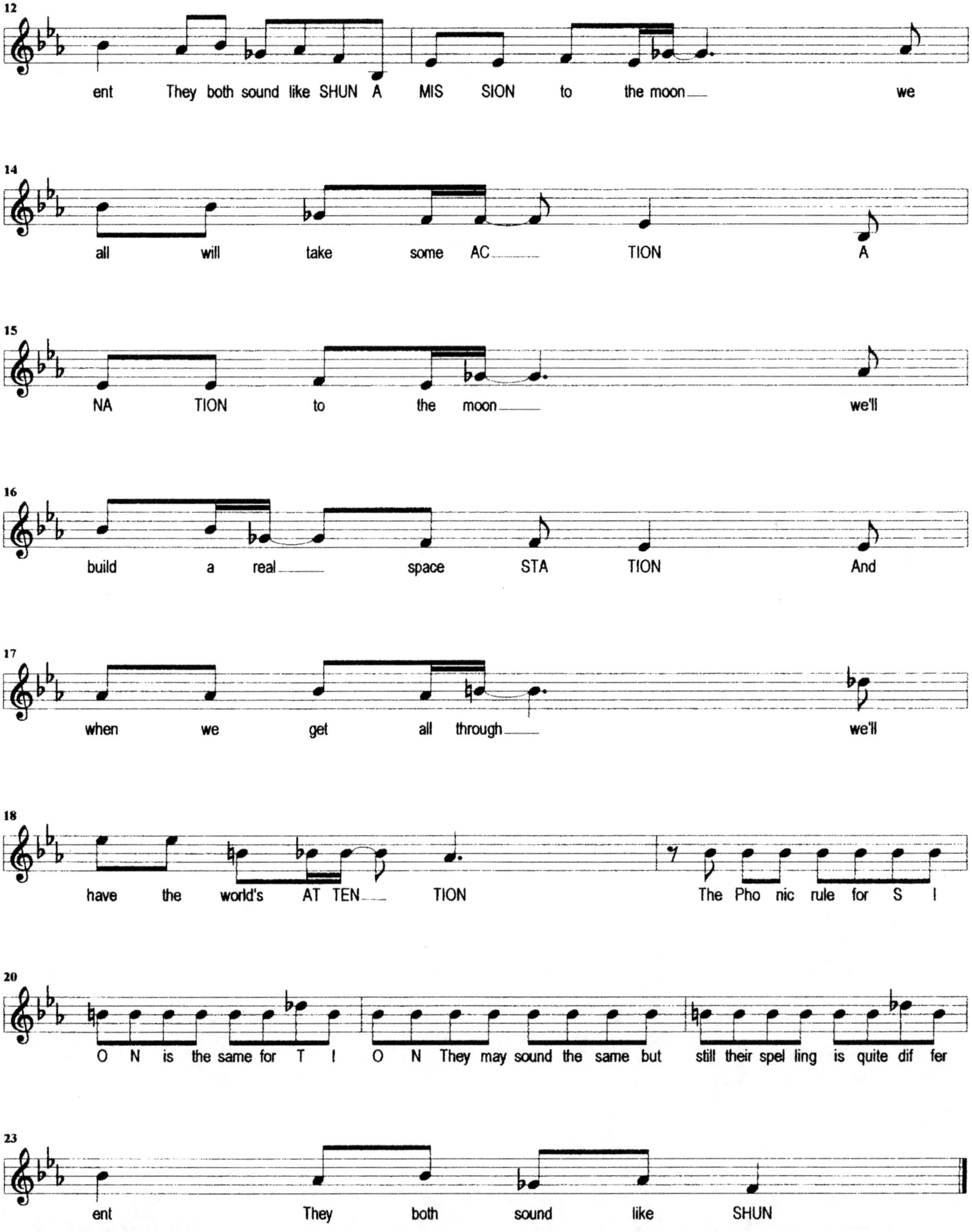
12
ent They both sound like SHUN A MIS SION to the moon we
14
all will take some AC TION A
15
NA TION to the moon we'll
16
build a real space STA TION And
17
when we get all through we'll
18
have the world's AT TEN TION The Pho nic rule for S I
20
O N is the same for T I O N They may sound the same but still their spel ling is quite dif fer
23
ent They both sound like SHUN

How Many Sounds?

(a/e/i/o/u/y)

A E I O U Y
A E I O U Y

How many sounds does A make
A has three main sounds
Then let me hear the sound A makes
A it sounds like this

You got A as in FAT
A as in FATE
AHHH as in FATHER
How many sounds does A make
A has three main sounds

How many sounds does E make
E has two main sounds
Then let me hear the sound E makes
E it sounds like this

You got E as in MET
E as in ME
How many sounds does E make
E has two main sounds

How many sounds does I make
I has two main sounds
Then let me hear the sound I makes
I it sounds like this

You got I as in PIN
I as in PINE
How many sounds does I make
I has two main sounds

A E I O U Y
A E I O U Y

How many sounds does O make
O has three main sounds
Then let me hear the sound O makes
O it sounds like this

You got O as in NOT
O as in NO
OOO as in MOVE
How many sounds does O make
O has three main sounds

How many sounds does U make
U has two main sounds
Then let me hear the sound U makes
U it sounds like this

You got U as in TUB
U as in TUBE
How many sounds does U make
U has two main sounds

How many sounds does Y make
Y has two main sounds
Then let me hear the sound Y makes
Y it sounds like this

You got Y as in DU TY
Y as in SHY
How many sounds does Y make
Y has two main sounds

A E I O U Y
A E I O U Y

HOW MANY SOUNDS?

Veritas Press

Upbeat

30
makes E it sounds like this You got
33
E as in MET E as in ME How ma ny sounds does E
37
make E has two main sounds How ma ny sounds does I
41
make I has two main sounds Then let me hear the sound I
45
makes I it sounds like this You got
48
I as in PIN I as in PINE How ma ny sounds does I
52
make I has two main sounds A E I
56
O U Y A E I O U Y

62
How ma ny sounds does O make O has three main sounds
66
Then let me hear the sound O makes
69
O it sounds like this You got O as in NOT
72
O as in NO OOO as in MOVE How ma ny sounds does O
76
make O has three main sounds How ma ny sounds does U
80
make U has two main sounds Then let me hear the sound U
84
makes U it sounds like this You got
87
U as in TUB U as in TUBE How ma ny sounds does U

91
make U has two main sounds
97
How ma ny sounds does Y make Y has two main sounds.
101
Then let me hear the sound Y makes
104
Y it sounds like this You got Y as in DU TY
107
Y as in SHY How ma ny sounds does Y make
111
Y has two main sounds A E I O U Y
115
A E I O U Y

THE ALPHABET CHASE

There was an A A A APPLE eaten by a M M MUMMY
Being chased from behind by a large B B B BULL

But then a big fat P P PIG jump up on the T T TABLE
And began to do a jig because he was a D D DANCER

And N N NUTS the G G GOAT went out in to the S S SUN
And got so hot they had to cool him off with a F F FAN

Now the R R RABBIT found the one and only colored E E EGG
While the I I INDIAN ran around his tent to get away
From the large O O OX

And when it started raining an U U UM BRELLA
Was used by L L LION and acted as his H H HAT
Who's heard of that a lion wearing a hat

You've heard of the C C COW who jumped over the moon
But a K K KANGAROO once flew in a balloon
You put flowers in a J J JAR see a Z Z ZEBRA at the zoo
And Y Y YELLOW is the color of the morning sun

A W W WIND MILL spins around creaking as it goes
A Q Q QUEEN sits down upon her high and lifted throne
And while the Jester sits and plays his V V VIOLIN
There's a X X BOXING match out in her court yard

TEACHER'S NOTE: This song may be sung as an alternative to singing *The Museum Song* for the sake of variety beginning in the second quarter.

THE ALPHABET CHASE

Veritas Press
Copyright 2000 Veritás Press

30
And act ed as his H H HAT Who's heard of that A lion
33
wear ing a hat You've heard of the C C COW
36
Who jumped o ver the moon But a K K KAN GA ROO
38
Once flew in a bal loon You put flo wers in a J J JAR See a Z Z ZE BRA at the zoo
41
And Y Y YEL LOW is the co lor Of the morn ing sun A W W WIND MILL spins a round
44
Crea king as it goes A Q Q QUEEN sits down u pon Her high and lif ted throne
47
And while the Jes ter sits and plays His V V VI O LIN There's a X X BOX ING match
50
Out in her court yard

Name

AaBbCcDdEeFfGgHhIiJjKkLlMmNnOoPpQqRrSsTtUuVvWwXxYyZz

VERITAS PRESS PHONICS MUSEUM PRIMERS *in sequence with the* VERITAS PRESS HISTORY CARDS

BOOK TITLE	VP HISTORY CARD SERIES	CARD #
Ella Sings Jazz	1815 to the Present	27
Alfred the King	Middle Ages, Renaissance and Reformation	9
My Clara	Middle Ages, Renaissance and Reformation	27–32
The Grand Cat	Middle Ages, Renaissance and Reformation	27–32
The Black Flag	Explorers to 1815	13
Up in the Sky	1815 to the Present	25
The Brave Monk	Middle Ages, Renaissance and Reformation	27
The Sailing Saint	Middle Ages, Renaissance and Reformation	2
Lexi's Hope	1815 to the Present	32
Red Hood	1815 to the Present	27
A Tale of Sir Galahad	Middle Ages, Renaissance and Reformation	12
Howard Saves a Hound	Middle Ages, Renaissance and Reformation	12
Queen of the Sea	Explorers to 1815	6
Serving in the Shadow of Death	Middle Ages, Renaissance and Reformation	20
Bright Night	Explorers to 1815	10
Cyrus the Archer	New Teatament, Greece and Rome	13
Moon Mission	1815 to the Present	31
Quothe the Prophet	Old Testament and Ancient Egypt	23
The Sword of Rob Roy	Explorers to 1815	13
Caught in Smiles	Explorers to 1815	13
Fathers' Faith	Middle Ages, Renaissance and Reformation	1

Name

Lower Case

a | begin at the center; curve around down, touch the ground, climb the column to close, down the column, and a curl.

b | begin at the top; down the column on a slant, touch the ground, curve around and up to close at the center.

c | begin under the center; curve up and around, touch the center and the ground, curve up, do not close.

d | begin at the center; curve around down, touch the ground, climb the column to the top, down the column, and a curl.

e | begin between the center and the ground, curve around and up, touch the center and the ground, curve up, do not close.

f | begin under the top, curve up and around, touch the top, down the column on a slant to the ground, cross at the center

g | begin at the center; curve around down, touch the ground, climb the column to close, down the column, underground, and a bend to the left in the tunnel.

h | begin at the top; down the column on a slant, touch the ground, climb the column, touch the center, curve around, down the column, and a curl.

i | begin at the center; down the column on a slant, touch the ground, and a curl; dot on top.

j | begin at the center; down the column on a slant, underground, and a bend to the left in the tunnel; dot on top.

k | begin at the top; down the column on a slant, touch the ground, climb the column, touch the center, curve around to close, to the ground with a curl.

l | begin at the top; down the column on a slant, touch the ground, and a curl.

m | begin at the center; down the column on a slant, touch the ground, climb the column, curve around, touch the center, down the column, climb the column, curve around, touch the center, down the column, and a curl.

n | begin at the center; down the column on a slant, touch the ground, climb the column, curve around, touch the center, down the column, and a curl.

o | begin at the center; curve around down, touch the ground, curve around and up to close.

p | begin at the center; down the column on a slant, underground, climb the column, touch the center, curve around to close on the ground.

q | begin at the center; curve around down, touch the ground, climb the column to close, down the column, underground, and a curl.

r | begin at the center; down the column on a slant, climb the column, touch the center, curve around with an arch.

s | begin under the center; curve up and around, touch the center and the ground, curve up, make a snake tail.

t | begin at the top; down the column on a slant, touch the ground, and a curl; cross at the center.

u | begin at the center; down the column on a slant, touch the ground, and a curl, climb a new column, down the column, and a curl.

v | begin at the center; down the column on a right slant, touch the ground, climb a new column on a slant.

w | begin at the center; down the column on a slant, touch the ground, and a curl, climb a new column, down the column, and a curl, climb a new column.

x | begin at the center; down the column on a right slant, and a curl; jump to the center, down the column on a left slant, to the ground.

y | begin at the center; down the column on a slant, touch the ground, and a curl, climb a new column, down the column, underground, and a bend to the left in the tunnel.

z | begin at the center; climb right on the center line, down the column on a slant, touch the ground, walk right along the ground.

Upper Case

A I begin at the top; down the column on a slant, touch the ground, jump to the top, straight to the ground, connect the columns on the center line.

B I begin at the top; down the column on a slant, touch the ground, climb the column to the top, curve around, close at the center, curve around, close on the ground.

C I begin under the top; curve up and around, touch the top and the ground, curve up, stop before the center.

D I begin at the top; down the column on a slant, touch the ground, climb the column to the top, curve around, close on the ground.

E I begin at the top; climb left on the top line, down the column on a slant, touch the ground, walk right along the ground, jump to the center and climb right on the line.

F I begin at the top; climb left on the top line, down the column on a slant, touch the ground, jump to the center and climb right on the line.

G I begin under the top; curve up and around, touch the top and the ground, curve up to the center, climb left on the line.

H I begin at the top; down the column on a slant, touch the ground, jump to the top, down a new column on a slant, touch the ground, connect the columns on the center line.

I I begin at the top; down the column on a slant, touch the ground, put a cap on the top, put a base on the ground.

J I begin at the top; down the column on a slant, touch the ground, and a bend to the left.

K I begin at the top; down the column on a slant, touch the ground, jump to the top, down to the center of the column, to the ground with a curl.

L I begin at the top; down the column on a slant, touch the ground, walk right along the ground.

M I begin at the top; down the column on a slant, touch the ground, jump to the top, down a new column on a right slant, touch the center, climb a new column on a right slant, down the column on a slant to the ground.

N I begin at the top; down the column on a slant, touch the ground, jump to the top, down a new column on a right slant, touch the ground, climb a new column on a slant.

O I begin at the top; curve around down, touch the ground, curve around and up to close.

P I begin at the top; down the column on a slant, climb the column, touch the top, curve around to close at the center.

Q I begin at the top; curve around down, touch the ground, curve around and up to close; give a tail on the right.

R I begin at the top; down the column on a slant, climb the column, touch the top, curve around to close at the center, to the ground with a curl.

S I begin under the top; curve up and around, touch the top and the ground, curve up, make a snake tail.

T I begin at the top; down the column on a slant, touch the ground, put a big cap on top.

U I begin at the top; down the column on a slant, touch the ground, and a curl, climb a new column, down the column, and a curl.

V I begin at the top; down the column on a right slant, touch the ground, climb a new column on a slant.

W I begin at the top; down the column on a right slant, touch the ground, climb a new column on a slant, down the column on a right slant, touch the ground, climb a new column on a slant.

X I begin at the top; down the column on a right slant, and a curl; jump to the top, down the column on a left slant, to the ground.

Y I begin at the top; down the column on a right slant to the center, jump to the top, down the column on a left slant, tag the first column, to the ground.

Z I begin at the top; climb right on the top line, down the column on a slant, touch the ground, walk right along the ground.

In a purely phonetic language there are as many letters in the alphabet as there are sounds. We might expect to have twenty-six sounds in our language, as we have twenty-six letters, but actually we have about forty-four sounds in our language. The vowels A,E,I,O and U represent many sounds, because the consonants with a few exceptions, do not vary the sounds they represent.

The list provided below is intended to help you know the various sounds that each letter makes. This is not here for you to spend hours laboring over, rather as a resource should you have questions.

Vowels are unobstructed sounds. Some would explain this by saying it is like water that flows from a garden hose. In making consonant sounds the breath is obstructed. To go back to the garden hose it would be like placing your finger at the end, partially obstructing the water. Consonants are referred to as voiced or unvoiced consonants. The pronunciation guide is intended to help you to make sure that you are saying each letter sound correctly.

Now that you have read over this list have fun as you begin your journey in teaching your child or students to read.

Aa *vowel*

Main sounds in order of frequency:

ă: apple, sad, pack
ā: late, nation, paste
ah: father, spa
(often sounds like a *schwa* in initial position)

PRONUNCIATION: *Open oral cavity, back of tongue raised, steady airflow*

Bb *Voiced consonant*

Main sound:

b: baby, about, cab

PRONUNCIATION: *Lips together, stopped airflow*

Cc *Unvoiced consonant*

Main sounds in order of frequency:

c(k): come, tactic
c(s): cent, acid, pace
Voiced equivalents: g, z

PRONUNCIATION: *Back of tongue raised to palate, stopped airflow (k); tip of tongue behind top teeth, steady restricted airflow (s)*

Common error substitutions: t

Dd *Voiced consonant*

Main sound:

d: doll, Adam, red
Unvoiced equivalent: t

PRONUNCIATION: *Tip of tongue behind top teeth, stopped airflow*

Common error substitutions: g

Ee *vowel*

Main sounds in order of frequency:

ĕ: end, fed
ē: me, emu, Peter

PRONUNCIATION: *Middle of tongue raised, steady airflow*

Ff *Unvoiced consonant*

Main sound:

f: fun, afar, puff
Voiced equivalent: v

PRONUNCIATION: *Bottom lip to top teeth, steady restricted airflow*

Common error substitutions: s

Gg *Voiced consonant*

Main sounds in order of frequency:

g: get, sugar, rug
g (j): general, diligent, rage
Unvoiced equivalents: k, ch)

PRONUNCIATION: *Back of tongue raised to palate, stopped airflow (g); tip and sides of tongue behind top teeth, stopped and restricted airflow (j)*

Common error substitutions: d

Hh *Unvoiced consonant*

Main sound:

h: heart, ahead

PRONUNCIATION: *Open oral cavity, steady airflow*

Ii *Vowel*

Main sounds in order of frequency:

ĭ: ill, pin
ī: island, line

PRONUNCIATION: *Open oral cavity, middle of tongue lifted*

Jj *Voiced consonant*

Main sound:

j (g): jump, pajamas
Unvoiced equivalent: ch

PRONUNCIATION:*Tip and sides of tongue behind top teeth, stopped and restricted airflow*

Common error substitutions: d

Kk *Unvoiced consonant*

Main sound:

k: kitten, locker, sack
Voiced equivalent: g

PRONUNCIATION: *Back of tongue raised to palate, stopped airflow*

Common error substitutions: t

Ll *Voiced consonant*

Main sound:

l: lips, salad, until

Tongue tip behind top teeth, steady airflow

Common error substitutions: w, y

Mm *Voiced consonant*

Main sound:

m: mother, animal, sum

Lips together, steady nasal airflow

Nn *Voiced consonant*

Main sound:

n: nose, panel, clean

PRONUNCIATION: *Tip of tongue behind top teeth, steady nasal airflow*

Oo *vowel*

Main sounds in order of frequency:

ŏ: operate, not

ō: open, total, no

o move, into

PRONUNCIATION: *Open oral cavity, steady airflow, lips rounded or pursed for second and third sounds above*

Pp *Unvoiced consonant*

Main sound:

p: pink, taper, sip

Voiced equivalent: b

PRONUNCIATION: *Lips together, stopped airflow*

Qq *Unvoiced consonant*

Main sound:

q (kw): quick, aqua

PRONUNCIATION: *Back of tongue raised to palate, stopped airflow, lips rounded*

Common error substitutions: k, t

Rr *Voiced consonant*

Main sound:

r: run, arise, stir

PRONUNCIATION: *Back of tongue raised to palate, steady airflow*

Common error substitutions: w, l, y, and various distortions

Ss *Unvoiced consonant*

Main sounds in order of frequency:

s: sin, listen, pass

s (z): laser, was

Voiced equivalent: z

PRONUNCIATION: *Tip of tongue behind top teeth, steady restricted airflow*

Common error substitutions: t, various distortions

Tt *Unvoiced consonant*

Main sound:

t: touch, later, sit

Voiced equivalent: d

PRONUNCIATION: *Tip of tongue behind top teeth, stopped airflow*

Common error substitutions: k

Uu *Vowel*

Main sounds in order of frequency:

ŭ: up, such

ū: tube, avenue

PRONUNCIATION: *Open oral cavity, middle of tongue raised, lips rounded for second sound*

Vv *Voiced consonant*

Main sound:

v: vine, lever, save

Unvoiced equivalent: f

PRONUNCIATION: *Bottom lip to top teeth, steady restricted airflow*

Common error substitutions: b

Ww *Unvoiced consonant*

Main sound:

w: wave, away

PRONUNCIATION: *Lips rounded, steady airflow*

Xx *Unvoiced consonant*

Main sounds in order of frequency:

x (ks): axle, box

x (z): xylophone, xylem

Voiced in initial position

PRONUNCIATION: *Back of tongue raised to palate, stopped airflow, tip behind top teeth, steady restricted airflow (ks); tip of tongue raised behind top teeth, steady restricted airflow (z)*

Common error substitutions: k, t

Yy *Voiced consonant or vowel*

Main sounds in order of frequency:

y *(as a consonant)*: yard, layer

y *(as a vowel)*:

ī: pyre, my

ē: duty

PRONUNCIATION: *Middle of tongue raised to palate, steady airflow*

Common error substitutions: w, l

Zz *Voiced consonant*

Main sound

z: zone, blazer, graze

Unvoiced equivalent: s

PRONUNCIATION: *Tip of tongue raised behind top teeth, steady restricted airflow*

Common error substitutions: d

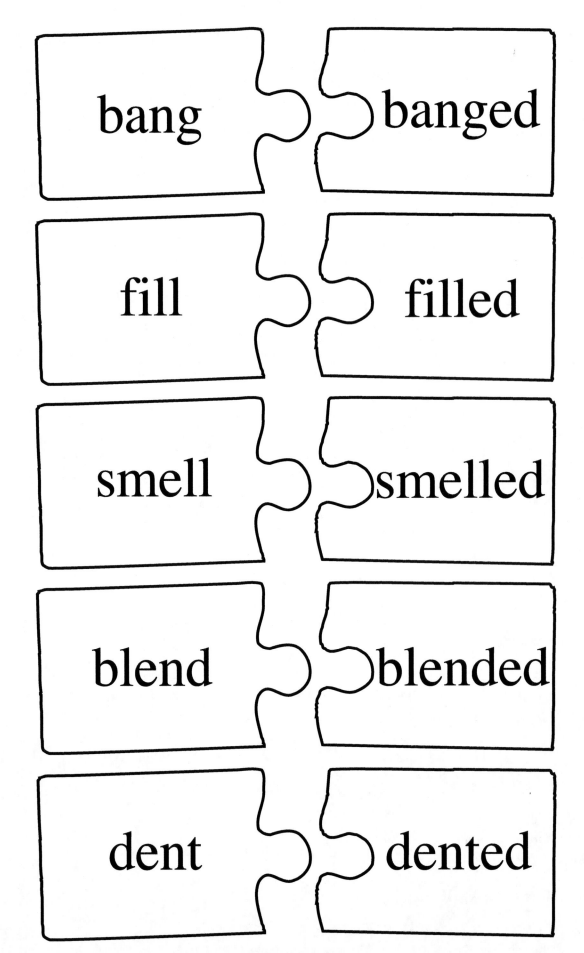

bang	banged
fill	filled
smell	smelled
blend	blended
dent	dented

frost	frosted
hand	handed
land	landed
melt	melted
drift	drifted

bebop	swing
hall	pop
budding	Saxons
bliss	brash

type of instrumental jazz music	musical form used in jazz
short for "popular," another musical form	large auditorium
the people who lived in Britain at this time	beginning, just starting
aggressive	happiness, joy

trash	trek
clash	quell
gruff	fret
glen	glum

trip, long journey	destroy
stop	fight
worry	angry, harsh
sad	clearing in the forest

gravel	bless
rush	prep
snapdragon	linens
drill	splendid

praise	dirt
to get ready	charge
sheets, bedclothes	a kind of flower
wonderful	practice

thrush	long spell
shrub	shrill
twitch	strip
status	snag

long time	small bird
high pitched sound	low growing bush
take off	quick, startled movement
catch	state of being

flash	flit
smock	thicket
trod	moss
thrust	black walnut

short flight	sudden burst of bright light
dense growth of bushes and woods	loose fitting dress
a small, leafy-stemmed plant that grows on moist ground	walked along
a type of tree with walnuts for fruit	to throw off with force

swish	squish
swell	spin
switch	lass
nix	spring-fed

to squeeze	the sound a bird makes with its wings
turn around	great
girl	turn into
watered by a spring	sprite; fairy-like fantasy creature

skillfull	Atlantic
Holland	windmill
dwelling	Dutch
slack	glint

ocean between North America and Europe	able to do something well
a machine that grinds or pumps using the wind for power	a country in Europe, also called The Netherlands
from Holland	home, place to "dwell"
sparkle or flash of light	lazy

blink	bunk
spring	loft
habit	stilts
swift	flicking

bed	to open and close the eyes quickly
an upper room under a sloping roof	jump
two poles with foot supports for walking above the ground	common way
pushing aside quickly	speedy, quick

scraps	sudden
aloft	alas
for a second	swept
instant	halt

quick, unexpected	bits of food; crumbs
a word used to express sorrow, grief or concern	into the air
passed over	for a short time
stop moving	short time

lit	spun
toss	gusting
rend	grasp
slinking	expect

went around and around	fell upon, saw
sudden strong blasting of wind	throw
tight hold	tear away
to plan on; anticipate	walking slowly in a crouch

lap	fend for
spunk	snatch
tact	shred
hissing	gasping

take care of	to lick up
to seize suddenly	spirit, mettle
destroy	being careful of somone else's feelings
taking sudden, short breaths	making a sound like the letter "s"

astonishment	clutching
pelt	wilt
limp	grip
brisk	gallant

seizing, grabbing	amazement
lose its shape and droop	hit with fierce blows
hold	without stiffness or firmness
brave, high-spirited	quick

grand	cutter
lurking	brig
buccaneers	port
rigging	lurching

swift single-masted sailing vessel	magnificent, splendid
a two-masted, square-rigged sailing ship	hiding
the left side of the ship	pirates
abruptly swaying	sails, ropes, etc.

in short order	mast
furl	spars
larder	sorting
deck	carting

the tall pole on a ship to which the sails are attached	quickly
poles that support sails and rigging	roll up
arranging according to kind	pantry, where food is stored
carrying	the upper level floor of the ship

charts	tarps
locker	silver dollars
smirk	stern
darting	swirling

protective canvas covers	maps
coins made of silver	storage chest
1) back of the ship; 2) firm, grim	insincere smile
twisting	moving suddenly

mist	arms
fort	start or stir
perch	barking
terms of surrender	herding

guns, cannons, ammunition	fog
move	a place strengthened with defensive armor and military men
commanding loudly and sharply	high sitting place
forcing them to walk in a group	requirements for giving up

harbor	Port of Boston
stern punish-ment	order
hang	pastor
Word of God	spat

a harbor in Massachusetts	a place of calm water where ships may anchor or tie up to a dock
command	severe penalty for a crime
a teaching elder in the church	to suspend by the neck until dead
past tense of "spit"	the Bible

snort	larks, storks and robins
hike	glide
whirl	labor
copper	rubber

kinds of birds	an angry laugh
fly smoothly and without effort	travel on foot
work	turn, spin
an elastic substance	a reddish-brown metal

bumper	shed
lumber	tire
model	lurch
jerk	suffer harm

an out-building	a horizontal metal guard that protects the front or the back of a car
become weary or weak	planks of wood
a sudden swaying to one side or the other	smaller version, toy
become damaged	a quick, sharp pull

motor	gas
propellers	shore
monk	holy
dare	brave

fuel	an engine that would propel the plane
beach	turning panels, like a windmill
without sin and accept-able to God	a person who leaves normal life and joins a religious group
courageous	have the necessary courage

square	pore over
bade	debate
state	take back
submit	abide

read carefully, think about	a public area in the center of town
argue politely	requested, asked
deny, be sorry for	say, write
live	obey

inquire	hare
snare	implore
relate	spades
manner	fare

rabbit	**ask**
fervently request	**trap**
shovels	**tell**
do	**way**

smite	assembly
mare	fortress
rare	never- ending
note	revere

group	hit, strike
strong building, castle	female horse
eternal	not common, outstanding
love and honor	take notice of, pay attention to

saint	blest
quest	oars
pilot	coast
dread	spinning

shown favor	one who is holy, set apart
wooden poles with flat ends, used for rowing a boat through the water	journey in pursuit of a goal
the shore, land next to the sea	guide, lead, direct
turning quickly	fright and sadness

cove	cheer
boar	gay
quay	soaking
cloaks	bail

joy	protected natural harbor
happy	large wild pig
making wet	landing dock
dump the water out of the boat by hand	clothes

pails	lush
tribe	beam
print	wise
sheaves	quaint

filled with abundant vegetation	buckets
to smile, respond with approval	a community of people
knowing what is right or true	write
charming	bundles

finch	steep
feast	oath
streaks	sweep
kin	glean

soak	a kind of bird
promise, covenant	an abundant, delicious meal
to spread across	lines, marks
to take what is left over	family

wed	boot
gleam	brook
sped	spooky
stoop	brood

trunk of the car	to marry
small stream of water	shine
frightful	ran quickly
group	crouch down

scooting	snuck
snoop	beheld
shoo	cruel
noose	brew

moved carefully so no one would see or hear	moving quickly
saw	look
mean, delighting in causing pain	leave, go away
bubbling mixture	hanging loop

rescue	infiltrator
grate	cue
swooping	flue
pursue	nook

spy	save from certain death
signal	a metal frame of crossed bars
conduit, vent	flying low and wide
small, hidden area	follow, chase

croon	loon
rue	strobe
swoon	self- destruct
sloop	sprang

wild bird, crazy person	sing or speak slowly
blinking light	regret, be sorry for
destroy itself	faint
leaped suddenly	a single-masted sailing boat

oysters	nets
marshes	tarry
quest	Hydra
fret	toying

meshed fabric used for catching fish	clam-like shellfish
stay, delay	wetlands, generally by the sea
multi-headed beast	journey with a goal
cruelly played with	worry

foil	hoisting
thrusting	toiling
fray	brutal
throbbing	joints

pulling	spoil, thwart
working	pushing forcibly
harsh, difficult	battle
shoulders, elbows, hips and knees	aching severely

coiling	curb
oozing	spoils
nay	farewell
bound	estate

slow down, stop	winding up
plunder, items given or taken after battle	flowing out slowly
goodbye, take care	no
large property	jump

kennels	huntsmen
grouse	fallow deer
sleek	browse
mount	howl

hunters	caged areas for animals
broad antlered deer found in Europe	wild game birds
graze	smooth and glossy
to cry out in a long, mournful way	to get up onto

scouting	prowl
thicket	bowmen
route	prow
scowl	dousing

hunt	searching
archers	many bushes grouped together
front of a boat	path
immersion in water	deep frown

sputter	stroke
snout	bravery
coward	crouch
drowsy	brisk

to pet	to spit explosively
act of courage	nose
sit in a curled up position	fearful person
sharp and biting	sleepy

bracing	grief
fleet	pounce
trounce	lance
prancing	razors

sadness	waiting, preparing
jump upon, take by surprise	a large group of ships
spear	defeat
sharp-edged blades	high stepping

straining	wincing
cease	hence
sour	stance
awful	fever

responding to a blow	working hard
therefore, as a result	stop, break
stand, firmly held position	bitter and sad
illness with a high temperature	very bad, horrible

raw	daunt
dawn	shawl
haul	staunch
brawny	squalid

deter, discourage	open, bleeding
garment that wraps around the shoulders and head	when the sun is just coming up
solid	pull
dirty	muscled

gaunt	drawn
paunch	haunt
taunting	mock
beggar	draw

tight with pain	thin
harass, go after	stomach, front of torso
to ridicule	mocking, unkind teasing
bring	one who asks for aid but offers nothing in return

cawing	fawn
burly	brawling
clearing	haunches
bawl	cheering

baby deer	making a loud call
fighting	big in size, stout
strong legs and back	an open area in the forest with no trees
heartening, pleasing	cry

slight	garden wren
sought out	gnomes
sigh	smallpox
shone	wreck

a little bird	slim
tiny, old men in legends who live in the earth and guard its treasure	looked for
a serious disease	to exhale with weariness or desire
crash to pieces	glowed with light

ought	knack
meek	spin
gnat	naught
chest	sobs

skill, talent	should
make yarn from wool	humble
nothing	small insect
deep cries	storage trunk

wretches	wrath
plight	speculate
dependent	fraught
might	newborn

anger	poor, abandoned ones
to assume or be doubtful about	difficult situation
full of	trusting, relying
a baby recently born	power

archer	diligent
enrage	grudge
purge	trudge
barge	planks

hard-working, applied	one who is skilled at shooting a bow
bitterness toward	make angry
march	get rid of
long, flat pieces of wood	a boat used for transporting freight

wedge	twinge
nudge	budge
sage	corral
intelligent	troops

small, sharp pain; a pang	push in between
move	push or prod
fenced-in area	clever, wise
soldiers	smart

inhale	pass
arrangement	combat
genius	Genesis
starvation	reflection

cut-out area through a mountain range	breathe in
fight	formation, lines
the first book of the Bible	very intelligent
return of light waves from a surface	lack of food

generations	imagination
innovation	transportation
invention	explosion
research	mission

creativity	ancestors/ descendants
mode of travel	development of new ideas
blast	development and building of new ideas or machines
trip with a goal	exploring, study

vision	determination
occupation	qualifications
education	tension
capsule	separation

desire to succeed	dream
abilities	job
stress	studying to gain knowledge
disconnection, taking apart	a compact compartment

section	fuel
portion	gravity
ignition	duration
division	coordination

gas	part
force of attraction which draws us to earth	part
length	start up
working together, team effort	split

translation	millions
commander	expression
interruptions	protection
foundation	traction

many thousands	changing from one language to another
emotion	captain
watchful care	breaks
ability to grip	solid base

connection	celebration
dreary	Pharaoh
pondered	weary
ragged	shepherd

party	hook-up, link
a king in ancient Egypt	miserable
tired	considered, thought
person who cares for sheep	humbly dressed

emphatic	reasonable
perhaps	prophet
philosopher	chime
emphasis	attack

level-headed	forceful
one who speaks God's truth	it may be, possibly
the sound a clock makes; loud and clear	someone who thinks about the meaning of life
strife, show aggression	force; importance

flee	decipher
foe	wrath
strayed	boils
lice	locusts

decode; make sense out of	run away
anger	enemy
oozing sores on the skin	wandered from
insects like grasshoppers	tiny insects which bite and suck blood

perished	cursed
hovered	wielded
kilts	tromped
toil	thatched

hated	died
held and used skillfully	hung in the air
walked purposefully, marched	skirt-like garment worn by Scottish men
made of interlocked grass used for roofing	work

especially	clan
resist	thieving
enraged	gathering
plotting	band

extended family group	particularly
taking something that is not yours	oppose, fight against
coming together	greatly angered
group of followers	planning

protectors	terrified
cast	dim
hulk	cleave
hilt	collapsed

greatly afraid	ones who defend
dark	threw
split apart	large form
fell	handle of a sword

dazed	aye
raided	plundered
in vain	spoiled
rejoice	drab

term for "yes!"	astonished
taken by force or unlawfully	attacked
ruined	without effect or result
dull, tarnished, faded	be glad

spoil	wretch
fawning	beaming
plush	flaunting
coy	blushing

person in great need	fail to discipline, give too many gifts to
smiling with pride	doting, devoted
prideful	costly and luxurious
having reddened cheeks	flirtatious, clever

chide	idols
phony	rude
tricky	flight
allowed	determined

false gods, worshipped images	correct, rebuke
without manners	fake
travel to escape or get away	clever
concluded, decided	permitted

eager	pagan
convinced	woodsman
chuckled	powerful
scoffed	tremble

unbeliever	enthusiastic
a lumberman or a man used to living in the woods	persuaded
strong, mighty	laughed
shake	laughed at, ridiculed

quake	observed
wondered	remarked
exclaimed	fend off
gigantic	festival

noticed	shake in fear
said	questioned
repel, push away	cried out
party, celebration	huge, grand

harshly	inquired
repent	stillness

asked	cruelly, severely
quietness, peacefullness	being sorry for sin and turn from it